THE SUPREME COURT:
ISSUES AND OPINIONS

THE SUPREME COURT:
ISSUES AND OPINIONS

D. ELLSWORTH BLANK
(EDITOR)

Nova Science Publishers, Inc.
Huntington, New York

Senior Editors: Susan Boriotti and Donna Dennis
Office Manager: Annette Hellinger
Graphics: Wanda Serrano and Jennifer Lucas
Information Editor: Tatiana Shohov
Book Production: LaToya Clay, Cathy DeGregory, and Lynette Van Helden
Circulation: Anna Cruz, Ave Maria Gonzalez, Ron Hedges, Andre Tillman

Library of Congress Cataloging-in-Publication Data
Available upon request

ISBN 1-56072-887-6

227 Main Street, Suite 100
Huntington, New York 11743
Tele. 631-424-6682 Fax 631-424-4666
e-mail: Novascience@earthlink.net
Web Site: http://www.nexusworld.com/nova

Printed in the United States of America

Contents

PREFACE

As the 21st Century gets underway, the Supreme Court seems to stand alone as the ly U.S. government branch worthy of the respect of the citizenry. The Presidency and ongress have been rocked by scandals and partisan bickering over and over again which ve degraded each place of honor. Yet, the Supreme Court continues to placidly reach s decisions which, at the least, sustains the image of a government interested in mocracy and progress.

This book brings together and summarizes Supreme Court decisions over the past 5 ars.

D. Ellsworth Blank

Supreme Court
Volume 1 pp. 1-40

SUPREME COURT OPINIONS: OCTOBER 1999 TERM

George Costello
Legislative Attorney
American Law Division

Adarand Constructors, Inc. v. Slater 120 S. Ct. 722, 68 USLW 3456 (1-12-00)

Mootness: The United States Court of Appeals for the Tenth Circuit erred in dismissing this case as moot. The case, stemming from the remand in *Adarand Constructors, Inc. v. Pena* (1995), involved petitioner low-bidder's challenge to racially discriminatory policies in award of highway construction contracts. In response to earlier phases of the litigation, the Colorado Department of Transportation (CDOT) eliminated its race-based presumptions of disadvantaged status and instead authorized applicants to self-certify the "disadvantaged" status of their majority owners. The petitioner did so self-certify, based on the fact that it had been the subject of racial discrimination under the old policy. The Court of Appeals then dismissed the underlying action as moot because CDOT had recognized the petitioner's disadvantaged status. But the Court of Appeals failed to take into account that Colorado's self-certification procedures had not yet been approved by the U.S. Department of Transportation (DOT) as required by federal regulation. Given the "patent incompatibility of the certification with the federal regulations," it was "not at all clear" that the procedures could be approved by DOT. The respondents did not meet their burden of establishing that it was "absolutely clear that the allegedly wrongful behavior could not reasonably be expected to recur."

9-0. *Per curiam.*

Apprendi v. New Jersey 120 S. Ct. 2348, 68 USLW 4576 (6-26-00)

Due Process, right to trial by jury, sentence enhancement: A New Jersey "hate crime" statute that allows a judge to extend a sentence upon finding by a preponderance of the evidence that the defendant, in committing a crime for which he has been found guilty, acted with a purpose to intimidate because of race, violates the Fourteenth Amendment's Due Process Clause and the Sixth Amendment's requirements of speedy and public trial by an impartial jury. Any fact that increases the penalty for a crime beyond the prescribed statutory maximum must be submitted to a jury and proved beyond a reasonable doubt. The hate crime law, which authorized the judge to extend imprisonment for a "second-degree" offense to imprisonment from 10 to 20 years, thereby authorized the judge to increase the defendant's penalty for the "second-degree" offense of possession of a firearm for an unlawful purpose, punishable by imprisonment of 5 to 10 years, beyond the prescribed statutory maximum for that offense. The effect is to turn a second-degree offense into a first-degree offense under New Jersey law. The constitutional principles are violated because the factual issue of whether the defendant acted with the purpose of intimidating is left to the judge rather than being submitted to the jury, and may be established by a preponderance of the evidence rather than by proof beyond a reasonable doubt. Characterizing the inquiry as one of "motive" does not save the statute as a sentencing measure, since "the defendant's intent in committing a crime is perhaps as close as one might hope to come to a core criminal offense 'element.'" The State's reliance on *McMillan v. Pennsylvania* (1986) and *Almendarez-Torres v. United States* (1998) is misplaced. *McMillan* dealt with a mandatory minimum sentence that did not authorize exceeding the statutory maximum for the underlying offense, and the recidivism-based exception to the general rule recognized in *Almendarez-Torres* is inapplicable to the New Jersey law.

5-4. Opinion of Court by Stevens, joined by Scalia, Souter, Thomas, and Ginsburg. Concurring opinions by Scalia; and by Thomas, joined in part by Scalia. Dissenting opinions by O'Connor, joined by Rehnquist, Kennedy, and Breyer; and by Breyer, joined by Rehnquist.

Arizona v. California 120 S. Ct. 2304, 68 USLW 4553 (6-19-00)

Water allocation, Colorado River: The claims of the Quechan Tribe, and of the United States on behalf of the Tribe, for increased rights to Colorado River water are not precluded by the Court's 1963 decision in *Arizona v. California* or by a consent judgment entered by the United States Claims Court in 1983. The case is remanded to the Special Master for consideration of the claims for additional water rights appurtenant to disputed boundary lands not attributed to the Fort Yuma Indian Reservation in earlier stages of the litigation. The Special Master's recommendations regarding allocation of water for the Fort Mojave Reservation and the Colorado River Indian Reservation are accepted.

6-3. Opinion of Court by Ginsburg, joined by Stevens, Scalia, Kennedy, Souter, and Breyer. Opinion by Rehnquist, concurring in part and dissenting in part, joined by O'Connor and Thomas.

Baral v. United States 120 S. Ct. 1006, 68 USLW 4119 (2-22-00)

Taxation, Federal: For purposes of determining the amount of credit or refund to which a taxpayer is entitled as compensation for overpayment of tax, the date on which withholding taxes and estimated tax payments are "paid" is the due date on the taxpayer's income tax return. Section 6511(b)(2)(A) of the Tax Code provides that the amount of credit or refund "shall not exceed the portion of the tax paid within the period, immediately preceding the filing of the claim, equal to 3 years plus the period of any extension." The "plain language" of section 6513(b) determines when withholding and estimated taxes are "paid." That section provides that "for purposes of section 6511 . . . [withholding taxes] shall . . . be deemed to have been paid on the 15th day of the fourth month following the close of his taxable year," and estimated taxes "shall be deemed to have been paid on the last day prescribed for filing the return." Here the taxpayer did not file his 1988 return and claim a refund until June 1, 1993. The three year "look-back" period, lengthened as a result of the four-month extension he had received in 1989, extended back to February 1, 1990. The taxpayer had paid no portion of his overpaid tax during that period, since by operation of section 6513 his payments were deemed to have been made on April 15, 1989.

9-0. Opinion for unanimous Court by Thomas.

Beck v. Prupis 120 S. Ct. 1608, 68 USLW 4320 (4-26-00)

RICO, conspiracy, nature of "overt act": A person injured by an "overt act" in furtherance of a RICO conspiracy has a cause of action under 18 U.S.C. § 1962(d), only if the "overt act" is an act of racketeering or otherwise unlawful under RICO. The provision makes it "unlawful for any person to conspire to violate"specified RICO provisions. When Congress uses language, not otherwise defined, with a settled common-law meaning, Congress is presumed to know and adopt that meaning. At the time of RICO's enactment in 1970, it was well established that a plaintiff could bring suit for civil conspiracy only if he had been injured by an act that was itself tortious. The RICO analogy to an act of a "tortious character" is an act that is "independently wrongful under RICO." In this case, the overt act of discharging from employment was not independently wrongful under RICO. This interpretation does not render the conspiracy language "mere surplusage," since, as long as one conspirator has committed an overt act, a plaintiff could use the provision to sue other co-conspirators who have not themselves committed an overt act.

7-2. Opinion of Court by Thomas, joined by Rehnquist, O'Connor, Scalia, Kennedy, Ginsburg, and Breyer. Dissenting opinion by Stevens, joined by Souter.

Board of Regents of the Univ. of Wisconsin System v. Southworth 120 S. Ct. 1346, 68 USLW 4220 (3-21-00)

First Amendment, mandatory student fees: The First Amendment permits a public university to charge its students an activity fee that is used to support student organizations that engage in expressive activities if the money is allocated to those groups by use of viewpoint-neutral criteria. Students opposed to the purposes and expression of some of the subsidized organizations brought this challenge, alleging they should not be required to subsidize speech they find objectionable. The parties stipulated that two of the three processes for reviewing and approving funding are administered in a viewpoint-neutral fashion. This viewpoint neutrality requirement "is in general sufficient to protect the rights of the objecting students." Rights recognized in the context of union and state bar association dues are implicated by the University's program, but the protections adopted for those contexts "are neither applicable nor workable" in the university context. In those contexts the Court limited the required subsidy to speech "germane" to the purposes of the union or bar association. The germaneness standard, difficult enough to apply to unions and bar associations, "becomes all the more unmanageable" in the university setting, where the purpose is "to stimulate the whole universe of speech and ideas." The University may if it chooses adopt an optional or refund system, but there is no constitutional requirement that it do so. Nor need the University distinguish between on-campus and off-campus expressive activities. The third process the University provides for allocating funds to student groups – a student referendum in which the student body can vote to approve or to disapprove an assessment – substitutes majority rule for viewpoint neutrality, and cannot be upheld along with the other aspects of the program.

9-0. Opinion of Court by Kennedy, joined by Rehnquist, O'Connor, Scalia, Thomas, and Ginsburg. Concurring opinion by Souter, joined by Stevens and Breyer.

Bond v. United States 120 S. Ct. 1462, 68 USLW 4255 (4-17-00)

Fourth Amendment, luggage search: Border Patrol agents violated the Fourth Amendment by feeling and squeezing carry-on luggage in the overhead storage compartment of a bus. The bus passenger in this case had exhibited an actual expectation of privacy by using an opaque bag and placing it directly above his seat. A bus passenger who places his bag in an overhead bin expects that other passengers will handle the bag in the process of making room for their own luggage, but does not expect that other passengers will "feel the bag in an exploratory manner." That expectation of privacy is one that society is prepared to recognize as reasonable, and the agent's physical manipulation of the bag therefore violated the passenger's Fourth Amendment rights.

7-2. Opinion of Court by Rehnquist, joined by Stevens, O'Connor, Kennedy, Souter, Thomas, and Ginsburg. Dissenting opinion by Breyer, joined by Scalia.

Boy Scouts of America v. Dale 120 S. Ct. 2446, 68 USLW 4625 (6-28-00)

First Amendment, freedom of association: Application of New Jersey's public accommodations law to require the Boy Scouts of America, a private, non-profit organization, to admit an avowed homosexual as an adult member and assistant scoutmaster violates the organization's First Amendment associational rights. The general mission of the Scouts, to instill values in young people, is expressive activity entitled to First Amendment protection. Although neither the Scout Oath nor the Scout Law expressly mentions sexuality or sexual orientation, they do require a scout to be "clean" and "morally straight." The Court "accept[s] the Boy Scouts' assertion" that the organization teaches that homosexual conduct is not morally straight. This assertion is documented by a 1978 "position statement" distributed to members of the Scouts' Executive Committee, and by other statements made after the respondent's membership in the Scouts was revoked. The Court also "give[s] deference to [the] association's view of what would impair its expression." Allowing a gay rights activist to serve in the Scouts would "force the organization to send a message . . . that the Boy Scouts accepts homosexual conduct as a legitimate form of behavior." In earlier cases the Court found that application of state public accommodations laws to the Jaycees and to the Rotary Club would not materially interfere with the ideas that these organizations sought to express. By contrast, application of New Jersey's public accommodations law does "significantly burden the Scouts' right to oppose or disfavor homosexual conduct." The Court's decision in *Hurley v. Irish-American Gay Group* (1995), in which the Court upheld the right of parade organizers to exclude a message with which parade organizers disagreed, is more on point. While homosexuality appears to have gained "greater societal acceptance," an organization is free to espouse an unpopular view.

5-4. Opinion of Court by Rehnquist, joined by O'Connor, Scalia, Kennedy, and Thomas. Dissenting opinions by Stevens, joined by Souter, Ginsburg, and Breyer; and by Souter, joined by Ginsburg and Breyer.

California Democratic Party v. Jones 120 S. Ct. 2402, 68 USLW 4604 (6-26-00)

First Amendment, right of association, "blanket" primary: California's "blanket" primary violates the First Amendment associational rights of political parties. Under the blanket primary law, adopted by initiative in 1996 as Proposition 198, each voter's primary ballot lists every candidate regardless of party affiliation, and allows the voter to choose freely among all the candidates. While the Court has held that racial discrimination in state-sanctioned primary elections is state action for purposes of the Fifteenth Amendment, these cases do not stand for any general proposition "that party affairs are public affairs" that states may freely regulate. Rather, political parties retain rights of association that include the "right to exclude" non-members in the process of selecting nominees for public office. Proposition 198 impinges on these rights by forcing political parties to "adulterate their candidate-selection process . . . by opening it up to persons wholly unaffiliated with the party." The law can be upheld, therefore, only if it is narrowly tailored to serve a compelling state interest. No compelling state interest is furthered by Proposition 198. Better representation of the electorate and expansion of candidate debate are "inadmissible" interests that reduce to "stark repudiation of freedom of political association." The interest in assuring an "effective" vote for "disenfranchised" independents and minority party voters in "safe" districts is "overborne by the countervailing and legitimate right of the party to determine its own membership qualifications." Other asserted interests in promoting fairness, voter choice, voter participation, and voter "privacy" are not compelling justifications for a blanket primary. Even if there were a compelling governmental interest, Proposition 198 is not "narrowly tailored." All of the asserted interests could be protected by a "nonpartisan blanket primary," in which parties might nominate candidates prior to the primary, so that primary voters would not choose a party's nominee.

7-2. Opinion of Court by Scalia, joined by Rehnquist, O'Connor, Kennedy, Souter, Thomas, and Breyer. Concurring opinion by Kennedy. Dissenting opinion by Stevens, joined in part by Ginsburg.

Carmell v. Texas 120 S. Ct. 1620, 68 USLW 4325 (5-1-00)

Ex Post Facto Clause, corroboration of evidence: A Texas law that eliminated a requirement that the testimony of a sexual assault victim age 14 or older must be corroborated by two other witnesses cannot constitutionally be applied to a crime committed while the earlier law was in effect. Such application violates the Ex Post Facto Clause of Art. I, sec. 10. The contours of the Ex Post Facto Clause were set forth in the 1798 case of *Calder v. Bull*, and included the category of "every law that alters the legal rules of evidence, and receives less, or different testimony, than the law required at the time of the commission of the offence, in order to convict the offender." The Texas law at issue is "unquestionably such a law." Under the old law, the petitioner could have been convicted only if the victim's testimony were corroborated by two other witnesses, while under the amended law, the petitioner could (and was) convicted on the victim's testimony alone. Neither Texas nor the United States, as amicus, offers persuasive reasons for abandoning this category of ex post facto law, which "resonates harmoniously" with one of the Clause's principal interests, that of "fundamental justice." .

5-4. Opinion of Court by Stevens, joined by Scalia, Souter, Thomas, and Breyer. Dissenting opinion by Ginsburg, joined by Rehnquist, O'Connor, and Kennedy.

Carter v. United States 120 S. Ct. 2159, 68 USLW 4513 (6-12-00)

Statutes, interpretation, lesser included offense: The crime defined by 18 U.S.C. § 2113(b) is not a lesser included offense of the crime defined by 18 U.S.C. § 2113(a). Subsection (b) penalizes anyone who "takes and carries away, with intent to steal or purloin, any property or money" exceeding $1,000 in value and belonging to a bank; subsection (a) penalizes anyone who "by force and violence, or by intimidation," takes from the person of another any money or property belonging to a bank. Generally, a crime is a lesser included offense of another crime only if the elements of the lesser offense are a subset of the elements of the charged offense. Three elements of section 2113(b) are not elements of section 2113(a): specific intent to steal, carrying away the stolen property, and valuation exceeding $1,000. Arguments for departing from this "straightforward reading of the text" are rejected. The fact that subsection (c) penalizes receipt of property taken from a bank in violation of subsection (b) but makes no mention of subsection (a) is an "anomaly," but does not rise to the level of an "absurdity." The fact that subsections (a) and (b) closely resemble the common law crimes of robbery and larceny does not require imputation of common-law meaning to the provisions. Common law meaning is imputed when Congress borrows terms of art with accumulated meaning, but neither the term "robbery" nor the term "larceny" appears in the statutory text. The word "robbery" does appear in the section's title, but words in a title are useful only when they shed light on some ambiguous word or phase in the text, and no such ambiguity exists. The "intent to steal or purloin" element of subsection (b) is not implicit in subsection (a). Only a general intent requirement – not the specific intent to steal or purloin – should be read into subsection (a). Taking property in violation of (a) should not be equated with taking and carrying away property in violation of (b); it would hardly have been "absurd" for Congress to have eliminated the asportation requirement from (a). The $1,000 valuation is clearly an offense element and not a sentencing factor.

5-4. Opinion of Court by Thomas, joined by Rehnquist, O'Connor, Scalia, and Kennedy. Dissenting opinion by Ginsburg, joined by Stevens, Souter, and Breyer.

Castillo v. United States 120 S. Ct. 2090, 68 USLW 4475 (6-5-00)

Statutes, interpretation; elements of offense: Language in 18 U.S.C. § 924(c) providing that a person who uses a machine gun during commission of a crime of violence shall be sentenced to imprisonment for thirty years defines a separate crime, and does not merely authorize an enhanced sentence. An indictment for the machine gun offense therefore must identify the firearm type and a jury must find that element proved beyond a reasonable doubt. The section provides that anyone who uses a "firearm" during commission of a crime of violence shall be sentenced to five years' imprisonment, and then increases the penalty sixfold if that firearm is a machine gun. While the literal language of the section is "neutral" as to whether the relevant words create a separate crime or merely authorize an enhanced penalty, the statutory structure "strongly favors the 'new crime' interpretation." The "machine gun" provision is contained in the same sentence that establishes the elements of the basic "uses a firearm" offense. It is the following three sentences that refer directly to sentencing factors, such as recidivism. Although use of a machine gun might be considered to fall within the traditional sentencing category relating to the manner in which a crime is carried out, the same could be said for use of a "firearm." To ask a jury rather than a judge to determine the type of weapon a defendant used will rarely complicate a trial or risk unfairness. On the other hand, leaving the decision to the sentencing judge may produce a conflict between the judge and jury when the jury must determine which of several weapons a defendant used. References to sentencing in the legislative history do not help the Government's interpretation, since the statute's basic "uses a firearm" provision also deals with sentencing. Finally, the "length and severity" of an added mandatory sentence weighs in favor of treating the language as referring to an element of an offense.

9-0. Opinion of Court by Breyer, joined by Rehnquist, Stevens, O'Connor, Kennedy, Souter, Thomas, and Ginsburg, and joined in part by Scalia.

Christensen v. Harris County 120 S. Ct. 1655, 68 USLW 4343 (5-1-00)

FLSA, forced use of compensatory time: The Fair Labor Standards Act (FLSA) does not prohibit the County from requiring its employees to schedule time off in order to reduce the amount of accrued compensatory time. Nothing in the FLSA expressly prohibits public employers from compelling employees to utilize accrued compensatory time, and the law's requirement that an employee "shall be permitted to use" compensatory time within a reasonable period of requesting to do so does not implicitly prohibit such compulsion. This latter grant of authority to employees to use compensatory time provided such use will not unduly disrupt the workplace does not implicitly preclude other methods of spending compensatory time. The provision should be read as safeguarding an employee's right to receive timely compensation, and as guaranteeing that an employee will get to use his compensatory time. No deference is due a Department of Labor opinion letter requiring advance agreement by an employee before an employer may compel use of comp time. Interpretations such as those contained in opinion letters are not arrived at after adjudication or notice-and-comment rulemaking, lack the force of law, and consequently do not warrant *Chevron*-type deference.

6-3 (merits); **5-4** (deference). Opinion of Court by Thomas, joined by Rehnquist, O'Connor, Kennedy, and Souter, and joined in part by Scalia. Concurring opinion by Souter. Opinion by Scalia concurring in part. Dissenting opinions by Stevens, joined by Ginsburg and Breyer; and by Breyer, joined by Ginsburg.

City of Erie v. Pap's A. M. 120 S. Ct. 1382, 68 USLW 4239 (3-29-00)

First Amendment, nude dancing: Erie, Pennsylvania's ordinance banning public nudity does not violate the First Amendment as applied to the operator of a nude dancing establishment open to the public. The ordinance permits dancers to perform wearing only pasties and a G-string, but not totally nude. One purpose of the ordinance was to combat negative "secondary effects," such as prostitution and other criminal activity, associated with the presence of adult entertainment establishments. As a general prohibition on public nudity, the ordinance is not aimed at suppression of expression, and consequently should be evaluated under the framework set forth in *United States v. O'Brien* (1968), for content-neutral restrictions on symbolic speech. There is no Court majority, however, on how the *O'Brien* test applies. The four-Justice plurality would allow the city to take "official notice of 'legislative facts,'" and to rely on earlier cases permitting zoning of adult establishments, and would not require a discrete evidentiary record in order to satisfy *O'Brien's* requirement that an incidental restriction on expression be no greater than essential to achieve the regulation's purpose. The two other Justices concurring on the merits would hold that there is no need to identify harmful secondary effects because "a general law regulating conduct and not specifically directed at expression is not subject to First Amendment scrutiny at all." Although the "Kandyland" establishment operated by the respondents has been closed, the case is not moot, since the respondents may have an interest in resuming operations, and the city has an interest in reversing the Pennsylvania Supreme Court's decision in order to allow enforcement of its ordinance.

6-3 (nudity ban); **7-2*** (mootness). Opinion of Court (mootness only) by O'Connor, joined by Rehnquist, Kennedy, Souter, and Breyer. Separate part of O'Connor opinion joined by Rehnquist, Kennedy, and Breyer. Opinion by Scalia, joined by Thomas, concurring in part (nudity ban) and dissenting in part (mootness), joined by Thomas. Opinion by Souter, concurring in part (applicability of *O'Brien*) and dissenting in part (evidentiary support). Dissenting opinion by Stevens, joined by Ginsburg. *Justice Stevens' dissent does not address mootness.

Cortez Bryd Chips, Inc. v. Bill Harbert Constr. Co. 120 S. Ct. 1331, 68 USLW 4214 (3-20-00)

Venue, Federal Arbitration Act: The venue provisions of the Federal Arbitration Act (FAA) are permissive, not exclusive. A case seeking to confirm, vacate, or modify an arbitration award may be brought in any district that is proper under the general venue statute or, as provided in the FAA, in the district where the award was made. Sections 9, 10, and 11 of the FAA provide that the district court in the district in which the award was made "may" enter appropriate orders. Use of the word "may" is not necessarily conclusive of congressional intent to provide for discretionary or permissive authority. In this case, however, statutory history points toward a permissive reading, and this conclusion is reinforced by consideration of the "practical consequences" of a restrictive reading. When the FAA was enacted in 1925, venue was ordinarily available only in the district of the defendant's residence. Against this background, the FAA's venue provisions "had an obviously liberalizing effect," there being no indication that Congress intended to take away the venue that is normally the most convenient for a defendant. The "practical consequences" of a restrictive reading would include "a needless tension" with § 3, which authorizes a court to stay, and retain jurisdiction over, any action that is referable to arbitration; and the creation of "anomalous results in the aftermath of arbitrations held abroad."

9-0. Opinion for unanimous Court by Souter.

Crosby v. National Foreign Trade Council 120 S. Ct. 2288, 68 USLW 4445 (6-19-00)

Preemption, Massachusetts Burma law: A Massachusetts law barring state agencies from buying goods or services from any entity listed as doing business with Burma (Myanmar) is preempted by the federal sanctions law. The Massachusetts law stands as "an obstacle to the accomplishment of Congress's full objectives under the federal act." The Massachusetts law undermines the federal law's conferral on the President of effective discretion to control economic sanctions against Burma. The President is authorized to terminate sanctions initially imposed by statute, and is empowered to impose additional sanctions limiting new investment in Burma. The presence of state sanctions as well as their perpetual nature limits the President's flexibility. The Massachusetts law, which applies to contracts for goods and services and to foreign as well as domestic companies, is broader in scope than the federal law. The Massachusetts law also frustrates the President's ability to engage in effective diplomacy in carrying out the federal law's directive to work with other nations to develop a "comprehensive, multilateral strategy" for improving democracy and human rights practices in Burma. The failure of Congress to include express preemption language in the federal law is not dispositive; lack of express congressional recognition does not preclude operation of "conflict" preemption based on frustration of congressional purpose.

9-0. Opinion of Court by Souter, joined by Rehnquist, Stevens, O'Connor, Kennedy, Ginsburg, and Breyer. Concurring opinion by Scalia, joined by Thomas.

Dickerson v. United States 120 S. Ct. 2326, 68 USLW 4566 (6-26-00)

***Miranda* rule, congressional power to abrogate**: *Miranda v. Arizona* (1966) was a constitutional decision that the Supreme Court declines to overrule, and that may not be overruled by statute. In *Miranda* the Court laid down "concrete constitutional guidelines" for the police to follow prior to custodial interrogation of a suspect: police must warn a suspect that he has the right to remain silent, that anything he says can be used against him in court, that he has the right to an attorney, and that if he cannot afford an attorney one can be appointed. Two years after the *Miranda* decision Congress enacted 18 U.S.C. § 3501, which purported to reinstate the voluntariness principle that had measured the validity of confessions prior to *Miranda*, and that the Court had found inadequate in *Miranda*. Section 3501 is an invalid attempt by Congress to redefine a constitutional protection. "Congress may not legislatively supersede [the Supreme Court's] decisions interpreting and applying the Constitution." Although there is language in some of the Court's decisions suggesting that the *Miranda* warnings are merely prophylactic rules, they are instead constitution-based rules. This is not to say that the *Miranda* warnings are necessarily immutable. The Court in *Miranda* invited a legislative rule that would be "at least as effective" in protecting a suspect's right to remain silent during custodial interrogation. Section 3501, however, is not an adequate substitute for the *Miranda* warnings. *Miranda* should not be overruled by the Court. Principles of *stare decisis* "weigh heavily against" its overruling, and "*Miranda* has become embedded in routine police practice to the point where the warnings have become part of our national culture." Moreover, subsequent cases have not undermined *Miranda's* "doctrinal underpinnings."

7-2. Opinion of Court by Rehnquist, joined by Stevens, O'Connor, Kennedy, Souter, Ginsburg, and Breyer. Dissenting opinion by Scalia, joined by Thomas.

Drye v. United States 120 S. Ct. 474, 68 USLW 4010 (12- 7-99)

Federal tax lien, disclaimer of inheritance under state law: Disclaimer of an inherited estate pursuant to state law does not operate to nullify a federal tax lien imposed on the heir's "property and rights to property" pursuant to 26 U.S.C. § 6321. The issue of whether the disclaimer right held under state law constitutes "property or rights to property" within the meaning of the federal tax lien statute is a matter of federal law. The language of the tax lien statute is broad, and reveals on its face that Congress intended to reach every interest in property that a taxpayer might have. Section 6334(a) of the Code, which lists property exempt from levy, corroborates this broad reading. Inheritances disclaimed under state law are not included in the listing of exempt property, and Congress provided that this listing is exclusive. Moreover, the tax lien treatment of disclaimers contrasts with that of section 2518(a), which expressly renders state-law disclaimers effective for federal wealth-transfer tax purposes. The important consideration in determining whether the disclaimer right constitutes a "property right" subject to tax lien is the breadth of control the taxpayer may exercise over the property. Here, Arkansas law conferred an unqualified right in the petitioner to receive the entire value of his mother's estate or to disclaim the inheritance and channel its entire value to his daughter. This control rendered the inheritance "property" or a "right to property" within the meaning of the statute.

9-0. Opinion for unanimous Court by Ginsburg.

Edwards v. Carpenter 120 S. Ct. 1587, 68 USLW 4308 (4-25-00)

Habeas corpus, ineffective assistance of counsel: A procedurally defaulted claim of ineffective assistance of counsel can serve as cause to excuse the procedural default of another habeas claim only if the habeas petitioner can satisfy the "cause and prejudice" standard with respect to the ineffective assistance claim itself. A prisoner must demonstrate cause (and prejudice resulting therefrom), for his state-court default of any federal claim, including a claim of ineffective assistance of counsel. The purposes of requiring "exhaustion" of state remedies before presenting a federal habeas corpus claim would be defeated if federal review were permitted to a prisoner who had presented his claim to state court, but not in a timely manner allowing the state court to consider it.

9-0. Opinion of Court by Scalia, joined by Rehnquist, O'Connor, Kennedy, Souter, Thomas, and Ginsburg. Concurring opinion by Breyer, joined by Stevens.

FDA v. Brown & Williamson Tobacco Corp. 120 S. Ct. 1291, 68 USLW 4194 (3-20-00)

FDA jurisdiction to regulate tobacco products: The FDA lacks authority under the Federal Food, Drug, and Cosmetic Act (FDCA) to regulate tobacco products. Congress has "directly spoken" to the issue of FDA jurisdiction within the meaning of *Chevron v. NRDC* (1984), and has precluded the FDA's assertion of jurisdiction. The issue is not determined solely by reference to the FDCA's definitions, but rather by reference to the Act as a whole, by reference to "tobacco-specific" legislation enacted after the FDCA, and to "common sense as to the manner in which Congress is likely to delegate a policy decision of such economic and political magnitude to an administrative agency." Tobacco products "simply do not fit" within the FDCA's regulatory scheme. A core purpose of the FDCA is to ensure that regulated products are "safe" and "effective" for their intended uses. Because the FDA exhaustively documented that tobacco products are unsafe and present extraordinary health risks, the agency would be required to remove these products from the market if it asserts jurisdiction to regulate them. Congress, however, has foreclosed the removal of tobacco products from the market. The six laws enacted since 1965 that directly address smoking and health all stop "well short of ordering a ban" on sale. Moreover, Congress' tobacco-specific statutes have "effectively ratified" the FDA's former, long-held position that it lacked authority to regulate tobacco products absent manufacturers' claims of therapeutic benefit. Congress has relied on the FDA's denial of jurisdiction in legislating to address smoking and health, has rejected bills that would have conferred such jurisdiction on the FDA, and has also acted to preclude other agencies from exercising regulatory authority in the area.

5-4. Opinion of Court by O'Connor, joined by Rehnquist, Scalia, Kennedy, and Thomas. Dissenting opinion by Breyer, joined by Stevens, Souter, and Ginsburg.

Fiore v. White 120 S. Ct. 469, 68 USLW 4001 (11-30-99)

Certification of state law question to state court: An issue involving the correct interpretation of a Pennsylvania statute at the time the petitioner's conviction became final is certified to the Pennsylvania Supreme Court. The petitioner, who owned and operated a hazardous waste facility, and his co-defendant, who was the facility's general manager, were both convicted of operating the facility without a permit. They possessed a permit, but had altered a monitoring pipe in order to hide a leakage problem. The petitioner's conviction was affirmed on appeal, and the Pennsylvania Supreme Court refused to review his case. After the petitioner's conviction became final, the Pennsylvania Supreme Court upheld an intermediate court's reversal of the facility manager's conviction, and ruled that violation of permit conditions did not constitute operation of the facility without a permit. The petitioner then initiated *habeas corpus* proceedings, alleging a due process deprivation. The question certified to the Pennsylvania Supreme Court is whether its interpretation in the facility manager's case stated the correct understanding of the statute at the time the petitioner's conviction became final, or whether it changed a prior understanding. Answer to this certified question will help the U.S. Supreme Court determine "the proper state law predicate" for resolving the constitutional issue raised.

9-0. Opinion for unanimous Court by Breyer.

Fischer v. United States 120 S. Ct. 1780, 68 USLW 4370 (5-15-00)

Federal bribery statute, scope: The federal bribery statute's prohibition on defrauding organizations that receive over $10,000 in "benefits" under a Federal program, 18 U.S.C. § 666, applies to hospital organizations that participate in the Medicare program. Language in section 666 providing that covered federal programs may involve a "grant, contract, subsidy, loan, guarantee, insurance, or other form of Federal assistance" reveals that Congress viewed many federal assistance programs as conferring benefits, and also reveals "Congress' expansive, unambiguous intent to ensure the integrity" of participating organizations. The fact that patients receive "benefits" under the program does not foreclose the possibility of other beneficiaries. Medicare payments to providers "are made for significant and substantial reasons in addition to compensation or reimbursement." Medicare is "a comprehensive federal assistance enterprise aimed at ensuring the availability of quality health care for the broader community." The Government has "a legitimate and significant interest in prohibiting financial fraud . . . being perpetrated upon Medicare providers," since fraudulent acts threaten the program's integrity and raise the risk that the providers will lack the resources necessary to maintain the desired level and quality of care.

7-2. Opinion of Court by Kennedy, joined by Rehnquist, Stevens, O'Connor, Souter, Ginsburg, and Breyer. Dissenting opinion by Thomas, joined by Scalia.

Flippo v. West Virginia 120 S. Ct. 7, 68 USLW 3260 (11-18-99)

Fourth Amendment, warrant requirement, crime scene search: There is no general "murder scene exception" to the warrant requirement. In *Mincey v. Arizona* (1978), the Court held that a warrantless search of an apartment "was not constitutionally permissible simply because a homicide had recently occurred there." The state trial court's finding in this case that a warrantless search of "anything and everything found within" a crime scene that had been secured for investigation was "within the law" is inconsistent with *Mincey*. The trial court in this case erred, therefore, in relying on such a principle to admit into evidence photographs found within a briefcase left at a crime scene.

9-0. Per curiam.

Florida v. J. L. 120 S. Ct. 1375, 68 USLW 4236 (3-28-00)

Fourth Amendment, *Terry* stop, anonymous tip: An anonymous tip that a person is carrying a gun is not, without more, sufficient to justify a police officer's stop and frisk of that person. Under some circumstances an anonymous tip, suitably corroborated, may exhibit sufficient indicia of reliability to provide reasonable suspicion necessary to justify an investigatory *Terry* stop. The tip in this case, however, contained no predictive information, and left the police with no means of testing the informant's knowledge or credibility about the alleged criminal activity. An accurate description of a subject's readily observable location and appearance does not demonstrate that the tipster has knowledge of concealed criminal activity. Reasonable suspicion requires that a tip be reliable in its assertion of illegality, and not merely reliable in its identification of someone. There is no "firearm exception" to this reasonable suspicion requirement. Such an exception would "rove too far" by enabling anyone to harass another person simply by placing an anonymous call to the police falsely accusing the person of carrying a firearm. The Court will not "speculate" about whether there are other circumstances (e.g., a report of a person carrying a bomb) where the danger might be so great as to justify a search without a showing of reliability.

9-0. Opinion for unanimous Court by Ginsburg. Concurring opinion by Kennedy, joined by Rehnquist.

Free v. Abbott Laboratories, Inc. 120 S. Ct. 1578, 68 USLW 4254 (4-3-00)

Federal courts, jurisdiction: The decision of the United States Court of Appeals for the Fifth Circuit, holding that the supplemental jurisdiction statute, 28 U.S.C. § 1367, overrules *Zahn v. International Paper Co.* (1973), and thus expands federal subject matter jurisdiction in a class action to encompass unnamed class members whose claims do not satisfy the amount-in-controversy requirement of 28 U.S.C. § 1332, as long as diversity jurisdiction exists for one named plaintiff, is affirmed by equally divided vote.

4-4. *Per curiam*. Justice O'Connor did not participate.

Friends of the Earth v. Laidlaw Envtl. Servs. 120 S. Ct. 693, 68 USLW 4044 (1-12-00)

Mootness, standing to sue: Environmental organizations had standing to assert the interests of their members in a Clean Water Act citizen suit seeking injunctive relief and civil penalties for violation of a discharge permit. The relevant showing for Article III standing is not injury to the environment, but rather injury to the plaintiffs. Here the environmental organizations established standing by documenting that the defendant's permit violations directly affected the recreational, aesthetic, and economic interests of their members. Redressability, one of the essential elements of standing, was present even though civil penalties are payable to the Government rather than to the plaintiffs. The civil penalties "carried with them a deterrent effect that made it likely, as opposed to merely speculative, that the penalties would redress [plaintiffs'] injuries by abating current violations and preventing future ones." The claims for civil penalties were not mooted by the defendant's compliance with its permit after the commencement of the litigation. Mootness is not merely "standing set in a time frame." There can be exceptions to mootness, *e.g.*, "capable of repetition, yet evading review," that cannot be recognized for standing. The district court's denial of injunctive relief and the plaintiffs' failure to appeal that denial did not moot the case; the district court's assessment of civil penalties recognized a need for deterrence.

7-2. Opinion of Court by Ginsburg, joined by Rehnquist, Stevens, O'Connor, Kennedy, Souter, and Breyer. Concurring opinions by Stevens and Kennedy. Dissenting opinion by Scalia, joined by Thomas.

Garner v. Jones 120 S. Ct. 1362, 68 USLW 4230 (3-28-00)

Ex Post Facto Clause, extension of time between parole hearings: Evidence was insufficient to determine whether action by the Georgia Board of Pardons and Paroles extending from three years to eight years the period between mandatory reconsideration of parole for inmates serving terms of life imprisonment violates the Ex Post Facto Clause, Art. I, § 10, cl. 1. A retroactive change in a law governing parole can violate the Clause if the change creates "a sufficient risk of increasing the measure of punishment" for a prisoner. In this case the rule changing the frequency of parole reviews was qualified in two respects. The law gave the Board discretion to determine how often within the eight-year period to reconsider an inmate's status, and the law also preserved the possibility of an earlier reconsideration based on a change of circumstances or new information. This discretion, allowing the Board to focus on prisoners deserving reconsideration, may result in some prisoners being released earlier than would have been the case otherwise. The record contained insufficient information to determine whether the change in the rule significantly increases the likelihood of prolonging the respondent's incarceration.

6-3. Opinion of Court by Kennedy, joined by Rehnquist, O'Connor, Thomas, and Breyer. Concurring opinion by Scalia. Dissenting opinion by Souter, joined by Stevens and Ginsburg.

Geier v. American Honda Motor Co. 120 S. Ct. 1913, 68 USLW 4425 (5-22-00)

Preemption, federal motor vehicle safety standard: Federal Motor Vehicle Safety Standard 208, which required auto manufacturers to equip some but not all of their 1987 vehicles with passive restraints, preempts a state common law action against a manufacturer for negligence for failure to equip a 1987 vehicle with a driver's side airbag. The express preemption provision of the National Traffic and Motor Vehicle Safety Act, which prohibits states from applying "any safety standard" different from an applicable federal standard, does not by itself preempt the state tort action. Preemption by statute is inconsistent with the

Act's "saving clause," which provides that "compliance with" a federal safety standard "does not exempt any person from any liability under common law." This saving clause, however, does not foreclose or limit the operation of ordinary preemption principles governing override of state laws – including common law tort rules – that conflict with federal statutes or regulations. Application of the tort rule would actually conflict with standard 208 because it would operate to frustrate the objectives of the federal rule. The federal standard sought variety, by allowing manufacturers to choose from among several different passive restraint systems, and also sought a gradual phase-in of passive restraints. Imposition of liability for failure to equip a particular car with an airbag is inconsistent with these approaches of dealer-choice and gradualism.

5-4. Opinion of Court by Breyer, joined by Rehnquist, O'Connor, Scalia, and Kennedy. Dissenting opinion by Stevens, joined by Souter, Thomas, and Ginsburg.

Gutierrez v. Ada 120 S. Ct. 740, 68 USLW 4066 (1-19-00)

Guam Organic Act, statutory construction: The Guam Organic Act does not require a runoff election when a candidate slate for Governor and Lieutenant Governor has received a majority of the votes cast for Governor and Lieutenant Governor, but not a majority of the number of ballots cast in the simultaneous general election. The Act provides for a runoff election "[i]f no candidates receive a majority of the votes cast in any election . . . ." In context, it is clear that "any election" refers to an election for Governor and Lieutenant Governor. The reference to "any election" is preceded by two references to gubernatorial election and followed by four. A word is known by the company it keeps. "Other clues" confirm this interpretation. The reference to "general election" later in the same provision suggests that Congress would not have used "any election" to mean "general election." Also, Congress has distinguished between "votes" and "ballots" in the same context of Guamanian elections. Equating the two terms would "impute to the Congress a strange preference for making it hard to select a Governor" by requiring a runoff "even though one slate already had a majority of all those who cared to make any choice among gubernatorial candidates." A law enacted four years later, referring to "a majority of votes cast for the office of Delegate" is more precise, but does not purport to differentiate between Delegate and gubernatorial elections. The term "any election" does not create a redundancy, since it may refer to the initial election and any elections held in the future.

9-0. Opinion for unanimous Court by Souter.

Harris Trust and Sav. Bank v. Salomon Smith Barney, Inc. 120 S. Ct. 2159, 68 USLW 4508 (6-12-00)

ERISA, action against nonfiduciaries: ERISA § 502(a)(3) authorizes a civil action against a nonfiduciary who participates in a transaction prohibited by ERISA § 406(a)(1). Section 406(a), which bars a fiduciary of an employee benefit plan from causing the plan to engage in certain transactions with a "party in interest," imposes a duty only on the fiduciary. Section 502(a)(3), however, which authorizes a civil action to obtain "appropriate equitable relief" to redress violations of title I, itself imposes certain duties. Liability under section 502(a)(3), therefore, does not depend on whether ERISA's substantive provisions impose a specific duty on the party being sued. The provision contains no limit on the universe of possible defendants, while, by contrast, other provisions of ERISA do address who may be a defendant. Because section 502(*l*) authorizes the Secretary to assess a civil penalty against "any other person" who knowingly participates in a fiduciary's breach, "it follows that a participant, beneficiary, or fiduciary may bring suit against an 'other person' under the similarly worded subsection (a)(3)." Concerns about possible misuse of section 502(a)(3) are alleviated by the limitation to "appropriate equitable relief." Also, the common law of trusts countenances the same sort of relief sought here, as, for example, when a trustee breaches his fiduciary duty by transferring trust property to a third person.

9-0. Opinion for unanimous Court by Thomas.

Hartford Underwriters Ins. Co. v. Union Planters Bank 120 S. Ct. 1942, 68 USLW 4441 (5-30-00)

Bankruptcy, administrative claim: 11 U.S.C. § 506(c) does not allow an administrative claimant of a bankruptcy estate to recover payment of its claim from property encumbered by a secured creditor's lien. The petitioner insurance company had provided workers' compensation insurance to respondent company during Chapter 11 reorganization proceedings, and the premiums were not paid. The reorganization was converted into a Chapter 7 liquidation, and the petitioner sought to recover the premiums as an administrative expense. Section 506(c), which provides that "the trustee may recover from property securing an allowed secured claim the reasonable, necessary costs . . . of preserving . . . such property," creates an exception to the normal rule that secured claims are superior to administrative claims. The plain language of the provision specifies that it is the "trustee" who may recover administrative costs, and the proper inference is that the trustee is the only party so empowered. The trustee's "unique role in bankruptcy proceedings makes it entirely plausible that Congress would provide a power to him and not to others." The fact that Congress did not use "only" or other restrictive language does not mean that parties other than the trustee may invoke the provision. In this case the language of the Code leaves no room for clarification by reference to pre-Code practice. It is also "far from clear" that policy implications favor petitioner's position. In any event, achieving a better policy outcome than that produced by a natural reading of the text "is a task for Congress, not the courts."

9-0. Opinion for unanimous Court by Scalia.

Hill v. Colorado 120 S. Ct. 2480, 68 USLW 4643 (6-28-00)

First Amendment, restrictions on speech near clinics: A Colorado statute making it unlawful within 100 feet of a health care facility to approach within eight feet of another person, without that person's consent, for the purpose of passing a leaflet or handbill, displaying a sign, or engaging in protest, education, or counseling, is constitutional. The measure is a valid content-neutral "time, place, or manner" regulation of speech that balances the rights of law-abiding speakers to attempt to persuade others to change their views and the recognized privacy interest of the unwilling listener in avoiding unwanted communication. The restrictions are content-neutral because they regulate only the places where some speech may occur, and because they apply equally to all demonstrators, regardless of viewpoint. Although the restrictions do not apply to all speech, the "kind of cursory examination" that might be required to distinguish casual conversation from protest, education, or counseling is not "problematic." The law is "narrowly tailored" to achieve the state's interests. The 8-foot restriction does not significantly impair the ability to convey messages by signs, and ordinarily allows speakers to come within a normal conversational distance of their targets. Because the statute allows the speaker to remain in one place, persons who wish to hand out leaflets may position themselves beside entrances near the path of oncoming pedestrians, and consequently are not deprived of the opportunity to get the attention of persons entering a clinic. The statute is neither overbroad nor unconstitutionally vague.

6-3. Opinion of Court by Stevens, joined by Rehnquist, O'Connor, Souter, Ginsburg, and Breyer. Concurring opinion by Souter, joined by O'Connor, Ginsburg, and Breyer. Dissenting opinions by Scalia, joined by Thomas; and by Kennedy.

Hunt-Wesson, Inc. v. Franchise Tax Bd. Of California 120 S. Ct. 1022, 68 USLW 4127
(2-22-00)

Taxation, State, "unitary" income, multistate corporation: California's rules for taxing its share of a multistate, nondomiciliary corporation's income violate the Due Process and Commerce Clauses by carving out an exception to its interest expense deduction measured by the amount of nonunitary dividend and interest income that the corporation has received. California uses a "unitary business" income calculation for determining its taxable share of a multistate corporation's income. Under that system the corporation's total income from its nationwide business is first determined, and the share appropriately attributed to California is then calculated by applying ratios reflecting instate property, payroll, and sales. The "unitary" income subject to tax excludes income derived from a business enterprise that is separate and "discrete" from that conducted instate. A state may not constitutionally tax this "nonunitary" business income. California specifies that the amount of interest that may be deducted is the amount by which "interest expense exceeds interest and dividend income . . . not subject to allocation by formula" – *i.e.*, the amount by which interest expense exceeds interest and dividends received from nonunitary business or investment. If California could show that its deduction limit actually reflects the portion of the expense properly attributable to nonunitary income, the tax would not, in fact, be a tax on nonunitary income. California cannot do so, however, and also cannot establish that its limit is a reasonable effort to allocate the deduction between taxable and tax-exempt income. Other approaches, such as ratio-based rules, recognize that borrowing may support nonunitary investment as well as the unitary business, but do not assume as California does that *all* borrowing first supports nonunitary business.

9-0. Opinion for unanimous Court by Breyer.

Illinois v. Wardlow 120 S. Ct. 673, 68 USLW 4031 (1-12-00)

Fourth Amendment, flight from police, *Terry* stop: Police officers did not violate the respondent's Fourth Amendment rights by pursuing him and subjecting him to a *Terry* stop after he fled from a high crime area upon the arrival of the officers' patrol. In *Terry v. Ohio* (1968), the Court held that a police officer may conduct a brief, investigatory stop of a person if the officer has a reasonable, articulable suspicion that the person is engaging in criminal activity. Here, the respondent's presence in a high-crime area was not enough, standing alone, to create such a reasonable suspicion, but his "unprovoked flight [from the area] when noticing the police," did create a reasonable suspicion that he was involved in criminal activity. "Headlong flight – wherever it occurs – is the consummate act of evasion; it is not necessarily indicative of wrongdoing, but it is certainly suggestive of such." A person approached by officers who lack probable cause or reasonable suspicion may refuse to cooperate, but "unprovoked flight is simply not a mere refusal to cooperate." The fact that there may be innocent reasons for flight does not prevent an investigative stop; even in *Terry* the conduct justifying the stop was ambiguous, and the officers were allowed to detain the individual to "resolve the ambiguity."

5-4. Opinion of Court by Rehnquist, joined by O'Connor, Scalia, Kennedy, and Thomas. Dissenting and concurring (concurring only as to rejection of *per se* approach) opinion by Stevens, joined by Souter, Ginsburg, and Breyer.

Johnson v. United States 120 S. Ct. 1795, 68 USLW 4378 (5-15-00)

Statutes, interpretation, retroactivity: A 1994 amendment to the Sentencing Reform Act (18 U.S.C. § 3583h)) does not apply retroactively, and hence there is no need to consider whether its retroactive application would violate the prohibition on *ex post facto* laws. There are no indications that Congress intended the provision to apply retroactively, and the normal rule, in the absence of contrary indications, is that the effective date is the date of enactment. The preexisting provision, 18 U.S.C. § 3583(e)(3), permits imposition of additional supervised release following revocation of supervised release and reimprisonment. The provision allows a court to "revoke a term of supervised release, and require the person to serve in prison all or part of the term of supervised release." Focus on the verb "revoke" would lead the Court to conclude that the language confers no authority to impose supervised release following the reincarceration. The "conventional" meaning of "revoke" is to annul by recalling or taking back. There are "some textual reasons," however, to conclude otherwise. Subsection (e)(1) authorizes a court when circumstances warrant to "terminate" a term of supervised release and discharge the supervised person. "If subsection (3) had likewise been meant to conclude any possibility of supervised release later, it would have been natural for Congress to write in like terms." Also, since subsection (3) provides that "all or part of the term of supervised release" may be served in prison, this means that "something about the term of supervised release survives" the revocation order. Moreover, there is an "unconventional" usage of "revoke," supported by a dictionary, that indicates that the "recall" need not be final, but may be "tentative for deliberation." Finally, this "unconventional" reading comports with the evident congressional purpose of improving the odds of a successful transition from prison to liberty.

8-1. Opinion of Court by Souter, joined by Rehnquist, Stevens, O'Connor, Ginsburg, and Breyer, and joined in part by Kennedy. Concurring opinions by Kennedy and by Thomas. Dissenting opinion by Scalia.

Jones v. United States 120 S. Ct. 1904, 68 USLW 4422 (5-22-00)

Commerce, arson of private residence: Arson of an owner-occupied private residence does not fall within the coverage of the federal arson statute, 18 U.S.C. § 844(i), which prohibits arson of "any building used in interstate or foreign commerce or in any activity affecting [such] commerce." The key word is "used," and the appropriate inquiry is into the function of the building. What is required is active employment of a building for commercial purposes. "Use" of the building as collateral to obtain a mortgage from an out-of-state lender, to obtain insurance from an out-of-state company, or to receive natural gas from another state, does not satisfy this test. Nor does the Court's decision in *Russell v. United States* (1985), in which the Court upheld application of the statute to arson of a 2-unit apartment building, require a different result. The *Russell* Court merely recognized that rental of real estate is "unquestionably" an activity that affects commerce. Were the Court to accept the Government's interpretation that owner-occupied private residences are covered, "hardly a building in the land would fall outside the federal statute's domain." Moreover, construing the statute as not applying to such private residences is consistent with the principle of constitutional doubt. A statute susceptible of two interpretations, one of which raises serious constitutional questions and one of which does not, should be interpreted to avoid the constitutional issue. Were the arson statute interpreted to apply to owner-occupied private residences, the issue of its validity under *United States v. Lopez* (1995) would be presented.

9-0. Opinion for unanimous Court by Ginsburg. Concurring opinions by Stevens, joined by Thomas; and by Thomas, joined by Scalia.

Kimel v. Florida Bd. of Regents 120 S. Ct. 631, 68 USLW 4016 (1-11-00)

Age Discrimination in Employment Act; 14th Amendment Enforcement Power: The Age Discrimination in Employment Act (ADEA) contains a clear statement of congressional intent to abrogate states' Eleventh Amendment immunity from suit in federal court, but that abrogation exceeded congressional authority under section 5 of the Fourteenth Amendment. Congressional intent to abrogate states' Eleventh Amendment immunity is "unmistakably clear" in the ADEA. The Act authorizes employees to maintain actions "against any employer (including a public agency) in any Federal or State court of competent jurisdiction," and defines the term "public agency" to include "the government of a State or political subdivision thereof." Because Congress lacks power under Article I to abrogate states' Eleventh Amendment immunity, but may do so pursuant to section 5 of the Fourteenth Amendment, the private petitioners in this case may maintain their federal court actions against states only if the ADEA is "appropriate" legislation under section 5. The test for appropriateness is whether there is a "congruence and proportionality between the [constitutional] injury to be prevented or remedied and the means adopted to that end." Age is not a suspect class under the Equal Protection Clause, and hence age classifications must be "irrational" before being held unconstitutional. Given this standard, the ADEA is "so out of proportion to a remedial or preventive object that it cannot be understood as responsive to, or designed to prevent, unconstitutional behavior." Congress pursuant to its section 5 power may enact "reasonably prophylactic legislation," but the legislative history of the ADEA falls "well short" of demonstrating any pattern of age discrimination by the states, let alone any discrimination rising to the level of a constitutional violation.

5-4 (section 5 power); **7-2** (unmistakable clarity of abrogation). Opinion of Court by O'Connor, joined in part by Rehnquist, Scalia, Kennedy, and Thomas; and joined in separate part by Rehnquist, Stevens, Scalia, Souter, Ginsburg, and Breyer. Opinion by Stevens, concurring in part and dissenting in part, joined by Souter, Ginsburg, and Breyer. Opinion by Thomas, concurring in part and dissenting in part, joined by Kennedy.

Los Angeles Police Dep't v. United Reporting Publishing Corp. 120 S. Ct. 483, 68 USLW 4005 (12-7-99)

First Amendment, overbreadth: A California statute restricting access to police-held information about the addresses of arrestees and crime victims is not subject to a First Amendment facial challenge by a company that obtains the information and sells it to others. The law requires that an entity requesting an address declare that the information will not be used to sell a product or service. At least for purposes of facial invalidity, the statute does not abridge anyone's speech, but instead merely regulates access to information. "California could decide not to give out arrestee information at all without violating the First Amendment." The traditional rule is that a person to whom a statute may constitutionally be applied may not challenge that statute on the ground that it may conceivably be applied unconstitutionally to others in situations not before the court. One of the exceptions to this traditional rule is based on First Amendment overbreadth but that exception is employed only sparingly, and the effect of the statute on the company's potential customers does not justify its invocation. Potential customers face no threat of prosecution, and there is no possibility that protected speech will be muted.

7-2. Opinion of Court by Rehnquist, joined by O'Connor, Scalia, Souter, Thomas, Ginsburg, and Breyer. Concurring opinions by Scalia, joined by Thomas; and by Ginsburg, joined by O'Connor, Souter, and Breyer. Dissenting opinion by Stevens, joined by Kennedy.

Martinez v. Court of Appeal of California, Fourth App. Dist. 120 S. Ct. 684, 68 USLW 4040 (1-12-00)

Appeals, self-representation: There is no constitutional right to self-representation on direct appeal from a criminal conviction. The rule of *Faretta v. California* (1975) that a criminal defendant has a constitutional right to proceed without counsel at trial, is inapplicable on appeal. The Court's conclusion in *Faretta* was based on three interrelated arguments, relying on historical evidence, the structure of the Sixth Amendment, and respect for the individual. The historical evidence supporting a trial right no longer has the same force, and, in any event, "there simply was no long-respected right of self-representation on appeal." The structure of the Sixth Amendment is not relevant; the Amendment identifies "rights that are available in preparation for trial and at the trial itself," but does not include any right to appeal. Respect for individual autonomy is applicable to an appellant as well as to a defendant at trial, but any right to self-representation based on autonomy must be grounded in the Due Process Clause, and there is insufficient risk of disloyal counsel or suspicion of disloyalty to justify recognition of a constitutional right. "The requirement of representation by trained counsel implies no disrespect for the individual inasmuch as it tends to benefit the appellant as well as the court."

9-0. Opinion of Court by Stevens, joined by Rehnquist, O'Connor, Kennedy, Souter, Thomas, Ginsburg, and Breyer. Separate concurring opinions by Kennedy, Breyer, and Scalia.

Miller v. French 120 S. Ct. 2246, 68 USLW 4535 (6-19-00)

Prison Litigation Reform Act, stay of injunctions, separation of powers: The automatic stay provision of the Prison Litigation Reform Act is mandatory, and the Act precludes courts from exercising equitable power to enjoin the stays. Under the provision, a motion to modify or terminate prospective relief "shall operate as a stay during the period . . . beginning on the 30th day after such motion is filed . . . and ending on the date the court enters a final order ruling on the motion." The statutory command that the motion "shall operate as a stay during [the specified time period]" indicates that the stay is mandatory throughout that time period. "To allow courts to exercise their equitable discretion to prevent the stay from 'operating' during this statutorily prescribed period would . . . contradict [the provision's] plain terms." Because Congress's intent to remove equitable discretion is "unmistakable," the doctrine of constitutional doubt is inapplicable and the constitutional issue raised by the provision must be faced. The automatic stay provision does not violate separation of powers principles. *Hayburn's Case* is inapplicable; the stay does not vest in Executive Branch officials review of the decisions of an Article III court. Although the stay provision can be viewed as legislatively suspending a final judgment of an Article III court, it operates to establish new standards for prospective injunctive relief. Prospective relief under a continuing injunction remains subject to alteration due to changes in conditions and changes in the law. Whether the automatic stay's deadline for judicial decisionmaking is so short as to deprive litigants of a meaningful opportunity to be heard is a due process question that is not before the Court.

7-2 (statutory interpretation); **5-2** (separation of powers). Opinion of Court by O'Connor, joined by Rehnquist, Scalia, Kennedy, and Thomas, and joined in part by Souter and Ginsburg. Opinion by Souter, concurring in part (statutory grounds) and dissenting in part (separation of powers), joined by Ginsburg. Dissenting opinion (statutory grounds) by Breyer, joined by Stevens.

Mitchell v. Helms 120 S. Ct. 2530, 68 USLW 4668 (6-28-00)

Establishment Clause, aid to parochial schools: Provision of federal assistance to private schools in the form of loans of educational materials and equipment does not violate the Establishment Clause, even though some of the private schools receiving assistance are religiously affiliated. The assistance, authorized by chapter 2 of the Education Consolidation and Improvement Act of 1981, is provided to public and private schools alike based on the number of children enrolled in each school. Because of these neutral, secular criteria, chapter 2 does not define its recipients by reference to religion in violation of the principle set forth in *Agostini v. Felton* (1997). Nor does chapter 2 result in "governmental indoctrination" of religion within the meaning of *Agostini*. The four-Justice plurality and the two-Justice concurrence disagree as to rationale, but agree that *Meek v. Pittenger* (1975) and *Wolman v. Walter* (1977) are overruled with respect to their holdings that governmental loan of instructional materials and equipment to religious schools is unconstitutional. The distinction drawn in those cases between loan of textbooks (held to be permissible) and loan of other instructional materials and equipment (held impermissible) is untenable.

6-3. No opinion of Court. Opinion by Thomas, joined by Rehnquist, Scalia, and Kennedy. Concurring opinion by O'Connor, joined by Breyer. Dissenting opinion by Souter, joined by Stevens and Ginsburg.

Mobil Oil Expl. & Prod. S.E., Inc. v. United States 120 S. Ct. 2423, 68 USLW 4615 (6-26-00)

Government contracts, OCS oil and gas lease: The Government has breached its outer continental shelf (OCS) oil and gas lease agreements with the petitioner oil companies, and the companies are therefore entitled to restitution of "bonus" payments made to the Government. In return for the bonus payments, the companies in 1981 received 10-year lease contracts with the United States that entitled them to explore for oil off the North Carolina coast and develop any oil that they found, subject to royalty payments and to compliance with specified statutes, including the Outer Continental Shelf Lands Act (OCSLA), and regulations. A new law enacted in 1990, the Outer Banks Protection Act (OBPA), imposed additional requirements. OBPA prohibited the Secretary of the Interior from approving any OCS exploration or development plan until new studies required by OBPA were completed and requisite findings had been made, and placed a minimum 13-month delay on approvals. Under the OCSLA, the Secretary had been required to approve within 30 days an exploration plan that satisfied that Act's requirements. After enactment of OBPA, the Secretary took no further action on the petitioners' plans. This inaction constituted a breach of the lease agreements. The lease agreements' explicit references to future regulations under specified laws means that the agreements were not subject to future regulations promulgated under other laws, including new statutes like OBPA. OBPA required Interior to impose the contract-violating delays, but "the fact that Interior's repudiation rested upon the enactment of a new statute makes no significant difference." The Government's breach was substantial and material. The companies did not waive their right to restitution, since they did not receive "substantial" post-repudiation performance from the Government. Whether the companies could ultimately have developed oil under the contracts is irrelevant, since the companies seek restitution of bonus payments rather than damages.

8-1. Opinion of Court by Breyer, joined by Rehnquist, O'Connor, Scalia, Kennedy, Souter, Thomas, and Ginsburg. Dissenting opinion by Stevens.

Nelson v. Adams 120 S. Ct. 1579, 68 USLW 4311 (4-25-00)

Due process, personal liability: The federal district court denied the petitioner due process and also violated Rule 15, Federal Rules of Civil Procedure, by simultaneously granting a motion to amend the pleadings to make the petitioner a party and subjecting him to liability for costs and attorney's fees in an action brought against a company of which he was president and sole shareholder. Rule 15 directs that, if a court grants leave to amend a pleading to add a party, that party must be given 10 days to respond on the merits after service of the amended pleading. Here, the district court granted permission to amend the pleading and altered the judgment "at a single stroke." The petitioner therefore was never given an opportunity to respond and contest his personal liability after he was made a party and before the entry of judgment against him.

9-0. Opinion for unanimous Court by Ginsburg.

New York v. Hill 120 S. Ct. 659, 68 USLW 4029 (1-11-00)

Interstate Agreement on Detainers: A defense counsel's agreement to a trial date outside the time period required by Article III of the Interstate Agreement on Detainers (IAD) bars the defendant from seeking dismissal because his trial did not occur within that period. Article III provides that a prisoner must be brought to trial within 180 days of the prisoner's request for disposition of the detainer, "provided that for good cause shown . . . , the prisoner and his counsel being present, the court . . . may grant any necessary or reasonable continuance." There is a general rule, applicable to most rights of a criminal defendant, that presumes the availability of waiver. "Scheduling matters" are among the rights that need not be waived personally by defendants, but instead may be waived by action of counsel. The "necessary or reasonable continuance" provision is the sole means by which the prosecution may obtain an extension over the defendant's objection, but it does not preclude a defendant from waiving his right by other means. There is no general principle that a private right that also benefits society may not be waived. Waiver is not allowed if it would contravene a statutory policy, but here there is no unalterable statutory policy barring waiver. There is no requirement that waiver of the speedy trial rights guaranteed by the IAD be effected by an affirmative request.

9-0. Opinion for unanimous Court by Scalia.

Nixon v. Shrink Missouri Government PAC 120 S. Ct. 897, 68 USLW 4102 (1-24-00)

First Amendment, campaign finance, contribution limitation: *Buckley v. Valeo* (1976), in which the Court upheld against First Amendment challenge restrictions on contributions to federal election campaigns and struck down limitations on expenditures linked to specific candidates, is authority for upholding state limits on contributions to state political candidates. State contribution limits need not, however, be pegged to the dollar amounts approved in *Buckley*. In distinguishing contribution limits from expenditure limits, the Court in *Buckley* determined that limiting the amount of contributions had little impact on speech and association rights protected by the First Amendment. The Court also determined that prevention of corruption and the appearance of corruption was a constitutionally sufficient justification for the contribution limits. Here Missouri espouses those same interests of preventing corruption and the appearance of corruption, and the respondents allege that Missouri failed to produce empirical evidence to justify invocation of those interests. This case "does not present a close call requiring further definition of whatever the State's evidentiary obligation may be." Missouri does not preserve legislative history. The record, however, consisting of an affidavit by a legislative leader, newspaper articles, and findings by the district court as well as the Eight Circuit, is sufficient to substantiate Missouri's concerns. The current Missouri limit of $1075 for statewide elections is not, as a result of inflation, violative of *Buckley*. In *Buckley*, the Court rejected the contention that the $1,000 limit then approved was a constitutional minimum. Rather, the issue is whether the limits are "so low as to impede the ability of candidates to amass the resources necessary for effective advocacy." Respondents have not established that Missouri's contribution limits so operate to suppress effective political advocacy.

6-3. Opinion of Court by Souter, joined by Rehnquist, Stevens, O'Connor, Ginsburg, and Breyer. Concurring opinions by Stevens; and by Breyer, joined by Ginsburg. Dissenting opinions by Kennedy; and by Thomas, joined by Scalia.

Norfolk So. Ry. v. Shanklin 120 S. Ct. 1467, 68 USLW 4258 (4-17-00)

Preemption, Federal Railroad Safety Act: A state tort action alleging negligence based on inadequate warning devices at a railway grade crossing is preempted if the warning devices at issue were installed with federal funds under a project approved by the federal government. Regulations promulgated under the FRSA set standards for warning devices installed with federal funds; these standards require automatic gates and flashing lights where certain conditions are present, and require approval by the Federal Highway Administration if those conditions are not present. The Court determined in *CSX Transportation, Inc. v. Easterwood* (1993) that state tort law is preempted if these regulations are applicable. The regulations are applicable and "mandatory for all warning devices installed with federal funds." The FHWA's new interpretation, that preemption is appropriate only for the "priority" or "hazard program" that is based on diagnostic studies and particularized analysis, and not for the "minimum protection" program, is not entitled to deference. The agency's new interpretation "contradicts the regulations' plain text," and departs from the previous interpretation that the Court adopted as "authoritative" in the *Easterwood* case. States are free to install more protective warning devices, but they may not hold the railroad responsible for the adequacy of devices installed with federal funds.

7-2. Opinion of Court by O'Connor, joined by Rehnquist, Scalia, Kennedy, Souter, Thomas, and Breyer. Concurring opinion by Breyer. Dissenting opinion by Ginsburg, joined by Stevens.

Ohler v. United States 120 S. Ct. 1851, 68 USLW 4396 (5-22-00)

Evidence, appeals: A defendant in a criminal trial who during direct examination voluntarily introduces evidence of a prior conviction may not on appeal challenge the admission of such evidence. This is so even though the testimony was offered only after an *in limine* ruling allowing the Government to introduce the prior conviction as impeachment evidence. Generally, a party introducing evidence cannot complain on appeal that the evidence was erroneously admitted. Neither Federal Rule of Evidence 103 nor Rule 609 addresses the question. Rule 609 has been amended to clarify that prior conviction evidence may be introduced on direct examination, but it does no more than that. Both the Government and the defendant must make choices as a criminal trial progresses, and there is nothing "unfair" about putting the defendant to her choice as to whether to forego the tactical advantage of preemptively introducing evidence of the conviction in order to preserve her right to appeal the *in limine* ruling. Nor does this waiver rule unconstitutionally burden her right to appeal.

5-4. Opinion of Court by Rehnquist, joined by O'Connor, Scalia, Kennedy, and Thomas. Dissenting opinion by Souter, joined by Stevens, Ginsburg, and Breyer.

Pegram v. Herdrich 120 S. Ct. 2143, 68 USLW 4501 (6-12-00)

ERISA, HMOs, fiduciary duty, treatment decisions: Treatment decisions made by a health maintenance organization (HMO), acting through its physician employees, are not fiduciary acts within the meaning of ERISA. In this case a patient who suffered a ruptured appendix following her HMO doctor's decision to delay treatment sued for malpractice, and also sued the HMO under ERISA for violation of a fiduciary duty by offering incentives to their doctors to hold down treatment costs. An HMO's treatment decisions are intertwined with eligibility decisions. Typically fiduciary responsibilities relate to managing assets and distributing property to beneficiaries, and it is doubtful whether Congress intended to extend fiduciary responsibilities to mixed eligibility and treatment decisions by HMO doctors. Consideration of the consequences of extending coverage confirms that Congress made no such choice. Allowing recovery for breach of fiduciary responsibility simply upon a showing that the profit incentive to ration health care would generally affect mixed eligibility and treatment decisions would have the effect of eliminating the for-profit HMO, yet Congress "has promoted the formation of HMO practices" for 27 years. Courts have "no warrant to precipitate [such an] upheaval." The appeals court's effort to confine the fiduciary breach to cases in which the financial motive was the "sole purpose" of delaying or withholding treatment "entails erroneous corruption of fiduciary obligation." ERISA was not enacted "in order to federalize malpractice litigation in the name of fiduciary duty."

9-0. Opinion for unanimous Court by Souter.

Portuondo v. Agard 120 S. Ct. 1119, 68 USLW 4176 (3-6-00)

Prosecutorial comments: A defendant who testified at his trial was not deprived of any constitutional rights as a result of the prosecutor's comments, during summation to the jury, that the defendant had had the opportunity to hear all the other witnesses testify and to tailor his testimony accordingly. *Griffin v. California (1965)*, holding that a prosecutor's comments about a defendant's failure to testify unconstitutionally burdened the defendant's privilege against self-incrimination, should not be extended to the present context. *Griffin* prohibited the prosecutor from urging the jury to do something the jury is not permitted to do. By contrast, it is "natural and irresistible" for a jury, in evaluating the credibility of a defendant who testified last, to take into account the fact that he had heard the testimony of those witnesses who preceded him. The comments prohibited by *Griffin* suggested evidence of guilt, while the comments here concerned the defendant's credibility as a witness. The Court, rejecting in *Brooks v. Tennessee* (1972) the "heavy-handed" approach of requiring a defendant to testify at the outset of his defense or not at all, had suggested that arguing credibility to the jury is "the preferred means of counteracting tailoring of the defendant's testimony." Because of the defendant's Sixth Amendment right to confront witnesses, the court cannot sequester the defendant, and allowing comment on the defendant's presence and "unique opportunity" to tailor testimony may sometimes be "essential" to discovering the truth. No due process denial stems from the fact that the defendant was required by state law to be present at his trial.

7-2. Opinion of Court by Scalia, joined by Rehnquist, O'Connor, Kennedy, and Thomas. Concurring opinion by Stevens, joined by Breyer. Dissenting opinion by Ginsburg, joined by Souter.

Public Lands Council v. Babbitt 120 S. Ct. 1815, 68 USLW 4387 (5-15-00)

Public Lands, Taylor Grazing Act regulations: Three challenged aspects of 1995 federal grazing regulations were within the Secretary of the Interior's authority under the Taylor Grazing Act. A new definition of "grazing preference" omits reference to a specified quantity of forage, and explicitly ties forage to that allocated by an applicable land use plan. Defining the privileges in relation to land use plans does not violate the Secretary's responsibility to "safeguard" previously recognized grazing privileges. The statute qualifies the duty to safeguard in several respects: it is to be achieved only "so far as consistent with the [Act's] purposes and provisions," and those purposes include preventing injury to the public grazing lands; and issuance of a grazing permit is said to create no "right, title, interest, or estate." Moreover, Congress has directed the development of land use plans for the rangelands, and "it is difficult to see how a definitional change that simply refers to the use of such plans could violate the Taylor Act." Other considerations are that the prior system, quantifying grazing privileges in terms of animal unit months, did not afford anything close to "absolute security," and the new definition does not automatically diminish the security of existing grazing privileges. The second challenged regulation eliminates the words "engaged in the livestock business" from the description of stock owners qualified to apply for permits. The statute itself limits the category to settlers, residents, "and other stock owners," and extends a preference to those engaged in the livestock business. The terms "stock owner" and "stock owner engaged in the livestock business" are not coextensive. The third challenge is to a change in the regulation that provides that ownership of range improvements made pursuant to cooperative agreements shall be in the name of the United States. Nothing in the statute denies the Secretary the authority to decide when or whether to grant title to those who make improvements.

9-0. Opinion for unanimous Court by Breyer. Concurring opinion by O'Connor, joined by Thomas.

Raleigh v. Illinois Dep't of Revenue 120 S. Ct. 1951, 68 USLW 4445 (5-30-00)

Bankruptcy, tax claims, burden of proof: When the substantive law creating a tax obligation puts the burden of proof on the taxpayer, the burden remains on the taxpayer (in this case the trustee in bankruptcy) in a proceeding in bankruptcy court. Creditors' entitlements in bankruptcy arise from the underlying substantive law creating the debtor's obligation, unless the Bankruptcy Code provides to the contrary. As a general matter, the burden of proof is a "substantive" aspect of a claim, and tax law is no candidate for exception. There is no indication in the Bankruptcy Code that Congress has altered the burden of proof on tax claims. The Code's silence on the matter does not require reliance on pre-Code practice; that practice was not well settled. Supreme Court precedent holding that "allowance" of claims is a federal matter is not helpful, since "allowance" refers to ordering of valid claims, not to the validity of claims in the first instance, and since the burden of proof rule here bears only on validity. A bankruptcy court's equitable powers are limited by what the Code provides, and, in any event, equitable principles do not necessarily favor the taxpayer's position.

9-0. Opinion for unanimous Court by Souter.

Ramdass v. Angelone 120 S. Ct. 2113, 68 USLW 4486 (6-12-00)

Habeas corpus, capital sentencing, parole ineligibility: The rule of *Simmons v. South Carolina* (1994), requiring that a capital sentencing jury be informed that a defendant is parole ineligible if the State has put the defendant's future dangerousness at issue and if the only alternative to a death sentences is life imprisonment without possibility of parole, is inapplicable to the present case. Here the defendant was not parole ineligible at the time of sentencing. Virginia has a three-strikes law providing that someone who has been convicted three times of felony offenses of murder, rape, or robbery with a deadly weapon is parole ineligible. At the time of sentencing in this case, the defendant had one such final conviction, but a second such conviction had not yet become final because the court had not entered judgment following the jury's verdict. Entry of a judgment order is not a purely ministerial act in Virginia because the court may set aside the jury verdict in response to a post-trial motion.

5-4. No opinion of Court. Opinion by Kennedy, joined by Rehnquist, Scalia, and Thomas. Concurring opinion by O'Connor. Dissenting opinion by Stevens, joined by Souter, Ginsburg, and Breyer.

Reeves v. Sanderson Plumbing Products, Inc. 120 S. Ct. 2097, 68 USLW 4480 (6-12-00)

Age Discrimination in Employment Act, burden of production: A plaintiff's prima facie case of discrimination, combined with sufficient evidence to reject the employer's nondiscriminatory explanation for its decision, is adequate to sustain a finding of liability for intentional discrimination under the Age Discrimination in Employment Act. The appeals court erred in assuming that a plaintiff must always introduce additional, independent evidence of discrimination once his prima facie case has been made and the employer's explanation has been disproved. It is permissible for the trier of fact to infer the ultimate fact of discrimination from the falsity of the employer's explanation. Proof of such falsity will not always be adequate to sustain a finding of liability, but discrimination "may well be the most likely alternative explanation" for the employer's action.

9-0. Opinion for unanimous court by O'Connor. Concurring opinion by Ginsburg.

Reno v. Bossier Parish School Bd. 120 S. Ct. 866, 68 USLW 4086 (1-24-00)

Voting Rights Act, preclearance: Section 5 of the Voting Rights Act does not prohibit preclearance of a redistricting plan enacted with a discriminatory but non-retrogressive purpose. Section 5 authorizes the Attorney General to preclear an election law change that "does not have the purpose and will not have the effect of denying or abridging the right to vote on account of race or color." This language requires a covered jurisdiction to make two distinct showings: that the proposed plan does not have the purpose of denying or abridging the right to vote, and that the plan will not have that effect. The Court had previously held that the no-effect requirement is limited to retrogressive effects. The purpose prong is also so limited. The Court "refuse[s] to adopt a construction that would attribute different meanings to the same phrase in the same sentence, depending upon which object it is modifying." For purposes of preclearance, the baseline for determining whether a voting practice "abridges" the right to vote is the status quo; if the change "abridges the right to vote relative to the status quo, then preclearance is denied, and the status quo (however discriminatory it may be) remains in effect." If a proposed voting change is not retrogressive, this means that it "cannot be stopped in advance under the extraordinary burden-shifting procedures of §5, but must be attacked through the normal means of a §2 action." "To deny preclearance to a plan that is not retrogressive – no matter how unconstitutional it may be – would risk leaving in effect a status quo that is even worse." The case is not moot. Although there will be a new census and presumably a new apportionment plan before the next scheduled school board election in 2002, the current plan will serve as the baseline against which the next plan will be measured for purposes of preclearance.

9-0 (mootness); **5-4** (merits). Opinion of Court by Scalia, unanimous as to mootness, and joined by Rehnquist, O'Connor, Kennedy, and Thomas on the merits. Concurring opinion by Thomas. Opinion by Souter concurring in part and dissenting in part, joined by Stevens, Ginsburg, and Breyer. Dissenting opinions by Stevens, joined by Ginsburg; and by Breyer.

Reno v. Condon 120 S. Ct. 666, 68 USLW 4037 (1-12-00)

Driver's Privacy Protection Act; Tenth Amendment: The Driver's Privacy Protection Act (DPPA) is a valid exercise of the commerce power, and does not violate the Tenth Amendment. The DPPA prohibits state departments of motor vehicles (DMVs) and others to whom the DMVs provide information from disclosing a driver's personal information (name, address, phone number, vehicle description, Social Security number, etc.) without the driver's consent. DMVs that violate the Act are subject to civil penalties. The drivers' information that the DPPA regulates is used by insurers, marketers, and others engaged in interstate commerce to contact drivers with customized solicitations, and therefore this information in this context constitutes "an article of commerce" subject to regulation under the commerce power. The DPPA does not violate the federalism principles reflected in the Tenth Amendment and set forth in *New York v. United States* (1992) and *Printz v. United States* (1997). *South Carolina v. Baker* (1988) governs instead. Although compliance with the DPPA will require time and effort on the part of state employees, the DPPA does not "commandeer" states in enforcing federal law applicable to private entities. The DPPA regulates state activities directly rather than seeking to control the manner in which states regulate private parties. Also, the DPPA is generally applicable, regulating both the states as initial suppliers and private entities that resell drivers' information – "the universe of entities that participate as suppliers to the market for motor vehicles."

9-0. Opinion for unanimous Court by Rehnquist.

Rice v. Cayetano 120 S. Ct. 1044, 68 USLW 4138 (2-23-00)

Fifteenth Amendment, voting restricted by ancestry: A provision of the Hawaii Constitution restricting the right to vote for trustees of the Office of Hawaiian Affairs (OHA) to persons who are descendants of people inhabiting the Hawaiian Islands in 1778 violates the Fifteenth Amendment. The OHA administers programs for the benefit of "Hawaiians" – the class of persons who may vote for trustees – as well as for a subclass of "Native Hawaiians." The State's electoral restriction enacts a race-based voting qualification forbidden by the Fifteenth Amendment. Ancestry can be a proxy for race, and that is the case here. The Court previously described racial discrimination as "singl[ing] out identifiable classes of persons solely because of their ancestry or ethnic characteristics," and that is what Hawaii's voting restriction does. Simply because a class defined by ancestry does not include all members of a race does not suffice to make the classification race-neutral. The State's arguments in support of the restriction are rejected. Cases upholding differential treatment of certain members of Indian tribes are inapplicable. Voting restrictions in tribal elections are "the internal affair of a quasi-sovereign," while the OHA elections are statewide elections to which the Fifteenth Amendment applies. *Morton v. Mancari* (1974), involving a hiring preference at the Bureau of Indian Affairs for members of federally recognized tribes, should not be extended to the election area. Cases exempting certain special district elections from the one person, one vote rule derived from the Fourteenth Amendment are inapplicable to the Fifteenth Amendment's command of race neutrality. Hawaii's restriction cannot be upheld as merely ensuring alignment of interests between the fiduciaries and beneficiaries of a trust, since the restriction rests "on the demeaning premise that citizens of a particular race are somehow more qualified than others to vote on certain matters."

> **7-2.** Opinion of Court by Kennedy, joined by Rehnquist, O'Connor, Scalia, and Thomas. Concurring opinion by Breyer, joined by Souter. Dissenting opinions by Stevens, joined by Ginsburg; and by Ginsburg.

Roe v. Flores-Ortega 120 S. Ct. 1029, 68 USLW 4132 (2-23-00)

Sixth Amendment, ineffective assistance of counsel: A defense counsel's failure to file a notice of appeal when the defendant has not clearly conveyed his wishes about whether to appeal does not constitute *per se* ineffective assistance of counsel in violation of the Sixth Amendment. Nor is representation deficient as a constitutional matter if counsel fails to consult with the defendant about an appeal. Instead, failure to appeal is measured by the general test for ineffective counsel set forth in *Strickland v. Washington* (1984): whether representation "fell below an objective standard of reasonableness," and whether counsel's deficient performance prejudiced the defendant. Counsel has a constitutionally mandated duty to consult with the defendant about an appeal when there is reason to believe that a rational defendant would want to appeal, or that this particular defendant has reasonably demonstrated that he is interested in an appeal. All relevant factors must be considered, *e.g.*, whether conviction followed a trial or a guilty plea, and whether a plea expressly reserved or waived rights to appeal. To show prejudice, a defendant must demonstrate that, "but for counsel's deficient conduct" in not consulting with him about an appeal, he would have appealed.

> **6-3** (duty to consult); **9-0** (prejudice). Opinion of Court by O'Connor, joined by Rehnquist, Scalia, Kennedy, Thomas, and Breyer, and joined in part by Stevens, Souter, and Ginsburg. Concurring opinion by Breyer. Opinion by Souter, joined by Stevens and Ginsburg, concurring in part and dissenting in part.

Rotella v. Wood 120 S. Ct. 1075, 68 USLW 4153 (2-23-00)

Civil RICO, limitations period: The injury discovery accrual rule – not the injury and pattern discovery rule – applies to the four-year limitations period applicable to civil RICO actions. This means that the statute of limitations begins to run when the plaintiff knew or should have known of his injury. Under the injury and pattern rule, the period would begin to run only after the plaintiff discovers, or should discover, both an injury and a pattern of RICO activity. This latter approach is "unsound for a number of reasons." Under RICO, predicate acts of racketeering can be 10 years apart, and remote from time of trial. Even in medical malpractice suits, "where the cry for a discovery rule is loudest," it is the discovery of the injury, not discovery of other aspects of the claim, that starts the clock. This rule places the burden on the victim of inadequate medical treatment to determine within the limitations period whether the inadequacy constituted malpractice. There is no reason for accepting a lesser degree of responsibility on the part of the RICO plaintiff. Also, Congress relied on the Clayton Act in formulating RICO, and at the time RICO was enacted the Clayton Act's injury-focused accrual rule was well established.

9-0. Opinion for unanimous Court by Souter.

Santa Fe Ind. School Dist. v. Doe 120 S. Ct. 2266, 68 USLW 4525 (6-19-00)

Establishment Clause, student-led prayer at high school football games: A Texas school district's policy permitting a student-led, student-initiated prayer delivered over public address systems at public high school football games violates the Establishment Clause. The policy authorizes students to determine by majority vote whether to select a student to deliver a "statement or invocation" at football games, and then, also by majority vote, to select the student who may do so. The policy "involves both perceived and actual endorsement of religion." The prayers are authorized by government policy, and take place on government property at government-sponsored school-related events. Moreover, "the policy, by its terms, invites and encourages religious messages." The government has not created the type of "public forum" at which the pre-game invocations could be considered to be private rather than government-sponsored speech. Selection of the speaker by majority vote does not cure the constitutional defect, but rather "guarantees . . . that minority candidates will never prevail and that their views will be effectively silenced." The policy cannot be justified by secular purposes, given the policy's approval of only one specific kind of message – an invocation – and given the evolution of the policy, which began with the "candid" title of "prayer at football games" and which originally created an office of "student chaplain." The football game venue does not distinguish the prayer from the graduation prayer held to violate the Establishment Clause in *Lee v. Weisman* (1992). Even though attendance at games is not compulsory, the prayer "has the improper effect of coercing those present to participate in an act of religious worship." Finally, the respondents' facial challenge is not premature. Although no invocation has yet been delivered under the policy, Establishment Clause values can be eroded in other ways, *e.g.*, by adoption of the policy and by subjecting the prayer issue to majoritarian vote.

6-3. Opinion of Court by Stevens, joined by O'Connor, Kennedy, Souter, Ginsburg, and Breyer. Dissenting opinion by Rehnquist, joined by Scalia and Thomas.

Shalala v. Illinois Council on Long Term Care 120 S. Ct. 1084, 68 USLW 4159 (2-29-00)

Judicial review, Medicare Act: The Medicare Act bars federal question jurisdiction over an action by provider nursing homes challenging the validity of certain Medicare-related regulations. A section of the Social Security Act, 42 U.S.C. § 405(h), as incorporated in the Medicare Act by 42 U.S.C. § 1395ii, provides that "no action . . . to recover on any claim" arising under the Medicare laws shall be brought "under section 1331 . . . of title 28," the section that confers federal question jurisdiction on federal courts. Instead, such challenges must be brought under a separate and exclusive system of administrative and judicial review for denials of Medicare claims. The nursing homes' challenge to the regulations is an action "to recover on any claim" within the meaning of section 405(h). The language clearly applies to a Medicare benefits case, and under the Court's precedents, applies as well to the challenge to the regulations. *Weinberger v. Salfi* (1975) and *Heckler v. Ringer* (1984) govern interpretation. In *Salfi* the Court held that section 405(h) barred federal question jurisdiction in an action challenging a statutory provision that denied the plaintiffs Social Security benefits. In *Ringer*, the Court reached the same conclusion about an action challenging the lawfulness of the agency's determination not to provide Medicare Part B reimbursement to persons who had undergone a particular medical operation. The appeals court erred in concluding that *Bowen v. Michigan Academy of Family Physicians* (1986) makes *Salfi* and *Ringer* inapplicable. The Court's holding in *Michigan Academy* that section 405(h) did not preclude federal question review of the lawfulness of regulations governing procedures used to calculate Medicare Part B benefits was not based on a general limitation of that provision to "amount determinations" – a construction that would render the provision inapplicable in the instant case – but instead was based on a narrower exception for instances in which application would result in a denial of all review rather than a channeling of review through the agency. The *Michigan Academy* precedent is inapplicable because, under a "legally permissible" interpretation by the Secretary of HHS, nursing home providers are entitled to review of a determination that they are not in compliance with governing law.

5-4. Opinion of Court by Breyer, joined by Rehnquist, O'Connor, Souter, and Ginsburg. Dissenting opinions by Stevens; by Scalia; and by Thomas, joined by Stevens and Kennedy, and joined in part by Scalia.

Sims v. Apfel 120 S. Ct. 2080, 68 USLW 4470 (6-5-00)

Judicial review, issue exhaustion, Social Security proceedings: A person whose claim for Social Security benefits is denied by an administrative law judge, and whose request for review by the Social Security Appeals Council is denied, may obtain judicial review of issues that he did not request the Appeals Council to review. Requirements for administrative issue exhaustion are for the most part contained in statutes or regulations. Neither the Social Security Act nor regulations implementing it require issue exhaustion. On occasion the Court has imposed an administrative issue exhaustion requirement in the absence of statute or regulation; but reasons for doing so are inapplicable here. The basis for a judicially imposed rule is an analogy to the rule that appellate courts refuse to consider issues that were not raised before the trial court. The rationale is that issue exhaustion is appropriate in an adversary proceeding. The administrative proceedings at issue are not sufficiently adversarial to require issue exhaustion.

5-4. Opinion of Court by Thomas, joined by Stevens, O'Connor, Souter, and Ginsburg. Separate part of Thomas opinion joined by Stevens, Souter, and Ginsburg. Concurring opinion by O'Connor. Dissenting opinion by Breyer, joined by Rehnquist, Scalia, and Kennedy.

Slack v. McDaniel 120 S. Ct. 1595, 68 USLW 4315 (4-26-00)

Habeas corpus, AEDPA, "second or successive petition": Provisions of the Antiterrorism and Effective Death Penalty Act of 1996 (AEDPA) that condition a *habeas corpus* petitioner's right to appeal on issuance of a certificate of appealability (COA) apply to appeals initiated after the Act's effective date, whether or not the *habeas* petition itself was filed in the district court before AEDPA's effective date. An appeal is a distinct step in litigation, and, under AEDPA, an appellate case is commenced when the application for a COA is filed. A COA may issue when the district court has denied a *habeas* petition on procedural grounds without reaching the petitioner's constitutional claims, if the prisoner shows that jurists of reason would find the constitutional claim and the procedural ruling at least debatable. A *habeas* petition that is filed after an initial petition was dismissed for failure to exhaust state remedies, and without adjudication on the merits, is not a "second or successive petition" as that term is understood in the habeas corpus context.

6-3 (effective date); **7-2** (second or successive petition). Opinion of Court by Kennedy, joined in par by Rehnquist, O'Connor, Scalia, Thomas, and Ginsburg; and joined in separate part by Rehnquist, Stevens, O'Connor, Souter, Ginsburg, and Breyer. Opinion by Stevens, concurring in part, joined by Souter and Breyer. Opinion by Scalia, concurring in part and dissenting in part, joined by Thomas.

Smith v. Robbins 120 S. Ct. 746, 68 USLW 4069 (1-19-00)

Equal Protection, indigents, frivolous appeals: California's procedures for evaluating the request of an appointed counsel not to pursue an appeal that would be frivolous are not unconstitutional simply because they diverge from the procedures set forth by the Court in *Anders v. California* (1967). Moreover, California's procedures, derived from *People v. Wende* (1979), satisfy all constitutional requirements. Under *Anders* procedures, the attorney requesting permission to withdraw must submit a brief pointing out anything in the record that might arguably support an appeal. Under California's *Wende* procedures, counsel summarizes the case's procedural and factual history. Counsel does not explicitly state that an appeal would be frivolous, and does not request to withdraw, but instead expresses availability to brief any issues on which the court desires briefing. The court, upon receiving a *Wende* brief, must conduct a review of the entire record. These *Wende* procedures satisfy the constitutional standard by providing a criminal appellant the minimum safeguards necessary to make the appeal adequate and effective. The *Wende* procedures are "undoubtedly far better than those procedures we have found inadequate," and "at least comparable to those procedures we have approved." On remand, respondent may still attempt to prove that his appellate counsel was constitutionally ineffective; this claim should be measured by the standards set forth in *Strickland v. Washington* (1984).

5-4. Opinion of Court by Thomas, joined by Rehnquist, O'Connor, Scalia, and Kennedy. Dissenting opinions by Stevens, joined by Ginsburg; and by Souter, joined by Stevens, Ginsburg, and Breyer.

Stenberg v. Carhart 120 S. Ct. 2597, 68 USLW 4702 (6-28-00)

Abortion: Nebraska's statute criminalizing the performance of "partial birth abortions" is unconstitutional under principles set forth in *Roe v. Wade* (1973) and *Planned Parenthood v. Casey (1992)*. The statute prohibits partial birth abortions "unless the procedure is necessary to save the life of the mother," and further defines partial birth abortion to mean "deliberately and intentionally delivering into the vagina a living unborn child, or a substantial portion thereof, for the purpose of performing a procedure that the person performing such procedure knows will kill the unborn child and does kill the unborn child." The statute is inconsistent with the Court's guidelines in *Planned Parenthood v. Casey* because it lacks an exception for those instances in which the banned procedure is necessary to preserve the health of the mother. The statute is also unconstitutional on the alternative ground that it imposes an "undue burden" on a woman's right to choose to terminate her pregnancy before viability. Nebraska's ban covers not only dilation and extraction (D&X), but also dilation and evacuation (D&E) procedures. D&E is the most commonly used method for performing pre-viability second trimester abortions, and prohibition of D&E would impose an undue burden on a woman's right to a pre-viability abortion.

5-4. Opinion of Court by Breyer, joined by Stevens, O'Connor, Souter, and Ginsburg. Concurring opinions by Stevens, joined by Ginsburg; O'Connor; and Ginsburg, joined by Stevens. Dissenting opinions by Rehnquist; Scalia; Kennedy, joined by Rehnquist; and Thomas, joined by Rehnquist and Scalia.

Texas v. Lesage 120 S. Ct. 467, 68 USLW 3351 (11-29-99)

Summary judgment; racial discrimination, college admissions: The fact that a public university rejected the application of a prospective student while operating a racially discriminatory admissions program does not establish a cause of action under 42 U.S.C. § 1983. The government can defeat liability by demonstrating that it would have made the same decision absent the forbidden discrimination. Because it was undisputed in this case that the respondent's application would have been rejected even if the university's admissions process had been completely color-blind, there was no factual issue, and the State's motion for summary judgment should have been granted.

9-0. *Per curiam.*

Troxel v. Granville 120 S. Ct. 2054, 68 USLW 4458 (6-5-00)

Due Process, grandparent visitation rights: A Washington State law allowing "any person" to petition a court "at any time" to obtain visitation rights whenever visitation "may serve the best interests" of a child is unconstitutional as applied to an order requiring a parent to allow her child's grandparents more extensive visitation than the parent wished. The Court has long recognized the "fundamental right of parents to make decisions concerning the care, custody, and control of their children." The Washington statute, as applied, infringes on that fundamental right by placing the "best-interests" determination solely in the hands of a judge, with no deference accorded a parent's decision that visitation would not be in her child's best interest.

6-3. No opinion of the Court. Opinion by O'Connor, joined by Rehnquist, Ginsburg, and Breyer. Separate concurring opinions by Souter and Thomas. Dissenting opinions by Stevens, Scalia, and Kennedy.

United States v. Hubbell 120 S. Ct. 2037, 68 USLW 4449 (6-5-00)

Self-Incrimination, personal papers, immunity: The Fifth Amendment privilege against self-incrimination protects a witness from being compelled to disclose the existence of incriminating documents that the Government is unable to describe with reasonable particularity. The Independent Counsel violated this principle by bringing criminal charges against the respondent based on information gained from documents obtained by virtue of the respondent's compliance with a subpoena to produce all records related to his and his family's income, employment, and relationship with professional clients. The district court's order compelling production of documents also extended use and derivative-use immunity pursuant to 18 U.S.C. § 6002, an immunity that has been interpreted to be coextensive with the scope of the privilege against self-incrimination. The act of producing documents that the Government identifies with particularity is not testimonial in nature, and ordinarily the privilege does not extend to the content of such documents. However, the act of producing documents in response to a subpoena can have a testimonial aspect if it communicates information about the existence, custody, or authenticity of documents. The broad scope of the subpoena in this case suggests that the Independent Counsel needed the respondent's assistance in identifying potential sources of information that could lead to his prosecution, and that is what happened. The respondent, in complying with the subpoena, provided the Independent Counsel with a mass of documents falling within 11 broadly worded subpoena categories, and prosecutors culled incriminating evidence from these documents. Because the Independent Counsel is unable to prove that the evidence used in obtaining the indictment and proposed to be used at trial was derived from legitimate sources wholly independent of the testimonial aspect of respondent's immunized conduct in selecting and producing documents described in the subpoena, the indictment must be dismissed.

8-1. Opinion of Court by Stevens, joined by O'Connor, Scalia, Kennedy, Souter, Thomas, Ginsburg, and Breyer. Concurring opinion by Thomas, joined by Scalia. Dissenting statement by Rehnquist.

United States v. Johnson 120 S. Ct. 1114, 68 USLW 4174 (3-1-00)

Prisoners, supervised release: A prisoner serving time in federal prison for multiple offenses, released after having served time under convictions held invalid, is not entitled to have his excess prison time credited against supervised release time still to be served on remaining convictions. The language of 18 U.S.C. § 3624(e) controls. That section provides that "[t]he term of supervised release commences on the day the person is released from imprisonment." The dictionary definition as well as the "ordinary, commonsense" meaning of "release" is "to be freed from confinement." The section does allow concurrent counting, but only for prison terms of less than 30 days. The "proper inference" is that Congress considered exceptions and intended to limit exceptions to those set forth. While the text of section 3624 "resolves the case," the result "accords with the statute's purpose and design," since supervised release serves "rehabilitative ends, distinct from those served by incarceration."

9-0. Opinion for unanimous Court by Kennedy.

United States v. Locke 120 S. Ct. 1135, 68 USLW 4184 (3-6-00)

Preemption, regulation of oil tankers: Four Washington State regulations imposed on oil tankers for the purpose of preventing oil spills are preempted by federal law. These four rules impose training requirements for tanker crews, require crews to be proficient in the English language, impose staffing requirements for navigation watch, and require reporting to state authorities of certain marine casualties. The State regulations intrude in an area where the federal interest in regulating navigation "without embarrassment from intervention of the separate States and resulting difficulties with foreign nations" is "manifest." Congress has enacted a series of statutes and has ratified international agreements governing oil tankers. Principal among the statutes are the Ports and Waterways Safety Act of 1972 (PWSA) and the Oil Pollution Act of 1990 (OPA). The Court's interpretation of the PWSA in *Ray v. Atlantic Richfield Co.* (1978) remains "correct and controlling." The Ninth Circuit erroneously relied on language in OPA Title I disclaiming any intent to preempt state laws imposing additional liability or additional requirements relating to the discharge of oil. Title I of the OPA does not regulate vessel operation, design, or manning, and its savings clause is similarly limited in scope. The preemptive reach of the PWSA and the regulations promulgated under it is not affected by the OPA. Under Title I of the PWSA, Congress preserved state authority to regulate the "peculiarities of local waters if there is no conflict with federal regulatory determinations." Uniformity is required under Title II of the PWSA for federal rules governing general seaworthiness of tankers and their crews – such things as construction, operation, maintenance, equipping, and manning of vessels. The first three Washington rules set forth above are subject to the "field preemption rule surrounding Title II." These training and crew qualification rules address matters that are not unique to the waters of Puget Sound, and impose requirements that affect tanker operations outside State waters. Other sources of federal regulation govern the reporting of marine incidents, and leave no room for duplicative or additional state requirements. The case is remanded for further evaluation of various other State regulations being challenged by tanker owners.

9-0. Opinion for unanimous Court by Kennedy.

United States v. Martinez-Salazar 120 S. Ct. 774, 68 USLW 4081 (1-19-00)

Peremptory challenges: A defendant charged with a federal offense who exercises a peremptory challenge to remove a potential juror following the trial court's erroneous refusal to dismiss that juror for cause is not deprived of any rule-based or constitutional right. Nothing in the Constitution requires Congress to provide for peremptory challenges. Rule 24, Federal Rules of Criminal Procedure, provides defendants with 10 peremptory challenges for the petit jury and one challenge for an alternate juror, and authorizes a district court to allow additional challenges in multiple-defendant cases. In this case the defendant and his co-defendant exercised their 11 challenges and did not request additional challenges, and defendant's counsel stated that he had no objection to the jurors who were seated. In *Ross v. Oklahoma* (1988), the Court held in a state-law setting that loss of a peremptory challenge exercised to cure the trial court's error in not dismissing a juror for cause did not deprive the defendant of any constitutional right "so long as the jury that sits is impartial." The same principle applies in the federal setting. Here the defendant "used the challenge in line with a principal reason for peremptories: to help secure the constitutional guarantee of trial by an impartial jury." The district court's error did not result in the seating of any juror who should have been dismissed for cause.

9-0. Opinion of Court by Ginsburg, joined by Rehnquist, Stevens, O'Connor, Souter, Thomas, and Breyer. Concurring opinions by Souter; and by Scalia, joined by Kennedy.

United States v. Morrison 120 S. Ct. 1740, 68 USLW 4351 (5-15-00)

Violence Against Women Act; Commerce power, 14th Amendment enforcement power: 42 U.S.C. § 13981, a provision of the Violence Against Women Act that creates a federal civil remedy for victims of gender-motivated violence, exceeds congressional power under the Commerce Clause and under section 5 of the Fourteenth Amendment. The guiding Commerce Clause principles were set forth in *United States v. Lopez* (1995), in which the Court held that the Gun-Free School Zones Act exceeded congressional power to regulate "activities that substantially affect interstate commerce." So far, the Court has upheld commerce-power regulation of intrastate activity only if that activity is economic in nature, and gender-motivated crimes of violence "are not, in any sense of the phrase, economic activity." Like the Gun-Free School Zones Act, section 13981 contains no jurisdictional element tying the regulated violence to interstate commerce. Unlike the Gun-Free School Zones Act, section 13981 contains "numerous" congressional findings about the impacts of gender-motivated crimes. Congressional findings, however, do not necessarily suffice to sustain Commerce Clause legislation. It is ultimately a judicial rather than a legislative question whether particular activities substantially affect interstate commerce. In this case the congressional findings rely heavily on a method of reasoning rejected in *Lopez*, a but-for causal chain that traces from violence to attenuated effects upon employment, production, transit, or consumption. Congress lacks the power to regulate "noneconomic, violent criminal conduct based solely on that conduct's aggregate effect on interstate commerce." Regulation and punishment of crime that is not directed at the instrumentalities, channels, or goods involved in interstate commerce has always been the province of the States. Similarly, there are limitations to Congress's power under section 5 of the Fourteenth Amendment to enforce that Amendment's guarantees. The Amendment prohibits only state action, and affords no protection against "merely private conduct." This principle, established in 1883 in *United States v. Harris* and the *Civil Rights Cases*, was not overruled by dicta in *United States v. Guest* (1966). Even if Congress's aim is to correct state officials' refusal or neglect in enforcing evenhanded laws, the remedy here is simply not corrective in character, and cannot be said to be congruent and proportional to the injury being addressed. Section 13981 is not aimed at proscribing discriminatory administration by state officials, but instead is aimed at private conduct. The section is "unlike any of the § 5 remedies" that the Court has upheld; it does not apply to state officials, and it applies uniformly throughout the nation rather than in targeted states.

> 5-4. Opinion of Court by Rehnquist, joined by O'Connor, Scalia, Kennedy, and Thomas. Concurring opinion by Thomas. Dissenting opinions by Souter, joined by Stevens, Ginsburg, and Breyer; and by Breyer, joined by Stevens, and joined in part by Souter and Ginsburg.

United States v. Playboy Entertainment Group, Inc. 120 S. Ct. 1878, 68 USLW 4409 (5-22-00)

First Amendment, regulation of indecent cable TV broadcasts: Section 505 of the Telecommunications Act of 1996, which required cable TV operators that offer channels primarily devoted to sexually oriented programming to prevent signal bleed either by fully scrambling those channels or by limiting their transmission to hours when children are unlikely to be viewing, violates the First Amendment. The provision, applicable to sexually explicit adult programming, is content-based, and therefore is subject to strict scrutiny: it must be "narrowly tailored to promote a compelling Government interest." Section 505 is not narrowly tailored in this sense, because section 504 offers a less restrictive alternative. Section 504 requires a cable operator, upon request by a subscriber, to fully scramble any channel the subscriber does not wish to receive. This key difference between cable television and the broadcasting media – the capacity to block unwanted channels on a household-by-household basis – enables the Government to support parental authority without affecting the First Amendment rights of other speakers and willing listeners. Here the only question is whether section 504, if adequately publicized, can be effective. The Government failed to meet its burden of proving that this alternative will not be effective in achieving its goals. Although there were very few blocking requests under section 504 before the addition of section 505, the Government did not establish the reason for this low utilization, nor did it establish that signal bleed was actually a pervasive problem.

> 5-4. Opinion of Court by Kennedy, joined by Stevens, Souter, Thomas, and Ginsburg. Concurring opinions by Stevens and Thomas. Dissenting opinions by Scalia; and by Breyer, joined by Rehnquist, O'Connor, and Scalia.

Vermont Agency of Nat. Res. v. United States ex rel. Stevens 120 S. Ct. 1858, 68 USLW 4399 (5-22-00)

False Claims Act, *qui tam* actions, standing to sue, state defendants: A private individual may not maintain an action against a state, on behalf of the United States, under the *qui tam* provision of the False Claims Act. A private individual who brings such a *qui tam* action has standing to sue. The provision allows an individual to sue any person who defrauds the Government, and to collect a portion of any civil penalty or treble damages assessed. The *qui tam* relator suffers no injury to a legally protected interest, but adequate basis for standing derives from the principle that the assignee of a claim has standing to assert the injury in fact suffered by the assignor. The United States suffers injury in fact, and the False Claims Act effects a partial assignment of the Government's damages claim. The long tradition of *qui tam* actions in England and in the American colonies supports this conclusion, since Article III's restriction of judicial power to "cases and controversies" has been interpreted to mean "cases and controversies of the sort traditionally amenable to, and resolved by, the judicial process." The False Claims Act, however, does not subject a state to liability in a *qui tam* action, because a state is not "person" within the meaning of the Act. The Act does not define the term "person," and there is a longstanding presumption that "person" does not include the sovereign. Nothing in the history and structure of the Act overcomes this presumption. Moreover, the conclusion is supported by two rules of construction: Congress may change the usual constitutional balance between states and the federal government only by unmistakably clear language, and statutes should be construed so as to avoid difficult constitutional issues (here the Eleventh Amendment issue).

7-2. Opinion of Court by Scalia, joined by Rehnquist, O'Connor, Kennedy, Thomas, and Breyer. Concurring opinions by Breyer; and by Ginsburg, joined by Breyer. Dissenting opinion by Stevens, joined by Souter.

Village of Willowbrook v. Olech 120 S. Ct. 1073, 68 USLW 4157 (2-23-00)

Equal Protection, "class of one": Successful equal protection claims may be brought by a "class of one" if the plaintiff establishes that she has been intentionally treated differently from others similarly situated and that there is no rational basis for the different treatment. The respondent in this case had asked the Village to connect her property to the municipal water supply, and the Village had conditioned the connection on a 33-foot easement rather than a 15-foot easement required of other property owners. The respondent alleged that the demand for a 33-foot easement was motivated by ill-will stemming from a previous, successful lawsuit she had brought against the Village; this allegation, if proved, would establish that the discriminatory treatment was intentional.

9-0. *Per curiam.* Separate opinion by Breyer, concurring in the result.

Wal-Mart Stores, Inc. v. Samara Bros., Inc. 120 S. Ct. 1339, 68 USLW 4217 (3-21-00)

Lanham Act, trade dress infringement: In an action for infringement of unregistered trade dress under section 43(a) of the Lanham Act, a product's design is distinctive, and therefore protectible, only upon a showing of secondary meaning. A mark can be distinctive in one of two ways – if it is inherently distinctive (*i.e.*, if its inherent nature serves to identify a particular source), or if it has developed secondary meaning. Secondary meaning is found if the primary significance of the mark in the public mind is to identify the source of a product rather than the product itself. Design, like color, is not inherently distinctive, "since consumer predisposition to equate product design with the source does not exist." Moreover, application of inherent distinctiveness to product design could harm consumer interests, since competition could be deterred "by the plausible threat of successful suit." Courts that have a difficult time in marginal cases distinguishing between product-design and product-packaging trade dress "should err on the side of caution and classify ambiguous trade dress as product design, thereby requiring secondary meaning."

9-0. Opinion for unanimous Court by Scalia.

Weeks v. Angelone 120 S. Ct. 727, 68 USLW 4060 (1-19-00)

Jury instruction, capital case, mitigating factors: A trial judge does not violate the Constitution by directing a jury's attention to a specific paragraph of a constitutionally sufficient sentencing instruction in response to the jury's question regarding the proper consideration of mitigating circumstances. After four hours of deliberation, the jury had asked the judge whether it was their "duty" to vote for the death penalty if they found the defendant "guilty" of at least one aggravating factor. Rather than answering the question directly, the judge referred the jury to language in the instruction providing that the jury "may" fix the punishment at death upon finding that the state had proved one aggravating factor, "or," the instruction continued, "if you believe from all the evidence that the death penalty is not justified, then you shall fix the punishment [at life imprisonment]." The jury also received a separate instruction that "you must consider a mitigating circumstance if you find there is evidence to support it." The Court had previously upheld the Virginia pattern instruction at issue. "Given that the jury was adequately instructed, and given that the trial judge responded to the jury's question by directing its attention to the precise paragraph of the constitutionally adequate instruction that answers its inquiry," there was no constitutional violation. Moreover, federal habeas corpus relief is precluded by 28 U.S.C. § 2254(d); affirmance of conviction was neither contrary to nor did it involve an unreasonable application of clearly established federal law.

5-4. Opinion of Court by Rehnquist, joined by O'Connor, Scalia, Kennedy, and Thomas. Dissenting opinion by Stevens, joined by Ginsburg and Breyer, and joined in part by Souter.

Weisgram v. Marley 120 S. Ct. 1011, 68 USLW 4122 (2-22-00)

Federal courts, appeals: Federal Rule of Civil Procedure 50 permits an appellate court to direct the entry of judgment as a matter of law when it determines that evidence was erroneously admitted at trial and that the remaining, properly admitted evidence is insufficient to constitute a submissible case. The Court had previously held in *Neely v. Martin K. Eby Constr. Co.* (1967) that there are situations in which an appellate court may appropriately enter judgment as a matter of law against the jury-verdict winner. Cases in which there remains insufficient evidence to support the jury's verdict after exclusion of erroneously admitted evidence can fall into this *Neely* category. The appellate court's "informed discretion" should guide its choice among the alternatives of ordering a new trial, remanding for the trial court to determine whether a new trial is warranted, or directing entry of judgment as a matter of law. Fairness to the parties is key to the exercise of the appellate court's discretion in the matter. A party whose verdict is set aside on appeal will have had notice at trial of any alleged evidentiary insufficiency, and it is "unconvincing" to suggest that allowing the appellate court to direct entry of judgment for the defendant will punish plaintiffs who could have shored up their cases by other means had they known that their expert testimony would be found inadmissible.

9-0. Opinion for unanimous Court by Ginsburg.

Williams v. Taylor 120 S. Ct. 1479, 68 USLW 4279 (4-18-00)

***Habeas corpus*, AEDPA, failure to develop factual basis in state court**: A *habeas corpus* petitioner has "failed" to develop the factual basis of his claim within the meaning of section 2254(e)(2) of the Antiterrorism and Effective

Death Penalty Act (AEDPA) only if there has been some lack of diligence on his part. The provision, which denies a federal court evidentiary hearing to a *habeas corpus* applicant who "has failed to develop the factual basis of [the] claim in State court proceedings," is not a no-fault standard. In ordinary usage the word "failed" connotes some omission, fault, or negligence by the person who has failed to do something. Moreover, this statutory language "echoes" the Court's characterization, in a case decided four years prior to AEDPA's enactment, of an attorney's negligent failure to develop a factual record. "When the words of the Court are used in a later statute governing the same subject matter, it is respectful of Congress and of the Court's own processes to give the words the same meaning in the absence of specific direction to the contrary." In this case there was lack of diligence as to one claim, involving the prosecution's failure to disclose the psychiatric report of a co-defendant and witness, since there were repeated references to the report in the transcript of the sentencing proceeding. The petitioner met his burden of showing diligence in efforts to develop facts supporting two other claims, one involving juror bias and the other involving prosecutorial misconduct.

9-0. Opinion for unanimous Court by Kennedy.

Williams v. Taylor 120 S. Ct. 1495, 68 USLW 4263 (4-18-00)

***Habeas corpus*, AEDPA, ineffective assistance of counsel**: Section 2254(d)(1) of the Antiterrorism and Effective Death Penalty Act (AEDPA), which provides that a federal court may grant *habeas corpus* relief to a prisoner who has already litigated the issue in state court only if the state-court adjudication was "contrary to," or involved an "unreasonable application of," clearly established federal law as determined by the Supreme Court, imposed new constraints on the federal court's power to grant relief. In this case, the claim of ineffective assistance of counsel due to counsel's failure to investigate and present substantial mitigating evidence to the sentencing jury involves law that had been "clearly established" by the Supreme Court's decision in *Strickland v. Washington* (1984). Counsel's representation during the sentencing phase fell short of the professional standards mandated by *Strickland*, and also "prejudiced" the petitioner by probably affecting the outcome of the proceeding. The Virginia Supreme Court's decision rejecting petitioner's ineffective assistance claim was both "contrary to" and involved an "unreasonable application" of *Strickland*. The "contrary to" and "unreasonable application" clauses carry independent meaning. The former clause requires that the state court's decision must be "substantially different from" the governing precedent. The "unreasonable application" clause requires an objective test; the "subjective" test that asks whether all jurists would agree that the state court's application was unreasonable is erroneous.

6-3 (result); **5-4** (applicable standard). Opinion of Court (in part) by Stevens, joined by O'Connor, Kennedy, Souter, Ginsburg, and Breyer. Separate part of Stevens opinion joined by Souter, Ginsburg, and Breyer. Separate part of Opinion of Court by O'Connor, joined by Rehnquist, Scalia, Kennedy, and Thomas. Separate part of O'Connor opinion joined by Kennedy. Opinion by Rehnquist, joined by Scalia and Thomas, concurring in part and dissenting in part.

Supreme Court
Volume 1 pp. 41-80

SUPREME COURT OPINIONS: OCTOBER 1998 TERM

George Costello
Legislative Attorney
American Law Division

Albertson's Inc. v. Kirkingburg 119 S. Ct. 2162, 67 USLW 4560 (6-22-99)

ADA, waivable federal safety regulation: The Americans with Disabilities Act of 1990 (ADA) does not require an employer to justify dismissal of an employee for failure to meet an applicable federal safety regulation, even if the regulation may be waived in an individual case. In this case the petitioner supermarket chain fired the respondent, a truck driver with monocular vision who failed to meet basic DOT vision standards for commercial drivers. The driver had applied to DOT for a waiver, but was fired before the waiver was granted. Persons with monocular vision who wish to invoke the ADA must prove a "disability" by establishing that their vision impairment "substantially limits" a major life activity such as seeing or working. Mitigating measures must be taken into account, and there is no principled basis for distinguishing between measures undertaken with artificial aids and measures undertaken by the body's own systems. Existence of the DOT's waiver program does not alter an employer's ability to impose the safety standard as a job qualification without having to justify its application on a case-by-case basis. The waiver program did not purport to modify the substance of the safety standard, but instead was designed as an experiment to gather data for use in determining the feasibility of relaxing the standard. The ADA does not require an employer to justify *de novo* an applicable government safety regulation.

9-0. Opinion of Court by Souter, unanimous in part (as to employer's imposition of safety regulation), and joined by Rehnquist, O'Connor, Scalia, Kennedy, Thomas, and Ginsburg in separate part (relating to proof of disability). Concurring opinion by Thomas.

Alden v. Maine 119 S. Ct. 2240, 67 USLW 4601 (6-23-99)

Federalism, state sovereign immunity: Congress lacks the authority, in exercise of Article I powers, to subject non-consenting states to private suits for damages in state courts. The history and structure of the Constitution make clear that States retain a "residual and inviolable sovereignty" under the Constitution. Fair Labor Standards Amendments of 1974 violate this principle of sovereign immunity by subjecting non-consenting states to suits for damages brought by employees in state courts. "Behind the words of the constitutional provisions are postulates which limit and control." The original Constitution's silence about state immunity is explained by the fact that no one at the time suggested that "the document might strip the States of [sovereign] immunity." The Eleventh Amendment's narrow terms, applicable only to cases brought in federal courts, did not by implication eliminate state sovereign immunity in state courts; that immunity derives not from the Eleventh Amendment, but from the structure of the original Constitution itself. Neither the Supremacy Clause nor the Necessary and Proper Clause authorizes Congress to override state sovereign immunity in exercise of Article I powers. To recognize such an Article I power would create an anomaly under which "the National Government would wield greater power in the state courts than in its own judicial instrumentalities."

5-4. Opinion of Court by Kennedy, joined by Rehnquist, O'Connor, Scalia, and Thomas. Dissenting opinion by Souter, joined by Stevens, Ginsburg, and Breyer.

American Manufacturers Mut. Ins. Co. v. Sullivan 119 S. Ct. 977, 67 USLW 4158 (3-3-99)

State action; Due Process, workers' compensation benefits: Private insurers who withhold payments under Pennsylvania's workers' compensation law while availing themselves of procedures for determining whether the underlying medical treatment was reasonable and necessary to treat the employee's condition are not state actors (persons acting "under color of" state law) subject to suit under 42 U.S.C. § 1983. The State authorizes but does not require insurers to withhold payments for disputed medical treatment. "Such permission of a private choice cannot support a finding of state action." The Due Process Clause of the Fourteenth Amendment does not require the insurers to pay the disputed bills prior to a determination that the medical treatment was reasonable and necessary. An employee obtains a protected property interest in the medical benefits only after two hurdles are met: the employer's initial liability must be established and any disputes over the reasonableness and necessity of particular treatment must be resolved. Only the first of these hurdles has been met in this case.

8-1. Opinion of Court by Rehnquist, joined in part by O'Connor, Scalia, Kennedy, Souter, Thomas, and Breyer; and joined in separate part by O'Connor, Kennedy, Thomas, and Ginsburg. Concurring opinions by Ginsburg and by Breyer, joined by Souter. Concurring and dissenting opinion by Stevens.

Amoco Production Co. v. Southern Ute Tribe 119 S. Ct. 1719, 67 USLW 4397 (6-7-99)

Public lands, patents, "coal" reservation: Reservation to the United States of "all coal" in lands patented pursuant to the Coal Lands Acts of 1909 and 1910 did not also reserve coalbed methane gas (CBM). Although CBM gas, generated during the formation of coal and retained in the coal, may be considered to be a constituent of coal, Congress did not so regard it in 1909 and 1910. Unless otherwise defined, statutory words are given their "ordinary, contemporary, common meaning." Dictionaries of the day defined coal as a solid rock substance, and "marsh gas" (one of the names by which CBM gas was known) as a distinct substance contained in or given off by coal. Congress viewed CBM gas not as a fuel resource, but as a dangerous waste product that necessitated ventilation safety standards for mines. Coal companies at that time made no effort to capture or preserve CBM gas. The limited nature of the reservation of "all coal" is confirmed by subsequent enactments containing broader reservations of "oil and gas" (1912) and of "coal and other minerals" (1916). The argument that Congress would not have intended to create such split estates, with coal and CBM gas in separate ownership, is unpersuasive; including coal and CBM gas under the same ownership would have led to a split gas estate "at least as difficult to administer," with ownership of CBM gas and "natural gas" being separated.

7-1. Opinion of Court by Kennedy, joined by Rehnquist, Stevens, O'Connor, Scalia, Souter, and Thomas. Dissenting opinion by Ginsburg. Breyer did not participate.

Arizona Dep't of Revenue v. Blaze Constr. Co. 119 S. Ct. 957, 67 USLW 4156 (3-2-99)

Taxation, State; federal contractors; Native Americans: The general rule announced in *United States v. New Mexico* (1982) that a state may impose a nondiscriminatory tax upon a private company's proceeds from a contract with the Federal Government applies when a private, non-Indian federal contractor has rendered its services on an Indian reservation. The Arizona Court of Appeals erred in applying a balancing test to conclude that federal laws regulating the welfare of Indians implicitly preempted the State's tax. "The need to avoid litigation and to ensure efficient tax administration counsels in favor of a bright-line standard for taxation of federal contracts, regardless of whether the contracted-for activity takes place on Indian reservations."

9-0. Opinion for unanimous Court by Thomas.

AT&T Corp. v. Iowa Utilities Bd. 119 S. Ct. 721, 67 USLW 4104 (1-25-99)

Telecommunications Act of 1996, regulation of local competition: The FCC has authority under section 201(b) of the Communications Act of 1934 to prescribe rules and regulations governing the restructuring of local telephone markets in accordance with the Telecommunications Act of 1996. The 1996 Act amends, and hence is part of, the 1934 Act; section 201(b) of the 1934 Act authorizes the Commission to "prescribe such rules and regulations as may be necessary in the public interest to carry out the provisions of this Act." Section 2(b) of the 1934 Act, which provides that "nothing in this Act shall be construed to apply or to give the Commission jurisdiction with respect to . . . intrastate communication service," does not restrict the Commission's jurisdiction to make rules governing matters to which the 1996 Act applies. The Commission has jurisdiction to design a pricing methodology that states must use in setting rates, and to promulgate rules regarding state review of interconnection agreements, rural exemptions, and dialing parity. The Commission's "unbundling" rules reasonably apply the Act's "network element" definition, but do not adequately take into account the Act's requirement that, in determining which network elements an incumbent carrier must provide to a requesting carrier, the Commission consider whether access is "necessary" and whether failure to provide access would "impair" the requesting carrier's ability to provide service. Two other aspects of the "unbundling" rules are upheld. The "all elements" rule, which allows competitors to rely completely on elements in an incumbent's network without owning any facilities themselves, is not unreasonable. Rule 315(b), which prohibits an incumbent from separating already-combined network elements before leasing them to a competitor, is a reasonable interpretation of ambiguous statutory language. The FCC's "pick and choose" rule, which "tracks the pertinent statutory language almost exactly," is upheld.

5-3 (jurisdiction generally); **8-0** (network element definition, "all elements" rule, rule 315(b), "pick and choose" rule); **7-1** ("necessary and impair" standards). Opinion of Court by Scalia, joined in part by Rehnquist, Stevens, Kennedy, Souter, Thomas, Ginsburg, and Breyer; joined in separate part by all of the above except Souter; and joined in separate part by Stevens, Kennedy, Souter, and

Ginsburg. Opinion by Souter, concurring in part and dissenting in part. Opinion by Thomas, concurring in part and dissenting in part, joined by Rehnquist and Breyer. Opinion by Breyer, concurring in part and dissenting in part. O'Connor did not participate.

Bank of America Nat'l Trust Ass'n v. 203 North Lasalle St. Partnership 119 S. Ct. 1411, 67 USLW 4275 (5-3-99)

Bankruptcy, reorganization, priorities: A reorganization plan under which a debtor's pre-bankruptcy equity holders are allowed the exclusive opportunity to contribute new capital and receive ownership interests in the reorganized entity is inconsistent with 11 U.S.C. § 1129(b)(2)(B)(ii), which provides that a plan is not fair and equitable if a junior claim holder receives any property "on account of such junior claim." In this case it is unnecessary to determine whether the "absolute priority rule" protected by the statutory language carries with it a "new value corollary." Under the new value corollary as it had developed prior to revision of the Bankruptcy Code, "old equity" holders who made a new contribution after reorganization could receive a participation reasonably equivalent to their contribution. Even assuming existence of this new value corollary, however, the current reorganization plan falls within the prohibition of § 1129(b)(2)(B)(ii) because it provides junior interest holders with "exclusive opportunities free from competition and without benefit of market valuation."

8-1. Opinion of Court by Souter, joined by Rehnquist, O'Connor, Kennedy, Ginsburg, and Breyer. Concurring opinion by Thomas. Dissenting opinion by Stevens.

Buckley v. American Constitutional Law Foundation 119 S. Ct. 636, 67 USLW 4043 (1-12-99)

First Amendment, conditions on ballot initiatives: Three conditions that Colorado placed on the petition process for ballot initiatives impermissibly restrict political speech in violation of the First and Fourteenth Amendments. The requirement that petition circulators be registered voters drastically reduces the number of persons available to circulate petitions, and is not warranted. Other requirements — that circulators be state residents and that they verify their addresses by affidavit — adequately protect the State's interest in insuring that circulators will be amenable to state process if they break the law. The requirement that petition circulators wear identification badges also restrains speech unnecessarily. By compelling identification "at the precise moment when the circulator's interest in anonymity is greatest," the requirement restrains speech more severely than did the prohibition on distribution of anonymous campaign literature struck down in *McIntyre v. Ohio Elections Comm'n* (1995). Here again, the affidavit requirement adequately serves the State's interest. Disclosure requirements are valid insofar as they require initiative sponsors to reveal the amount of money they have spent, but are invalid in requiring identification of paid circulators and the amounts paid to each.

9-0 (identification badges); **6-3** (registration and disclosure requirements). Opinion of Court by Ginsburg, joined by Stevens, Scalia, Kennedy, and Souter. Concurring opinion by Thomas. Opinion by O'Connor, joined by Souter, concurring in part and dissenting in part. Dissenting opinion by Rehnquist.

Calderon v. Coleman 119 S. Ct. 500, 67 USLW 3390 (12-14-98)

Death penalty, jury instruction: The Ninth Circuit erred in failing to apply the harmless error analysis of *Brecht v. Abrahamson* (1990) to determine whether to grant *habeas corpus* relief to a prisoner sentenced to death following an erroneous jury instruction about the power of California's governor to commute a sentence of life without possibility of parole. Under *Brecht*, relief may be granted only if the unconstitutional instruction had a "substantial and injurious effect or influence on the jury's sentence of death." This requirement assures that a state will not be put to the "arduous task" of retrial "based on mere speculation that the defendant was prejudiced by trial error." Instead of pursuing the *Brecht* inquiry, the Ninth Circuit applied *Boyde v. California* (1990) to determine whether there was a "reasonable likelihood that the jury has applied the challenged instruction in a way that prevents the consideration of constitutionally relevant evidence." This *Boyde* analysis "is not a harmless-error test at all," but merely asks whether constitutional error has occurred.

5-4. *Per curiam*. Dissenting opinion by Stevens, joined by Souter, Ginsburg, and Breyer.

California Dental Ass'n v. FTC 119 S. Ct. 1605, 67 USLW 4365 (5-25-99)

Federal Trade Commission, jurisdiction: The Federal Trade Commission has jurisdiction over the California Dental Association (CDA), a nonprofit association that provides substantial economic benefits to its for-profit members. The Federal Trade Commission Act gives the FTC jurisdiction over "corporations," and defines "corporation" to include an association organized to carry on business for profit of its members. The CDA contributes to the profits of its members in a variety of ways that are proximate and apparent. The "logic and purpose" of the FTC Act, as well as its legislative history, support the conclusion that the FTC has jurisdiction over such nonprofit entities. The Court of Appeals erred, however, when it concluded that "quick-look" analysis was an appropriate basis for concluding that the CDA's restrictions on price and quality advertising by its members were anticompetitive. "Quick-look" analysis under the rule of reason is appropriate only if the likelihood of anticompetitive effects is obvious. The CDA's advertising restrictions might plausibly be thought to have a pro-competitive rather than an anticompetitive effect. In any event, restrictions on professional advertising that arguably protect patients from misleading or irrelevant claims "call for more than cursory treatment."

9-0 (jurisdiction); **5-4** (merits). Opinion of Court by Souter, unanimous in part, and joined in separate part by Rehnquist, O'Connor, Scalia, and Thomas. Concurring and dissenting opinion by Breyer, joined by Stevens, Kennedy, and Ginsburg.

California Pub. Employees' Retirement Sys. v. Felzen 119 S. Ct. 720, 67 USLW 4090 (1-20-99)

Appeals, derivative shareholder action: The decision of the U.S. Court of Appeals for the Seventh Circuit, holding that shareholders who have appeared in response to a notice provided under Federal Rule of Civil Procedure 23.1 in order to provide objections to a proposed dismissal or settlement of a derivative action, but who have not formally intervened as parties, have no right to appeal an adverse decision, is affirmed by equally divided vote.

4-4. *Per curiam*. Justice O'Connor did not participate.

Cedar Rapids Community Sch. Dist. v. Garret F. 119 S. Ct. 992, 67 USLW 4165 (3-3-99)

IDEA, "related services" and "medical services": A state that accepts federal funding under the Individuals with Disabilities Education Act (IDEA) must provide continuous, one-on-one nursing care to a ventilator-dependent student. IDEA requires provision of a free appropriate public education and "related services," and defines "related services" to include various supportive services that enable a child to remain in school during the day, but to exclude "medical services" that are not diagnostic or evaluative. Continuous nursing care clearly falls within the general terms of "related services," and does not fit within the regulatory understanding of "medical services." In *Irving Indep. Sch. Dist. v. Tatro* (1984), the Court upheld as reasonable an administrative determination that "medical services" means services that must be performed by a physician, and does not apply to procedures such as catheterization that can performed by school health personnel. None of the services required by the respondent in this case need be performed by a physician, and consequently none are "medical." The combined and continuous character of the required care may make care more costly and may require additional school personnel, but does not transform the care into "medical services."

7-2. Opinion of Court by Stevens, joined by Rehnquist, O'Connor, Scalia, Souter, Ginsburg, and Breyer. Dissenting opinion by Thomas, joined by Kennedy.

Central State Univ. v. American Ass'n of Univ. Professors 119 S. Ct. 1162, (3-22-99)

Equal Protection, preclusion of collective bargaining: An Ohio law directing state universities to develop standards for faculty workloads to emphasize undergraduate instruction, and exempting such standards from collective bargaining, does not violate the Equal Protection Clause of the Fourteenth Amendment. Depriving state-employed professors of the right, otherwise available to public employees, to bargain collectively over their workload implicates neither fundamental rights nor suspect classifications, so the rational basis test applies. Imposition of the faculty workload policy was intended to increase the amount of time that professors spend in the classroom, and exempting the policy from collective bargaining was "an entirely rational step to accomplish this objective." The legislature rationally could have concluded that their objective "would have been undercut and likely varied if it were subject to collective bargaining."

8-1. *Per curiam*. Concurring opinion by Ginsburg, joined by Breyer. Dissenting opinion by Stevens.

City of Chicago v. Morales 119 S. Ct. 1849, 67 USLW 4415 (6-10-99)

Due Process, anti-loitering ordinance: Chicago's Gang Congregation Ordinance, which prohibits "criminal street gang members" from "loitering" with one another or with other persons in any public place after being ordered by a police officer to disperse, violates the Due Process Clause of the Fourteenth Amendment. "Loitering" is defined as "remain[ing] in any one place with no apparent purpose." The ordinance directs the police, if they reasonably believe that at least one of the congregating persons is a street gang member, to order "all" of the persons to disperse, without first making any inquiries about their possible purposes. The broad sweep of the ordinance violates the requirement that a legislature establish minimal guidelines for law enforcement. The ordinance reaches a substantial amount of innocent conduct. Also, the Court is bound by the Illinois Supreme Court's interpretation of the ordinance as conferring "absolute discretion" on police officers to determine what activities constitute loitering. The ordinance requires no harmful purpose, and applies to non-gang members as well as to suspected gang members. The ordinance also excludes from coverage much of the intimidating conduct that motivated its enactment, since it has no application to loiterers whose purpose is apparent — even if that purpose is threatening or illicit.

6-3. Opinion of Court by Stevens, joined by O'Connor, Kennedy, Souter, Ginsburg, and Breyer. Separate part of Stevens opinion joined by Souter and Ginsburg. Concurring opinions by O'Connor, joined by Breyer; by Kennedy; and by Breyer. Dissenting opinions by Scalia; and by Thomas, joined by Rehnquist and Scalia.

City of Monterey v. Del Monte Dunes at Monterey, Ltd. 67 USLW 4345 (5-24-99)

Regulatory taking, § 1983 action, right to jury trial: Respondent's regulatory takings claim, brought under 42 U.S.C. § 1983, was properly submitted to the jury. Section 1983 does not itself confer a right to jury trial, but the Seventh Amendment does for such actions. The Seventh Amendment applies not only to "common law" causes of action, but also to statutory actions analogous to common law actions that in late 18th century England were tried in courts of law rather than in courts of equity or in admiralty courts. A section 1983 action seeking "legal relief" is an action at law within the meaning of the Seventh Amendment. Section 1983 actions "sound in tort," and a claim for just compensation seeks "legal relief," since as a general rule monetary relief is legal. The particular issue of liability presented in this case — whether a landowner has been deprived of all economically viable use of his property — was proper for determination by the jury. The "rough proportionality" test of *Dolan v. City of Tigard* (1994), previously applied only in the context of property exactions, is inappropriate for cases such as this.

5-4 (Seventh Amendment); **9-0** (proportionality). Opinion of Court by Kennedy, unanimous in part, and joined in separate part by Rehnquist, Stevens, Scalia, and Thomas. Separate part of Kennedy opinion joined only by Rehnquist, Stevens, and Thomas. Concurring opinion by Scalia. Concurring and dissenting opinion by Souter, joined by O'Connor, Ginsburg, and Breyer.

City of West Covina v. Perkins 119 S. Ct. 678, 67 USLW 4058 (1-13-99)

Due Process, seizure of property, notice of remedies: The Due Process Clause of the Fourteenth Amendment does not require that police, when they have lawfully seized property, notify the property owners about state procedures for the return of the seized property. Law enforcement agents who seize property must take reasonable steps to notify the owner that the property has been taken, but need not provide the owner with additional information about state law remedies. In cases such as this, when the owner is not present when property is seized, notice of the seizure is necessary to inform the owner about what has happened to the missing property. No similar rationale requires notice of remedies; information about remedies is generally available in published form as state statutes and case law. The notice required by the appeals court in this case lacks support in Supreme Court precedent and "far exceeds that which the States and the Federal Government have traditionally required." The appeals court's analysis would render constitutionally inadequate, for example, the notice mandated by Federal Rule of Criminal Procedure 41(d), which requires that agents seizing property give the dispossessed a copy of the warrant and a receipt for the property.

9-0. Opinion of Court by Kennedy, joined by Rehnquist, Stevens, O'Connor, Souter, Ginsburg, and Breyer. Concurring opinion by Thomas, joined by Scalia.

Cleveland v. Policy Management Systems Corp. 67 USLW 4375 (5-24-99)

SSDI, ADA, compatibility of claims: Pursuit and receipt of Social Security Disability Insurance (SSDI) benefits does not automatically estop the recipient from pursuing a claim under the Americans With Disabilities Act (ADA). Nor do the claims inherently conflict to the point where courts should apply a special negative presumption. There are many situations in which an SSDI claim and an ADA claim can coexist. While the ADA defines a "qualified individual" to include a disabled person who can perform the essential functions of her job "with reasonable accommodation," the total disability determination under SSDI takes no account of the possibility of a "reasonable accommodation." In other cases, however, an earlier SSDI claim may turn out to conflict with an ADA claim. For this reason, an ADA plaintiff may not simply ignore the apparent contradiction, but must explain her earlier SSDI claim. To defeat summary judgment, that explanation must be sufficient to warrant a reasonable juror's conclusion that, assuming the truth of, or the plaintiff's good-faith belief in, the earlier SSDI claim, the plaintiff could nonetheless perform the essential functions of her job, with or without accommodation.

9-0. Opinion for unanimous Court by Breyer.

Clinton v. Goldsmith 119 S. Ct. 1538, 67 USLW 4302 (5-17-99)

All Writs Act, Court of Appeals for the Armed Forces: The Court of Appeals for the Armed Forces (CAAF) lacked jurisdiction to enjoin the President and various military officers from dropping the respondent from the rolls of the Air Force. The respondent had been court-martialed, and his conviction became final after the Air Force Court of Criminal Appeals (AFCCA) affirmed and he sought no review in the CAAF. When the Air Force notified respondent that it was taking action to drop him from its rolls, he challenged that action in the AFCCA, and, following dismissal for lack of jurisdiction, appealed to the CAAF. The CAAF relied on the All Writs Act in enjoining the President and the Air Force officers from proceeding against the respondent. The All Writs Act authorizes issuance of extraordinary writs only "in aid of" the issuing court's jurisdiction. The CAAF's jurisdiction is limited to review of specified sentences imposed by courts-martial. The Air Force's action to drop the respondent was an executive action, not a finding or sentence that was or could have been imposed in a court-martial proceeding, so the action was beyond the CAAF's jurisdiction and hence also beyond the "aid" of the All Writs Act. Even if the CAAF had jurisdiction, resort to the All Writs Act would still have been unjustifiable because it was neither "necessary" nor "appropriate." Both the federal courts and various administrative bodies in the military would have authority to review the challenged action.

9-0. Opinion for unanimous Court by Souter.

College Savings Bank v. Florida Prepaid Postsecondary Educ. Expense Bd. 119 S. Ct. 2219, 67 USLW 4590 (6-23-99)

State sovereign immunity, abrogation by Congress, trademarks: The Trademark Remedy Clarification Act (TRCA), which amended the Lanham Act to subject states to suits for false and misleading advertising, did not validly abrogate state sovereign immunity, and Florida in this case has not waived its immunity. Congress may abrogate state sovereign immunity in exercise of its power to enforce the Fourteenth Amendment, but the TRCA is not such an enforcement action. The assertion that the TRCA was enacted to remedy and prevent state deprivations of property rights is "without merit." Neither the right to be free from a business competitor's false advertising nor a more generalized right to be secure in one's business interests qualifies as a "property" right protected by the Due Process Clause. The essence of a property right is the right to exclude others, yet the Lanham Act's false advertising provisions bear no relationship to a right to exclude. Analogies to equity jurisdiction and to the common-law tort of unfair competition are unpersuasive. Business assets are property, but the activity of doing business — the only aspect of property impinged upon by a competitor's false advertising — is not property in the ordinary sense. Florida did not waive its immunity from Lanham Act suits by selling and advertising in interstate commerce a for-profit educational investment vehicle. *Parden v. Terminal Ry.* (1964), which recognized a constructive waiver of immunity, has been limited by subsequent decisions, and is now expressly overruled. *Parden* was premised on the now-discredited notion that state sovereign immunity is not constitutionally based.

5-4. Opinion of Court by Scalia, joined by Rehnquist, O'Connor, Kennedy, and Thomas. Dissenting opinions by Stevens; and by Breyer, joined by Stevens, Souter, and Ginsburg.

Conn v. Gabbert 119 S. Ct. 1292, 67 USLW 4219 (4-5-99)

Due Process, right to practice profession: An attorney's Fourteenth Amendment right to practice his profession is not impaired when the prosecutor requires that the attorney be searched at the same time that his client is testifying before a grand jury, even if the search was calculated to annoy or to prevent the attorney from consulting with his client. Cases in which the Court has recognized a right to choose and follow one's field of private employment have all dealt with a complete prohibition of that right, and not with the sort of brief interruption that occurred here. The attorney has no standing to allege infringement of his client's right to assistance of counsel during the grand jury proceeding. The attorney may challenge the reasonableness of the timing of the search, but this is a Fourth Amendment issue rather than a Due Process issue.

9-0. Opinion of Court by Rehnquist, joined by O'Connor, Scalia, Kennedy, Souter, Thomas, Ginsburg, and Breyer. Concurring opinion by Stevens.

Cunningham v. Hamilton County 119 S. Ct. 1915, 67 USLW 4458 (6-14-99)

Appeals, "final decision": An order imposing sanctions on an attorney pursuant to Federal Rule of Civil Procedure 37(a)(4) for failure to comply with discovery orders is not a "final decision" appealable under 28 U.S.C. § 1291 prior to final judgment in the underlying action. The Rule 37 sanction did not end the litigation or leave the district court with only the task of executing its judgment. Nor does the sanction fit within the small category of orders that are appealable even though they do not terminate litigation. The order was conclusive, but cannot be separated completely from the merits of the case. Also, the order is not effectively unreviewable on appeal from a final judgment on the merits. The congruence of interests between attorneys and clients "counsels against treating attorneys like other nonparties for purposes of appeal." To permit an immediate appeal would undermine the purposes of Rule 37(a), which was designed to protect courts and opposing parties from delaying or harassing tactics during the discovery process. The same rule applies when the attorney no longer represents a party in the case. The efficiency interests served by limiting immediate appeals "far outweigh" any costs that sanctioned attorneys might bear in monitoring the progress of the litigation.

9-0. Opinion for unanimous Court by Thomas. Concurring opinion by Kennedy.

Davis v. Monroe County Bd. of Educ. 119 S. Ct. 1661, 67 USLW 4329 (5-24-99)

Title IX, "student-on-student" sexual harassment: A recipient of federal educational funds can be held liable under Title IX of the Education Amendments of 1972 in a private damages action arising from student-on-student sexual harassment. Funding recipients are properly held liable, however, only if they are "deliberately indifferent to sexual harassment, of which they have actual knowledge, that is so severe, pervasive, and objectively offensive that it can be said to deprive the victims of access to the educational opportunities or benefits provided by the school." Earlier cases have established that private damages actions are available only if funding recipients had adequate notice that they can be held liable, and only if their own actions or indifference effectively caused the "discrimination" at issue and therefore constituted an intentional violation of Title IX. Such an intentional violation can occur even when the harasser is a student rather than a teacher, so long as the funding recipient "exercises substantial control over both the harasser and the context in which the known harassment occurs." This is the case when student-on-student sexual harassment occurs during school hours and on school grounds, and the alleged harasser is under the school's disciplinary authority. A further limitation is that funding recipients will be deemed to be "deliberately indifferent" only if their response or lack of response to alleged harassment "is clearly unreasonable in light of the known circumstances." And the recipient's indifference is actionable only when the alleged harassment is so severe, pervasive, and objectively offensive as to effectively deprive the victim of the educational opportunities provided by the school.

5-4. Opinion of Court by O'Connor, joined by Stevens, Souter, Ginsburg, and Breyer. Dissenting opinion by Kennedy, joined by Rehnquist, Scalia, and Thomas.

Department of Commerce v. United States House of Representatives
Clinton v. Glavin 119 S. Ct. 765, 67 USLW 4090 (1-25-99)

Standing to sue; Census Act: Plaintiffs in *Clinton v. Glavin*, consolidated with the House of Representative's suit for purposes of review, had standing to sue to challenge the use of statistical sampling in the Department's proposed Census 2000 plan. An Indiana citizen had standing because of the "virtual certainty" that Indiana would lose a seat in the House under the Department's plan, and citizens of several counties had standing by virtue of the likelihood that their counties would suffer vote dilution as a result of census-based redistricting for state, local, and congressional elections. The Census Act does not permit the use of statistical sampling in calculating the population for purposes of apportioning Representatives among the states. Section 195 of the Act, as amended in 1976, provides that, "except for the determination of population for purposes of apportionment of Representatives . . . , the Secretary shall, if he considers it feasible, authorize the use of the statistical method known as 'sampling.'" General language added in 1976 authorizes the Secretary to take the decennial census "in such form and content as he may determine, including the use of sampling procedures." The broad grant of authority in section 141 is limited "by the narrower and more specific §195," and section 195 must be interpreted in the broader context of a 200-year-long prohibition on the use of statistical sampling. Because the Census Act prohibits the use of sampling in calculating population for purposes of apportionment, it is unnecessary to consider the constitutionality of sampling. Because the disposition of *Clinton v. Glavin* also resolves the substantive issues presented in the House of Representatives' action, that case (98-404) is dismissed as no longer presenting a substantial federal question.

9-0 (standing); **5-4** (Census Act). Opinion of Court by O'Connor, joined in part by Rehnquist, Scalia, Kennedy, Thomas, and Breyer, and joined in separate part by Rehnquist, Scalia, Kennedy, and Thomas. Separate part of O'Connor opinion joined only by Rehnquist and Kennedy. Opinion by Scalia, joined by Thomas, and joined in part by Rehnquist and Kennedy, concurring in part. Opinion by Breyer, concurring in part and dissenting in part. Dissenting opinion by Stevens, joined in part by Souter and Ginsburg, and joined in separate part by Breyer. Dissenting opinion by Ginsburg, joined by Souter.

Department of the Army v. Blue Fox, Inc. 119 S. Ct. 687, 67 USLW 4073 (1-20-99)

Sovereign immunity: Section 10(a) of the Administrative Procedure Act, 5 U.S.C. § 702, does not nullify the long-settled rule that sovereign immunity bars creditors from enforcing liens on Government property. In this case, a subcontractor on a Government contract, unable to recover from the contractor, sought an "equitable lien" on any Government funds still available for payment to the contractor or for completion of the project. Section 702 waives sovereign immunity for certain claims "seeking relief other than money damages." In this context, "money damages" means compensatory or substitute relief, and "other than money damages" refers to specific relief, e.g., enforcement of a statutory mandate. The goal of the equitable lien sought by the subcontractor in this case is to attach money held by the Government in order to compensate for the loss resulting from the default of the contractor. This is a claim for "substitute" rather than "specific" relief, and therefore amounts to a claim for "money damages" within the meaning of the APA. The action therefore falls outside of section 702's waiver of sovereign immunity.

9-0. Opinion for unanimous Court by Rehnquist.

Dickinson v. Zurko 119 S. Ct. 1816, 67 USLW 4445 (6-10-99)

Patents and trademarks, standard of review: The Federal Circuit, when it reviews findings of fact made by the Patent and Trademark Office (PTO), must apply the "arbitrary, capricious, [or] abuse of discretion [or] unsupported by substantial evidence" standards set forth in section 706 of the Administrative Procedure Act (APA), and not the "clearly erroneous" standard set forth in Federal Rule of Civil Procedure 52(a) for appellate court review of lower court decisions. A reviewing court must apply the APA standard in the absence of an exception authorized by section 559, which provides that the APA does "not limit or repeal additional requirements . . . recognized by law." The "clearly erroneous" standard was not "recognized by law" when the APA was enacted in 1946. The 89 pre-APA cases involving judicial review of a PTO administrative decision do not reflect a well-established "court/court" standard of judicial review. Use of such terms as "clear case of error" or "manifest error" is not conclusive, since the "relevant linguistic conventions were less firmly established before adoption of the APA." The Supreme Court's 1884 decision in *Morgan v. Daniels* does not support application of the court/court standard. Rather, the Court, in determining the appropriate standard for review of Patent Office decisions, rejected reliance on the then-governing standard for an appellate court's review of a lower court's factual findings.

6-3. Opinion of Court by Breyer, joined by Stevens, O'Connor, Scalia, Souter, and Thomas. Dissenting opinion by Rehnquist, joined by Kennedy and Ginsburg.

El Al Israel Airlines v. Tsui Yuan Tseng 119 S. Ct. 662, 67 USLW 4036 (1-12-99)

Warsaw Convention, preemption: The Warsaw Convention precludes a passenger from maintaining an action for personal injury damages under local law when her claim does not satisfy the conditions for liability under the Convention. The plaintiff in this action alleged that she suffered emotional distress, but no bodily injury, from an intrusive airport security search conducted before she boarded an El Al flight. The Convention does not permit recovery for emotional distress unaccompanied by bodily injury. Article 24 of the Convention provides that "cases covered by Article 17" may only be brought subject to the conditions and limits set out by the Convention. Article 17 creates a cause of action for personal injuries suffered as a result of an "accident . . . in the course of any of the operations of embarking or disembarking." Although the security search was not an "accident" within the meaning of Article 17, Article 24's reference to "cases covered by Article 17" applies generically to all personal injury cases stemming from occurrences on board an aircraft or in embarking or disembarking. The "cardinal purpose" of the Convention was "to achieve uniformity of rules governing claims arising from international air transportation." Decisions of the courts of other signatory nations support a broad reading of the Convention's preemptive effect.

8-1. Opinion of Court by Ginsburg, joined by Rehnquist, O'Connor, Scalia, Kennedy, Souter, Thomas, and Breyer. Dissenting opinion by Stevens.

El Paso Natural Gas Co. v. Neztsosie 119 S. Ct. 1430, 67 USLW 4286 (5-3-99)

Price-Anderson Act, preemption, tribal court exhaustion: The doctrine of tribal court exhaustion, under which federal district courts abstain from deciding issues of tribal court jurisdiction until the tribal courts themselves have addressed them, is inapplicable to suits involving claims under the Price-Anderson Act. In this case the district court should have decided whether the claims at issue were Price-Anderson claims. The Act's "unusual preemption provision," which gives federal courts jurisdiction over "any public liability action arising out of . . . a nuclear incident, provides for removal to federal court if a putative Price-Anderson action is brought in state court, but is silent about actions brought in tribal courts. It seems most likely that congressional silence on tribal courts is due to "inadvertence." Because there were no nuclear testing labs or reactors on reservation lands, Congress probably did not foresee the possibility that a nuclear incident might occur on tribal lands. There is no reason to believe, however, that Congress would have favored tribal exhaustion in Price-Anderson suits. The Act, amended in the aftermath of the Three-Mile Island accident, sought speed and efficiency in managing claims, and authorized a special caseload management panel to consolidate and expedite claims. The panel, explained a Senate report, would help avoid inefficiencies resulting from "duplicative determinations . . . in multiple jurisdictions." Application of tribal exhaustion would defeat these purposes.

9-0. Opinion for unanimous Court by Souter.

Federal Republic of Germany v. United States 119 S. Ct. 1016, 67 USLW 3559 (3-3-99)

International Court of Justice, enforcement of order: The Federal Republic of Germany's motions for leave to file a complaint, and for issuance of a preliminary injunction, are denied. Germany sought enforcement of an *ex parte* order issued by the International Court of Justice directing the United States to prevent the execution of Walter LaGrand, a German citizen, by the State of Arizona. See also *Stewart v. LaGrand* (1999). The United States has not waived its sovereign immunity, and it is "doubtful" that Article III, § 2, cl. 2, which extends jurisdiction to cases affecting ambassadors and consuls, "provides an anchor" for the action. The Federal Republic's suit against the State of Arizona, as was Paraguay's suit against Virginia in *Breard v. Greene* (1998), "is without evident support in the Vienna Convention and in probable contravention of the Eleventh Amendment."

7-2. *Per curiam.* Concurring opinion by Souter, joined by Ginsburg. Dissenting opinion by Breyer, joined by Stevens.

Florida Prepaid Postsecondary Educ. Expense Bd. v. College Savings Bank 119 S. Ct. 2199, 67 USLW 4580 (6-23-99)

State sovereign immunity, abrogation by Congress, patents: The Patent and Plant Variety Protection Remedy Clarification Act's amendment of the patent laws to expressly abrogate states' sovereign immunity from patent infringement suits cannot be upheld as an exercise of congressional power to enforce the Fourteenth Amendment's Due Process Clause. While Congress in exercise of its enforcement power may abrogate state sovereign immunity, it must do so through legislation that is "appropriate" within the meaning of § 5 of the 14th

Amendment. The Court's decision in *City of Boerne v. Flores* (1997) established that "appropriate" legislation must be "remedial": Congress must identify conduct that violates the Fourteenth Amendment and must tailor its legislation to remedying or preventing such conduct. In enacting the Patent Remedy Act, however, Congress identified no pattern of patent infringement by states. Moreover, Congress barely considered the availability of state remedies for patent infringement. Patent infringement alone does not constitute a due process violation; "only where the State provides no remedy, or only inadequate remedies . . . could a deprivation of property without due process occur." The legislative record thus "at best offers scant support" for a conclusion that states were engaging in due process violations. Consequently, the provisions of the Act are "so out of proportion to a supposed remedial or preventive object" that they cannot be upheld as an exercise of Fourteenth Amendment enforcement power.

5-4. Opinion of Court by Rehnquist, joined by O'Connor, Scalia, Kennedy, and Thomas. Dissenting opinion by Stevens, joined by Souter, Ginsburg, and Breyer.

Florida v. White 119 S. Ct. 1555, 67 USLW 4311 (5-17-99)

Fourth Amendment, seizure of automobile, contraband forfeiture: The Fourth Amendment does not require the police to obtain a warrant before seizing an automobile from a public place when they have probable cause to believe that the automobile itself is forfeitable contraband. The Court has long recognized that when law enforcement officers have probable cause to believe than an automobile contains contraband, the Fourth Amendment does not require them to obtain a warrant prior to searching the car and seizing the contraband. This principle derives from laws and cases involving customs inspections of vessels, and reflects the need to seize "readily movable contraband before it is spirited away." The same principle applies if it is the vehicle itself that is the contraband. The Court also recognizes that law enforcement officers have "greater latitude in exercising their duties in public places" than they have when searching private premises. In this case police officers had observed the respondent using his car to transport illegal drugs. Several months later, after arresting the respondent on unrelated charges, the officers, acting under authority of the Florida Contraband Forfeiture Act, seized respondent's car from his employer's parking lot. No warrant was required under these circumstances.

7-2. Opinion of Court by Thomas, joined by O'Connor, Scalia, Kennedy, Souter, and Breyer. Concurring opinion by Souter, joined by Breyer. Dissenting opinion by Stevens, joined by Ginsburg.

Greater New Orleans Broadcasting Ass'n v. United States 119 S. Ct. 1923, 67 USLW 4451 (6-14-99)

First Amendment, commercial speech: 18 U.S.C. § 1304, which prohibits radio and television broadcasters from carrying advertisements for privately operated casino gambling regardless of the station's or casino's location, may not constitutionally be applied to prohibit advertising of private casino gambling broadcast by stations located within a state where such gambling is legal. The provision fails to satisfy the *Central Hudson* test for restrictions on commercial speech. If the commercial speech relates to lawful activity and is not misleading, restrictions must directly advance a substantial governmental interest and must not be more extensive than necessary to serve that interest. The government has identified substantial interests that are served by the prohibition on ads for casino gambling, but the underlying policy "is now decidedly equivocal." When section 1304 was enacted in 1934, the federal anti-gambling policy was uniform. Now, however, with various exemptions for gambling conducted by Indian tribes and state governments, federal statutes promote both pro-gambling and anti-gambling policies. "The operation of § 1304 and its attendant regulatory regime is so pierced by exemptions and inconsistencies that the Government cannot hope to exonerate it." Moreover, while there may be valid reasons for regulating tribal casino gambling more closely than non-tribal casino gambling, there is "no convincing reason" for restricting the speech of non-tribal owners more than that of tribal owners.

9-0. Opinion of Court by Stevens, joined by Rehnquist, O'Connor, Scalia, Kennedy, Souter, Ginsburg, and Breyer. Concurring opinions by Rehnquist and Thomas.

Grupo Mexicano de Desarollo v. Alliance Bond Fund 119 S. Ct. 1961, 67 USLW 4490
(6-17-99)

Federal courts, injunctive powers; mootness: A federal district court lacks the authority, in an action for money damages, to issue a preliminary injunction preventing the defendant from transferring assets in which no lien or equitable interest is claimed. The relief sought has no basis in the traditional powers of the equity courts. It is well established that a general creditor (one without a judgment) has no cognizable interest, at law or in equity, in the property of his debtor. There is no analogy to the equitable action known as a "creditor's bill," since that action could be brought only by a creditor who had already obtained a judgment establishing the debt. The merger of law and equity did not alter substantive rights. While policy arguments may be made for and against creating the preliminary injunctive remedy to freeze a debtor's assets pending adjudication, the Court lacks authority under the Judiciary Act of 1789 to create remedies previously unknown to equity jurisprudence. Congress is the appropriate forum for deciding whether "this formidable power over debtors" should be created. Appeal of the preliminary injunction in this case was not rendered moot by decision on the merits and issuance of a permanent injunction. The basis for arguing that the preliminary injunction was wrongfully issued — that the court lacked power to restrain use of assets pending a money judgment — was independent of the breach of contract claim adjudicated on the merits.

5-4 (authority to issue preliminary injunction); **9-0** (mootness). Opinion of Court by Scalia, unanimous in part, and joined by Rehnquist, O'Connor, Kennedy, and Thomas in separate part. Dissenting opinion by Ginsburg, joined by Stevens, Souter, and Breyer.

Haddle v. Garrison 119 S. Ct. 489, 67 USLW 4029 (12-14-98)

Civil rights, conspiracy to deter testimony: Termination of at-will employment as part of a conspiracy to deter testimony before a federal grand jury is actionable under 42 U.S.C. § 1985(2) as injuring a citizen "in his person or property." The Eleventh Circuit was mistaken that a citizen must suffer an injury to a constitutionally protected interest in order to recover damages under § 1985(2). The case is not resolved, therefore, by the fact that loss of at-will employment is not "property" for purposes of the Due Process Clause. The "gist of the wrong" at which the provision is directed is not deprivation of property, but intimidation of witnesses. For this purpose, it is sufficient that interference with at-will employment has long been compensable under tort law.

9-0. Opinion for unanimous Court by Rehnquist.

Hanlon v. Berger 119 S. Ct. 1706, 67 USLW 4329 (5-24-99)

Fourth Amendment, media "ride-along", qualified immunity: Fish and Wildlife Service agents violated the Fourth Amendment when they allowed a media camera crew to accompany them in executing a warrant to search respondents' ranch for evidence of illegal taking of wildlife. The principles announced in *Wilson v. Layne* control. The agents are entitled to the defense of qualified immunity since the right to be free of media intrusion during a search was not clearly established in 1993 when this search occurred.

9-0. Per curiam.

Holloway v. United States 119 S. Ct. 966, 67 USLW 4148 (3-2-99)

Carjacking, intent: The federal carjacking statute, 18 U.S.C. § 2119, which prohibits carjacking "with the intent to cause death or serious bodily harm," applies to someone who seizes a car with the intent to kill or harm only if necessary to accomplish the carjacking. The statute applies to both conditional and unconditional intent to harm the victim, so the trial court did not err in instructing the jury to find requisite intent upon concluding that the defendant had intended to cause death or serious bodily harm if the victims had refused to turn over their cars. A "commonsense" reading of the statute counsels that Congress intended to criminalize carjacking generally, and did not intend to enact a "truncated" law applicable only to a limited subset of carjackings in which the offender intends to harm or kill the driver regardless of whether the driver surrenders his car. The statute as a whole reflects a deterrent purpose, and that purpose is better served by construing the statute to cover both conditional and unconditional intent. Also, it is reasonable to presume that Congress was aware of state court decisions recognizing that specific intent to commit a crime may be conditional.

7-2. Opinion of Court by Stevens, joined by Rehnquist, O'Connor, Kennedy, Souter, Ginsburg, and Breyer. Dissenting opinions by Scalia and Thomas.

Hughes Aircraft Co. v. Jacobson 119 S. Ct. 755, 67 USLW 4122 (1-25-99)

ERISA, amendment of defined benefit plan: Hughes did not violate ERISA by suspending its own contributions to a retirement plan with a large surplus and by amending the plan to provide for an early retirement program and a noncontributory benefit structure applicable to new employees and optional for existing plan members. The existing plan members had no vested interest in the plan's surplus. The plan was a "defined benefit plan" under which qualified employees are entitled to a fixed periodic payment and the employer was obligated to cover any underfunding. Hughes did not violate ERISA's anti-inurement provision; amending the plan did not create a second plan, and fund assets were being used to pay benefits to plan participants, not for the benefit of the employer. ERISA's fiduciary provisions are inapplicable to plan amendments; this principle, already applied to welfare benefit plans, applies as well to pension benefit plans. The plan amendments did not work an effective termination based on the common-law theory of a wasting trust. ERISA's enormously complex and detailed text should not be supplemented by common-law remedies, and, in any event, the doctrine is inapplicable by its own terms.

9-0. Opinion for unanimous Court by Thomas.

Humana Inc. v. Forsyth 119 S. Ct. 710, 67 USLW 4085 (1-20-99)

Insurance; RICO compatibility with McCarran-Ferguson: The McCarran-Ferguson Act does not bar recourse to RICO in a treble damages action for health insurance fraud in Nevada. In this action beneficiaries of group health insurance policies alleged that their insurance company and a hospital committed fraud by agreeing to discounts on the insurance company's 80% share of hospital charges, thereby increasing the beneficiaries' share above the 20% agreed to in the insurance contract. Section 2(b) of the McCarran-Ferguson Act permits application of general federal legislation not specifically directed at insurance regulation if the law does not "invalidate, impair, or supersede" state laws regulating insurance. RICO is not a law that specifically relates to the business of insurance, and it does not "invalidate" or "supersede" Nevada law. The principal issue is whether RICO "impairs" Nevada law, and this issue depends on whether application of RICO would "frustrate any declared State policy or interfere with [the] State's administrative regime." There is no frustration of state policy or interference with state administration in this case. Instead, RICO "appears to complement" Nevada's provision of relief. Nevada allows insured parties to sue for insurance fraud and to obtain punitive damages that may exceed the treble damages obtainable under RICO.

9-0. Opinion for unanimous Court by Ginsburg.

Hunt v. Cromartie 119 S. Ct. 1545, 67 USLW 4306 (5-17-99)

Congressional districting, summary judgment, proof of racial motivation: The three-judge district court should not have granted a summary judgment to the appellees on their claim that North Carolina's Twelfth Congressional District, as redrawn in 1997, constituted an unconstitutional racial gerrymander in violation of the Equal Protection Clause. A redistricting law, facially neutral as to race, warrants strict scrutiny only if it can be proved to have been motivated by a racial purpose or object. Assessing a jurisdiction's motivation is an "inherently complex endeavor," requiring a "sensitive inquiry" by the trial court. In this case there was evidence supporting conflicting inferences — one that the legislature was primarily motivated by race, the other that the principal motivation was partisan politics. Summary judgment is appropriate only if there is no genuine issue of material fact. Because the legislature's motivation was in dispute, summary judgment on that issue was inappropriate.

9-0. Opinion of Court by Thomas, joined by Rehnquist, O'Connor, Scalia, and Kennedy. Concurring opinion by Stevens, joined by Souter, Ginsburg, and Breyer.

INS v. Aguirre-Aguirre 119 S. Ct. 1439, 67 USLW 4270 (5-3-99)

Deportation, political persecution: The Court of Appeals for the Ninth Circuit failed to accord appropriate deference to the determination of the Board of Immigration Appeals that a person who committed a serious nonpolitical crime before entering the United States, and whose political opinions would subject him to persecution in his country of origin, is not entitled to withholding of deportation. The court should have applied principles announced in *Chevron v. NRDC* (1984), and should have deferred to the Board's interpretation of the exception for serious nonpolitical crimes. Deference is "especially appropriate in the immigration context where officials 'exercise especially sensitive political functions that implicate questions of foreign relations.'" The provision in question, 8 U.S.C. § 1253(h)(2)(C), directs that withholding of deportation does not apply if the Attorney General finds "serious reasons for considering that the alien has committed a serious nonpolitical crime . . . prior to [his] arrival." In finding that the respondent's actions in burning buses and vandalizing stores in Guatemala were "nonpolitical," the Board (to which the Attorney General had delegated her authority) determined that the criminal nature of the respondent's actions outweighed their political motivation. The Board did not, however, balance the criminal nature of the respondent's actions against the persecution that he would face if he were forced to return to Guatemala. The Board's interpretation is a reasonable one that comports with the plain language of the statute. The fact that this interpretation conflicts with that set forth in a United Nations handbook that was prepared as guidance for interpreting the treaty that the statute implements is not dispositive: the handbook "is not binding on the Attorney General, the [Board], or United States courts."

9-0. Opinion for unanimous Court by Kennedy.

Jefferson County v. Acker 119 S. Ct. 2069, 67 USLW 4521 (6-21-99)

County occupational tax, application to federal judges: An occupational tax imposed by Jefferson County, Alabama, on persons working within the county is not invalid as applied to federal judges. The case was properly removed to federal court under the federal officer removal statute. The judges made an "adequate threshold showing that the suit is 'for an act under color of office,'" since the act requires payment of a fee before they engage in their occupation. The Tax Injunction Act does not bar federal court adjudication of the case. The Act does not bar collection suits, nor does it prevent taxpayer-defendants in collection suits from challenging the validity of the tax. The occupation tax operates as a non-discriminatory tax on judges' salaries to which the Public Salary Tax Act of 1939 consents. That Act applies the intergovernmental tax immunity doctrine, now interpreted to allow one sovereign to tax the salaries of another sovereign's employees as long as the tax is not discriminatory. The tax is a tax on "pay or compensation" within the meaning of the Act, and is not an invalid licensing measure. Because the tax does not discriminate against federal judges in particular, or federal officeholders in general, based on the federal source of their compensation, and the record shows no discrimination between similarly situated federal and state judges, the tax does not discriminate in violation of the Act.

5-4 (removal); 9-0 (Tax Injunction Act); 7-2 (intergovernmental immunity). Opinion of Court by Ginsburg, unanimous in part; joined in part by Stevens,

O'Connor, Kennedy, and Breyer; and joined in separate part by Rehnquist, Stevens, Scalia, Kennedy, Souter, and Thomas. Opinion by Scalia, concurring in part and dissenting in part, joined by Rehnquist, Souter, and Thomas. Opinion by Breyer, concurring in part and dissenting in part, joined by O'Connor.

Jones v. United States 119 S. Ct. 1215, 67 USLW 4204 (3-24-99)

Carjacking, elements of offense: The federal carjacking statute, 18 U.S.C. § 2119, establishes three separate offenses rather than a single offense with a choice of three maximum penalties. The section provides that whoever takes a motor vehicle by force and violence "shall — (1) be fined . . . or imprisoned not more than 15 years, . . . (2) if serious bodily injury results, be . . . imprisoned not more than 25 years, and (3) if death results, be . . . imprisoned for any number of years up to life . . . ." The additional elements added by subsections (2) and (3) must be charged in the indictment, submitted to a jury, and proven beyond a reasonable doubt. At first glance, the section's structure suggests that the numbered subsections are only sentencing provisions. It is "questionable," however, whether specification of facts sufficient to drastically increase a penalty range was intended to carry none of the safeguards associated with elements of an offense. Moreover, the first paragraph of the section does not "stand on [its] own grammatical feet," as most offense-defining provisions do, because there is no language such as "shall be guilty of" that completes the sentence. Use of the word "shall" does not resolve the issue, because the word is not "invariably" used to separate offense-defining clauses from sentencing provisions. Also, the provision was enacted against the backdrop of many federal and state criminal statutes that identify serious bodily injury as an offense element. Most important, the statute would be open to constitutional doubt if the subsections were interpreted as sentencing provisions. Precedent under both the Due Process Clause and the Sixth Amendment can be read as imposing limits on a legislature's ability to omit traditional elements from the definition of crimes and to diminish the jury's role in making factual determinations on which sentencing limits are based. The decision last Term in *Almendarez-Torres v. United States*, holding that recidivism increasing the maximum penalty need not be charged in the indictment, is distinguished. Recidivism has traditionally been regarded as a sentencing factor, whereas infliction of serious bodily injury has not been.

5-4. Opinion of Court by Souter, joined by Stevens, Scalia, Thomas, and Ginsburg. Concurring opinions by Stevens and Scalia. Dissenting opinion by Kennedy, joined by Rehnquist, O'Connor, and Breyer.

Jones v. United States 119 S. Ct. 2090, 67 USLW 4508 (6-21-99)

Death penalty, jury instructions on consequences of deadlock: In a sentencing hearing conducted under the Federal Death Penalty Act of 1994, the court's refusal to instruct the jury that the court would impose a sentence of life imprisonment without possibility of parole if the jury was unable to reach unanimous agreement on a sentence did not violate the Eighth Amendment. The Supreme Court declines to exercise its supervisory power to require that an instruction on the consequences of deadlock be given in every capital case. In this case the court gave the jury three options: it could by unanimous vote recommend the death penalty, life imprisonment without possibility of parole, "or . . . some other lesser sentence." If the jury recommended "some other lesser sentence," the instruction explained, "the court is required to impose a sentence that is authorized by law." The instruction did not constitute "plain error," even though a "lesser sentence" was not authorized in this case. There is "no reasonable likelihood that the jury applied the instructions incorrectly." The instructions, read in their entirety, were not misleading as to the consequences of the jury's failure to reach a unanimous verdict. Any confusion over the effect of a lesser sentence recommendation was allayed by the court's instruction that the jury should not concern itself with such matters. Loose drafting of "nonstatutory" aggravating factors was harmless error if it constituted error at all.

5-4. Opinion of Court by Thomas, joined in part by Rehnquist, O'Connor, Scalia, and Kennedy, and in separate part by Rehnquist, O'Connor, and Kennedy. Dissenting opinion by Ginsburg, joined by Stevens and Souter, and joined in part by Breyer.

Knowles v. Iowa 119 S. Ct. 484, 67 USLW 4027 (12-8-98)

Fourth Amendment, search incident to traffic citation: A search authorized by an Iowa statute permitting officers to conduct a full-blown search of an automobile when issuing a traffic citation violates the Fourth Amendment. Neither of the rationales that justifies a search incident to arrest justifies a full search of an automobile incident to a traffic citation. The threat to officer safety is "a good deal less" in the case of a routine traffic stop than it is in the case of a custodial arrest. The "relatively brief encounter" of a traffic stop contrasts with an officer's "extended exposure" to a suspect who is placed in custody and transported to the police station. Officers conducting a routine traffic stop may order driver and passengers out of the car and may even conduct a patdown search if there is reasonable suspicion that the driver or any passengers may be armed and dangerous, but there is no such justification for a full search of the car. The second justification for a search incident to arrest — the need to preserve evidence — is "not present at all" in a routine traffic stop.

9-0. Opinion for unanimous Court by Rehnquist.

Kolstad v. American Dental Ass'n 119 S. Ct. 2118, 67 USLW 4552 (6-22-99)

Punitive damages, Title VII of Civil Rights Act: A plaintiff in an action brought under Title VII of the Civil Rights Act need not show "egregious" misconduct in order to recover punitive damages. 1991 amendments to Title VII authorized awards of compensatory and punitive damages in cases of "intentional misconduct," and further limited punitive awards to acts undertaken "with malice or with reckless indifference to . . . federally protected rights." The terms "malice" and "reckless" focus on the actor's state of mind. There is no additional requirement of egregiousness, although egregious misconduct is often associated with the award of punitive damages, and may serve as evidence supporting an inference of the requisite evil motive. Agency principles place limits on recovery of punitive damages from employers for the acts of employees. While the Restatement (Second) of Agency provides "a useful starting point," its principles must be modified so that an employer may not be held vicariously liable for discriminatory employment decisions of managerial agents when those decisions are contrary to the employer's good-faith efforts to comply with Title VII.

7-2 ("egregious" standard); **5-4** (agency). Opinion of Court by O'Connor, joined in part by Stevens, Scalia, Kennedy, Souter, Ginsburg, and Breyer; and joined in separate part by Rehnquist, Scalia, Kennedy, and Thomas. Opinion concurring in part and dissenting in part by Rehnquist, joined by Thomas. Opinion concurring in part and dissenting in part by Stevens, joined by Souter, Ginsburg, and Breyer.

Kumho Tire Co. v. Carmichael 119 S. Ct. 1167, 67 USLW 4179 (3-23-99)

Evidence, expert testimony: The standards announced in *Daubert v. Merrell Dow Pharmaceuticals* (1993) for admissibility of opinion testimony by qualified scientific experts apply as well to testimony based on technical and other specialized knowledge that is not "scientific." Federal Rule of Evidence 702, which allows admission of expert testimony "[i]f scientific, technical, or other specialized knowledge will assist the trier of fact," affords no basis for distinguishing between admissibility of "scientific" knowledge and "technical" or "other specialized" knowledge. Whatever the specialized discipline, the trial judge must determine whether the testimony has "a reliable basis in the knowledge and experience of [the] discipline." Trial judges need considerable leeway in making this determination. The *Daubert* standards are "flexible,"and do not constitute a mandatory checklist. Whether or not the expert is applying scientific principles, the trial judge may, if appropriate, consider any of the specific factors identified in *Daubert* as possibly bearing on reliability. In this case, the district court's decision not to admit the testimony of an expert in motor vehicle tire failure analysis was reasonable. The court did not question the expert's qualifications, but instead found his methodology unreliable as applied to the facts of this case.

9-0 (general principles); **8-1** (disposition of case). Opinion of Court by Breyer, joined by Rehnquist, O'Connor, Scalia, Kennedy, Souter, Thomas, and Ginsburg, and joined in part by Stevens. Concurring opinion by Scalia, joined by O'Connor and Thomas. Concurring and dissenting opinion by Stevens.

Lilly v. Virginia 119 S. Ct. 1887, 67 USLW 4435 (6-10-99)

Confrontation Clause: The defendant's Sixth Amendment right to be confronted with the witnesses against him was violated by admission into evidence at his trial of a confession made by a non-testifying accomplice. The accomplice confessed to participating in a burglary, but stated that the defendant was the one who shot and killed a person whose car they had stolen during their crime spree. The fact that portions of the confession were "against penal interest" does not place the non-self-inculpatory portions incriminating the defendant within a firmly rooted exception to the hearsay rule; the latter portions are presumptively unreliable. The case is remanded to Virginia courts to determine whether the violation of the defendant's Confrontation Clause rights was harmless beyond a reasonable doubt.

9-0. Opinion of Court by Stevens, one part of which was joined by Scalia, Souter, Thomas, Ginsburg, and Breyer, and a separate part of which was joined by Scalia, Souter, Ginsburg, and Breyer. Separate part of Stevens opinion joined by only by Souter, Ginsburg, and Breyer. Concurring opinions by Rehnquist, joined by O'Connor and Kennedy; by Scalia; by Thomas; and by Breyer.

Lopez v. Monterey County 119 S. Ct. 693, 67 USLW 4076 (1-20-99)

Voting Rights Act, preclearance: A political subdivision covered by the Voting Rights Act must seek preclearance before giving effect to voting changes required by state law, even if the state is not covered by the Act. The Act's plain meaning and its history of interpretation support this conclusion. Section 5 of the Voting Rights Act requires preclearance "whenever a [covered] State or political subdivision . . . shall enact or seek to administer any voting [change]." The phrase "seek to administer" does not limit preclearance obligations to discretionary acts of a covered jurisdiction. "Administer" comprehends non-discretionary acts, and the word "seek" is used merely to make a "temporal distinction" between enactment and implementation of legislation: preclearance need not be obtained before enactment, but must be before implementation. The Attorney General's interpretation to the same effect is entitled to deference. Although the Act intrudes on state sovereignty by requiring federal approval of state enactments, "the Fifteenth Amendment permits this intrusion."

8-1. Opinion of Court by O'Connor, joined by Stevens, Scalia, Souter, Ginsburg, and Breyer. Concurring opinion by Kennedy, joined by Rehnquist. Dissenting opinion by Thomas.

Marquez v. Screen Actors Guild 119 S. Ct. 292, 67 USLW 4001 (11-3-98)

Labor, union security clause: A union does not breach its duty of fair representation by negotiating a union security clause that uses the language of § 8(a)(3) of the National Labor Relations Act without explaining in the agreement itself the Supreme Court's interpretation of that language. Section 8(a)(3) permits unions to negotiate collective bargaining agreements that require union "membership" for all employees on or after the 30th day following the beginning of "such employment." The Court has interpreted this language to mean merely that the union may require the payment of core fees and dues necessary to support the union's representational activities. There is no requirement that these qualifications be spelled out in the security clause; the clause is enforceable as written because the statutory provisions have become terms of art that incorporate case law interpretations. The union did not breach its duty of fair representation; there was no claim of discriminatory conduct in this case, and the union's negotiation of the security clause was neither arbitrary nor in bad faith. The District Court lacked jurisdiction over the petitioner's second claim. That claim, that the security clause violates § 8(a)(3) by providing that the 30-day grace period begins to run with any employment in the industry rather than with the particular employment at issue, is at base a statutory issue within the NLRB's primary jurisdiction.

9-0. Opinion for unanimous Court by O'Connor. Concurring opinion by Kennedy, joined by Thomas.

Martin v. Hadix 119 S. Ct. 1998, 67 USLW 4500 (6-21-99)

Retroactivity, Prison Litigation Reform Act, attorney's fees: Section 803(d) of the Prison Litigation Reform Act (PLRA), which limits the fees that may be awarded to attorneys who litigate prisoner lawsuits, applies to services that were performed after the PLRA's effective date, but not to services performed prior to that date. Principles announced in *Landgraf v. USI Film Products* (1994) govern the retroactivity issue. The statute does not address "the temporal reach" of the provision. The language of the provision sets substantive limits, and "falls short of demonstrating a 'clear congressional intent' favoring retroactive application of the fees limitations." The structure and history of the PLRA should not be read to mean that the fees limitations are inapplicable to pending cases. Section 802, governing "appropriate remedies" in prison litigation, explicitly provides that it applies to pending cases, while section 803 is silent in this regard. Because, however, sections 802 and 803 "address wholly distinct subject matters," no negative inference should be made about section 803's application to pending cases. The fact that the fees limitations were moved out of section 802 and placed in section 803 during congressional consideration does not mean that Congress intended the provisions to apply to pending cases, since there could have been "a variety of other reasons" for the move. In the absence of congressional guidance on the retroactivity issue, the next question in this case is whether application to fees for postjudgment monitoring would be "inconsistent with the usual rule that legislation is deemed to be prospective." Application to monitoring performed before the effective date would be contrary to the rule, since it would "attach new legal consequences to completed conduct." Application to monitoring performed after the PLRA's effective date creates no such retroactivity problem, because enactment of the PLRA put attorneys on notice that their hourly rate had been adjusted.

7-2. Opinion of Court by O'Connor, joined by Rehnquist, Kennedy, Souter, Thomas, and Breyer; joined in part by Scalia; and joined in separate part by Stevens and Ginsburg. Concurring opinion by Scalia. Opinion by Ginsburg, joined by Stevens, concurring in part and dissenting in part.

Maryland v. Dyson 119 S. Ct. 2013, 67 USLW 3770 (6-21-99)

Fourth Amendment, automobile search: The Fourth Amendment does not require police to obtain a search warrant before searching a vehicle that they have probable cause to believe contains illegal drugs. Under established precedent, the "automobile exception" to the warrant requirement has no separate exigency requirement. The Court held in *United States v. Ross* (1982) that a search of an automobile is not unreasonable, even though a warrant has not been obtained, if the search is based on facts that would support a warrant.

Per curiam. Dissenting opinion by Breyer, joined by Stevens.

Minnesota v. Carter 119 S. Ct. 469, 67 USLW 4017 (12-1-98)

Fourth Amendment, persons protected in home: A person present in someone else's apartment for a few hours for the purpose of bagging cocaine for later sale is not entitled to Fourth Amendment protection. In some circumstances a person in someone else's house has a legitimate expectation of privacy, and hence is entitled to Fourth Amendment protection. The Court has extended protection, for example, to overnight guests. At the other extreme, persons who are merely "legitimately on the premises" are not entitled to protection. The purely commercial nature of the transaction here, the relatively brief period of time on the premises, and the lack of any previous connection with the householder make the respondent's situation in this case closer to that of one simply permitted on the premises. Because the respondent had no legitimate expectation of privacy in the apartment, there is no need to decide whether a police officer's observations through a window constituted a "search."

5-4 (Fourth Amendment protection); 6-3 (result). Opinion of Court by Rehnquist, joined by O'Connor, Scalia, Kennedy, and Thomas. Concurring opinions by Scalia, joined by Thomas; by Kennedy; and by Breyer (concurring in result, but agreeing with dissent on Fourth Amendment coverage). Dissenting opinion by Ginsburg, joined by Stevens and Souter.

Minnesota v. Mille Lacs Band of Chippewa Indians 119 S. Ct. 1187, 67 USLW 4189 (3-24-99)

Native Americans, treaty rights: Several Bands of Chippewa Indians retain rights guaranteed by an 1837 Treaty "during the pleasure of the President" to hunt, fish, and gather rice on lands ceded to the United States. These usufructuary rights were not eliminated by an 1850 Executive Order, by an 1855 Treaty, or by admission of Minnesota into the Union in 1858. The 1850 Executive Order purported to revoke these hunting, fishing, and gathering "privileges granted temporarily to the Chippewa Indians," but the Order was understood as a "removal" order requiring relocation of the Indians, and as such exceeded the President's authority. Neither the Removal Act nor the Treaty itself authorized the President to order removal of the Indians. The portion of the Executive Order revoking the usufructuary rights is not severable from the invalid removal order because "it is clear that President Taylor intended the 1850 order to stand or fall as a whole." The 1855 Treaty, by which the Indians "relinquish[ed] and convey[ed] . . . any and all right, title, and interest [in] lands," relinquished lands, not usufructuary rights. Minnesota's enabling act does not abrogate the 1837 Treaty, nor does the "equal footing doctrine." Statehood by itself is insufficient to extinguish Indian treaty rights to hunt, fish, and gather, because such treaty rights are still subject to reasonable and non-discriminatory state conservation regulations. The contrary interpretation of the equal footing doctrine in *Ward v. Race Horse* (1896) is rejected.

5-4. Opinion of Court by O'Connor, joined by Stevens, Souter, Ginsburg, and Breyer. Dissenting opinions by Rehnquist, joined by Scalia, Kennedy, and Thomas; and by Thomas.

Mitchell v. United States 119 S. Ct. 1307, 67 USLW 4230 (4-5-99)

Self-incrimination: A guilty plea does not waive the privilege against self-incrimination at the sentencing phase of a federal trial. Incrimination is not complete once guilt has been adjudicated. Rather, a defendant may have a legitimate fear of adverse consequences from testimony at sentencing. The Court has already held that the privilege against self-incrimination applies in a capital sentencing hearing, and there is no reason not to apply the principle to non-capital sentencing hearings as well. A district court's explanation, pursuant to Rule 11, that a defendant who pleads guilty will lose the right to remain silent at trial, does not suggest to a defendant that he could also lose the right to remain silent at sentencing. The rule applicable at trial that no negative inference may be drawn from the defendant's failure to testify applies with equal force at sentencing. The district court may not make an adverse inference, based on the defendant's silence at sentencing, about circumstances and details of the crime that bear on sentencing — in this case the amount of drugs sold by the defendant. The Government retains the burden at the sentencing phase of proving facts relevant to the crime, and may not "enlist the defendant in this process at the expense of the self-incrimination privilege."

9-0 (effect of guilty plea); **5-4** (adverse inference). Opinion of Court by Kennedy, joined by Stevens, Souter, Ginsburg, and Breyer. Opinions concurring in part and dissenting in part by Scalia, joined by Rehnquist, O'Connor, and Thomas; and by Thomas.

Murphy Bros. v. Michetti Pipe Stringing, Inc. 119 S. Ct. 1322, 67 USLW 4238 (4-5-99)

Removal, timing, service of process: The 30-day period established by 28 U.S.C. § 1446(b) for removal of actions from state to federal court does not begin to run until formal service of process, even if the defendant has already received a copy of the complaint. Section 1446(b) provides that notice of removal "shall be filed within thirty days after the receipt by the defendant, through service or otherwise, of a copy of the initial pleading." In this case the plaintiff filed a complaint in an Alabama court and 3 days later faxed a file-stamped copy of the complaint to the defendant; the defendant was not formally served until two weeks later. The defendant's notice of removal, filed 30 days after service of process and 44 days after receipt of the complaint, complied with section 1446(b). Historically, service of process has been the official trigger for responsive action by the party named as a defendant. Nothing in the legislative history of enactment of the modern version of the section indicates that Congress intended to dispense with this historic function. Rather, the accompanying Senate report explained that the measure was intended to correct a problem that could occur in New York and other states, in which the period for removal might end before the defendant obtained access to the complaint. Similar language in Federal Rule of Civil Procedure 81, governing the time allowed a defendant to answer a complaint, has been interpreted to afford the defendant the specified number of days after service of process.

6-3. Opinion of Court by Ginsburg, joined by Stevens, O'Connor, Kennedy, Souter, and Breyer. Dissenting opinion by Rehnquist, joined by Scalia and Thomas.

Murphy v. United Parcel Service 119 S. Ct. 2133, 67 USLW 4549 (6-22-99)

ADA, "regarded as" disabled: An individual fired from his job as a mechanic because of high blood pressure that prevented him from receiving DOT certification to drive a commercial vehicle – an essential function of this particular mechanic's job – is not "regarded as" disabled within the meaning of the ADA definition of "disability." As the Court determined in *Sutton v. United Airlines*, the initial issue of whether the petitioner was "disabled" should be determined with reference to the mitigating measures he employs. A person is "regarded as" disabled if a covered employer believes that the person's actual, nonlimiting impairment substantially limits one or more major life activities. No such showing was made in this case. The petitioner established that he is regarded as unable to perform the job of mechanic only when that job requires driving a commercial motor vehicle, but it is undisputed that he is generally employable as a mechanic. At most, the petitioner is regarded as unable to perform only a particular job – not an entire class or broad range of jobs.

7-2. Opinion of Court by O'Connor, joined by Rehnquist, Scalia, Kennedy, Souter, Thomas, and Ginsburg. Dissenting opinion by Stevens, joined by Breyer.

NASA v. FLRA 119 S. Ct. 1979, 67 USLW 4468 (6-17-99)

Inspector General Act, employee examinations, FSLMRS: An investigator employed in NASA's Office of Inspector General can be considered a "representative" of NASA when examining a NASA employee, and consequently the right to union representation guaranteed by the Federal Service Labor-Management Relations Statute, 5 U.S.C. § 7114(a)(2)(B), applies. By its terms, the provision is not limited to agency investigators representing an "entity" within the agency that collectively bargains with the employee's union. Neither the fact that the relevant language is contained in a larger section addressing collective bargaining rights, nor the fact that the phrase "representative of the agency" is used elsewhere in the statute to refer to management representatives responsible for collective bargaining requires a different reading. Moreover, there is no basis in the history and purpose of the FSLMRS to give § 7114(a)(2)(B) a narrow construction that covers some, but not all, interviews by agency representatives. Nor does the Inspector General Act (IGA) require a limiting construction. Rather, the IGA provides that Inspectors General "shall report to and be under the general supervision of the head of the establishment involved," and also refers to the agency "within which [an IG's] Office is established." Although enforcing § 7114(a)(2)(B) may lessen an Inspector General's ability to maintain the confidentiality of its investigations, the provision "vindicates obvious countervailing federal policies" favoring fair treatment of employees under investigation.

5-4. Opinion of Court by Stevens, joined by Kennedy, Souter, Ginsburg, and Breyer. Dissenting opinion by Thomas, joined by Rehnquist, O'Connor, and Scalia.

National Fed'n of Fed. Employees v. Department of the Interior 119 S. Ct. 1003, 67 USLW 4170 (3-3-99)

Labor, federal employees, midterm bargaining: The Federal Service Labor-Management Relations Statute is ambiguous as to the duty of federal employers to bargain midterm (*i.e.*, while the basic collective bargaining agreement is in effect) over matters not included in the basic agreement. The statute, 5 U.S.C. § 7114(a)(4), simply provides that the federal agency employer and the union representative "shall meet and negotiate in good faith for the purposes of arriving at a collective bargaining agreement." The "arriving at" language is not dispositive, because there is nothing in the circular definition of "collective bargaining agreement" to exclude a midterm agreement. The statutory ambiguity is consistent with the conclusion that Congress delegated to the Federal Labor Relations Authority the power to determine whether, where, and when midterm bargaining is required. The statute also grants the Authority power to determine whether an agency must bargain "endterm" over including in the basic collective bargaining agreement a clause requiring midterm bargaining.

5-4. Opinion of Court by Breyer, joined by Stevens, Kennedy, Souter, and Ginsburg. Dissenting opinion by O'Connor, joined by Rehnquist, and joined in part by Scalia and Thomas.

NCAA v. Smith 119 S. Ct. 924, 67 USLW 4130 (2-23-99)

Sex discrimination, Title IX, scope of coverage: Receipt of dues from member colleges and universities that receive federal funds does not bring the National Collegiate Athletic Association (NCAA) within the scope of Title IX of the Education Amendments of 1972. A private action based on this theory, and challenging application of NCAA rules governing postgraduate eligibility for participation in intercollegiate athletics, cannot be maintained. Title IX prohibits sex discrimination in "any education program or activity receiving Federal financial assistance," and a regulation defines a "recipient" of such assistance as any entity "to whom Federal financial assistance is extended directly or through another recipient." Federal assistance is received "through another recipient" if it is earmarked for such payments, as is the case with a college that enrolls students who receive federal funds earmarked for college expenses. There is no allegation, however, that NCAA member institutions pay their dues with federal funds earmarked for the purpose of paying NCAA dues. Entities such as the NCAA that merely benefit economically from federal assistance are not "recipients" covered by Title IX.

9-0. Opinion for unanimous Court by Ginsburg.

Neder v. United States 119 S. Ct. 1827, 67 USLW 4404 (6-10-99)

Harmless error; fraud statutes, materiality: The district court's error in failing to submit to the jury the issue of materiality in a tax fraud case was "harmless error." The error at issue — a jury instruction that omits an element of the offense — differs markedly from the constitutional violations that have been held to defy harmless-error review. Errors that require reversal affect the framework in which the trial proceeds, and "necessarily render a trial fundamentally unfair." An instruction that omits an element of an offense does not *necessarily* render a criminal trial fundamentally unfair or unreliable. In this case, in which the defendant failed to report over $5 million in income and filed false returns, the evidence supporting materiality was "overwhelming," and the court's failure to submit the materiality issue to the jury was harmless error. Materiality of falsehood is an element of a "scheme or artifice to defraud" under the federal mail fraud, wire fraud, and bank fraud statutes. Under a natural reading of the statutory text itself, materiality would not be an element of the fraud statutes. However, where Congress uses terms that have accumulated a settled meaning under the common law, a court must infer, unless the statute dictates otherwise, that Congress intended to incorporate the established meaning. The well-settled meaning of "fraud" required a misrepresentation or concealment of a material fact. Nothing in the fraud statutes dictates a different conclusion, so it is presumed that Congress intended to incorporate materiality.

6-3 (harmless error); **9-0** (materiality). Opinion of Court by Rehnquist, unanimous on materiality issue, and joined by O'Connor, Kennedy, Thomas, and Breyer on harmless error issue. Concurring opinion by Stevens. Opinion by Scalia, concurring in part and dissenting in part, joined by Souter and Ginsburg.

Nynex Corp. v. Discon, Inc. 119 S. Ct. 493, 67 USLW 4031 (12-14-98)

Antitrust, group boycotts: The rule that group boycotts are illegal *per se* does not apply to a buyer's decision to buy from one seller instead of another, whenever that decision cannot be justified in terms of ordinary competitive objectives. In this case, a purchaser of telephone removal services allegedly switched purchases from the respondent to a competitor because the respondent refused to participate in a scheme to defraud phone service customers. The group boycott *per se* rule is limited to cases involving horizontal agreements among direct competitors. This case does not involve any horizontal agreement, but instead involves a "vertical" agreement between supplier and customer. There is no special feature of this case to distinguish it from precedents limiting the *per se* rule.

9-0. Opinion for unanimous Court by Breyer.

Olmstead v. L.C. 119 S. Ct. 2176, 67 USLW 4567 (6-22-99)

ADA, mentally disabled, community placement: The ADA's general prohibition on discrimination against disabled persons in the provision of public services requires placement of persons with mental disabilities in community settings rather than institutions if the state's treatment professionals have determined that community placement is appropriate, if the transfer is not opposed by the affected individual, and if the placement can be reasonably accommodated, taking into account the resources available to the state. Unjustified institutionalization is properly regarded as discrimination by reason of disability. The Department of Justice regulations requiring public entities to administer services in "the most integrated setting appropriate" are entitled to deference under *Chevron v. NRDC* (1984). Moreover, congressional findings in the ADA explicitly identify unjustified "segregation" of disabled persons as a form of "discrimination."

6-3. Opinion of Court by Ginsburg, joined by Stevens, O'Connor, Souter, and Breyer. Separate part of Ginsburg opinion joined by O'Connor, Souter, and Breyer. Concurring opinions by Stevens; and by Kennedy, joined in part by Breyer. Dissenting opinion by Thomas, joined by Rehnquist and Scalia.

Ortiz v. Fibreboard Corp. 119 S. Ct. 2295, 67 USLW 4632 (6-23-99)

Class actions, asbestos settlement: Applicants for certification of a mandatory settlement class on a limited fund theory under Federal Rule of Civil Procedure 23(b)(1)(B) must show that the settlement fund is limited by more than the agreement of the parties, and will be allocated to claimants belonging within the class by a process addressing any conflicting interests of class members. The record on which the district court in this case rested its class certification did not support these essential premises of mandatory limited fund actions. There is good reason to treat these limited fund characteristics as "presumptively necessary," since the Advisory Committee that developed Rule 23 did not contemplate that the mandatory class action codified in subdivision (b)(1)(B) would be used to aggregate unliquidated tort claims on a limited fund rationale, and since serious constitutional concerns (jury trial and due process rights of absent class members) are implicated. There was no evaluation of the amount of insurance money that would be available to pay claims, and consequently there was no adequate demonstration of the fund's upper limit. There was also inadequate consideration of the inclusiveness of the class and of equity among class members. Several groups, including persons who had previously settled but retained the right to sue again upon development of asbestos-related malignancy, plaintiffs with claims pending at the time of an initial settlement agreement, and "inventory" plaintiffs, were excluded from the class. There was no division of plaintiffs between holders of present and future claims, and thus there was inadequate protection against conflicting interests of counsel. The class also did not accommodate the different interests of plaintiffs whose claims arose while Fibreboard maintained insurance, and those whose claims arose after the insurance was discontinued. Another departure from "limited fund antecedents" is that Fibreboard's net worth was not taken into account in determining the size of the fund.

7-2. Opinion of Court by Souter, joined by Rehnquist, O'Connor, Scalia, Kennedy, Thomas, and Ginsburg. Concurring opinion by Rehnquist, joined by Scalia and Kennedy. Dissenting opinion by Breyer, joined by Stevens.

O'Sullivan v. Boerckel 119 S. Ct. 1728, 67 USLW 4389 (6-7-99)

Habeas corpus, exhaustion of state remedies: Before a federal court may grant habeas relief to a state prisoner, that prisoner must exhaust his remedies in state court, and this required exhaustion includes petitioning a state court of last resort that has discretionary control over its docket. The governing statute, 28 U.S.C. § 2254(c), provides that a habeas petitioner shall not be deemed to have exhausted his state remedies "if he has the right under [state law] to raise, by any available procedure, the question presented." This does not require state prisoners to invoke every possible avenue of state review, but it does require that prisoners give state courts "one full opportunity to resolve any constitutional issues by invoking one complete round of the State's appellate review process." Because the respondent raised three issues in his federal habeas petition that he had not raised in his petition for leave to appeal to the Illinois Supreme Court, and because the time for filing in Illinois had long passed, he procedurally defaulted on those claims.

6-3. Opinion of Court by O'Connor, joined by Rehnquist, Scalia, Kennedy, Souter, and Thomas. Concurring opinion by Souter. Dissenting opinions by Stevens, joined by Ginsburg and Breyer; and by Breyer, joined by Stevens and Ginsburg.

Peguero v. United States 119 S. Ct. 961, 67 USLW 4154 (3-2-99)

***Habeas corpus*, harmless error**: A district court's failure to advise a defendant of his right to appeal his sentence, as required by Federal Rule of Criminal Procedure 32(a)(2), does not provide a basis for *habeas corpus* relief if the defendant was aware of his right to appeal when the trial court failed to give the advice. Because the defendant was aware of his right to appeal, he suffered no prejudice from the trial court's omission.

9-0. Opinion for unanimous Court by Kennedy. Concurring opinion by O'Connor, joined by Stevens, Ginsburg, and Breyer.

Pfaff v. Wells Electronics, Inc. 119 S. Ct. 304, 67 USLW 4009 (11-10-98)

Patents, invention "on sale" more that a year: A product can be "on sale" within the meaning of section 102(b) of the Patent Act of 1952, 35 U.S.C. § 102 (b), if it has been offered for sale, even if it has not yet been reduced to practice. Section 102(b) provides that an "invention" may not be patented if it has been "on sale" for more than one year before the patent application was filed. An "invention" is an inventor's conception rather than a physical embodiment of that idea. It is well settled that an invention may be patented before it is reduced to practice. Two conditions must be satisfied before an invention is "on sale." First, the product must be the subject of a commercial sale. In this case, the product had been offered for sale more than a year prior to patent application. Second, the invention must be ready for patenting. This latter condition may be satisfied in at least two ways — by proof of reduction to practice, or by proof that the inventor had prepared drawings or other descriptions of the invention that were sufficiently specific to enable a person skilled in the art to practice the invention. Here, the second condition was satisfied by drawings that the inventor had provided to a manufacturer before the critical date.

9-0. Opinion for unanimous Court by Stevens.

Reno v. American-Arab Anti-Discrimination Comm. 119 S. Ct. 936, 67 USLW 4133 (2-24-99)

Immigration, deportation, judicial review, selective enforcement: Provisions of the Illegal Immigration Reform and Immigrant Responsibility Act of 1996 (IIRIRA) limiting judicial review apply to certain types of challenges to deportation proceedings that were ongoing at the time of enactment of IIRIRA. The "supposed tension" between 8 U.S.C. § 309(c)(1), which sets a general rule of inapplicability to pending cases, and § 306(c)(1), which provides that §1252(g) applies to pending cases, is resolved by a "narrow reading" of the latter provision. 8 U.S.C. §1252(g) should be read as barring judicial review, prior to a final deportation order, of a limited subset of claims challenging three discrete types of actions by the Attorney General — commencing proceedings, adjudicating cases, or executing removal orders. The instant case, involving a claim that respondents were targeted for deportation because of their affiliation with a politically unpopular group, fits squarely within the first category as a challenge to the commencement of proceedings. The three categories should not be treated as all-encompassing. Nowhere in the U.S. Code is precise and narrow language of this nature used as a shorthand means of imposing a general jurisdictional limitation. Also, there is "good reason" for Congress to insulate these particular actions from judicial review, since each involves a stage at which the Attorney General may exercise nonreviewable discretion to abandon deportation proceedings. The doctrine of constitutional doubt is inapplicable because there is no constitutional right implicated. "As a general matter . . . an alien unlawfully in this country has no constitutional right to assert selective enforcement as a defense against his deportation."

8-1. Opinion of Court by Scalia, joined by Rehnquist, O'Connor, Kennedy, and Thomas, and joined in part by Ginsburg and Breyer. Concurring opinion by Ginsburg, joined in part by Breyer. Concurring opinion by Stevens. Dissenting opinion by Souter.

Richardson v. United States 67 USLW 4381 (6-1-99)

Jury unanimity, "continuing criminal enterprise": A jury in a case brought under 18 U.S.C. § 848, which forbids any person from engaging in a "continuing criminal enterprise," must unanimously agree not only that the defendant committed some "continuing series of violations," but also which specific violations make up that continuing series. It is well settled that a federal jury may convict only if it finds unanimously that the Government has proved each element of an offense. A jury may, however, disagree as to which of several possible means the defendant used to commit an element of the crime. For purposes of section 848, each violation making up a "series of violations" should be considered to be a separate "element" of the offense, and not merely the possible "means" by which the offense was committed. The statute provides that a person is engaged in a continuing criminal enterprise if he violates any provision of the federal drug laws, and if "such violation is a part of a continuing series of violations." Use of the word "violation" suggests that each "violation" amounts to a separate element of the offense that requires jury unanimity. Also, the breadth of possible drug law violations that could comprise a "series" means that, absent a unanimity requirement, there could be wide disagreement among jurors as to just what the defendant did or did not do. Finally, the statute should be construed so as to avoid possible constitutional issues that could be raised under the alternative construction.

6-3. Opinion of Court by Breyer, joined by Rehnquist, Stevens, Scalia, Souter, and Thomas. Dissenting opinion by Kennedy, joined by O'Connor and Ginsburg.

Roberts v. Galen of Virginia, Inc. 119 S. Ct. 685, 67 USLW 4062 (1-13-99)

Emergency Medical Treatment and Active Labor Act: Recovery in an action brought under the Emergency Medical Treatment and Active Labor Act for a hospital's failure to provide necessary stabilizing treatment for an emergency medical condition is not contingent upon proof of improper motive. Section 1395dd(b) of the Act requires hospitals to provide "for such further medical examination and such treatment as may be required to stabilize the medical condition." The provision is not qualified by a requirement of "appropriateness," and cannot "reasonably be read to require an improper motive."

9-0. *Per curiam.*

Ruhrgas AG v. Marathon Oil Co. 119 S. Ct. 1563, 67 USLW 4315 (5-17-99)

Federal courts, priority of jurisdictional issues: There is "no unyielding jurisdictional hierarchy" in cases removed from state to federal court, or in cases originating in federal court. Federal district courts have discretion to dismiss a removed case for lack of personal jurisdiction without reaching the issue of subject matter jurisdiction. The principles that require a court to find subject matter jurisdiction before proceeding to the merits do not necessarily require a set sequencing of jurisdictional issues. The possibility of issue preclusion in subsequent state-court litigation merits consideration, but is not dispositive. In most instances, "both expedition and sensitivity to state courts' coequal stature" should impel the federal court to consider subject matter jurisdiction before personal jurisdiction. However, if the court has a "straightforward" issue of personal jurisdiction that presents "no complex question of state law," and if the alleged defect in subject matter jurisdiction raises a "difficult and novel question," the court does not abuse its discretion by first addressing personal jurisdiction.

9-0. Opinion for unanimous Court by Ginsburg.

Saenz v. Roe 119 S. Ct. 1518, 67 USLW 4291 (5-17-99)

Right to travel, durational residency requirement for welfare: A provision of the California Welfare and Institutions Code limiting new residents, for the first year they live in California, to the level of welfare benefits that they would have received in the state of their prior residence, abridges the right to travel in violation of the Fourteenth Amendment. The right to travel is "firmly embedded in our jurisprudence." A component of the right to travel is the right of a newly arrived citizen to the same privileges and immunities enjoyed by other citizens of that state. Privileges and immunities of citizenship are protected under Article IV by virtue of the new arrival's status as a state citizen, and under the Fourteenth Amendment by virtue of her status as a citizen of the United States. The Court recognized in the *Slaughter-House Cases* in 1873 that the Fourteenth Amendment's Privileges or Immunities Clause guarantees that United States citizens who establish *bona fide* residence in a state are entitled to the same rights as other citizens of that state. Classification based upon the period of residency in California and the location of prior residence penalizes the citizen's right to be treated equally in her new state of residence. Such penalties may not be judged by mere rationality or by an "intermediate" standard of review; instead, the standard must be "no less strict" than the compelling governmental interest test applied in *Shapiro v. Thompson* (1969). The Court in *Shapiro* held that the purpose of deterring welfare applicants from migrating into a state is impermissible. Here, California's professed purpose of saving money is legitimate, but cannot justify its discrimination among equally eligible citizens. Federal approval of such durational residency requirements in the Personal Responsibility and Work Opportunity Reconciliation Act of 1996 cannot resuscitate the constitutionality of California's law. Congress may not authorize the states to violate the Fourteenth Amendment. Article I powers may not be exercised in a manner that violates other specific provisions of the Constitution, and congressional enforcement power under section 5 of the Fourteenth Amendment encompasses no power to restrict, abrogate, or dilute the Amendment's guarantees.

7-2. Opinion of Court by Stevens, joined by O'Connor, Scalia, Kennedy, Souter, Ginsburg, and Breyer. Dissenting opinions by Rehnquist, joined by Thomas; and by Thomas, joined by Rehnquist.

South Central Bell Tel. Co. v. Alabama 119 S. Ct. 1180, 67 USLW 4186 (3-23-99)

Commerce Clause; Taxation, State: Alabama's franchise tax law discriminates against foreign corporations in violation of the Commerce Clause. The law establishes a domestic corporation's tax base as the par value of its capital stock, a value that the corporation may set at whatever level it chooses. The tax base of a foreign corporation, on the other hand, contains balance sheet items that the corporation cannot so manipulate. Denial to foreign corporations of the ability afforded domestic corporations to reduce their tax liability constitutes facial discrimination against interstate commerce and can be upheld only if the State offers sufficient justification. Alabama has not justified the discrimination. The tax is not a "compensatory" tax that offsets the tax burden imposed on domestic corporations. The burdens on foreign and domestic corporations are neither "roughly approximate" nor similar in substance, the one being a tax on the decision to do business in the state, the other being a tax on ownership of a certain form of property. The Eleventh Amendment does not deprive the Supreme Court of appellate jurisdiction over cases such as this arising from state courts. Nor may Alabama apply "*res judicata*" principles to deny relief simply because the same issue had been decided by the Alabama Supreme Court in an earlier case involving different parties.

9-0. Opinion for unanimous Court by Breyer. Concurring opinions by O'Connor and Thomas.

Stewart v. LaGrand 119 S. Ct. 1018, 67 USLW 3557 (3-3-99)

***Habeas corpus*, waiver of challenge to execution by lethal gas**: A convicted murderer who was sentenced to death and who exercised his option under Arizona law to be executed by lethal gas rather than by lethal injection has waived any objection he might have had to the constitutionality of execution by gas. The prisoner in this case also procedurally defaulted by failing to raise this claim on direct appeal after having been sentenced to death by lethal gas prior to the State's adoption of the lethal injection alternative. At the time of the prisoner's direct appeal (1987) there had been sufficient debate about the constitutionality of lethal gas executions that he cannot show cause for his failure to raise the issue on appeal.

8-1. *Per curiam*. Concurring opinion by Souter, joined by Ginsburg and Breyer. Dissenting opinion by Stevens.

Strickler v. Greene 119 S. Ct. 1936, 67 USLW 4477 (6-17-99)

Prosecutorial misconduct; habeas corpus, procedural default: Virginia did not violate the rule derived from *Brady v. Maryland* (1963) that suppression by the prosecution of evidence favorable to an accused violates due process where the evidence is material either to guilt or to punishment. In this case the prosecution withheld an initial statement made to police by a prosecution witness. The statement, much less definite about the defendant's role in the crime than her later testimony, could have been used by the defendant to impeach her credibility. Petitioner's procedural default in not raising this *Brady* claim in state courts is excused by an adequate showing of cause and prejudice; the petitioner had relied on the prosecution's "open file" policy and on assurances that "everything known to the government" had been disclosed. Petitioner could not, however, establish the underlying *Brady* violation. Two of the three components of a violation were established: the evidence was favorable to the accused and was suppressed by the State. The petitioner failed, however, to demonstrate the prejudice necessary to establish "materiality" because he failed to show that there is a reasonable probability that his conviction or sentence would have been different if the materials had been disclosed. Even if the one witness had been "severely impeached," there was other evidence in the record lending "strong support" for the conclusion that the petitioner still would have been convicted and sentenced to death. Moreover, the testimony in question did not relate to the petitioner's eligibility for the death sentence, and was not relied upon by the prosecution in its closing argument during the penalty phase of the trial.

7-2 (*Brady* violation); **9-0** (excusal of procedural default). Opinion of Court by Stevens, joined by Rehnquist, O'Connor, Scalia, Ginsburg, and Breyer, and joined in part by Kennedy, Souter, and Thomas. Opinion by Souter, joined by Kennedy, concurring in part and dissenting in part.

Sutton v. United Airlines 119 S. Ct. 2139, 67 USLW 4537 (6-22-99)

ADA, definition of "disability": The determination of whether an individual is "disabled" for purposes of the Americans with Disabilities Act of 1990 (ADA) should be made with reference to corrective measures that mitigate the individual's impairment, including, for instance, eyeglasses and contact lenses. The ADA defines "disability" as "a physical or mental impairment that substantially limits one or more of [that individual's] major life activities." No agency has been delegated the authority to interpret the term "disability." EEOC guidelines, however, define "major life activities" to include "working," and also provide that individuals are to be evaluated in their hypothetical uncorrected state. This latter EEOC interpretation is "impermissible." The present indicative verb form of the statutory definition ("substantially limits") requires that the individual be presently – not potentially – limited by an impairment. The evaluation as to disability must be individualized, but focus on an uncorrected impairment would require instead that persons be judged as members of a group with similar impairments. Finally, congressional "findings" written into the ADA declare that "some 43,000,000 Americans have one or more physical or mental disabilities." This figure is inconsistent with a definition of disability that would treat all impairments in their uncorrected form; estimates available in 1990 produced a significantly larger number (approximately 160 million) for a nonfunctional "health conditions" approach to defining disability. Because it is included in the ADA's text, the congressional finding "gives content to the ADA's terms, specifically the definition of disability." A second aspect of the statutory definition includes individuals who are "regarded as" having a disability. The petitioners in this case, individuals whose corrected vision was 20/20 or better, were rejected for employment as airline pilots because their uncorrected vision did not meet the airline's minimum requirement of 20/100 uncorrected vision. The ADA allows employers to establish physical criteria for jobs. The fact that petitioners were rejected for employment in one particular job does not establish that the employer regarded them as having an impairment "substantially limiting" their ability to work. The definition requires an allegation that an individual's impairment makes her unable to work in a "broad class of jobs." There are a number of other positions – such as regional pilot and pilot instructor – utilizing petitioners' skills.

7-2. Opinion of Court by O'Connor, joined by Rehnquist, Scalia, Kennedy, Souter, Thomas, and Ginsburg. Concurring opinion by Ginsburg. Dissenting opinions by Stevens, joined by Breyer; and by Breyer.

United States v. Haggar Apparel Co. 119 S. Ct. 1392, 67 USLW 4249 (4-21-99)

Administrative law, deference to agency interpretation: A Customs Service regulation is subject to analysis under principles set forth in *Chevron v. NRDC* (1984). The statute grants importers a partial exemption from customs duties for manufactured articles that are assembled abroad and that have not been enhanced in value "except by being assembled and except by operations incidental to the assembly process." The regulation deems permapressing operations to be an additional step in manufacturing of textiles, and not an incidental part of the assembly process. The regulation is not limited in application to customs officers who classify imported merchandise, but applies to refund suits in the Court of International Trade. "The tariffs do not mean one thing for customs officers and another for importers." Statutes authorizing the Court of International Trade to conduct *de novo* review do not displace the customary *Chevron* deference to agency interpretations. "*De novo* proceedings presume a foundation of law," and deference may be given to the regulations without impairing the court's authority to make factual determinations *de novo* or to apply the regulations to those determinations. The case is remanded for determination of whether the regulation is entitled to deference under application of *Chevron* principles.

9-0; 7-2. Opinion of Court by Kennedy, unanimous with respect to whether *Chevron* principles apply, and joined by Rehnquist, O'Connor, Scalia, Souter, Thomas, and Breyer on the remand issue. Opinion by Stevens, joined by Ginsburg, concurring in part and dissenting in part.

United States v. Rodriguez-Moreno 119 S. Ct. 1239, 67 USLW 4219 (3-30-99)

Venue, using firearm during crime of violence: Venue in a prosecution for using or carrying a firearm "during and in relation to any crime of violence," in violation of 18 U.S.C. § 924(c)(1), is proper in any district where the crime of violence was committed, even if the firearm was used or carried only in one district. In this case the defendant participated in a kidnaping that began in Texas and continued with transportation of the victim to New Jersey and then to Maryland; in Maryland the defendant used a gun to threaten the victim. Venue was proper in New Jersey even though there was no evidence that the defendant used a gun in New Jersey. Section 924(c)(1) is not a point-in-time offense that can only be committed in the place where the underlying violent crime and the gun use coincide. Rather, where a crime consists of distinct parts that have different localities, the whole may be tried where any part can be proved to have been done. Venue is appropriate for the section 924(c)(1) offense wherever venue is appropriate for the underlying crime of violence.

7-2. Opinion of Court by Thomas, joined by Rehnquist, O'Connor, Kennedy, Souter, Ginsburg, and Breyer. Dissenting opinion by Scalia, joined by Stevens.

United States v. Sun-Diamond Growers 119 S. Ct. 1402, 67 USLW 4265 (4-27-99)

Illegal gratuity statute: The illegal gratuity statute, 18 U.S.C. § 201(c)(1)(A), which prohibits giving "anything of value" to a public official "for or because of any official act performed or to be performed by such public official," requires a showing beyond the mere fact that a gratuity was given because of the recipient's official position. Under the "more natural reading" of this language, an indictment is defective if it does not allege a specific connection between the gratuities and some official act. The provision could have been worded more simply and directly if the aim had been to proscribe all gifts for or because of official position. Broad prohibitions on gift giving found elsewhere in the Code are "more precise and more administrable." Moreover, the Government's position could produce "peculiar results," such as prohibiting a sports team visiting the White House from giving the President a replica jersey, or prohibiting a farmers group before whom the Secretary of Agriculture is speaking from offering him a complimentary lunch in connection with his speech. The illegal gratuity statute is but "one strand of an intricate web of regulations" that includes many "precisely targeted prohibitions." Given this statutory context, the Court will not "expand . . . one piece of the regulatory puzzle so dramatically as to make many other pieces misfits."

9-0. Opinion for unanimous Court by Scalia.

Unum Life Ins. Co. v. Ward 119 S. Ct. 1380, 67 USLW 4243 (4-20-99)

ERISA, preemption: California's "notice-prejudice" rule, under which an insurer may avoid liability for an untimely claim only by establishing that a claimant's delay in filing was prejudicial, is a "law . . . which regulates insurance" within the meaning of ERISA's saving clause, and therefore is not preempted as a law that "relate[s] to any employee benefit plan." The notice-prejudice rule fits a common-sense understanding of insurance regulation. The rule applies to insurance contracts, and is not a general principle applicable outside the insurance context. Moreover, the rule is grounded in policy concerns specific to the insurance industry. Two of the three criteria used to determine whether a state law regulates "the business of insurance" within the meaning of the McCarran-Ferguson Act are also met — the rule serves as "an integral part of the policy relationship between the insurer and the insured," and it is "limited to entities within the insurance industry." California's *Elfstrom* rule, under which the employer could be deemed to be the agent of the insurer (and by application of which the notice in this case would have been timely), is preempted as a law that "relate[s] to [an] employee benefit plan." Deeming the policyholder-employer the agent of the insurer "would have a marked effect on plan administration."

9-0. Opinion for unanimous Court by Ginsburg.

West v. Gibson 119 S. Ct. 1906, 67 USLW 4462 (6-14-99)

Title VII, compensatory damages in administrative proceedings: The Equal Employment Opportunity Commission (EEOC) possesses the authority to require federal agencies to pay compensatory damages when they discriminate in employment in violation of Title VII of the Civil Rights Act of 1964. Section 717(b), added in 1972, grants the EEOC authority to enforce the Act "through appropriate remedies, including reinstatement or hiring of employees with or without back pay." Section 717(c) authorizes an employee or job applicant to "file a civil action." A Compensatory Damages Amendment (CDA) enacted in 1991 authorized award of compensatory damages "[i]n an action brought under section . . . 717." "Read literally," the language of the statutes is consistent with a grant of authority to the EEOC to award compensatory damages. After enactment of the CDA in 1991, award of compensatory damages is a remedy that is "appropriate." The meaning of "appropriate" was not frozen as of 1972; rather, the meaning of the word permits its scope to expand or contract to reflect later changes in the law. Recognizing this authority in the EEOC is consistent with the purposes of the 1972 amendments to encourage administrative resolution of discrimination complaints. While the CDA made no mention of the EEOC, and use of the word "action" often refers to judicial cases and not to administrative proceedings, Congress could have referenced section 717(c) had it desired to limit the remedy to court actions. Conferral of a right to a jury trial (unavailable in an EEOC proceeding) if a complaining party seeks compensatory damages does not preclude a holding that the EEOC may award compensatory damages; the provision merely makes a jury trial available if a complaining party brings a court action under § 717(c). Finally, the provision meets the standard for waiver of sovereign immunity. "[T]he statutory language, taken together with statutory purposes, history, and the absence of any convincing reason for denying the EEOC the relevant power, produce evidence of a waiver that satisfies the [appropriate] standard."

5-4. Opinion of Court by Breyer, joined by Stevens, O'Connor, Souter, and Ginsburg. Dissenting opinion by Kennedy, joined by Rehnquist, Scalia, and Thomas.

Wilson v. Layne 67 USLW 4322 (5-24-99)

Fourth Amendment, media "ride-along", qualified immunity: Police officers violate the Fourth Amendment by bringing members of the media or other third parties into a home during the execution of a warrant if the presence of the third parties in the home was not in aid of the execution of the warrant. Respect for privacy of the home lies at the "core" of the Fourth Amendment; absent exigent circumstances, a warrant is required before officers may enter a home to search or to make an arrest. Moreover, police actions in execution of a warrant must be related to the objectives of the authorized intrusion. In this case the reporters were not present to identify stolen property or otherwise to assist in execution of the warrant, and consequently their presence in the home was not related to the objectives of the authorized intrusion. Generalized interests in furthering law enforcement objectives and publicizing crime-fighting efforts do not suffice to override the right of residential privacy. However, because this right to be free from media intrusion during a search of the home was not "clearly established" at the time of the search in this case, the law enforcement officers (deputy federal marshals and local sheriff's deputies) are entitled to "qualified immunity." A reasonable officer could have believed that it was legal to bring media observers along during the execution of an arrest warrant in the home. At that time (1992) media "ride-alongs" were common, and there were no court decisions holding the practice unlawful. Also, the policy of the U.S. Marshal's Service explicitly contemplated the practice.

9-0 (Fourth Amendment); **8-1** (qualified immunity). Opinion of Court by Rehnquist, unanimous in part, and joined in separate part by O'Connor, Scalia, Kennedy, Souter, Thomas, Ginsburg, and Breyer. Opinion by Stevens concurring in part and dissenting in part.

Wright v. Universal Maritime Service Corp. 119 S. Ct. 391, 67 USLW 4009 (11-16-98)

Labor, arbitration clause, ADA: A generally worded arbitration clause in a collective bargaining agreement, providing only for arbitration of "matters under dispute," does not require a covered employee to use the arbitration procedure for an alleged violation of the Americans with Disabilities Act. The presumption of arbitrability derived from section 301 of the Labor Management Relations Act is inapplicable; that presumption applies only to disputes about the applicability or interpretation of a collective bargaining agreement, and the underlying dispute here involves interpretation of the ADA. A union's waiver of the rights of represented employees to a judicial forum for claims of employment discrimination must be "clear and unmistakable." The collective bargaining agreement in this case does not meet that standard. The arbitration clause is "very general," and the agreement contains no antidiscrimination language, statutory or otherwise. General language to the effect that no provision shall be violative of federal or state law is inadequate to constitute a clear waiver of ADA rights, especially when contrasted with specific language stating that OSHA requirements "shall be binding on both Parties."

9-0. Opinion for unanimous Court by Scalia.

Wyoming v. Houghton 119 S. Ct. 1297, 67 USLW 4225 (4-5-99)

Fourth Amendment, search of auto passenger's belongings: Police officers with probable cause to search a car may search a passenger's personal belongings inside the car if those belongings are capable of concealing the object of the search, even if it is the driver and not the passenger who is under suspicion. The initial step in evaluating the constitutionality of a search is to determine whether the search would have been regarded as unlawful under the common law at the time the Fourth Amendment was adopted. There is a long history that allows officers with probable cause but without a warrant to search for contraband in a vessel, and the same principle has been applied to allow search of containers within motor vehicles. Cases allowing such searches have expressed no qualification based on ownership of the containers. A second inquiry is the reasonableness of the search, and this is determined by balancing the intrusion on individual privacy against the governmental interests at stake. This balancing "must be conducted with an eye to the generality of cases." Passengers "possess a reduced expectation of privacy with regard to the property that they transport in cars," and a search of such property is far less intrusive than a search of the person. On the other hand, the governmental interest in effective law enforcement is "substantial," and the "ready mobility" of cars often makes obtaining a warrant impractical. Also impractical is requiring police officers to determine whether property belongs to the driver or to a passenger, whether the driver and passenger are confederates in crime, and whether the driver may have hidden contraband among a passenger's possessions without the passenger's knowledge.

6-3. Opinion of Court by Scalia, joined by Rehnquist, O'Connor, Kennedy, Thomas, and Breyer. Concurring opinion by Breyer. Dissenting opinion by Stevens, joined by Souter and Ginsburg.

Your Home Visiting Nurse Servs. v. Shalala 119 S. Ct. 930, 67 USLW 4127 (2-23-99)

Medicare Act; Administrative law, judicial review of agency action: A provider of Medicare services has no right to judicial review of a fiscal intermediary's refusal to reopen an annual determination of the amount of reimbursement to which the provider is entitled. The Medicare Act gives a provider the right to an administrative appeal within 180 days of the intermediary's original determination, and the Provider Reimbursement Review Board's decision is subject to review in federal district court. The provider may also, within three years, request the intermediary to reopen the reimbursement determination, and any new decision is subject to review. The regulation says nothing, however, about a refusal to reopen. The Medicare Act authorizes a hearing before the Board if the provider is dissatisfied with an intermediary's "final determination . . . as to the amount" of reimbursement. The Secretary's interpretation of this language to mean that a refusal to reopen is not a "final determination . . . as to the amount," but rather a refusal to make such a determination, is a reasonable interpretation entitled to deference under *Chevron v. NRDC* (1984). These review provisions, authorizing direct appeal and a request for reopening, are not inconsistent with a separate statutory directive that regulations provide for making "suitable" retroactive corrective adjustments.

9-0. Opinion for unanimous Court by Scalia.

Supreme Court
Volume 1 pp. 81-148

SUPREME COURT OPINIONS: OCTOBER 1996 TERM

George Costello
Legislative Attorney
American Law Division

Abrams v. Johnson 65 USLW 4478 (6-19-97)

Congressional districting, court-ordered plan: Georgia's congressional districting plan, imposed by a federal district court after the legislature deadlocked and was unable to adopt a new districting law in conformity with the Supreme Court's ruling in *Miller v. Johnson* (1995), is valid. The district court did not exceed its remedial power, either by changing district lines statewide or by failing to create more than one majority-black district. The constitutional violations in the legislature's original plan affected a large geographic area, and legislative plans incorporating either two or three majority-black districts were constitutionally flawed by evidence of predominant racial motive. The court-ordered plan did not dilute minority voting strength in violation of section 2 of the Voting Rights Act. The black population was not sufficiently compact for a second majority-black district, and the record failed to demonstrate chronic bloc voting. Nor was the plan "retrogressive" in violation of section 5 of the Voting Rights Act; the appropriate benchmark is the 1982 plan, and there is no evidence that black voters in any district suffered a retrogression in their voting strength. Finally, the court-ordered plan does not violate the one-person, one-vote requirement of Article I, § 2. The plan had lower deviation from population equality (.35% overall, .11% average) than any other valid plan presented to the court, and these slight deviations from mathematical equality were justified by deference to state policies favoring use of political subdivision lines.

5-4. Opinion of Court by Kennedy, joined by Rehnquist, O'Connor, Scalia, and Thomas. Dissenting opinion by Breyer, joined by Stevens, Souter, and Ginsburg.

Agostini v. Felton 65 USLW 4524 (6-23-97)

Religion, public school teachers in parochial schools: The First Amendment's Establishment Clause does not bar use of public school teachers in parochial schools to provide remedial education to disadvantaged children pursuant to Title I of the Elementary and Secondary Education Act of 1965. *Aguilar v. Felton* (1985) is overruled, as is that portion of *Grand Rapids School Dist. v. Ball* (1985) that invalidated the "Shared Time" program. The petitioners, parties bound by the injunction in *Aguilar*, are entitled to relief under Federal Rule of Civil Procedure 60(b)(5), which allows relief when "it is no longer equitable that the judgment should have prospective application." Decisions since *Aguilar* and *Grand Rapids* have so undermined those holdings that they are no longer good law. New York City's Title I program does not run afoul of any of the three criteria employed by the Court in Establishment Clause cases. The Court has abandoned the presumptions that public employees working in a parochial school setting will necessarily inculcate religion, that their mere placement on parochial school grounds creates a symbolic union between church and state, and that any public assistance to the educational function of parochial schools will impermissibly finance religious indoctrination. In the latter regard, Title I assistance is made available to students at whatever school they choose to attend, so any particular school's receipt of that assistance can be attributed to the private decisions of parents. The program does not result in "excessive entanglement"; because the Court no longer presumes that public employees will inculcate religion, pervasive monitoring is no longer required.

5-4. Opinion of Court by O'Connor, joined by Rehnquist, Scalia, Kennedy, and Thomas. Dissenting opinions by Souter, joined by Stevens and Ginsburg, and joined in part by Breyer; and by Ginsburg, joined by Stevens, Souter, and Breyer.

Amchem Products, Inc. v. Windsor 65 USLW 4635 (6-25-97)

Class action, certification, asbestos-related claims: Class certification, for settlement purposes only, of "the sprawling class" of persons who have been or may be adversely affected by past exposure to asbestos products does not satisfy the requirements of Federal Rule of Civil Procedure 23. While settlement can be "relevant" to class certification, the criteria for certification extend beyond a mere finding that a settlement is fair. Rule 23(b)(3) requires a finding that common questions of law or fact "predominate" over any questions affecting only individual members. The shared experience of asbestos exposure and the common interest in receiving prompt and fair compensation do not meet this predominance requirement. The disparate interests of different class members -- e.g., the exposure-only plaintiffs and the presently injured plaintiffs -- undermine class cohesion. For similar reasons, the approved class cannot satisfy Rule 23(a)(4)'s requirement that named parties "will fairly and adequately protect the interests of the class." The named parties sought to act on behalf of the single, undifferentiated class, yet the interest of presently injured plaintiffs in immediate payments "tugs against" the interest of exposure-only plaintiffs in ensuring an ample fund for future payments.

6-2. Opinion of Court by Ginsburg, joined by Rehnquist, Scalia, Kennedy, Souter, and Thomas. Opinion by Breyer, joined by Stevens, concurring in part and dissenting in part. O'Connor did not participate.

Arizonans for Official English v. Arizona 117 S. Ct. 1055, 65 USLW 4169 (3-3-97)

Mootness: This case, involving a challenge to Article 28 of the Arizona Constitution, which declares that English is the official language of the State and requires that English be used for "government functions and actions," should have been dismissed as moot by the Ninth Circuit court of appeals. The Court has "grave doubts" as to whether two parties granted intervenor status -- Arizonans for Official English and its chairman -- had standing to seek appellate review. AOE and its members were not agents of the state for litigation purposes, and AOE's standing to represent its members' interests is undercut by the fact that AOE members had no evident basis for standing. The AOE standing issue need not be decided, however, because the case had become moot. The originating plaintiff had resigned from public employment prior to the Ninth Circuit's consideration of the case, and her plea for nominal damages was insufficient to keep the case alive. That plea was based on 42 U.S.C. § 1983, yet such actions do not lie against a state. The appropriate remedy is vacatur "down the line," including the district court's holding of unconstitutionality. The State Attorney General had requested certification so that the Arizona Supreme Court could give a definitive construction to Article 28, and that process could "greatly simplif[y]" the federal constitutional issues.

9-0. Opinion for unanimous Court by Ginsburg.

Arkansas v. Farm Credit Servs. 117 S. Ct. 1776, 65 USLW 4414 (6-2-97)

Tax Injunction Act, federal instrumentalities: Production Credit Associations (PCAs), corporations chartered under the Farm Credit Act, are barred by the Tax Injunction Act from challenging state taxation in federal court. The judicial exception that allows the United States to sue in federal court to protect itself and its instrumentalities from state taxation is not available to PCAs when they sue without the United States as co-plaintiff. The Tax Injunction Act creates a jurisdictional barrier that protects states in administering their tax laws from "undue interference" by federal courts. The Farm Credit Act provides that PCAs are instrumentalities of the United States, and further provides for limited tax immunity, but these facts alone do not entitle PCAs to challenge state taxation in federal court. Appeals court precedents have recognized exceptions for Federal Reserve banks, and, under the analogous Anti-Injunction Act, for the NLRB, but PCAs are not similar entities clothed with substantial regulatory authority. Rather, the interests of PCAs, which make commercial loans and whose stock is owned by private entities, "are not coterminous with those of the Government any more than most commercial interests." Denying access to PCAs will promote the purposes of the Tax Injunction Act without sacrificing the interests of the United States.

9-0. Opinion for unanimous Court by Kennedy.

Associates Commercial Corp. v. Rash 65 USLW 4451 (6-16-97)

Bankruptcy, valuation of property: When a debtor exercises the "cram down" option under § 1325(a)(5)(B) of the Bankruptcy Code and keeps property over the objection of the creditor, the value of that property is not its foreclosure value, but rather its replacement value -- "the price a willing buyer in the debtor's trade, business, or situation would pay to obtain like property from a willing seller." Section 506(a) of the Code governs valuation in this case, but the Fifth Circuit inappropriately focused on the first sentence rather than the second sentence of that section. The first sentence merely provides that a secured creditor's claim is to be divided into secured and unsecured portions, with the secured portion limited to the value of the collateral. The second sentence provides that "such value shall be determined in light of the purpose of the valuation and of the proposed disposition or use of the property." Application of the replacement-value rather than the foreclosure-value standard recognizes the different consequences of the debtor's choice to retain rather than surrender the property, and thereby "renders meaningful the key words 'disposition or use.'" If a debtor surrenders the property to the creditor, then the creditor can sell it and reinvest the proceeds. If the debtor retains the property and uses it to generate income for himself, then the replacement-value standard accurately gauges that use. There is "no warrant" in the Code for the intermediate, "split-the-difference" standard adopted by the Seventh Circuit in a different case.

8-1. Opinion of Court by Ginsburg, joined by Rehnquist, O'Connor, Kennedy, Souter, Thomas, and Breyer, and joined in part by Scalia. Dissenting opinion by Stevens.

Atherton v. FDIC 117 S. Ct. 666, 65 USLW 4062 (1-14-97)

Banks, officers, standard of care: State law sets the standard of conduct applicable to officers and directors of federally insured savings institutions as long as the state standard is "stricter" than the "gross negligence" standard set by federal law. Federal common law standards once applicable to officers of federally chartered banks did not survive the Court's decision in *Erie R.R. v. Tompkins* (1938). 12 U.S.C. § 1821(k) provides that an officer or director "may be held personally liable . . . for gross negligence, including any similar conduct or conduct that demonstrates a greater disregard of a duty of care (than gross negligence) . . . as such terms are defined and determined under applicable State law." This language does not immunize from liability conduct, such as simple negligence, that is less culpable than gross negligence. Rather, it sets a liability "floor" that does not preclude states from applying a stricter standard. A savings clause, providing that "[n]othing in this paragraph shall impair or affect any right of the [FDIC] under other applicable law," is broad enough to save rights conferred by state law. Also, legislative history, although "not all on one side," supports the conclusion that wholesale preemption of state law was not intended.

9-0. Opinion of Court by Breyer, joined by Rehnquist, Stevens, Kennedy, Souter, and Ginsburg, and joined in part by O'Connor, Scalia, and Thomas. Concurring opinion by O'Connor, joined by Scalia and Thomas.

Auer v. Robbins 117 S. Ct. 905, 65 USLW 4136 (2-19-97)

FLSA, deference to administrative interpretation: The Secretary of Labor's regulation setting a "salary-basis" test for exemption under the Fair Labor Standards Act as a "bona fide executive, administrative, or professional" employee is a permissible reading of the FLSA as applied to public-sector employees, and is entitled to deference. The essence of the test is that the employee receives a regular salary that "is not subject to reduction because of variations in the quality or quantity of work performed." The Secretary's interpretation of the regulation as applying only if there is an "actual practice" or "significant likelihood" of salary reductions is not "plainly erroneous or inconsistent with the regulation," and is therefore controlling.

9-0. Opinion for unanimous Court by Scalia.

Babbitt v. Youpee 117 S. Ct. 727, 65 USLW 4069 (1-21-97)

Taking of property, right to leave property to one's heirs: Section 207 of the Indian Land Consolidation Act, as amended in 1984, effects an unconstitutional taking of property without compensation by restricting a property owner's right to pass on property to his heirs. The amended section, like an earlier version held unconstitutional in *Hodel v. Irving* (1987), provides that certain small interests in Indian land will escheat to the tribe upon death of the owner. None of the changes made in 1984 cures the constitutional defect. In classifying property subject to escheat, the amended provision still focuses on the amount of income generated from the land, and ignores the land's value. Revision of the section to allow transmission of fractional interests to successors who already own an interest in the allotment still severely restricts the right of an individual to direct the descent of his property, since it is unlikely that the group of permissible devisees will contain any lineal descendants. And the provision continues to operate even when the government's purpose of preventing further "fractionation" of Indian land will not be advanced; in this case the respondent's will had bequeathed each fractional interest to only one heir.

8-1. Opinion of Court by Ginsburg, joined by Rehnquist, O'Connor, Scalia, Kennedy, Souter, Thomas, and Breyer. Dissenting opinion by Stevens.

Bennett v. Spear 117 S. Ct. 1154, 65 USLW 4201 (3-19-97)

Endangered Species Act, standing to sue: Two irrigation districts and a rancher within one of those districts who assert economic rather than environmental injury have standing to sue under the Endangered Species Act (ESA) and the Administrative Procedure Act (APA) to challenge a Biological Opinion recommending that the Bureau of Reclamation maintain minimum water levels at two reservoirs in order to protect endangered species. The petitioners alleged that the Secretary failed to comply with the ESA's mandates that critical habitat decisions be based on "the best scientific data available" and that "economic impact" be taken into account. The ESA's citizen suit provision authorizes "any person" to sue to compel the Secretary to perform a non-discretionary duty under § 4 of the Act. One of the petitioners' three claims involves a challenge to the Secretary's implementation of section 4, and therefore may be brought as a citizen suit. The other two claims challenge implementation of section 7, and may be brought under the APA, which authorizes challenges to final agency action for which there is no other adequate remedy. The "zone of interests" test, a prudential principle limiting standing to persons asserting injuries within the zone of interests sought to be protected by the particular statutory provision at issue, is overridden by the broad language of the citizen suit provision, but applies under the APA. The petitioners have satisfied that test. An "obvious purpose" of the requirements that the Secretary employ the best scientific data available and take economic impact into account was "to avoid needless economic dislocation" of the sort that petitioners allege will befall them.

9-0. Opinion for unanimous Court by Scalia.

Blessing v. Freestone 117 S. Ct. 1353, 65 USLW 4265 (4-21-97)

Social Security Act, right of beneficiaries to sue: Individuals whose children are eligible to receive child support services from a state pursuant to Title IV-D of the Social Security Act may not sue under 42 U.S.C. § 1983 to require the state to operate the program in "substantial compliance" with

Title IV-D. The requirement that a state operate its child support program in "substantial compliance" with Title IV-D was not intended to benefit individual children and custodial parents, and therefore does not create a "federal right" enforceable under section 1983. Rather, the "substantial compliance" standard is simply a yardstick by which the Secretary measures a state's system-wide performance and determines whether to increase audits or decrease a state's grant. Title IV-D is not so comprehensive as to demonstrate congressional intent to preclude the possibility of remedy under section 1983. However, it is incumbent upon plaintiffs in a section 1983 action to identify with particularity the rights they claim. This case is remanded so that the district court can determine exactly what specific rights the plaintiffs are asserting.

9-0. Opinion for unanimous Court by O'Connor. Concurring opinion by Scalia, joined by Kennedy.

Boggs v. Boggs 117 S. Ct. 1754, 65 USLW 4418 (6-2-97)

ERISA, preemption, community property: ERISA preempts a Louisiana community property law that allows a non-participant spouse to transfer by will interests in undistributed pension plan benefits. ERISA provides for payment of an annuity to a surviving spouse, and a state may not authorize a predeceasing spouse to diminish the surviving spouse's entitlement through a testamentary transfer. To this extent, there is a "direct clash" between state and federal law, and the state law is superseded by operation of "conventional conflict pre-emption principles." The Louisiana law is also preempted to the extent that it allows testamentary transfer by a non-participant spouse of rights to other ERISA benefits, including the participant's monthly annuity, a lump-sum retirement payment he rolled over into an IRA, and shares of stock from the company's employee stock ownership plan. ERISA's principal object is to protect plan participants and beneficiaries. In this case the first spouse and her sons, to whom she attempted to devise her community property rights in the retirement plans, do not qualify as ERISA beneficiaries. Moreover, the attempted devise violates ERISA's anti-alienation section, which provides that benefits "may not be assigned or alienated."

7-2 (surviving spouse annuity); **5-4** (other benefits). Opinion of Court by Kennedy, joined by Stevens, Scalia, Souter, and Thomas; and joined in part by Rehnquist and Ginsburg. Dissenting opinion by Breyer, joined by O'Connor; and joined in part by Rehnquist and Ginsburg.

Bracy v. Gramley 117 S. Ct. 1793, 65 USLW 4435 (6-9-97)

Habeas corpus, "good cause" showing, judicial bias: The petitioner has made a sufficient factual showing to establish "good cause," as required by Habeas Corpus Rule 6(a), for discovery on his claim of actual judicial bias in his criminal trial in state court. The claim, based on the due process right to a fair trial in a fair tribunal before an unbiased judge, alleged that the judge had taken bribes in other criminal cases and that he engaged in "compensatory bias" against defendants who, like the petitioner, did not attempt to bribe him. Proof of the judge's conviction on bribery charges, and additional evidence raising the possibility of collusion between the judge and the petitioner's trial attorney, a former associate of the judge who was appointed by the judge to defend the petitioner in this case, suffice to establish "good cause" for discovery.

9-0. Opinion for unanimous Court by Rehnquist.

California Div. of Labor Stds. Enf. v. Dillingham Constr. 117 S. Ct. 832, 65 USLW 4097 (2-18-97)

ERISA, preemption: California's prevailing wage law, as applied to a public contractor who was paying apprentices a wage lower than that required for a non-approved apprenticeship program, does not "relate to" an employee benefit plan within the meaning of ERISA § 514, 29 U.S.C. § 1144(a), and thus is not preempted by ERISA. The apprenticeship agreement was an "employee welfare benefit plan" under ERISA, but the wage law did not "relate to" that plan. A state law "relates to" a benefit plan, the Court has held, if the law has a reference to, or connection with, a benefit plan. The California law makes no reference to ERISA plans. Nor does the law have sufficient "connection" with the ERISA plan. The wages paid to apprenticeship training programs are "quite remote" from ERISA's central concerns -- "reporting, disclosure, fiduciary responsibility, and the like." Moreover, the law does not require ERISA plans to employ apprentices or, if they do, to hire apprentices from an approved program, but merely "alters the incentives" for doing so.

9-0. Opinion for unanimous Court by Thomas. Concurring opinion by Scalia, joined by Ginsburg.

California v. Roy 117 S. Ct. 337, 65 USLW 3338 (11-4-96)

Harmless error, habeas corpus: When federal courts in habeas corpus proceedings are asked to overturn state convictions on the basis of "trial errors" such as an invalid jury instruction, they should apply a harmless error standard that inquires "whether the error had substantial and injurious effect or influence on the jury's verdict." The habeas court need grant the petition only if it has "grave doubt as to the harmlessness of an error." The appeals court here imposed too high a standard for harmless error in requiring a finding that the jury would "necessarily" have found the element omitted from the jury instruction. The appropriate standard in habeas corpus cases is also less demanding than the "harmless-beyond-a reasonable-doubt" standard applicable on direct review.

9-0. *Per curiam*. Concurring opinion by Scalia, joined in part by Ginsburg.

Camps Newfound/Owatonna v. Town of Harrison 117 S. Ct. 1590, 65 USLW 4337 (5-19-97)

Commerce Clause, discriminatory state property tax: Maine's property tax law, which contains an exemption for charitable institutions but limits that exemption to institutions serving principally Maine residents, violates the "dormant" Commerce Clause as applied to deny exemption status to a nonprofit corporation that operates a summer camp for children, most of whom are not Maine residents. The camp is unquestionably engaged in commerce, not only as a purchaser, but also as a provider of goods and services. A tax on real estate, like any other tax, may impermissibly burden interstate commerce. The Maine tax facially discriminates against interstate commerce, and the only novel question is whether the nonprofit character of the enterprise should exclude it from protection. Any such distinction is "wholly illusory." Protectionism, whether targeted at for-profit or not-for-profit entities, is prohibited. Maine's further arguments are also rejected. Case law does not equate tax exemptions with direct subsidies, and the tax exemption is not a proprietary activity falling within the market-participant exception to dormant Commerce Clause restraint.

5-4. Opinion of Court by Stevens, joined by O'Connor, Kennedy, Souter, and Breyer. Dissenting opinions by Scalia, joined by Rehnquist, Thomas, and Ginsburg; and by Thomas, joined by Scalia, and joined in part by Rehnquist.

Caterpillar Inc. v. Lewis 117 S. Ct. 467, 65 USLW 4021 (12-10-96)

Federal courts, jurisdiction, removal: A federal district court's error in failing to remand a case improperly removed from state court is not fatal to the ensuing adjudication if federal jurisdictional requirements are met at the time judgment is entered. Even though the plaintiff in this case, by timely moving for remand, did all that was required to preserve his objection to removal, "considerations of finality, efficiency, and economy" are overriding. To "wipe out the [federal court] adjudication post-judgment" and require re-adjudication in state court "would impose an exorbitant cost on our dual court system [that is] incompatible with the fair and unprotracted administration of justice."

9-0. Opinion for unanimous Court by Ginsburg.

Chandler v. Miller 117 S. Ct. 1295, 65 USLW 4243 (4-15-97)

Fourth Amendment, drug testing of candidates: Georgia's requirement that candidates for state office certify that they have passed a drug test does not fit within the "closely guarded category of constitutionally permissible suspicionless searches," and hence violates the Fourth Amendment. The requirement effects a "search" that is plainly not tied to individualized suspicion. Georgia has failed to establish existence of a "special need, beyond the normal need for law enforcement," that can justify such a search. There is nothing in the record to indicate any actual fear or suspicion of drug use by state officials, the required certification is not well designed to detect illegal drug use, and candidates for state office, unlike the customs officers held subject to drug testing in *Treasury Employees v. von Raab* (1989), are subject to "relentless" public scrutiny. Under these circumstances, Georgia's need to display a public commitment to the struggle against drug abuse is "symbolic" rather than "special."

8-1. Opinion of Court by Ginsburg, joined by Stevens, O'Connor, Scalia, Kennedy, Souter, Thomas, and Breyer. Dissenting opinion by Rehnquist.

City of Boerne v. Flores 65 USLW 4612 (6-25-97)

Religious Freedom Restoration Act, Congressional power: The Religious Freedom Restoration Act (RFRA) exceeds congressional power under section 5 of the Fourteenth Amendment. Section 5 gives Congress the power to "enforce" the Fourteenth Amendment's due process and other guarantees by "appropriate legislation." This includes the power to enforce the right to the free exercise of religion, protected against state interference by the Due Process Clause. In exercising its enforcement authority,

Congress may legislate to deter or remedy constitutional violations even if in the process it prohibits conduct that is not itself unconstitutional. Congress' authority does not extend, however, to defining the substance of the Amendment's restrictions. This RFRA appears to do, expressly disapproving the Court's approach in *Employment Division v. Smith* (1990) and instead imposing on state and federal legislation the compelling interest test -- "the most demanding test known to constitutional law." While the distinction between remedial and substantive legislation is not always easy to draw, there must be "a congruence and proportionality" between the means adopted and the injury to be remedied. RFRA "is so far out of proportion to a supposed remedial or preventive object that it cannot be understood as responsive to, or designed to prevent, unconstitutional behavior." RFRA's reach and scope distinguish it from other legislation, such as the Voting Rights Act, passed pursuant to section 5 enforcement power. There are no termination dates or geographic restrictions limiting RFRA's reach, and there was no history of religious persecution constituting an "egregious predicate" for such far-reaching legislation.

6-3. Opinion of Court by Kennedy, joined by Rehnquist, Stevens, Thomas, and Ginsburg, and joined in part by Scalia. Concurring opinions by Stevens; and by Scalia, joined by Stevens. Dissenting opinions by O'Connor, joined in part by Breyer; and by Souter, joined by Breyer.

Clinton v. Jones 117 S. Ct. 1636, 65 USLW 4372 (5-27-97)

President, immunity from civil suit: Trial of the respondent's civil action against the President need not be deferred until after petitioner Clinton is no longer President. There is no basis for granting the President temporary immunity from civil damages litigation arising out of events that occurred before he took office. The principal rationale for conferring immunity on officials -- to enable them to perform their official functions efficiently without fear of personal liability -- has no application to unofficial conduct. Separation of powers principles also do not require a postponement of trial. The doctrine of separation of powers is concerned with the allocation of official power among the branches. Here the only claim is that the burden of defending the action will hamper the President in performance of his official duties. But it is settled that the President is subject to judicial process in appropriate circumstances, including cases involving the legality of his official conduct, so it "must follow that the federal courts have power to determine the legality of [the President's] unofficial conduct." The district court abused its discretion in granting a categorical stay until after the President leaves office. That stay "takes no account whatever of the respondent's interest in bringing the case to trial," and was also "premature," since there was nothing in the record to allow the judge to assess the potential harm that could ensue from a prompt trial. The Court "assume[s]" that the President's trial testimony "could be taken at the White House at a time that will accommodate his busy schedule."

9-0. Opinion of Court by Stevens, joined by Rehnquist, O'Connor, Scalia, Kennedy, Souter, Thomas, and Ginsburg. Concurring opinion by Breyer.

Commissioner v. Estate of Hubert 117 S. Ct. 1124, 65 USLW 4183 (3-18-97)

Taxation, Federal, estate tax, deductions: Under the "unusual" facts of this case, the amount deducted from estate taxes for marital or charitable bequests need not be reduced by the amount of estate administration expenses paid from income generated by estate assets allocated to those bequests. If administration expenses are paid from marital and charitable residue principal, then the marital and charitable deductions must be correspondingly reduced. When those expenses are paid from income, however, the issue under IRS regulations applicable to the marital deduction becomes whether the payments reflect a "material limitation" on the spouse's right to income from the property. The marital and charitable deductions should be treated similarly in this respect. In this case, with the residue principal assumed to be worth $26 million and with administrative expenses of $1.5 million paid from interest, the Commissioner did not establish that payment of the administrative expenses was quantitatively material.

7-2. No opinion of Court. Opinion by Kennedy, announcing the Court's judgment, joined by Rehnquist, Stevens, and Ginsburg. Concurring opinion by O'Connor, joined by Souter and Thomas. Dissenting opinions by Scalia, joined by Breyer; and by Breyer.

Commissioners of Bryan County v. Brown 117 S. Ct. 1382, 65 USLW 4286 (4-28-97)

Municipal liability, 42 U.S.C. § 1983: The County is not liable under 42 U.S.C. § 1983 for personal injury resulting from the use of excessive force by a police officer who had been hired in spite of an arrest record for various misdemeanors that included assault and battery, resisting arrest, and public drunkenness. Municipalities and other local governments are "persons" subject to liability under section 1983, but, under previous Court rulings, may not be held liable under a theory of *respondeat superior*. Instead, someone injured by actions of a municipal employee must show that the municipality, through some kind of deliberate policy or conduct, was the moving force behind the injury. If the municipality did not authorize deprivation of federal rights, but instead the injury is alleged to have resulted because of inadequate training of employees or inadequate screening before hiring of employees, the plaintiff must demonstrate "deliberate indifference" to the risk that a violation of a particular federal right will follow the decision. The required culpability cannot depend on a finding that an inadequately screened officer will inflict some constitutional injury, but rather "must depend on a finding that *this* officer was highly likely to inflict the *particular* injury suffered by the plaintiff."

5-4. Opinion of Court by O'Connor, joined by Rehnquist, Scalia, Kennedy, and Thomas. Dissenting opinions by Souter, joined by Stevens and Breyer; and by Breyer, joined by Stevens and Ginsburg.

De Buono v. NYSA-ILA Medical Servs. Fund 117 S. Ct. 1747, 65 USLW 4410 (6-2-97)

ERISA, preemption, state tax: New York may impose its Health Facility Assessment, a tax on gross receipts for patient services, on the income of medical centers operated with ERISA funds. The HFA does not "relate to any employee benefit plan," and hence is not preempted by operation of ERISA § 514. The Court's decision in *New York Conf. of Blue*

Cross v. Travelers Ins. Co. (1995), rejected emphasis on the "unhelpful text" of § 514 in favor of an approach looking to the objectives of the statute. Although the HFA burdens plan administration somewhat by raising the cost, it is a tax of general applicability that does not target hospitals owned or operated by ERISA funds. Such general tax laws are not the type of state laws that Congress intended ERISA to supersede.

7-2. Opinion of Court by Stevens, joined by Rehnquist, O'Connor, Kennedy, Souter, Ginsburg, and Breyer. Dissenting opinion by Scalia, joined by Thomas.

Dunn v. CFTC 117 S. Ct. 913, 65 USLW 4141 (2-25-97)

Commodity Exchange Act, foreign currency options: Transactions in options to buy or sell foreign currency are "transactions in currency" within the meaning of the "Treasury Amendment" to the Commodity Exchange Act, 7 U.S.C. § 2(ii), and hence, if they are off-exchange, are exempt from regulation by the Commodity Futures Trading Commission. The Commission's distinction between futures contracts, which concededly come within the exemption, and options contracts, which the Commission argues do not, is untenable in view of the plain statutory meaning. For that reason, deference to the administrative interpretation is inappropriate. The statutory phrase "encompasses all transactions in which foreign currency is the fungible good whose fluctuating market price provides the motive for trading." The provision's legislative history supports this interpretation. The Act does not, as the Commission alleges, consistently distinguish between transactions "involving" a commodity and transactions "in" a commodity.

9-0. Opinion of Court by Stevens, joined by Rehnquist, O'Connor, Kennedy, Souter, Thomas, Ginsburg, and Breyer. Concurring opinion by Scalia.

Edmond v. United States 117 S. Ct. 1573, 65 USLW 4362 (5-19-97)

Appointments, military judges: Congress has authorized the Secretary of Transportation to appoint civilian members of the Coast Guard Court of Criminal Appeals, and this authorization is consistent with the Appointments Clause of Article II, § 2, cl. 2. Article 66(a) of the Uniform Code of Military Justice, which authorizes the Judge Advocate General to assign judges to the CG Court of Criminal Appeals, does not authorize appointment of civilian judges to that court. Rather, the Secretary of Transportation may appoint such civilian judges pursuant to the general authority in 49 U.S.C. § 323(a) to appoint officers and employees of the Department. Congress "has repeatedly and consistently distinguished" between offices that require separate appointment and other positions to which one may be assigned or detailed by a superior officer. Military officers, who have already been appointed in the constitutionally prescribed manner, may be assigned to these military courts, but civilians, who have not been previously appointed, may not be so assigned. The judges in question are "inferior officers" within the meaning of the Appointments Clause, and hence their appointment by a head of a Department is valid. The term "inferior officer" connotes a relationship to a superior officer. These military appeals court judges are supervised by the Judge Advocate General, who exercises administrative oversight and has removal power, and by the Court of Appeals for the Armed Forces, which reviews every decision. The Court of Criminal Appeals has no authority to render a final decision on behalf of the United States unless permitted to do so by other executive officers.

9-0. Opinion of Court by Scalia, joined by Rehnquist, Stevens, O'Connor, Kennedy, Thomas, Ginsburg, and Breyer, and joined in part by Souter. Concurring opinion by Souter.

Edwards v. Balisok 117 S. Ct. 1584, 65 USLW 4359 (5-19-97)

Prison discipline, 42 U.S.C. § 1983: A prisoner's claim for declaratory relief and money damages, based on allegations of deceit and bias on the part of the decisionmaker in excluding defense testimony in a prison disciplinary hearing, is not cognizable under 42 U.S.C. § 1983 because the claim necessarily implies the invalidity of the punishment imposed, and because that decision imposing punishment has not previously been invalidated. The Court in *Heck v. Humphrey* (1994) ruled that section 1983 actions are inappropriate vehicles for challenging the validity of criminal judgments. Although that case involved a challenge to the substance of the underlying judgment and this action alleges a denial of procedural due process, the procedural defect complained of would, if established, necessarily imply the invalidity of the deprivation of the prisoner's good-time credits.

9-0. Opinion for unanimous Court by Scalia. Concurring opinion by Ginsburg, joined by Souter and Breyer.

General Motors Corp. v. Tracy 117 S. Ct. 811, 65 USLW 4086 (2-18-97)

Commerce Clause, discriminatory state tax: Ohio's imposition of its sales and use tax on all sales of natural gas except sales by regulated public utilities does not amount to an unconstitutional discrimination against interstate commerce, even though petitioner GMC bought virtually all of its natural gas from out-of-state independent marketers subject to the tax. The regulated public utilities enjoy monopoly protection and provide natural gas "bundled" with various rights and benefits for their captive residential users, while the independent marketers sell "unbundled" gas in a competitive market, primarily to large industrial users. Because the public utilities and the independent marketers provide different services to different markets, they are not similarly situated for purposes of dormant Commerce Clause analysis. The fact that the public utilities, in addition to supplying residential customers, also compete with independent marketers in the competitive market, does not require bifurcated analysis. There are strong reasons to give the greater weight to a state's interest in protecting the captive market. Congress rather than the Court has the "institutional competence" to determine the economic effects of a required equalization of taxation. GMC's separate claim based on the Equal Protection Clause is without merit.

8-1. Opinion of Court by Souter, joined by Rehnquist, O'Connor, Scalia, Kennedy, Thomas, Ginsburg, and Breyer. Concurring opinion by Scalia. Dissenting opinion by Stevens.

Gilbert v. Homar 117 S. Ct. 1807, 65 USLW 4442 (6-9-97)

Due Process, procedure, suspension of public employee: A state does not violate the Due Process Clause of the Fourteenth Amendment by failing to provide notice and a hearing before suspending without pay a tenured police officer who has been arrested and charged with a felony. Due process is flexible, and the limited hearing required before termination of a public employee is not required prior to suspension. The Court balances three factors in determining what process is constitutionally due: the private interest that will be affected, the risk of an erroneous deprivation of that interest and the likely value of any additional procedures, and the government's interest. Here, if the suspended employee receives "a sufficiently prompt post-suspension hearing," his interest in continued income is "relatively insubstantial." On the other hand, the government's interest in immediately suspending an employee accused of serious crime is "significant." In this case the purpose of a pre-suspension hearing would be to determine whether there are reasonable grounds to support the suspension, but that determination "has already been assured by the arrest and the filing of charges." The government "does not have to give an employee charged with a felony a paid leave at taxpayer expense."

9-0. Opinion for unanimous Court by Scalia.

Glickman v. Wileman Bros. & Elliott, Inc. 65 USLW 4597 (6-25-97)

First Amendment, generic advertising: A requirement imposed by marketing orders promulgated under authority of the Agricultural Marketing Agreement Act of 1937 that California fruit growers finance generic advertising does not offend the First Amendment. Rather, the compelled funding "is simply a question of economic policy for Congress and the Executive to resolve." Application of the *Central Hudson* test for validity of restrictions on commercial speech "is inconsistent with the very nature and purpose of the collective action program," of which the generic advertising was a component. The Appeals Court erred in imposing an obligation on the Secretary to establish that generic advertising was more effective than independent advertising in stimulating consumer demand for the commodities. That purpose of stimulating consumer demand in a regulated market is legitimate, and the means of doing so is a policy judgment "better made by producers and administrators than by judges." The marketing orders are "a species of economic regulation [entitled to a] strong presumption of validity." Cases involving union dues have established that assessments to fund a lawful collective program may sometimes be used to pay for speech over the objections of some members. The test developed in those cases is satisfied here, because the generic advertising of California fruit "is unquestionably germane to the purposes of the marketing orders," and because "the assessments are not used to fund ideological activities."

5-4. Opinion of Court by Stevens, joined by O'Connor, Kennedy, Ginsburg, and Breyer. Dissenting opinions by Souter, joined by Rehnquist and Scalia, and joined in part by Thomas; and by Thomas, joined in part by Scalia.

Harbor Tug & Barge Co. v. Papai 117 S. Ct. 1535, 65 USLW 4330 (5-12-97)

Jones Act seaman: A worker on a vessel is not a Jones Act seaman unless his work on a particular vessel, or for an identifiable fleet of vessels, involves "regular exposure to the perils of the sea." For these purposes there is not an identifiable fleet of vessels unless there is a requisite degree of common ownership or control. The fact that a group of vessels hires deckhands on a job-by-job basis from the same union hiring hall does not establish such common ownership or control. Classification of a worker as a deckhand by the union hiring hall agreement also does not create seaman status. That status is based on actual duties, and in this case the deckhand's duties did not include any seagoing activities.

6-3. Opinion of Court by Kennedy, joined by Rehnquist, O'Connor, Scalia, Souter, and Thomas. Dissenting opinion by Stevens, joined by Ginsburg and Breyer.

Hughes Aircraft Co. v. United States ex rel. Schumer 65 USLW 4447 (6-16-97)

Retroactivity, False Claims Act, *qui tam* actions: A 1986 amendment to the *qui tam* provision of the False Claims Act may not be applied in an action brought in 1989 but based on allegedly false claims submitted to the Government between 1982 and 1984. The *qui tam* provision permits suits by private parties, on behalf of the United States, against anyone submitting a false claim to the Government. The 1986 amendments partially lifted a previous barrier to any such actions that are based on information already possessed by the Government. There is a general presumption against retroactive legislation, reiterated in *Landgraf v. USI Film Products* (1994). Nothing in the 1986 amendment evidences a congressional intent that it be applied retroactively. The amendment would have retroactive effect if applied in this case because it would authorize a cause of action that was barred at the time the allegedly unlawful conduct took place. The exception allowing retroactive application of "jurisdictional" statutes that merely reallocate jurisdiction among courts is inapplicable; instead, the 1986 amendment "*creates* jurisdiction where none previously existed."

9-0. Opinion for unanimous Court by Thomas.

Idaho v. Coeur d'Alene Tribe 65 USLW 4540 (6-23-97)

Eleventh Amendment, declaratory judgment action: The Tribe's action against the State for a declaratory judgment and an injunction establishing the Tribe's ownership and control of the submerged lands and bed of Lake Coeur d'Alene is barred by the Eleventh Amendment. The action does not fall within the exception the Court has recognized under *Ex parte Young* (1908), for certain suits seeking declaratory and injunctive relief against state officers in their individual capacities. The Tribe's suit is the functional equivalent of a quiet title action because, if the suit is successful, substantially all benefits of ownership and control would shift from the State to the Tribe. The result would affect Idaho's sovereign interest in its lands and waters "in a degree fully as intrusive as almost any conceivable retroactive levy upon funds in its Treasury."

5-4. Opinion of Court by Kennedy, joined by Rehnquist, O'Connor, Scalia, and Thomas. Separate parts of Kennedy opinion joined only by Rehnquist. Concurring opinion by O'Connor, joined by Scalia and Thomas. Dissenting opinion by Souter, joined by Stevens, Ginsburg, and Breyer.

Ingalls Shipbuilding v. Director, OWCP 117 S. Ct. 796, 65 USLW 4077 (2-18-97)

LHWCA, death benefits; appeals: Prior to an injured worker's death, the worker's spouse is not a "person entitled to compensation" for death benefits within the meaning of § 33(g) of the Longshore and Harbor Workers' Compensation Act, 33 U.S.C. § 933(g). The spouse, therefore, does not forfeit the right to collect death benefits under the Act for failure to obtain the worker's employer's approval of settlements entered into before the worker's death. The provision is phrased in the present tense, requiring forfeiture "if the person entitled to compensation . . . *enters* into a settlement . . . ," and consequently the issue is whether that person was entitled to compensation at the time she settled. The Director, OWCP, may appear as a respondent before the courts of appeals. The statute is silent on the issue, but Federal Rule of Appellate Procedure 15 governs. That Rule provides that "the agency" whose order is subject to review is to be named the respondent. This case involved an appeal from the Benefits Review Board. The relevant agency, however, is the Department of Labor, since the Department oversees the Benefits Review Board. The Secretary has designated the Director as the Department's litigant for such cases.

9-0 (compensation issue); **7-2** (representation issue). Opinion of Court by O'Connor, unanimous as to compensation issue, and joined by Rehnquist, Stevens, Kennedy, Souter, Ginsburg, and Breyer on representation issue. Opinion by Scalia, joined by Thomas, concurring in part and dissenting in part.

INS v. Yang 117 S. Ct. 350, 65 USLW 4009 (11-13-96)

Immigration, deportation waiver: In determining whether to grant a waiver of deportation under 8 U.S.C. § 1251(a)(1)(H) to an alien who fraudulently entered the United States but who was "otherwise admissible" at that time, the Attorney General may distinguish between aliens who have committed a single, isolated act of fraud to obtain entry, and those who have engaged in a pattern of immigration fraud removed in time and circumstance from actual entry. The statute sets certain prerequisites for eligibility for a waiver, but places no limitations on the factors that the Attorney General may consider in determining who among that eligible class may be granted a waiver. It was "rational, and therefore lawful," for the Attorney General to distinguish between an isolated act of misrepresentation and a pattern of immigration fraud.

9-0. Opinion for unanimous Court by Scalia.

Inter-Modal Rail Employees v. Atchison, T. & S.F. Ry. 117 S. Ct. 1513, 65 USLW 4319 (5-12-97)

ERISA: Section 510 of ERISA, which makes it unlawful to discharge an employee benefit plan participant "for the purpose of interfering with the attainment of any right to which such participant may become entitled under the plan," applies regardless of whether the rights at issue are capable of vesting. The section thus protects against interference with welfare benefits (rights to which do not vest) as well as pension benefits (rights to which can vest). The Ninth Circuit's holding that section 510 bars interference only with vested rights "is contradicted by the [section's] plain language." ERISA defines a "plan" to include both employee welfare benefit plans and pension benefit plans, so use of the word "plan" in section 510 "all but forecloses the argument that the section's protections extend only to "vested" rights.

9-0. Opinion for unanimous Court by O'Connor.

Johnson v. Fankell 117 S. Ct. 1800, 65 USLW 4438 (6-9-97)

42 U.S.C. § 1983, qualified immunity, interlocutory appeals: A defendant in an action brought in state court under 42 U.S.C. § 1983 does not have a federal right to an interlocutory appeal from a denial of qualified immunity. In this case Idaho courts, relying on an Idaho appellate rule, determined that the defendant was not entitled to an interlocutory appeal. Idaho law, not federal law, governs procedure in Idaho courts. Idaho need not apply the same definition of the term "final decision" that governs qualified immunity claims in federal court; that definition derives from interpretation of 28 U.S.C. § 1291, which is applicable only in federal courts. The Idaho appellate rule is not preempted by 42 U.S.C. § 1983. The normal presumption against preemption is buttressed by the fact that the governing Idaho rule is a neutral one that does not target immunity claims or civil rights actions for adverse treatment. As applied in this case, involving a claim of immunity by a state official, the rule balances competing state interests more than it interferes with a federal interest. Implementation of the rule is not "outcome determinative," since it does not affect the "ultimate disposition" of the case. 42 U.S.C. § 1983 "presumably" confers a right to have a qualified immunity claim considered by the trial court, but does not confer the asserted right to prevail in advance of trial.

9-0. Opinion for unanimous Court by Stevens.

Johnson v. United States 117 S. Ct. 1544, 65 USLW 4305 (5-12-97)

Criminal procedure: Under Federal Rule of Criminal Procedure 52(b), an appellate court can correct an error not raised at trial if the error is "plain," and if it affects "substantial rights." The Court ruled in *United States v. Olano* (1993), however, that this discretion should be exercised only if the error "substantially affects the fairness, integrity, or public reputation of judicial proceedings." Plain error was committed in this case, involving a perjury prosection under 18 U.S.C. § 1623, because the judge rather than jury determined the materiality of a false statement made to a grand jury. The *Olano* test was not met, however, since evidence supporting materiality was "overwhelming."

9-0. Opinion of Court by Rehnquist, joined by Stevens, O'Connor, Kennedy, Souter, Thomas, Ginsburg, and Breyer, and joined in part by Scalia.

Kansas v. Hendricks 65 USLW 4564 (6-23-97)

Sexual predator law, due process, double jeopardy: Kansas' Sexually Violent Predator Act, which provides for civil commitment of persons who have been convicted or charged with a sexually violent offense, and who, due to a "mental abnormality" or "personality disorder," are likely to engage in "predatory acts of sexual violence," does not offend the substantive requirements of the Due Process Clause. The required finding of future dangerousness, coupled with a finding of mental abnormality indicating volitional impairment, satisfies due process. The Constitution's double jeopardy and ex post facto prohibitions are not implicated because confinement under the Act does not constitute punishment. A legislature's intent to establish civil rather than criminal proceedings can be overcome only by "the clearest proof," and that proof is lacking. The Act's purpose is neither retribution nor deterrence. Confinement of mentally unstable persons who present a danger to the public is not punitive. The fact that the Act provides for various procedural safeguards normally associated with criminal trials does not make the proceedings criminal in nature. The validity of the respondent's confinement does not depend on the availability of treatment; persons who pose a danger to others may be confined even if no treatment is available to them. The Act, however, does make some provision for treatment, and the fact that treatment is "at least an ancillary goal of the Act . . . easily satisfies any test for determining that the Act is not punitive."

5-4. Opinion of Court by Thomas, joined by Rehnquist, O'Connor, Scalia, and Kennedy. Concurring opinion by Kennedy. Dissenting opinion by Breyer, joined by Stevens and Souter, and joined in part by Ginsburg.

Klehr v. A. O. Smith Corp. 65 USLW 4514 (6-19-97)

RICO, limitations period: The Third Circuit's "last predicate act" rule, under which the limitations period for civil RICO actions begins to run from the time when the plaintiff knew or should have known of the last injury or the last predicate act that is part of the same pattern of racketeering activity, is not a proper interpretation of the law. This rule creates a limitations period longer than Congress could have contemplated, and would allow plaintiffs to "sleep on their rights" as the racketeering continues and damages accumulate. Moreover, civil RICO was patterned after the Clayton Act, and the last predicate act rule is inconsistent with the accrual rule that governs Clayton Act cases. There is no need to decide which of the divergent limitations rules does apply to civil RICO cases, however, since the last predicate act rule is the only one that could benefit the plaintiffs in this case. The doctrine of "fraudulent concealment," which tolls the statute of limitations when the defendant takes affirmative steps to conceal his unlawful activity, applies only if the plaintiff is "reasonably diligent" in discovering his cause of action.

9-0. Opinion of Court by Breyer, joined by Rehnquist, Stevens, O'Connor, Kennedy, Souter and Ginsburg. Concurring opinion by Scalia, joined by Thomas.

Lambert v. Wicklund 117 S. Ct. 1169, 65 USLW 3662 (3-31-97)

Abortion, parental notification, judicial bypass: The Ninth Circuit appeals court erred in holding invalid Montana's parental notification of abortion law. The law prohibits a physician from performing an abortion on an unemancipated minor unless the physician has notified one of the minor's parents, but allows a judicial bypass exception if a youth court finds that notification "is not in the best interests of the [minor]." The case is controlled by *Ohio v. Akron Center (Akron II)* (1990), in which the Court upheld a parental notification statute "indistinguishable in any relevant way from the Montana statute at issue here." In *Akron II* the Court determined that the "not in the best interests of the minor" criterion for judicial bypass of parental notification satisfied an earlier standard that authorized judicial bypass of a parental consent requirement upon a finding that an abortion would be in the best interests of the minor.

9-0. *Per curiam.* Concurring opinion by Stevens, joined by Ginsburg and Breyer.

Lambrix v. Singletary 117 S. Ct. 1517, 65 USLW 4322 (5-12-97)

Habeas corpus, new rule limitation: A state prisoner whose conviction became final before the Court's decision in *Espinosa v. Florida* (1992), is foreclosed from relying on that decision in a federal habeas corpus proceeding because *Espinosa* announced a "new rule" within the meaning of *Teague v. Lane* (1989). A "new rule" is a rule not "dictated by precedent" existing at the time the petitioner's conviction became final. *Espinosa* held that, if a state requires the decisionmaker in a capital trial to weigh aggravating and mitigating factors, and also requires the judge to give deference to the jury's advisory recommendation, neither the judge nor jury is constitutionally permitted to weigh an invalid aggravating factor. There are several reasons for concluding that *Espinosa* was not dictated by existing precedent. First, the decision did not purport to rely on existing precedent. Also, a reasonable jurist considering the issue in 1986, when the petitioner's conviction became final, might have concluded either that Florida had sufficient means for cabining the trial court's discretion, that the trial court and not the jury was the actual sentencer in Florida, or that the trial court's weighing of properly narrowed aggravating and mitigating circumstances was sufficiently independent of the jury to cure any error in the jury's consideration of any invalid aggravating circumstances.

5-4. Opinion of Court by Scalia, joined by Rehnquist, Kennedy, Souter, and Thomas. Dissenting opinions by Stevens, joined by Ginsburg and Breyer; and by O'Connor.

Lawyer v. Department of Justice 65 USLW 4629 (6-25-97)

State legislative redistricting, court-approved settlement: A federal district court did not err in approving a settlement agreement imposing new districts for election of members of the Florida Senate and House without first holding unconstitutional the existing plan. The existing plan had been imposed by the State Supreme Court after the Legislature had declined its invitation to meet Justice Department objections based on the Voting Rights Act. It is well established that, before a federal court declares a state redistricting plan unconstitutional, it should afford the legislature a "reasonable opportunity" to revise its plan to meet constitutional requirements. In this case the State was afforded an opportunity and availed itself of its opportunity; the State, represented in the settlement by its attorney general, was a party to the agreement, and each legislative chamber was also represented. The settlement is not invalid because one party, the appellant in this case, did not agree to it. The appellant had his views considered in the district court, was granted part of the relief he sought (elimination of the earlier plan), and may still litigate the constitutionality of the settlement plan. The settlement plan did not subordinate traditional districting principles to race in creating Senate District 21.

5-4. Opinion of Court by Souter, joined by Rehnquist, Stevens, Ginsburg, and Breyer. Dissenting opinion by Scalia, joined by O'Connor, Kennedy, and Thomas.

Lindh v. Murphy 65 USLW 4557 (6-23-97)

Retroactivity, Antiterrorism and Effective Death Penalty Act: Amendments made by the Antiterrorism and Effective Death Penalty Act (the Act) to the general habeas corpus provisions of chapter 153 of Title 28 do not apply to cases that were pending on the date of enactment. There is a negative inference from the fact that section 107(c) of the Act provided that amendments to chapter 154, which governs habeas corpus actions in capital cases, "shall apply to cases pending on or after the date of enactment of this Act." The implication is that the amendments to chapter 153 were not intended to apply to pending cases. Negative implications "are strongest when portions of a statute treated differently [are] joined together and . . . considered simultaneously." That was the case here, since section 107(c) was added to the bill only after the amendments to chapters 153 and 154 had been joined together and introduced as a single bill. A competing explanation for the significance of section 107(c) -- that it was an indirect fix for an alleged minor ambiguity -- is not plausible.

5-4. Opinion of Court by Souter, joined by Stevens, O'Connor, Ginsburg, and Breyer. Dissenting opinion by Rehnquist, joined by Scalia, Kennedy, and Thomas.

Lopez v. Monterey County 117 S. Ct. 340, 65 USLW 4003 (11-6-96)

Voting Rights Act, § 5 preclearance: A three-judge federal district court in California lacked authority to order that the county's judicial elections be conducted under an at-large districting plan essentially identical to one that, four years earlier, had been challenged as not having been precleared under section 5 of the Voting Rights Act. The original at-large districting had replaced a system under which judges had been elected from single-judge districts. Section 5 requires that covered jurisdictions obtain preclearance of proposed election law changes by one of two means: submission of the changes to the Attorney General or to the U.S. District Court for the District of Columbia. Other federal district courts lack authority to rule on the discriminatory effect of proposed changes subject to preclearance, and may determine only whether the contested changes are subject to section 5 preclearance, whether preclearance has been obtained, and, if not, what temporary remedy is appropriate. Here, the three-judge court "interposed itself into the §5 approval process in a way that the statute does not contemplate."

9-0. Opinion for unanimous Court by O'Connor.

Lynce v. Mathis 117 S. Ct. 891, 65 USLW 4131 (2-19-97)

Ex Post Facto Clause: A Florida statute canceling early release credits awarded to prisoners as a result of prison overcrowding violates the Ex Post Facto Clause, Art. I, § 10, cl. 1, as applied to a prisoner who had already been awarded the credits and released from custody. The cancellation of early release credits met the two-part test for an ex post facto law: it was "clearly retrospective" and it disadvantaged the petitioner by lengthening his period of incarceration. The tests are objective; the motivation of the legislature in avoiding overcrowding rather than rewarding prisoners for good behavior is irrelevant. The overcrowding statute was in effect at the time of petitioner's offense, and slight modifications in subsequent years do not affect the core of petitioner's ex post facto claim, although they may affect calculation of credits to which he was entitled.

9-0. Opinion of Court by Stevens, joined by Rehnquist, O'Connor, Kennedy, Souter, Ginsburg, and Breyer. Concurring opinion by Thomas, joined by Scalia.

M. L. B. v. S. L. J. 117 S. Ct. 555, 65 USLW 4035 (12-16-96)

Appeals, poverty, parental rights termination: Mississippi may not, consistent with the Equal Protection and Due Process Clauses of the Fourteenth Amendment, condition appeals from trial court decrees terminating parental rights on the affected parent's ability to pay for preparation of a transcript. As a general matter, fee requirements are upheld if rational. Beginning with *Griffin v. Illinois* (1956), however, exceptions have been recognized. Neither the right of access to judicial processes in criminal cases nor the right to participate in political processes as candidates and voters may be limited to those who can pay. Decrees terminating parental rights belong in this same "category of cases in which the State may not bolt the door to equal justice." Parents have a fundamental interest in their relationship with their children, and the Court closely scrutinizes state intrusions on family relationships. The state's countervailing interest in recouping court costs is, in this instance, outweighed. While government need not, as a general matter, provide funds so that people may exercise every right that is fundamental, the scales are tipped when a person is trying to defend against a "devastatingly adverse action" by government.

6-3. Opinion of Court by Ginsburg, joined by Stevens, O'Connor, Souter, and Breyer. Concurring opinion by Kennedy. Dissenting opinions by Rehnquist; and by Thomas, joined by Scalia and joined in part by Rehnquist.

Maryland v. Wilson 117 S. Ct. 882, 65 USLW 4124 (2-19-97)

Fourth Amendment, traffic stop, passengers: Police officers who have lawfully stopped a car may order passengers to get out of the car pending completion of the stop. The rule announced in *Pennsylvania v. Mimms* (1977), allowing officers to order a driver of a lawfully stopped car to exit his vehicle, extends to passengers as well. "[T]he same weighty interest in officer safety is present regardless of whether the occupant of the stopped car is a driver or passenger." On the other hand, there is not the same basis for ordering a passenger out of a car as there is for ordering the driver out, since a stop is ordinarily premised on probable cause to believe that the driver has committed an offense. Nevertheless, as a practical matter, the passengers are already stopped, and "the additional intrusion on the passenger is minimal."

7-2. Opinion of Court by Rehnquist, joined by O'Connor, Scalia, Souter, Thomas, Ginsburg, and Breyer. Dissenting opinions by Stevens, joined by Kennedy; and by Kennedy.

Mazurek v. Armstrong 65 USLW 3822 (6-16-97)

Abortion, state law, preliminary injunction: The Court of Appeals for the Ninth Circuit erred in vacating a district court's refusal to grant a preliminary injunction against enforcement of Montana's 1995 statute restricting the performance of abortions to licensed physicians. The district court applied the correct standard in ruling that there was insufficient evidence to establish that the Montana law would create "a substantial obstacle to a woman seeking an abortion." On the other hand, the appeals court lacked evidence supporting its conclusion that the law was enacted for the purpose of imposing substantial obstacles on abortions. The Ninth Circuit's decision is contradicted by "repeated statements in past cases" to the effect that states may restrict performance of abortions to physicians.

6-3. *Per curiam*. Dissenting opinion by Stevens, joined by Ginsburg and Breyer.

McMillian v. Monroe County 117 S. Ct. 1734, 65 USLW 4403 (6-2-97)

42 U.S.C. § 1983, municipal liability: Sheriffs in Alabama, when exercising policymaking authority in a law enforcement capacity, represent the State and not the county. Alabama counties, therefore, are not liable under 42 U.S.C. § 1983 for actions of sheriffs that constitute "policy." Under the Alabama Constitution a sheriff is an officer of the executive department, impeachable by the State Supreme Court. Tort claims brought against sheriffs based on their official acts have been held to constitute suits against the State, not suits against the sheriff's county. Moreover, sheriffs, subject to supervision by the governor and attorney general, are given authority to enforce state criminal law in their counties, and the counties themselves have no powers in the area of law enforcement. While Alabama sheriffs are elected locally, are limited in jurisdiction to county borders, and are paid and supplied by the counties, these facts do not convert sheriffs into policymakers for the county.

5-4. Opinion of Court by Rehnquist, joined by O'Connor, Scalia, Kennedy, and Thomas. Dissenting opinion by Ginsburg, joined by Stevens, Souter, and Breyer.

Metro-North Commuter R.R. v. Buckley 65 USLW 4586 (6-23-97)

FELA, recovery for emotional distress: A railroad worker negligently exposed to a carcinogen but without symptoms of any disease may not recover for emotional distress under the Federal Employers' Liability Act. In *Consolidated Rail Corp. v. Gottshall* (1994), the Court ruled that plaintiffs who sustain a negligently inflicted "physical impact" may recover for emotional distress. Not every form of physical contact constitutes such "physical impact," however. Simple physical exposure to asbestos-laden insulation dust that might cause disease at a substantially later time does not satisfy this requirement of "physical impact." General policy concerns underlying common law precedent counsel against recovery when no symptoms of disease are present. Separating meritorious from trivial claims of emotional distress is generally difficult. Moreover, exposure to carcinogens is common, the risk of dying from cancer is relatively high to begin with, and measuring emotional reaction to an increased risk is all the more difficult. Respondent in this case is not entitled to recover costs for extra medical check-ups to monitor his condition for onset of asbestos-related disease.

9-0 (emotional distress); **7-2** (medical monitoring). Opinion of Court by Breyer, joined by Rehnquist, O'Connor, Scalia, Kennedy, Souter, and Thomas. Opinion by Ginsburg, joined by Stevens, concurring in part and dissenting in part.

Metropolitan Stevedore Co. v. Rambo 65 USLW 4498 (6-19-97)

Longshore and Harbor Workers' Compensation Act: The LHWCA allows nominal compensation to a worker who presently earns as much as he had earned before his injury if there is a significant possibility that his wage-earning capacity will fall below his pre-injury wages sometime in the future. The Act ties benefits to a percentage of the difference between pre-injury wages and wage-earning capacity, and allows wage-earning capacity to be set at a "reasonable" level if "actual earnings do not fairly and reasonably represent . . . wage-earning capacity." This provision, considered along with other provisions that require a prompt filing of a claim, that bar second applications more than a year after denial or termination of benefits, and that allow for modification of awards in response to changed conditions, favors a wait-and-see approach over a one-time calculation. Ordering nominal compensation holds open the possibility of a modified award if and when circumstances change.

6-3. Opinion of Court by Souter, joined by Rehnquist, Stevens, Kennedy, Ginsburg, and Breyer. Dissenting opinion by O'Connor, joined by Scalia and Thomas.

O'Dell v. Netherland 65 USLW 4506 (6-19-97)

Habeas corpus, new rule limitation: The rule set forth in *Simmons v. South Carolina* (1994) -- that a capital defendant must be permitted to inform his sentencing jury that he is ineligible for parole if the prosecution argues that the defendant should receive the death penalty rather than life imprisonment because of his alleged future dangerousness to society -- was a "new rule" that cannot be used to "disturb" a death sentence that had become final before *Simmons* was decided. A state court considering the issue when the petitioner's sentence became final would not have felt compelled by existing precedent to conclude that the *Simmons* rule was required by the Constitution. Both *Skipper v. South Carolina* (1986), which had cited the Due Process Clause as well as the Eighth Amendment in concluding that a defendant, after the prosecution had relied on a prediction of future dangerousness in seeking the death penalty, could not be sentenced to death "on the basis of information which he had no opportunity to deny or explain," and *Gardner v. Florida* (1977), which had overturned a death sentence based in part on a presentence report not made available to the defendant, involved evidence of the defendant's past behavior rather than information about "the extant legal regime." Also, *Simmons* was not a "watershed" decision falling within an exception to the "new rule" limitation on habeas corpus relief.

5-4. Opinion of Court by Thomas, joined by Rehnquist, O'Connor, Scalia, and Kennedy. Dissenting opinion by Stevens, joined by Souter, Ginsburg, and Breyer.

O'Gilvie v. United States 117 S. Ct. 452, 65 USLW 4026 (12-10-96)

Taxation, Federal, damages excludable from gross income: In a tort action for personal injuries, punitive damages are not excludable from gross income under former language of 26 U.S.C. § 104(a)(2), which provided an exclusion for the "amount of any damages received . . . on account of personal injuries or sickness." The phrase "on account of" is better read as meaning "by reason of" rather than "but for." While compensatory damages are awarded "by reason of" personal injuries, punitive damages, which are levied to punish reprehensible conduct, are not. The Court's 1995 decision in *Commissioner v. Schleier*, holding that liquidated damages received in settlement of an age discrimination claim are not excludable, lends support for this interpretation. Further support can be found in the history of the statutory provision, which traces to tax rulings based on the principle that restoration of capital is not income. Also, there is "no very good answer" to the question why Congress might have wanted to exclude punitive damages from income.

6-3. Opinion of Court by Breyer, joined by Rehnquist, Stevens, Kennedy, Souter, and Ginsburg. Dissenting opinion by Scalia, joined by O'Connor and Thomas.

Ohio v. Robinette 117 S. Ct. 417, 65 USLW 4013 (11-18-96)

Fourth Amendment, traffic stop, consent to search auto: The Fourth Amendment does not require that police officers must always inform detainees that they are free to go before a consent to search may be deemed voluntary. The Ohio Supreme Court erred, therefore, in ruling that a search was invalid because an officer, following issuance of a warning to a motorist for a traffic offense, and without clearly informing the motorist that he was legally free to go, proceeded to ask the motorist for permission to search his car. The touchstone of the Fourth Amendment is reasonableness, and the Court has consistently eschewed bright-line rules in emphasizing the fact-specific nature of the reasonableness inquiry. Similarly, the voluntariness of consent to search is a question of fact to be determined from all of the circumstances. Under principles announced in *Michigan v. Long* (1983), the U.S. Supreme Court had jurisdiction to review this case. Although the Ohio Supreme Court purported to rest its decision on the Ohio Constitution as well as the Fourth Amendment, the adequacy and independence of the state law ground was not clear from the face of the opinion.

8-1. Opinion of Court by Rehnquist, joined by O'Connor, Scalia, Kennedy, Souter, Thomas, and Breyer. Concurring opinion by Ginsburg. Dissenting opinion by Stevens.

Old Chief v. United States 117 S. Ct. 644, 65 USLW 4049 (1-7-97)

Evidence, unfair prejudice, nature of prior felony: The district court abused its discretion under Rule 403, Federal Rules of Evidence, in ruling that the United States Attorney, in a prosecution for possession of a firearm by someone with a prior felony conviction, need not agree to the defendant's stipulation that he had a prior felony conviction. Rule 403 authorizes exclusion of relevant evidence when its probative value is outweighed by the danger of unfair prejudice. Under the circumstances of this case, the prosecution's introduction of the name and nature of the prior offense -- assault causing serious bodily injury -- would create the risk of "unfair prejudice" within the meaning of Rule 403. A jury might well believe that the circumstances of the earlier felony evidence a propensity to commit the crime at issue. On the other hand, the probative value of the offered stipulation conceding a prior felony conviction is fully equal to the probative value of the government's evidence when the point at issue is merely the defendant's legal status. "For purposes of Rule 403 . . . , the functions of the competing evidence are distinguishable only by the risk inherent in the one and wholly absent from the other."

5-4. Opinion of Court by Souter, joined by Stevens, Kennedy, Ginsburg, and Breyer. Dissenting opinion by O'Connor, joined by Rehnquist, Scalia, and Thomas.

Printz v. United States 65 USLW 4731 (6-27-97)

Congressional power, Brady Act: Interim provisions of the Brady Handgun Violence Prevention Act that require state and local law enforcement officers to conduct background checks on prospective handgun purchasers and to perform certain related tasks are unconstitutional. No constitutional text speaks directly to the issue, so it is resolved by reference to historical understanding and practice, to the structure of the Constitution, and to the jurisprudence of the Court. Early congressional enactments reveal an understanding that state judges could be required to enforce federal law, but there was an "utter lack of statutes imposing obligations on the States' executive." Enactments in the past few decades imposing obligations on state and local officials are too recent to be "probative . . . of a constitutional tradition that lends meaning to text." The structure of the Constitution creates a "dual sovereignty" under which federal and state governments exercise concurrent authority directly over the people; the Framers rejected the Articles of Confederation structure under which the central government operated on and through the states. The Brady Act also is inconsistent with separation of powers principles that recognize "unity in the Federal Executive," since the Act "transfers the President's responsibility to thousands of [law enforcement officers] in the 50 States." The Brady Act is not authorized by the Necessary and Proper Clause; a law that "violates the principle of state sovereignty" is not a "proper" means of effectuating the commerce power. Nor does Supreme Court precedent support the Brady Act. The Court has upheld laws that allowed states to avoid preemption by complying with federal standards, but not laws mandating such compliance. In *New York v. United States* (1992), the Court ruled that Congress cannot compel states to enact or enforce a federal regulatory program, and "Congress cannot circumvent that prohibition by conscripting the State's officers directly."

5-4. Opinion of Court by Scalia, joined by Rehnquist, O'Connor, Kennedy, and Thomas. Concurring opinions by O'Connor and Thomas. Dissenting opinions by Stevens, joined by Souter, Ginsburg, and Breyer; by Souter; and by Breyer, joined by Stevens.

Raines v. Byrd 65 USLW 4705 (6-26-97)

Standing to sue, Line Item Veto Act: Members of Congress who voted against the Line Item Veto Act lack standing to challenge the Act's constitutionality. The standing requirement, derived from Article III's "case" or "controversy" limitation on exercise of judicial power, requires that plaintiffs establish a particularized personal injury. This the Members have failed to do. Their case is distinguishable from that of former Rep. Powell, who was held to have standing to challenge his exclusion from the House (*Powell v. McCormack* (1969)); they are suing solely because they are Members of Congress, not because they have been deprived of something to which they are personally entitled. Nor does their claim fall within the ambit of *Coleman v. Miller* (1939), upholding standing for members of a state legislature to challenge the tie-breaking vote of the Lieutenant Governor in approving a constitutional amendment. The votes of those state legislators were completely nullified; here the plaintiffs' votes were given full effect, and "they simply lost." The argument that the Line Item Veto Act operates to dilute a vote on an appropriation bill by giving the President a third option in addition to blanket approval or blanket disapproval "pulls *Coleman* too far from its moorings."

7-2. Opinion of Court by Rehnquist, joined by O'Connor, Scalia, Kennedy, Thomas, and Ginsburg. Concurring opinion by Souter, joined by Ginsburg. Dissenting opinions by Stevens and by Breyer.

Regents of University of California v. Doe 117 S. Ct. 900, 65 USLW 4129 (2-19-97)

Eleventh Amendment: The fact that the Federal Government has agreed to indemnify a state instrumentality against the costs of litigation, including adverse judgments, does not divest the state agency of its Eleventh Amendment immunity from suit in federal court. It is the state instrumentality's potential legal liability, not its ability or inability to require a third party to reimburse it, or to discharge the liability in the first instance, that is relevant for Eleventh Amendment purposes. Here, the issue involved breach of an employment contract for work at the Lawrence Livermore National Laboratory, operated by the University under contract with the Energy Department, which had assumed liability for employment-related judgments against the University.

9-0. Opinion for unanimous Court by Stevens.

Reno v. ACLU. 65 USLW 4715 (6-26-97)

First Amendment, Communications Decency Act: Two provisions of the Communications Decency Act of 1996 -- one that prohibits knowing transmission on the Internet of obscene or indecent messages to any recipient under 18 years of age, and the other that prohibits the knowing sending or displaying of patently offensive messages in a manner that is available to anyone under 18 years of age -- violate the First Amendment. Earlier decisions relied on by the Government are distinguishable. The CDA ban is far broader than a ban on sale of obscene material to minors, and an analogy to zoning of adult movie theaters is inappropriate because the CDA is a content-based regulation of speech that cannot properly be analyzed as a time, place, and manner regulation. Special justifications for regulation of broadcast media are not present in cyberspace; the *Sable* decision invalidating restrictions on indecent "dial-a-porn" messages is a closer analogy. The vagueness of the CDA "undermines the likelihood that [it] has been carefully tailored to the congressional goal of protecting children." The CDA suppresses a large amount of speech that adults have a constitutional right to receive, and the Government has not met its heavy burden of establishing that less restrictive alternatives are unavailable. The only way in which the CDA's severability clause can be employed is to sever the word "indecent" from the first prohibition noted above, leaving intact the prohibition on transmission of "obscene" messages.

7-2. Opinion of Court by Stevens, joined by Scalia, Kennedy, Souter, Thomas, Ginsburg, and Breyer. Opinion by O'Connor, joined by Rehnquist, concurring in part and dissenting in part.

Reno v. Bossier Parish School Bd. 117 S. Ct. 1491, 65 USLW 4308 (5-12-97)

Voting Rights Act, preclearance: Preclearance under section 5 of the Voting Rights Act may not be denied solely on the basis that the voting procedure at issue constitutes vote dilution in violation of section 2. The Attorney General's regulation authorizing denial of preclearance in order to prevent a violation of section 2 would contradict the Court's longstanding interpretation of the two sections, and is not entitled to deference. Section 5 and section 2 "combat different evils and . . . impose very different duties." Section 5 focuses on changes in voting plans, and prohibits implementation of new plans that would lead to retrogression in exercise of the franchise by racial minorities. The benchmark for section 5 is the existing plan. Section 2, on the other hand, prohibits maintenance of any plan that has the effect of diluting the voting strength of racial minorities. The benchmark for section 2 is any reasonable alternative that does not lead to vote dilution. To hold that preclearance can be denied on the basis of a section 2 violation would "shift the focus of § 5 from nonretrogression to vote dilution, and . . . change the § 5 benchmark from a jurisdiction's existing plan to a hypothetical, undiluted plan." Some section 2 evidence may be relevant, however, to establish a jurisdiction's intent to retrogress, and thereby to establish discriminatory "purpose" within the meaning of section 5.

7-2. Opinion of Court by O'Connor, joined by Rehnquist, Scalia, Kennedy, and Thomas, and joined in part by Breyer and Ginsburg. Concurring opinions by Thomas; and by Breyer, joined by Ginsburg. Opinion by Stevens, joined by Souter, dissenting in part and concurring in part.

Richards v. Wisconsin 117 S. Ct. 1416, 65 USLW 4283 (4-28-97)

Fourth Amendment, knock-and-announce rule: The Fourth Amendment does not permit a blanket exception to the knock-and-announce rule when police officers are executing a search warrant in a felony drug investigation. Instead, a case-by-case analysis is required to determine whether the circumstances present a threat of physical violence, or whether officers have reason to believe that evidence would likely be destroyed if advance notice is given. There are two "serious concerns" raised by a blanket exception. One is that of "overgeneralization": not every drug search will pose risks justifying no-knock entry. The other is the difficulty of distinguishing drug searches from other categories of searches that often involve danger to officers or possible destruction of evidence; blanket exceptions could swallow the knock-and-announce rule. In this case, however, the entry was permissible. The officers knocked, but did not announce themselves as police. The petitioner's reaction of slamming his door shut when he saw police confronting him justified immediate entry before evidence could be destroyed.

9-0. Opinion for unanimous Court by Stevens.

Richardson v. McKnight 65 USLW 4579 (6-23-97)

Immunity from suit, private prison guards: Employees of private prison management companies are not entitled to the qualified immunity that is extended to publicly employed state prison guards in suits brought under 42 U.S.C. § 1983. Entitlement of private defendants to immunity is decided on the basis of history and on the basis of the purposes that underlie government employee liability. There is no firmly rooted common law tradition of immunity applicable to privately employed prison guards. Private companies operated jails and prisons in this country in the 18th and 19th centuries, and the common law provided remedies for mistreatment of prisoners, but there is no evidence that these private concerns enjoyed any special immunity from suit. The purposes of providing immunity to government employees, which include ensuring that talented candidates are not deterred from government service and that the public is protected from unwarranted timidity on the part of government employees, do not carry over to privately employed prison guards. Marketplace pressures as well as privatization law, which requires liability insurance coverage and frees private firms from civil service laws, distinguish the private and public employment settings, and render immunity unnecessary in the former.

5-4. Opinion of Court by Breyer, joined by Stevens, O'Connor, Souter, and Ginsburg. Dissenting opinion by Scalia, joined by Rehnquist, Kennedy, and Thomas.

Robinson v. Shell Oil Co. 117 S. Ct. 843, 65 USLW 4103 (2-18-97)

Civil rights, Title VII, "employee": The term "employees" as used in section 704(a) of the Civil Rights Act of 1964, which makes it unlawful "for an employer to discriminate against any of his employees or applicants for employment," includes former employees. Consequently, a former employee may sue his former employer under Title VII for post-employment actions (here a negative reference) allegedly taken in retaliation for the employee's having filed a charge with the EEOC. Title VII's general definition of "employee" has no temporal qualifier, and it is plain that some sections of Title VII use the term "employees" to include former employees, and other sections use the term to refer only to current employees. The usage in section 704(a) is ambiguous, but the Act's broader context resolves this ambiguity. The Act provides remedies for discriminatory discharge, and such actions must necessarily be brought by former employees. Also, exclusion of former employees from protection would undermine the effectiveness of Title VII by allowing the threat of post-employment retaliation to deter discrimination victims from complaining to the EEOC.

9-0. Opinion for unanimous Court by Thomas.

Saratoga Fishing Co. v. J. M. Martinac & Co. 117 S. Ct. 1783, 65 USLW 4429 (6-2-97)

Admiralty, defective product: Under the Court's decision in *East River S.S. v. Transamerica Delaval* (1986), an admiralty plaintiff may not recover in tort for economic loss caused when a defective product damages only itself, but may recover for personal injuries and for damage caused to other property. Property added to the defective product, not by the plaintiff-purchaser himself, but by an earlier purchaser in the chain of ownership, constitutes "other property" for purposes of this *East River* rule. The premise of *East River* is that loss of value to a product that does not work properly implicates contract and warranty law, but that additional losses may be covered by tort law. Property added to the product by the initial user would constitute "other property" if damages occur before resale, and there is no reason to reduce a manufacturer's tort liability because of the "fortuity" of resale by the initial user. The subsequent user does not contract directly with the manufacturer, and a consumer/purchaser will have more difficulty than the manufacturer in offering an appropriate warranty.

6-3. Opinion of Court by Breyer, joined by Rehnquist, Stevens, Kennedy, Souter, and Ginsburg. Dissenting opinions by O'Connor; and by Scalia, joined by Thomas.

Schenck v. Pro-Choice Network 117 S. Ct. 855, 65 USLW 4109 (2-19-97)

First Amendment, abortion protest, injunctions: An injunction restricting demonstrations outside abortion clinics is consistent with the First Amendment insofar as it creates "fixed buffer zones" around clinic doorways, driveways, and driveway entrances, but violates the First Amendment insofar as it creates a "floating buffer zone" around people and vehicles entering and leaving the clinics. The governmental interests here -- ensuring public safety and order, promoting the free flow of traffic on streets and sidewalks, protecting property, and protecting a woman's freedom to seek pregnancy-related services -- are significant enough to justify an appropriately tailored injunction. The floating buffer zones, however, burden more speech than necessary to serve these governmental interests. The floating buffer zones prevent demonstrators from handing out leaflets or from communicating a message from a normal conversational distance, and are also difficult to interpret and comply with. The fixed buffer zones, on the other hand, are necessary to ensure that people and vehicles trying to enter or exit clinics can do so. The district court was entitled to conclude, based on the record of obstruction in this case before and after entry of a temporary restraining order, that the only way to ensure access was to remove protesters from driveways and doorways. Another aspect of the injunction, requiring that the two "sidewalk counselors" allowed inside the fixed buffer zones "cease and desist" their counseling on request of the target, is also permissible, given the history of harassment and intimidation in the case.

8-1 (floating buffer zones); **6-3** (fixed buffer zones). Opinion of Court by Rehnquist, joined in part by Stevens, O'Connor, Scalia, Kennedy, Souter, Thomas, and Ginsburg; and joined in separate part by Stevens, O'Connor, Souter, Ginsburg, and Breyer. Opinion by Scalia, joined by Kennedy and Thomas, concurring in part and dissenting in part. Opinion by Breyer concurring in part and dissenting in part.

Strate v. A-1 Contractors 117 S. Ct. 1404, 65 USLW 4298 (4-28-97)

Native Americans, tribal court jurisdiction: When a traffic accident occurs on a portion of a public highway maintained by the state under a federally granted right-of-way across an Indian reservation, tribal courts generally have no jurisdiction over a civil action against an allegedly negligent driver and the driver's employer, neither of whom is a member of the tribe. No statute or treaty confers such jurisdiction in this case, which involves a North Dakota highway that crosses land held in trust for the Three Affiliated Tribes. The controlling general principle, set forth in *Montana v. United States* (1981), is that the powers of a tribe do not extend to the activities of nonmembers. Neither of the exceptions to *Montana* is applicable. The case does not involve activities of nonmembers who have entered consensual relationships with the tribe or its members, and the underlying conduct does not threaten or directly affect the tribe's political integrity, economic security, or health and welfare.

9-0. Opinion for unanimous Court by Ginsburg.

Suitum v. Tahoe Regional Planning Agency 117 S. Ct. 1659, 65 USLW 4385 (5-27-97)

Taking of property, ripeness of compensation claim: The landowner's action for compensation for a regulatory taking of her property is ripe for adjudication even though she has not attempted to sell the transferable development rights (TDRs) she is entitled to receive as a result of the regulatory action. Classification of the land as a "stream environment zone" barred further development of the land, and constituted a "final decision" on use of the land sufficient to satisfy the prudential test for ripeness. Decision on a possible application by the landowner to transfer the TDRs to a particular buyer does not involve discretion about development of the land, and is not the type of "final decision" required to establish ripeness. Precedent governing "fitness for review" is not on point, and, in any event, would not bar review if applicable.

9-0. Opinion of Court by Souter, joined by Rehnquist, Stevens, Kennedy, Ginsburg, and Breyer. Concurring opinion by Scalia, joined by O'Connor and Thomas.

Timmons v. Twin Cities Area New Party 117 S. Ct. 1364, 65 USLW 4273 (4-28-97)

Elections, First Amendment, prohibition on "fusion" candidacies: Minnesota may constitutionally prohibit a candidate from appearing on the ballot as the candidate of more than one party. In considering First Amendment challenges to ballot access restrictions, the character and magnitude of the burden imposed by a state's rule must be weighed against the interests the state seeks to protect. Regulations imposing "severe" burdens must be narrowly tailored and advance a compelling state interest. Lesser burdens, however, trigger less exacting review. The burdens imposed by Minnesota's prohibitions on a political party's associational rights are not "severe." The ban on "fusion" candidacies does not prohibit a political party from trying to persuade a candidate to be its nominee rather than the nominee of a different party, and a party remains free to communicate by means other than ballot identification its endorsement of another party's candidate. The State's interests in ballot integrity and political stability are "sufficiently weighty" to justify the limitations.

6-3. Opinion of Court by Rehnquist, joined by O'Connor, Scalia, Kennedy, Thomas, and Breyer. Dissenting opinions by Stevens, joined by Ginsburg and joined in part by Souter; and by Souter.

Turner Broadcasting System v. FCC 117 S. Ct. 1174, 65 USLW 4209 (3-31-97)

Cable TV, "must-carry" rules, First Amendment: Sections 4 and 5 of the Cable Television Consumer Protection and Competition Act of 1992, which require cable systems to carry local broadcast television stations, are consistent with the First Amendment. Following remand from an earlier decision in the case, in which the Supreme Court identified the appropriate standard for reviewing content-neutral regulations, the district court found that the record supports Congress' predictive judgment that the must-carry provisions further important governmental interests, and that the provisions are narrowly tailored to further those interests. The district court's judgment is affirmed. The government's interests in preserving the benefits of free, over-the-air broadcast television for the 40% of American households without cable, and in promoting the widespread dissemination of information from a multiplicity of sources, are both important, and the must-carry rules promote those interests without burdening substantially more speech than necessary. The actual burdens on cable broadcasters are "modest," the evidence indicating that cable operators nationwide carry 99.8% of the programming they carried before imposition of must-carry, and that broadcast stations gained access on 5,880 cable channels as a result of must-carry. The Court will not "displace Congress' judgment respecting content-neutral regulations with [its] own, so long as [Congress'] policy is grounded on reasonable factual findings supported by evidence that is substantial."

5-4. Opinion of Court by Kennedy, joined by Rehnquist, Stevens, and Souter, and joined in part by Breyer. Concurring opinions by Stevens and by Breyer. Dissenting opinion by O'Connor, joined by Scalia, Thomas, and Ginsburg.

United States v. Alaska 65 USLW 4457 (6-19-97)

Submerged Lands Act; Alaska Statehood Act: Alaska's various exceptions to the report of a Special Master recommending resolution of a dispute between the United States and Alaska over ownership of submerged lands along Alaska's Arctic coast are overruled. The baseline for calculation of the State's three-mile belt of submerged lands is the normal baseline for purposes of the Convention on the Territorial Sea and the Contiguous Zone, and barrier islands have their own three-mile belts. Enclaves in Stefansson Sound formed because barrier islands are more than six miles offshore or more than six miles apart remain in federal ownership, since at the time of Alaska statehood the United States did not have a well-established rule treating waters between the mainland and fringing islands as inland waters. The Master also did not err in concluding that a gravel and ice formation in the Flaxman Island chain, known as Dinkum Sands, is not an island constituting part of Alaska's coastline. At statehood, the United States retained ownership of submerged lands beneath certain coastal features within the boundaries of the National Petroleum Reserve. Congress has power to reserve submerged lands under federal control for an appropriate public purpose. The Executive Order creating the Reserve in 1923 reflected a clear intent to include submerged lands within the Reserve, and section 11(b) of the Alaska Statehood Act reflected Congress' intent to ratify that inclusion of submerged lands and defeat the State's title to those lands. Finally, the United States' exception to the Master's ruling that submerged lands within the Arctic National Wildlife Refuge passed to Alaska at statehood is sustained. The disputed lands were included in an application for creation of an Arctic Wildlife Range that was pending at the time of statehood; a regulation then in effect operated to "segregate" such lands; and section 6(e) of the Statehood Act excepted from transfer to Alaska "lands withdrawn or otherwise set apart as refuges or reservations for the protection of wildlife."

9-0 (Stefansson Sound and Dinkum Sands); **6-3** (petroleum reserve and wildlife refuge). Opinion of Court by O'Connor,. joined by Stevens, Kennedy, Souter, Ginsburg, and Breyer, and joined in part by Rehnquist, Scalia, and Thomas. Opinion by Thomas, joined by Rehnquist and Scalia, concurring in part and dissenting in part.

United States v. Brockamp 117 S. Ct. 849, 65 USLW 4106 (2-18-97)

Taxation, Federal, equitable tolling, refund claim: Courts may not toll, for nonstatutory equitable reasons, the time limitations for filing tax refund claims set forth in § 6511 of the Internal Revenue Code. Even assuming that the appropriate test for tax cases is that set forth in a 1990 civil rights case, application of the test leads to the conclusion that there is "good reason to believe that Congress did not want the equitable tolling doctrine to apply." The limitations set forth in section 6511 are unusually technical and detailed, and are reiterated several times. Explicit exceptions to the time limits do not include equitable tolling. Moreover, to read equitable tolling into the provision could create "serious administrative problems" for the IRS and might undermine the tax collection process.

9-0. Opinion for unanimous Court by Breyer.

United States v. Gonzales 117 S. Ct. 1032, 65 USLW 4157 (3-3-97)

Sentencing, statutory construction: A federal court may not direct that a prison sentence under 18 U.S.C. § 924(c) run concurrently with a state-imposed sentence. Section 924(c) imposes an additional sentence of five years' imprisonment on anyone who uses a firearm in the commission of a drug trafficking offense, and provides that such punishment shall not "run concurrently with any other term of imprisonment including that imposed for the . . . drug trafficking crime for which the firearm was used . . . ." The unqualified phrase "any other term of imprisonment" means what it says, and therefore refers to all terms of imprisonment, including those imposed by state courts. Given the straightforward statutory language, there is no reason to resort to legislative history. A committee report statement that the § 924(c) sentence should be served prior to the start of the sentence for the underlying offense is "in no way anchored to the text of the statute," and should be disregarded. Section 924(c) does not conflict with 18 U.S.C. § 3584, which grants courts general discretion to determine whether federal sentences are to run concurrently or consecutively.

7-2. Opinion of Court by O'Connor, joined by Rehnquist, Scalia, Kennedy, Souter, Thomas, and Ginsburg. Dissenting opinions by Stevens, joined by Breyer; and by Breyer, joined by Stevens.

United States v. Hyde 117 S. Ct. 1630, 65 USLW 4369 (5-27-97)

Criminal procedure, guilty plea withdrawal: A defendant who attempts to withdraw a guilty plea between the time the district court accepted that plea and the time the court determines whether to accept or reject a plea agreement may withdraw that guilty plea only by establishing a "fair and just reason" as required by Federal Rule of Criminal Procedure 32(e). While plea agreements and guilty pleas are linked in some ways, acceptance of a guilty plea and acceptance of a plea agreement can be separated in time. Rule 11 sets the prerequisites for the court's acceptance of a plea, and prior acceptance of a plea agreement is not among them. Moreover, Rule 11 provides that, if the court rejects the plea agreement, the defendant may "then" withdraw his guilty plea. The necessary implication, if the court has not rejected the plea agreement, is that the defendant may not "then" withdraw his plea without satisfying Rule 32(e)'s requirement of a "fair and just reason."

9-0. Opinion for unanimous Court by Rehnquist.

United States v. LaBonte 117 S. Ct. 1673, 65 USLW 4392 (5-27-97)

Sentencing, guidelines; Statutes, plain meaning: The requirement of 28 U.S.C. § 994(h) that the Sentencing Commission assure that Sentencing Guidelines specify a sentence for categories of repeat offenders "at or near the maximum term authorized" means the maximum term available, including any applicable statutory sentencing enhancements. The Commission's interpretation precluding consideration of sentencing enhancements "is inconsistent with § 994(h)'s plain language," and must give way. The word "categories" does not refer to one broad category of repeat offenders, but rather contemplates two distinct categories -- those who have received the requisite notice that the U.S. Attorney intends to rely on previous convictions to seek an enhanced sentence, and those who have not received such notice and who therefore are not subject to enhanced sentences. To read the reference as eliminating this distinction "would largely eviscerate" the statutory penalty enhancements that Congress has enacted.

6-3. Opinion of Court by Thomas, joined by Rehnquist, O'Connor, Scalia, Kennedy, and Souter. Dissenting opinion by Breyer, joined by Stevens and Ginsburg.

United States v. Lanier 117 S. Ct. 1219, 65 USLW 4232 (3-31-97)

Due Process, notice of criminal conduct: The Sixth Circuit appeals court erred in ruling that criminal liability may be imposed under 18 U.S.C. § 242 for deprivation of a constitutional right under color of state law only if the constitutional right said to have been violated is first identified in a Supreme Court decision, and only if the right has been held to apply in a factual situation fundamentally similar to the one at issue. Rather, the right must have been "made specific," either by the express terms of the statute or by decisions interpreting those terms. There is no categorical rule that the interpreting decisions must be Supreme Court decisions, or that precedent must trace to a "fundamentally similar" factual situation. What is required under section 242 is "reasonable warning that the conduct at issue violated constitutional rights"; reasonable warning exists if "unlawfulness . . . is apparent" under the circumstances. The case is remanded for consideration of whether prior judicial decisions gave fair warning that respondent's actions violated a due process right to be free from willful sexual assault.

9-0. Opinion for unanimous Court by Souter.

United States v. O'Hagan 65 USLW 4650 (6-25-97)

Securities, insider trading: An attorney who worked for a law firm representing the bidder in a tender offer and who relied on confidential information to purchase securities issued by the target company was properly held liable for securities violations. Criminal liability under section 10(b) of the Securities Exchange Act of 1934 may be predicated on the misappropriation theory, which prohibits trading on the basis of nonpublic information by a corporate outsider in breach of a duty owed not to a trading party, but to the source of the information. This theory satisfies section 10(b)'s two basic requirements: that the charged conduct involves a "deceptive device or contrivance," and that the device or contrivance be used "in connection with" the purchase or sale of securities. Further, the Securities and Exchange Commission did not exceed its rulemaking authority under § 14(e) when it adopted Rule 14e-3(a) without requiring a showing that the trading at issue entailed a breach of fiduciary duty. Section 14(e) prohibits fraudulent acts in connection with a tender offer, and authorizes the SEC to "define, and prescribe means reasonably designed to prevent, such acts"; the Rule requires that persons who trade on the basis of nonpublic information abstain or disclose, without regard to whether the trader owes a preexisting fiduciary duty to respect the confidentiality of the information. The Rule qualifies under § 14(e) as a "means reasonably designed to prevent fraudulent trading." The Rule is neither arbitrary, capricious, nor manifestly contrary to the statute, so the SEC's interpretation must be accorded deference in accordance with *Chevron U.S.A. v. NRDC* (1984). Resolution of the securities issues compels reversal of the Appeals Court's ruling overturning the lawyer's conviction for mail fraud.

6-3 (§10(b)); **7-2** (§ 14(e)); **9-0** (mail fraud). Opinion of Court by Ginsburg, joined by Stevens, O'Connor, Kennedy, Souter, and Breyer, and joined in part by Scalia. Opinion by Scalia, concurring in part and dissenting in part. Opinion by Thomas, joined by Rehnquist, concurring in part and dissenting in part.

United States v. Watts 117 S. Ct. 633, 65 USLW 3461 (1-6-97)

Sentence enhancement, consideration of acquitted conduct: A jury's verdict of acquittal does not prevent a court sentencing for a different crime from considering conduct underlying the acquitted charge, so long as that conduct has been proved by a preponderance of the evidence. An acquittal does not necessarily mean that a jury has rejected certain facts, and it "does not prove that a defendant is innocent; it merely proves the existence of a reasonable doubt as to his guilt." It follows that the Government may relitigate a factual issue in a subsequent action governed by a lower standard of proof. 18 U.S.C. § 3661 codifies the longstanding principle that "no limitation shall be placed on the information concerning the [defendant's] background, character, and conduct" that a sentencing court may consider. The Sentencing Guidelines did not narrow this aspect of a sentencing court's discretion, but instead reiterate the principle.

7-2. *Per curiam*. Concurring opinions by Scalia and Breyer. Dissenting opinions by Stevens and Kennedy.

United States v. Wells 117 S. Ct. 921, 65 USLW 4146 (2-26-97)

Criminal law, materiality: Materiality of falsehood is not an element of the crime, set forth in 18 U.S.C. § 1014, of "knowingly mak[ing] any false statement . . . for the purpose of influencing in any way the action" of a federally insured bank. Under a natural reading of the full text of the provision, materiality is not an element. The prohibition applies to "any" false statement, and the term "false statement" carries no connotation of influential significance. Statutory history confirms this natural reading. The original version of section 1014 consolidated 13 separate provisions, 10 of which, like section 1014, contained no express materiality provision, and 3 of which did. The most likely inference is that Congress dropped the materiality requirement of the latter 3 laws. A reviser's note explaining that the consolidation involved no substantive change "was simply wrong." Prior to enactment of section 1014, the Supreme Court had interpreted one of the 10 earlier laws with no express materiality provision as having no implied materiality element, and the Court "presume[s] that Congress expects its statutes to be read in conformity with [Supreme Court] precedents."

8-1. Opinion of Court by Souter, joined by Rehnquist, O'Connor, Scalia, Kennedy, Thomas, Ginsburg, and Breyer. Dissenting opinion by Stevens.

Vacco v. Quill 65 USLW 4695 (6-26-97)

Equal Protection, physician-assisted suicide: New York's prohibition on assisting suicide does not violate the Equal Protection Clause by distinguishing between mentally competent, terminally ill patients who are on life-support systems and who are allowed to direct the removal of such systems, and other patients in similar condition who are not on life support systems and who are not allowed to hasten death by self-administering prescribed drugs. The Equal Protection Clause requires states to "treat like cases alike," but allows states to "treat unlike cases accordingly." Because New York's prohibition on assisting suicide neither infringes fundamental rights nor involves suspect classifications, it is entitled to a "strong presumption of validity." The distinction between assisting suicide and withdrawing life-sustaining treatment is both important and logical, and is "certainly rational." The prohibition serves "valid and important public interests," detailed in *Washington v. Glucksberg*, and therefore the classification easily satisfies the requirement that it bear a rational relation to legitimate ends.

9-0. Opinion of Court by Rehnquist, joined by O'Connor, Scalia, Kennedy, and Thomas. Concurring opinions by O'Connor, joined in part by Ginsburg and Breyer; and by Stevens; Souter; Ginsburg; and Breyer.

Walters v. Metropolitan Educ. Enterprises 117 S. Ct. 660, 65 USLW 4059 (1-14-97)

Employment discrimination, Title VII: A company "has fifteen or more employees for each working day of twenty or more calendar weeks" of a given year, and thus is an "employer" subject to Title VII of the Civil Rights Act, if that company has an employment relationship with the required number of employees for the required period of time. The count is not limited to days on which employees actually performed work or were being compensated despite their absence. This "payroll method," based on existence of an employment relationship, represents the fair reading of the statutory language. Giving the words their "ordinary, contemporary, common meaning," an employer "has" an employee if he has an employment relationship with that individual. The added qualification "for each working day" of a week is not superfluous; instead, the phrase eliminates ambiguity over whether to count persons whose employment begins or ends in the midst of a workweek.

9-0. Opinion for unanimous Court by Scalia.

Warner-Jenkinson Co. v. Hilton Davis Chem. Co. 117 S. Ct. 1040, 65 USLW 4162 (3-3-97)

Patents, doctrine of equivalents: The "doctrine of equivalents," announced by the Court in the *Graver Tank* decision in 1950, was not eliminated by the 1952 revision of the Patent Act, and remains a part of the Act. The 1952 Act did not make material changes in the relevant parts of the 1870 Act interpreted in *Graver Tank*. Under the doctrine, infringement can be found if there is an "equivalence" between elements of the infringing product and claimed elements of the patented invention, even though there is not literal infringement of the express terms of the claim. Application of the doctrine is an objective inquiry in which intent plays no role. The Court declines to rule on whether application of the doctrine is a jury issue, or whether the judge should perform the task. "Prosecution history estoppel," a limitation on the doctrine of equivalents that bars recapture of subject matter surrendered by a claim amendment, also survived *Graver Tank*. Properly understood, this estoppel principle bars departure from the express terms of a claim amendment only if the amendment was made in order to avoid a ruling against patentability. If no explanation for a claim amendment is established, there is a presumption that the reason related to patentability and that estoppel applies. The patent holder in this case has not given any reason for a claim amendment that set a lower limit to a pH range in a filtration system used in purifying dyes. The judgment of infringement is reversed, and the case is remanded for reconsideration of issues relating to equivalence and prosecution history estoppel.

9-0. Opinion for unanimous Court by Thomas. Concurring opinion by Ginsburg, joined by Kennedy.

Washington v. Glucksberg 65 USLW 4669 (6-26-97)

Due Process, right to assisted suicide: Washington State's statutory prohibition on causing or aiding a suicide does not violate the Due Process Clause of the Fourteenth Amendment. The Due Process Clause recognizes no liberty interest that includes a right to commit suicide with another's assistance. There is no tradition recognizing such a right; instead "a consistent and almost universal tradition has long rejected the right. Cases that have recognized certain "basic and intimate exercises of personal autonomy," e.g., the right to refuse life-prolonging hydration and nutrition, and the right to be free of undue governmental interference in aborting a non-viable fetus, do not establish any broad principle that "all important, intimate, and personal decisions are so protected." Washington's ban on assisted suicide is rationally related to various legitimate governmental interests, including the preservation of human life, protecting persons who suffer from depression or other mental disorders, protecting other vulnerable groups, protecting the integrity of the medical profession, and refusing to start down a path that could lead to approval of euthanasia. Refusing to recognize a constitutional right to assisted suicide permits public debate on the issue to continue, "as it should in a democratic society."

9-0. Opinion of Court by Rehnquist, joined by O'Connor, Scalia, Kennedy, and Thomas. Concurring opinions by O'Connor, joined by Ginsburg and Breyer; and by Stevens; Souter; Ginsburg; and Breyer.

Young v. Fordice 117 S. Ct. 1228, 65 USLW 4236 (3-31-97)

Voting Rights Act, preclearance: Mississippi has not precleared, and must preclear under section 5 of the Voting Rights Act, changes in its voter registration procedures that it made in order to comply with the National Voter Registration Act (NVRA). The Attorney General's preclearance of a provisional plan, premised on the State's application of changes to both state and federal elections, did not insulate the State's final changes from preclearance review after the Legislature tabled a bill that would have applied the changes to state as well as federal elections. Preclearance is required even if changes in voting laws are made in an effort to comply with federal law, so long as those changes reflect policy choices made by state officials. The fact that the NVRA applies only to registration for federal elections does not necessarily insulate from Voting Rights Act review the State's decision to maintain a dual registration system. Discretionary changes must be examined in context in order to evaluate whether they have the purpose or effect of denying or abridging the right to vote on the basis of race.

9-0. Opinion for unanimous Court by Breyer.

Young v. Harper 117 S. Ct. 1148, 65 USLW 4197 (3-18-97)

Parole: Parole by any other name is parole, and revocation must be accompanied by the procedural protections set forth by the Court in *Morrissey v. Brewer* (1972). Oklahoma's Preparole Conditional Supervision Program was equivalent to parole as understood in *Morrissey*. Both involved early release from prison, substantial liberty in finding and maintaining a job, and certain curtailments on liberty such as periodic reporting to a parole officer. Most alleged differences were "phantom." While the purpose of preparole was to relieve prison overcrowding, parole may also be employed for that purpose, and both programs served to reintegrate the prisoner into society. A preparolee remained no more "within the custody" of the Corrections Department than did a parolee. An analogy to furlough is "inapposite," and there is no indication in this case that the parolee was informed in advance that he would be reincarcerated if the Governor denied him parole. Actual differences (e.g., different proceeding. The attorney may challenge the reasonableness of the timing of the search, but this is a Fourth Amendment issue rather than a Due Process issue.

9-0. Opinion of Court by Rehnquist, joined by O'Connor, Scalia, Kennedy, Souter, Thomas, Ginsburg, and Breyer. Concurring opinion by Stevens.

Cunningham v. Hamilton County 119 S. Ct. 1915, 67 USLW 4458 (6-14-99)

Appeals, "final decision": An order imposing sanctions on an attorney pursuant to Federal Rule of Civil Procedure 37(a)(4) for failure to comply with discovery orders is not a "final decision" appealable under 28 U.S.C. § 1291 prior to final judgment in the underlying action. The Rule 37 sanction did not end the litigation or leave the district court with only the task of executing its judgment. Nor does the sanction fit within the small category of orders that are appealable even though they do not terminate litigation. The order was conclusive, but cannot be separated completely from the merits of the case. Also, the order is not effectively unreviewable on appeal from a final judgment on the merits. The congruence of interests between attorneys and clients "counsels against treating attorneys like other nonparties for purposes of appeal." To permit an immediate appeal would undermine the purposes of Rule 37(a), which was designed to protect courts and opposing parties from delaying or harassing tactics during the discovery process. The same rule applies when the attorney no longer represents a party in the case. The efficiency interests served by limiting immediate appeals "far outweigh" any costs that sanctioned attorneys might bear in monitoring the progress of the litigation.

9-0. Opinion for unanimous Court by Thomas. Concurring opinion by Kennedy.

Davis v. Monroe County Bd. of Educ. 119 S. Ct. 1661, 67 USLW 4329 (5-24-99)

Title IX, "student-on-student" sexual harassment: A recipient of federal educational funds can be held liable under Title IX of the Education Amendments of 1972 in a private damages action arising from student-on-student sexual harassment. Funding recipients are properly held liable, however, only if they are "deliberately indifferent to sexual harassment, of which they have actual knowledge, that is so severe, pervasive, and objectively offensive that it can be said to deprive the victims of access to the educational opportunities or benefits provided by the school." Earlier cases have established that private damages actions are available only if funding recipients had adequate notice that they can be held liable, and only if their own actions or indifference effectively caused the "discrimination" at issue and therefore constituted an intentional violation of Title IX. Such an intentional violation can occur even when the harasser is a student rather than a teacher, so long as the funding recipient "exercises substantial control over both the harasser and the context in which the known harassment occurs." This is the case when student-on-student sexual harassment occurs during school hours and on school grounds, and the alleged harasser is under the school's disciplinary authority. A further limitation is that funding recipients will be deemed to be "deliberately indifferent" only if their response or lack of response to alleged harassment "is clearly unreasonable in light of the known circumstances." And the recipient's indifference is actionable only when the alleged harassment is so severe, pervasive, and objectively offensive as to effectively deprive the victim of the educational opportunities provided by the school.

5-4. Opinion of Court by O'Connor, joined by Stevens, Souter, Ginsburg, and Breyer. Dissenting opinion by Kennedy, joined by Rehnquist, Scalia, and Thomas.

Department of Commerce v. United States House of Representatives
Clinton v. Glavin 119 S. Ct. 765, 67 USLW 4090 (1-25-99)

Standing to sue; Census Act: Plaintiffs in *Clinton v. Glavin*, consolidated with the House of Representative's suit for purposes of review, had standing to sue to challenge the use of statistical sampling in the Department's proposed Census 2000 plan. An Indiana citizen had standing because of the "virtual certainty" that Indiana would lose a seat in the House under the Department's plan, and citizens of several counties had standing by virtue of the likelihood that their counties would suffer vote dilution as a result of census-based redistricting for state, local, and congressional elections. The Census Act does not permit the use of statistical sampling in calculating the population for purposes of apportioning Representatives among the states. Section 195 of the Act, as amended in 1976, provides that, "except for the determination of population for purposes of apportionment of Representatives . . . , the Secretary shall, if he considers it feasible, authorize the use of the statistical method known as `sampling.'" General language added in 1976 authorizes the Secretary to take the decennial census "in such form and content as he may determine, including the use of sampling procedures." The broad grant of authority in section 141 is limited "by the narrower and more specific §195," and section 195 must be interpreted in the broader context of a 200-year-long prohibition on the use of statistical sampling. Because the Census Act prohibits the use of sampling in calculating population for purposes of apportionment, it is unnecessary to consider the constitutionality of sampling. Because the disposition of *Clinton v. Glavin* also resolves the substantive issues presented in the House of Representatives' action, that case (98-404) is dismissed as no longer presenting a substantial federal question.

9-0 (standing); **5-4** (Census Act). Opinion of Court by O'Connor, joined in part by Rehnquist, Scalia, Kennedy, Thomas, and Breyer, and joined in separate part by Rehnquist, Scalia, Kennedy, and Thomas. Separate part of O'Connor opinion joined only by Rehnquist and Kennedy. Opinion by Scalia, joined by Thomas, and joined in part by Rehnquist and Kennedy, concurring in part. Opinion by Breyer, concurring in part and dissenting in part. Dissenting opinion by Stevens, joined in part by Souter and Ginsburg, and joined in separate part by Breyer. Dissenting opinion by Ginsburg, joined by Souter.

Department of the Army v. Blue Fox, Inc. 119 S. Ct. 687, 67 USLW 4073 (1-20-99)

Sovereign immunity: Section 10(a) of the Administrative Procedure Act, 5 U.S.C. § 702, does not nullify the long-settled rule that sovereign immunity bars creditors from enforcing liens on Government property. In this case, a subcontractor on a Government contract, unable to recover from the contractor, sought an "equitable lien" on any Government funds still available for payment to the contractor or for completion of the project. Section 702 waives sovereign immunity for certain claims "seeking relief other than money damages." In this context, "money damages" means compensatory or substitute relief, and "other than money damages" refers to specific relief, e.g., enforcement of a statutory mandate. The goal of the equitable lien sought by the subcontractor in this case is to attach money held by the Government in order to compensate for the loss resulting from the default of the contractor. This is a claim for "substitute" rather than "specific" relief, and therefore amounts to a claim for "money damages" within the meaning of the APA. The action therefore falls outside of section 702's waiver of sovereign immunity.

9-0. Opinion for unanimous Court by Rehnquist.

Dickinson v. Zurko 119 S. Ct. 1816, 67 USLW 4445 (6-10-99)

Patents and trademarks, standard of review: The Federal Circuit, when it reviews findings of fact made by the Patent and Trademark Office (PTO), must apply the "arbitrary, capricious, [or] abuse of discretion [or] unsupported by substantial evidence" standards set forth in section 706 of the Administrative Procedure Act (APA), and not the "clearly erroneous" standard set forth in Federal Rule of Civil Procedure 52(a) for appellate court review of lower court decisions. A reviewing court must apply the APA standard in the absence of an exception authorized by section 559, which provides that the APA does "not limit or repeal additional requirements . . . recognized by law." The "clearly erroneous" standard was not "recognized by law" when the APA was enacted in 1946. The 89 pre-APA cases involving judicial review of a PTO administrative decision do not reflect a well-established "court/court" standard of judicial review. Use of such terms as "clear case of error" or "manifest error" is not conclusive, since the "relevant linguistic conventions were less firmly established before adoption of the APA." The Supreme Court's 1884 decision in *Morgan v. Daniels* does not support application of the court/court standard. Rather, the Court, in determining the appropriate standard for review of Patent Office decisions, rejected reliance on the then-governing standard for an appellate court's review of a lower court's factual findings.

6-3. Opinion of Court by Breyer, joined by Stevens, O'Connor, Scalia, Souter, and Thomas. Dissenting opinion by Rehnquist, joined by Kennedy and Ginsburg.

El Al Israel Airlines v. Tsui Yuan Tseng 119 S. Ct. 662, 67 USLW 4036 (1-12-99)

Warsaw Convention, preemption: The Warsaw Convention precludes a passenger from maintaining an action for personal injury damages under local law when her claim does not satisfy the conditions for liability under the Convention. The plaintiff in this action alleged that she suffered emotional distress, but no bodily injury, from an intrusive airport security search conducted before she boarded an El Al flight. The Convention does not permit recovery for emotional distress unaccompanied by bodily injury. Article 24 of the Convention provides that "cases covered by Article 17" may only be brought subject to the conditions and limits set out by the Convention. Article 17 creates a cause of action for personal injuries suffered as a result of an "accident . . . in the course of any of the operations of embarking or disembarking." Although the security search was not an "accident" within the meaning of Article 17, Article 24's reference to "cases covered by Article 17" applies generically to all personal injury cases stemming from occurrences on board an aircraft or in embarking or disembarking. The "cardinal purpose" of the Convention was "to achieve uniformity of rules governing claims arising from international air transportation." Decisions of the courts of other signatory nations support a broad reading of the Convention's preemptive effect.

8-1. Opinion of Court by Ginsburg, joined by Rehnquist, O'Connor, Scalia, Kennedy, Souter, Thomas, and Breyer. Dissenting opinion by Stevens.

penalties for violation) were "minor," and did not change "the fundamentally parole-like nature of the Program."

9-0. Opinion for unanimous Court by Thomas.

El Paso Natural Gas Co. v. Neztsosie 119 S. Ct. 1430, 67 USLW 4286 (5-3-99)

Price-Anderson Act, preemption, tribal court exhaustion: The doctrine of tribal court exhaustion, under which federal district courts abstain from deciding issues of tribal court jurisdiction until the tribal courts themselves have addressed them, is inapplicable to suits involving claims under the Price-Anderson Act. In this case the district court should have decided whether the claims at issue were Price-Anderson claims. The Act's "unusual preemption provision," which gives federal courts jurisdiction over "any public liability action arising out of . . . a nuclear incident, provides for removal to federal court if a putative Price-Anderson action is brought in state court, but is silent about actions brought in tribal courts. It seems most likely that congressional silence on tribal courts is due to "inadvertence." Because there were no nuclear testing labs or reactors on reservation lands, Congress probably did not foresee the possibility that a nuclear incident might occur on tribal lands. There is no reason to believe, however, that Congress would have favored tribal exhaustion in Price-Anderson suits. The Act, amended in the aftermath of the Three-Mile Island accident, sought speed and efficiency in managing claims, and authorized a special caseload management panel to consolidate and expedite claims. The panel, explained a Senate report, would help avoid inefficiencies resulting from "duplicative determinations . . . in multiple jurisdictions." Application of tribal exhaustion would defeat these purposes.

9-0. Opinion for unanimous Court by Souter.

Federal Republic of Germany v. United States 119 S. Ct. 1016, 67 USLW 3559 (3-3-99)

International Court of Justice, enforcement of order: The Federal Republic of Germany's motions for leave to file a complaint, and for issuance of a preliminary injunction, are denied. Germany sought enforcement of an *ex parte* order issued by the International Court of Justice directing the United States to prevent the execution of Walter LaGrand, a German citizen, by the State of Arizona. See also *Stewart v. LaGrand* (1999). The United States has not waived its sovereign immunity, and it is "doubtful" that Article III, § 2, cl. 2, which extends jurisdiction to cases affecting ambassadors and consuls, "provides an anchor" for the action. The Federal Republic's suit against the State of Arizona, as was Paraguay's suit against Virginia in *Breard v. Greene* (1998), "is without evident support in the Vienna Convention and in probable contravention of the Eleventh Amendment."

7-2. *Per curiam*. Concurring opinion by Souter, joined by Ginsburg. Dissenting opinion by Breyer, joined by Stevens.

Florida Prepaid Postsecondary Educ. Expense Bd. v. College Savings Bank 119 S. Ct. 2199, 67 USLW 4580 (6-23-99)

State sovereign immunity, abrogation by Congress, patents: The Patent and Plant Variety Protection Remedy Clarification Act's amendment of the patent laws to expressly abrogate states' sovereign immunity from patent infringement suits cannot be upheld as an exercise of congressional power to enforce the Fourteenth Amendment's Due Process Clause. While Congress in exercise of its enforcement power may abrogate state sovereign immunity, it must do so through legislation that is "appropriate" within the meaning of § 5 of the 14th

Amendment. The Court's decision in *City of Boerne v. Flores* (1997) established that "appropriate" legislation must be "remedial": Congress must identify conduct that violates the Fourteenth Amendment and must tailor its legislation to remedying or preventing such conduct. In enacting the Patent Remedy Act, however, Congress identified no pattern of patent infringement by states. Moreover, Congress barely considered the availability of state remedies for patent infringement. Patent infringement alone does not constitute a due process violation; "only where the State provides no remedy, or only inadequate remedies . . . could a deprivation of property without due process occur." The legislative record thus "at best offers scant support" for a conclusion that states were engaging in due process violations. Consequently, the provisions of the Act are "so out of proportion to a supposed remedial or preventive object" that they cannot be upheld as an exercise of Fourteenth Amendment enforcement power.

5-4. Opinion of Court by Rehnquist, joined by O'Connor, Scalia, Kennedy, and Thomas. Dissenting opinion by Stevens, joined by Souter, Ginsburg, and Breyer.

Florida v. White 119 S. Ct. 1555, 67 USLW 4311 (5-17-99)

Fourth Amendment, seizure of automobile, contraband forfeiture: The Fourth Amendment does not require the police to obtain a warrant before seizing an automobile from a public place when they have probable cause to believe that the automobile itself is forfeitable contraband. The Court has long recognized that when law enforcement officers have probable cause to believe than an automobile contains contraband, the Fourth Amendment does not require them to obtain a warrant prior to searching the car and seizing the contraband. This principle derives from laws and cases involving customs inspections of vessels, and reflects the need to seize "readily movable contraband before it is spirited away." The same principle applies if it is the vehicle itself that is the contraband. The Court also recognizes that law enforcement officers have "greater latitude in exercising their duties in public places" than they have when searching private premises. In this case police officers had observed the respondent using his car to transport illegal drugs. Several months later, after arresting the respondent on unrelated charges, the officers, acting under authority of the Florida Contraband Forfeiture Act, seized respondent's car from his employer's parking lot. No warrant was required under these circumstances.

7-2. Opinion of Court by Thomas, joined by O'Connor, Scalia, Kennedy, Souter, and Breyer. Concurring opinion by Souter, joined by Breyer. Dissenting opinion by Stevens, joined by Ginsburg.

Greater New Orleans Broadcasting Ass'n v. United States 119 S. Ct. 1923, 67 USLW 4451 (6-14-99)

First Amendment, commercial speech: 18 U.S.C. § 1304, which prohibits radio and television broadcasters from carrying advertisements for privately operated casino gambling regardless of the station's or casino's location, may not constitutionally be applied to prohibit advertising of private casino gambling broadcast by stations located within a state where such gambling is legal. The provision fails to satisfy the *Central Hudson* test for restrictions on commercial speech. If the commercial speech relates to lawful activity and is not misleading, restrictions must directly advance a substantial governmental interest and must not be more extensive than necessary to serve that interest. The government has identified substantial interests that are served by the prohibition on ads for casino gambling, but the underlying policy "is now decidedly equivocal." When section 1304 was enacted in 1934, the federal anti-gambling policy was uniform. Now, however, with various exemptions for gambling conducted by Indian tribes and state governments, federal statutes promote both pro-gambling and anti-gambling policies. "The operation of § 1304 and its attendant regulatory regime is so pierced by exemptions and inconsistencies that the Government cannot hope to exonerate it." Moreover, while there may be valid reasons for regulating tribal casino gambling more closely than non-tribal casino gambling, there is "no convincing reason" for restricting the speech of non-tribal owners more than that of tribal owners.

9-0. Opinion of Court by Stevens, joined by Rehnquist, O'Connor, Scalia, Kennedy, Souter, Ginsburg, and Breyer. Concurring opinions by Rehnquist and Thomas.

Grupo Mexicano de Desarollo v. Alliance Bond Fund 119 S. Ct. 1961, 67 USLW 4490
(6-17-99)

Federal courts, injunctive powers; mootness: A federal district court lacks the authority, in an action for money damages, to issue a preliminary injunction preventing the defendant from transferring assets in which no lien or equitable interest is claimed. The relief sought has no basis in the traditional powers of the equity courts. It is well established that a general creditor (one without a judgment) has no cognizable interest, at law or in equity, in the property of his debtor. There is no analogy to the equitable action known as a "creditor's bill," since that action could be brought only by a creditor who had already obtained a judgment establishing the debt. The merger of law and equity did not alter substantive rights. While policy arguments may be made for and against creating the preliminary injunctive remedy to freeze a debtor's assets pending adjudication, the Court lacks authority under the Judiciary Act of 1789 to create remedies previously unknown to equity jurisprudence. Congress is the appropriate forum for deciding whether "this formidable power over debtors" should be created. Appeal of the preliminary injunction in this case was not rendered moot by decision on the merits and issuance of a permanent injunction. The basis for arguing that the preliminary injunction was wrongfully issued — that the court lacked power to restrain use of assets pending a money judgment — was independent of the breach of contract claim adjudicated on the merits.

5-4 (authority to issue preliminary injunction); **9-0** (mootness). Opinion of Court by Scalia, unanimous in part, and joined by Rehnquist, O'Connor, Kennedy, and Thomas in separate part. Dissenting opinion by Ginsburg, joined by Stevens, Souter, and Breyer.

Haddle v. Garrison 119 S. Ct. 489, 67 USLW 4029 (12-14-98)

Civil rights, conspiracy to deter testimony: Termination of at-will employment as part of a conspiracy to deter testimony before a federal grand jury is actionable under 42 U.S.C. § 1985(2) as injuring a citizen "in his person or property." The Eleventh Circuit was mistaken that a citizen must suffer an injury to a constitutionally protected interest in order to recover damages under § 1985(2). The case is not resolved, therefore, by the fact that loss of at-will employment is not "property" for purposes of the Due Process Clause. The "gist of the wrong" at which the provision is directed is not deprivation of property, but intimidation of witnesses. For this purpose, it is sufficient that interference with at-will employment has long been compensable under tort law.

9-0. Opinion for unanimous Court by Rehnquist.

Hanlon v. Berger 119 S. Ct. 1706, 67 USLW 4329 (5-24-99)

Fourth Amendment, media "ride-along", qualified immunity: Fish and Wildlife Service agents violated the Fourth Amendment when they allowed a media camera crew to accompany them in executing a warrant to search respondents' ranch for evidence of illegal taking of wildlife. The principles announced in *Wilson v. Layne* control. The agents are entitled to the defense of qualified immunity since the right to be free of media intrusion during a search was not clearly established in 1993 when this search occurred.

9-0. Per curiam.

Holloway v. United States 119 S. Ct. 966, 67 USLW 4148 (3-2-99)

Carjacking, intent: The federal carjacking statute, 18 U.S.C. § 2119, which prohibits carjacking "with the intent to cause death or serious bodily harm," applies to someone who seizes a car with the intent to kill or harm only if necessary to accomplish the carjacking. The statute applies to both conditional and unconditional intent to harm the victim, so the trial court did not err in instructing the jury to find requisite intent upon concluding that the defendant had intended to cause death or serious bodily harm if the victims had refused to turn over their cars. A "commonsense" reading of the statute counsels that Congress intended to criminalize carjacking generally, and did not intend to enact a "truncated" law applicable only to a limited subset of carjackings in which the offender intends to harm or kill the driver regardless of whether the driver surrenders his car. The statute as a whole reflects a deterrent purpose, and that purpose is better served by construing the statute to cover both conditional and unconditional intent. Also, it is reasonable to presume that Congress was aware of state court decisions recognizing that specific intent to commit a crime may be conditional.

7-2. Opinion of Court by Stevens, joined by Rehnquist, O'Connor, Kennedy, Souter, Ginsburg, and Breyer. Dissenting opinions by Scalia and Thomas.

Hughes Aircraft Co. v. Jacobson 119 S. Ct. 755, 67 USLW 4122 (1-25-99)

ERISA, amendment of defined benefit plan: Hughes did not violate ERISA by suspending its own contributions to a retirement plan with a large surplus and by amending the plan to provide for an early retirement program and a noncontributory benefit structure applicable to new employees and optional for existing plan members. The existing plan members had no vested interest in the plan's surplus. The plan was a "defined benefit plan" under which qualified employees are entitled to a fixed periodic payment and the employer was obligated to cover any underfunding. Hughes did not violate ERISA's anti-inurement provision; amending the plan did not create a second plan, and fund assets were being used to pay benefits to plan participants, not for the benefit of the employer. ERISA's fiduciary provisions are inapplicable to plan amendments; this principle, already applied to welfare benefit plans, applies as well to pension benefit plans. The plan amendments did not work an effective termination based on the common-law theory of a wasting trust. ERISA's enormously complex and detailed text should not be supplemented by common-law remedies, and, in any event, the doctrine is inapplicable by its own terms.

9-0. Opinion for unanimous Court by Thomas.

Humana Inc. v. Forsyth 119 S. Ct. 710, 67 USLW 4085 (1-20-99)

Insurance; RICO compatibility with McCarran-Ferguson: The McCarran-Ferguson Act does not bar recourse to RICO in a treble damages action for health insurance fraud in Nevada. In this action beneficiaries of group health insurance policies alleged that their insurance company and a hospital committed fraud by agreeing to discounts on the insurance company's 80% share of hospital charges, thereby increasing the beneficiaries' share above the 20% agreed to in the insurance contract. Section 2(b) of the McCarran-Ferguson Act permits application of general federal legislation not specifically directed at insurance regulation if the law does not "invalidate, impair, or supersede" state laws regulating insurance. RICO is not a law that specifically relates to the business of insurance, and it does not "invalidate" or "supersede" Nevada law. The principal issue is whether RICO "impairs" Nevada law, and this issue depends on whether application of RICO would "frustrate any declared State policy or interfere with [the] State's administrative regime." There is no frustration of state policy or interference with state administration in this case. Instead, RICO "appears to complement" Nevada's provision of relief. Nevada allows insured parties to sue for insurance fraud and to obtain punitive damages that may exceed the treble damages obtainable under RICO.

9-0. Opinion for unanimous Court by Ginsburg.

Hunt v. Cromartie 119 S. Ct. 1545, 67 USLW 4306 (5-17-99)

Congressional districting, summary judgment, proof of racial motivation: The three-judge district court should not have granted a summary judgment to the appellees on their claim that North Carolina's Twelfth Congressional District, as redrawn in 1997, constituted an unconstitutional racial gerrymander in violation of the Equal Protection Clause. A redistricting law, facially neutral as to race, warrants strict scrutiny only if it can be proved to have been motivated by a racial purpose or object. Assessing a jurisdiction's motivation is an "inherently complex endeavor," requiring a "sensitive inquiry" by the trial court. In this case there was evidence supporting conflicting inferences — one that the legislature was primarily motivated by race, the other that the principal motivation was partisan politics. Summary judgment is appropriate only if there is no genuine issue of material fact. Because the legislature's motivation was in dispute, summary judgment on that issue was inappropriate.

9-0. Opinion of Court by Thomas, joined by Rehnquist, O'Connor, Scalia, and Kennedy. Concurring opinion by Stevens, joined by Souter, Ginsburg, and Breyer.

INS v. Aguirre-Aguirre 119 S. Ct. 1439, 67 USLW 4270 (5-3-99)

Deportation, political persecution: The Court of Appeals for the Ninth Circuit failed to accord appropriate deference to the determination of the Board of Immigration Appeals that a person who committed a serious nonpolitical crime before entering the United States, and whose political opinions would subject him to persecution in his country of origin, is not entitled to withholding of deportation. The court should have applied principles announced in *Chevron v. NRDC* (1984), and should have deferred to the Board's interpretation of the exception for serious nonpolitical crimes. Deference is "especially appropriate in the immigration context where officials 'exercise especially sensitive political functions that implicate questions of foreign relations.'" The provision in question, 8 U.S.C. § 1253(h)(2)(C), directs that withholding of deportation does not apply if the Attorney General finds "serious reasons for considering that the alien has committed a serious nonpolitical crime . . . prior to [his] arrival." In finding that the respondent's actions in burning buses and vandalizing stores in Guatemala were "nonpolitical," the Board (to which the Attorney General had delegated her authority) determined that the criminal nature of the respondent's actions outweighed their political motivation. The Board did not, however, balance the criminal nature of the respondent's actions against the persecution that he would face if he were forced to return to Guatemala. The Board's interpretation is a reasonable one that comports with the plain language of the statute. The fact that this interpretation conflicts with that set forth in a United Nations handbook that was prepared as guidance for interpreting the treaty that the statute implements is not dispositive: the handbook "is not binding on the Attorney General, the [Board], or United States courts."

9-0. Opinion for unanimous Court by Kennedy.

Jefferson County v. Acker 119 S. Ct. 2069, 67 USLW 4521 (6-21-99)

County occupational tax, application to federal judges: An occupational tax imposed by Jefferson County, Alabama, on persons working within the county is not invalid as applied to federal judges. The case was properly removed to federal court under the federal officer removal statute. The judges made an "adequate threshold showing that the suit is 'for an act under color of office,'" since the act requires payment of a fee before they engage in their occupation. The Tax Injunction Act does not bar federal court adjudication of the case. The Act does not bar collection suits, nor does it prevent taxpayer-defendants in collection suits from challenging the validity of the tax. The occupation tax operates as a non-discriminatory tax on judges' salaries to which the Public Salary Tax Act of 1939 consents. That Act applies the intergovernmental tax immunity doctrine, now interpreted to allow one sovereign to tax the salaries of another sovereign's employees as long as the tax is not discriminatory. The tax is a tax on "pay or compensation" within the meaning of the Act, and is not an invalid licensing measure. Because the tax does not discriminate against federal judges in particular, or federal officeholders in general, based on the federal source of their compensation, and the record shows no discrimination between similarly situated federal and state judges, the tax does not discriminate in violation of the Act.

5-4 (removal); **9-0** (Tax Injunction Act); **7-2** (intergovernmental immunity). Opinion of Court by Ginsburg, unanimous in part; joined in part by Stevens,

O'Connor, Kennedy, and Breyer; and joined in separate part by Rehnquist, Stevens, Scalia, Kennedy, Souter, and Thomas. Opinion by Scalia, concurring in part and dissenting in part, joined by Rehnquist, Souter, and Thomas. Opinion by Breyer, concurring in part and dissenting in part, joined by O'Connor.

Jones v. United States 119 S. Ct. 1215, 67 USLW 4204 (3-24-99)

Carjacking, elements of offense: The federal carjacking statute, 18 U.S.C. § 2119, establishes three separate offenses rather than a single offense with a choice of three maximum penalties. The section provides that whoever takes a motor vehicle by force and violence "shall — (1) be fined . . . or imprisoned not more than 15 years, . . . (2) if serious bodily injury results, be . . . imprisoned not more than 25 years, and (3) if death results, be . . . imprisoned for any number of years up to life . . . ." The additional elements added by subsections (2) and (3) must be charged in the indictment, submitted to a jury, and proven beyond a reasonable doubt. At first glance, the section's structure suggests that the numbered subsections are only sentencing provisions. It is "questionable," however, whether specification of facts sufficient to drastically increase a penalty range was intended to carry none of the safeguards associated with elements of an offense. Moreover, the first paragraph of the section does not "stand on [its] own grammatical feet," as most offense-defining provisions do, because there is no language such as "shall be guilty of" that completes the sentence. Use of the word "shall" does not resolve the issue, because the word is not "invariably" used to separate offense-defining clauses from sentencing provisions. Also, the provision was enacted against the backdrop of many federal and state criminal statutes that identify serious bodily injury as an offense element. Most important, the statute would be open to constitutional doubt if the subsections were interpreted as sentencing provisions. Precedent under both the Due Process Clause and the Sixth Amendment can be read as imposing limits on a legislature's ability to omit traditional elements from the definition of crimes and to diminish the jury's role in making factual determinations on which sentencing limits are based. The decision last Term in *Almendarez-Torres v. United States*, holding that recidivism increasing the maximum penalty need not be charged in the indictment, is distinguished. Recidivism has traditionally been regarded as a sentencing factor, whereas infliction of serious bodily injury has not been.

5-4. Opinion of Court by Souter, joined by Stevens, Scalia, Thomas, and Ginsburg. Concurring opinions by Stevens and Scalia. Dissenting opinion by Kennedy, joined by Rehnquist, O'Connor, and Breyer.

Jones v. United States 119 S. Ct. 2090, 67 USLW 4508 (6-21-99)

Death penalty, jury instructions on consequences of deadlock: In a sentencing hearing conducted under the Federal Death Penalty Act of 1994, the court's refusal to instruct the jury that the court would impose a sentence of life imprisonment without possibility of parole if the jury was unable to reach unanimous agreement on a sentence did not violate the Eighth Amendment. The Supreme Court declines to exercise its supervisory power to require that an instruction on the consequences of deadlock be given in every capital case. In this case the court gave the jury three options: it could by unanimous vote recommend the death penalty, life imprisonment without possibility of parole, "or . . . some other lesser sentence." If the jury recommended "some other lesser sentence," the instruction explained, "the court is required to impose a sentence that is authorized by law." The instruction did not constitute "plain error," even though a "lesser sentence" was not authorized in this case. There is "no reasonable likelihood that the jury applied the instructions incorrectly." The instructions, read in their entirety, were not misleading as to the consequences of the jury's failure to reach a unanimous verdict. Any confusion over the effect of a lesser sentence recommendation was allayed by the court's instruction that the jury should not concern itself with such matters. Loose drafting of "nonstatutory" aggravating factors was harmless error if it constituted error at all.

5-4. Opinion of Court by Thomas, joined in part by Rehnquist, O'Connor, Scalia, and Kennedy, and in separate part by Rehnquist, O'Connor, and Kennedy. Dissenting opinion by Ginsburg, joined by Stevens and Souter, and joined in part by Breyer.

Knowles v. Iowa 119 S. Ct. 484, 67 USLW 4027 (12-8-98)

Fourth Amendment, search incident to traffic citation: A search authorized by an Iowa statute permitting officers to conduct a full-blown search of an automobile when issuing a traffic citation violates the Fourth Amendment. Neither of the rationales that justifies a search incident to arrest justifies a full search of an automobile incident to a traffic citation. The threat to officer safety is "a good deal less" in the case of a routine traffic stop than it is in the case of a custodial arrest. The "relatively brief encounter" of a traffic stop contrasts with an officer's "extended exposure" to a suspect who is placed in custody and transported to the police station. Officers conducting a routine traffic stop may order driver and passengers out of the car and may even conduct a patdown search if there is reasonable suspicion that the driver or any passengers may be armed and dangerous, but there is no such justification for a full search of the car. The second justification for a search incident to arrest — the need to preserve evidence — is "not present at all" in a routine traffic stop.

9-0. Opinion for unanimous Court by Rehnquist.

Kolstad v. American Dental Ass'n 119 S. Ct. 2118, 67 USLW 4552 (6-22-99)

Punitive damages, Title VII of Civil Rights Act: A plaintiff in an action brought under Title VII of the Civil Rights Act need not show "egregious" misconduct in order to recover punitive damages. 1991 amendments to Title VII authorized awards of compensatory and punitive damages in cases of "intentional misconduct," and further limited punitive awards to acts undertaken "with malice or with reckless indifference to . . . federally protected rights." The terms "malice" and "reckless" focus on the actor's state of mind. There is no additional requirement of egregiousness, although egregious misconduct is often associated with the award of punitive damages, and may serve as evidence supporting an inference of the requisite evil motive. Agency principles place limits on recovery of punitive damages from employers for the acts of employees. While the Restatement (Second) of Agency provides "a useful starting point," its principles must be modified so that an employer may not be held vicariously liable for discriminatory employment decisions of managerial agents when those decisions are contrary to the employer's good-faith efforts to comply with Title VII.

7-2 ("egregious" standard); 5-4 (agency). Opinion of Court by O'Connor, joined in part by Stevens, Scalia, Kennedy, Souter, Ginsburg, and Breyer; and joined in separate part by Rehnquist, Scalia, Kennedy, and Thomas. Opinion concurring in part and dissenting in part by Rehnquist, joined by Thomas. Opinion concurring in part and dissenting in part by Stevens, joined by Souter, Ginsburg, and Breyer.

Kumho Tire Co. v. Carmichael 119 S. Ct. 1167, 67 USLW 4179 (3-23-99)

Evidence, expert testimony: The standards announced in *Daubert v. Merrell Dow Pharmaceuticals* (1993) for admissibility of opinion testimony by qualified scientific experts apply as well to testimony based on technical and other specialized knowledge that is not "scientific." Federal Rule of Evidence 702, which allows admission of expert testimony "[i]f scientific, technical, or other specialized knowledge will assist the trier of fact," affords no basis for distinguishing between admissibility of "scientific" knowledge and "technical" or "other specialized" knowledge. Whatever the specialized discipline, the trial judge must determine whether the testimony has "a reliable basis in the knowledge and experience of [the] discipline." Trial judges need considerable leeway in making this determination. The *Daubert* standards are "flexible,"and do not constitute a mandatory checklist. Whether or not the expert is applying scientific principles, the trial judge may, if appropriate, consider any of the specific factors identified in *Daubert* as possibly bearing on reliability. In this case, the district court's decision not to admit the testimony of an expert in motor vehicle tire failure analysis was reasonable. The court did not question the expert's qualifications, but instead found his methodology unreliable as applied to the facts of this case.

9-0 (general principles); 8-1 (disposition of case). Opinion of Court by Breyer, joined by Rehnquist, O'Connor, Scalia, Kennedy, Souter, Thomas, and Ginsburg, and joined in part by Stevens. Concurring opinion by Scalia, joined by O'Connor and Thomas. Concurring and dissenting opinion by Stevens.

Lilly v. Virginia 119 S. Ct. 1887, 67 USLW 4435 (6-10-99)

Confrontation Clause: The defendant's Sixth Amendment right to be confronted with the witnesses against him was violated by admission into evidence at his trial of a confession made by a non-testifying accomplice. The accomplice confessed to participating in a burglary, but stated that the defendant was the one who shot and killed a person whose car they had stolen during their crime spree. The fact that portions of the confession were "against penal interest" does not place the non-self-inculpatory portions incriminating the defendant within a firmly rooted exception to the hearsay rule; the latter portions are presumptively unreliable. The case is remanded to Virginia courts to determine whether the violation of the defendant's Confrontation Clause rights was harmless beyond a reasonable doubt.

9-0. Opinion of Court by Stevens, one part of which was joined by Scalia, Souter, Thomas, Ginsburg, and Breyer, and a separate part of which was joined by Scalia, Souter, Ginsburg, and Breyer. Separate part of Stevens opinion joined by only by Souter, Ginsburg, and Breyer. Concurring opinions by Rehnquist, joined by O'Connor and Kennedy; by Scalia; by Thomas; and by Breyer.

Lopez v. Monterey County 119 S. Ct. 693, 67 USLW 4076 (1-20-99)

Voting Rights Act, preclearance: A political subdivision covered by the Voting Rights Act must seek preclearance before giving effect to voting changes required by state law, even if the state is not covered by the Act. The Act's plain meaning and its history of interpretation support this conclusion. Section 5 of the Voting Rights Act requires preclearance "whenever a [covered] State or political subdivision . . . shall enact or seek to administer any voting [change]." The phrase "seek to administer" does not limit preclearance obligations to discretionary acts of a covered jurisdiction. "Administer" comprehends non-discretionary acts, and the word "seek" is used merely to make a "temporal distinction" between enactment and implementation of legislation: preclearance need not be obtained before enactment, but must be before implementation. The Attorney General's interpretation to the same effect is entitled to deference. Although the Act intrudes on state sovereignty by requiring federal approval of state enactments, "the Fifteenth Amendment permits this intrusion."

8-1. Opinion of Court by O'Connor, joined by Stevens, Scalia, Souter, Ginsburg, and Breyer. Concurring opinion by Kennedy, joined by Rehnquist. Dissenting opinion by Thomas.

Marquez v. Screen Actors Guild 119 S. Ct. 292, 67 USLW 4001 (11-3-98)

Labor, union security clause: A union does not breach its duty of fair representation by negotiating a union security clause that uses the language of § 8(a)(3) of the National Labor Relations Act without explaining in the agreement itself the Supreme Court's interpretation of that language. Section 8(a)(3) permits unions to negotiate collective bargaining agreements that require union "membership" for all employees on or after the 30th day following the beginning of "such employment." The Court has interpreted this language to mean merely that the union may require the payment of core fees and dues necessary to support the union's representational activities. There is no requirement that these qualifications be spelled out in the security clause; the clause is enforceable as written because the statutory provisions have become terms of art that incorporate case law interpretations. The union did not breach its duty of fair representation; there was no claim of discriminatory conduct in this case, and the union's negotiation of the security clause was neither arbitrary nor in bad faith. The District Court lacked jurisdiction over the petitioner's second claim. That claim, that the security clause violates § 8(a)(3) by providing that the 30-day grace period begins to run with any employment in the industry rather than with the particular employment at issue, is at base a statutory issue within the NLRB's primary jurisdiction.

9-0. Opinion for unanimous Court by O'Connor. Concurring opinion by Kennedy, joined by Thomas.

Martin v. Hadix 119 S. Ct. 1998, 67 USLW 4500 (6-21-99)

Retroactivity, Prison Litigation Reform Act, attorney's fees: Section 803(d) of the Prison Litigation Reform Act (PLRA), which limits the fees that may be awarded to attorneys who litigate prisoner lawsuits, applies to services that were performed after the PLRA's effective date, but not to services performed prior to that date. Principles announced in *Landgraf v. USI Film Products* (1994) govern the retroactivity issue. The statute does not address "the temporal reach" of the provision. The language of the provision sets substantive limits, and "falls short of demonstrating a 'clear congressional intent' favoring retroactive application of the fees limitations." The structure and history of the PLRA should not be read to mean that the fees limitations are inapplicable to pending cases. Section 802, governing "appropriate remedies" in prison litigation, explicitly provides that it applies to pending cases, while section 803 is silent in this regard. Because, however, sections 802 and 803 "address wholly distinct subject matters," no negative inference should be made about section 803's application to pending cases. The fact that the fees limitations were moved out of section 802 and placed in section 803 during congressional consideration does not mean that Congress intended the provisions to apply to pending cases, since there could have been "a variety of other reasons" for the move. In the absence of congressional guidance on the retroactivity issue, the next question in this case is whether application to fees for postjudgment monitoring would be "inconsistent with the usual rule that legislation is deemed to be prospective." Application to monitoring performed before the effective date would be contrary to the rule, since it would "attach new legal consequences to completed conduct." Application to monitoring performed after the PLRA's effective date creates no such retroactivity problem, because enactment of the PLRA put attorneys on notice that their hourly rate had been adjusted.

7-2. Opinion of Court by O'Connor, joined by Rehnquist, Kennedy, Souter, Thomas, and Breyer; joined in part by Scalia; and joined in separate part by Stevens and Ginsburg. Concurring opinion by Scalia. Opinion by Ginsburg, joined by Stevens, concurring in part and dissenting in part.

Maryland v. Dyson 119 S. Ct. 2013, 67 USLW 3770 (6-21-99)

Fourth Amendment, automobile search: The Fourth Amendment does not require police to obtain a search warrant before searching a vehicle that they have probable cause to believe contains illegal drugs. Under established precedent, the "automobile exception" to the warrant requirement has no separate exigency requirement. The Court held in *United States v. Ross* (1982) that a search of an automobile is not unreasonable, even though a warrant has not been obtained, if the search is based on facts that would support a warrant.

Per curiam. Dissenting opinion by Breyer, joined by Stevens.

Minnesota v. Carter 119 S. Ct. 469, 67 USLW 4017 (12-1-98)

Fourth Amendment, persons protected in home: A person present in someone else's apartment for a few hours for the purpose of bagging cocaine for later sale is not entitled to Fourth Amendment protection. In some circumstances a person in someone else's house has a legitimate expectation of privacy, and hence is entitled to Fourth Amendment protection. The Court has extended protection, for example, to overnight guests. At the other extreme, persons who are merely "legitimately on the premises" are not entitled to protection. The purely commercial nature of the transaction here, the relatively brief period of time on the premises, and the lack of any previous connection with the householder make the respondent's situation in this case closer to that of one simply permitted on the premises. Because the respondent had no legitimate expectation of privacy in the apartment, there is no need to decide whether a police officer's observations through a window constituted a "search."

5-4 (Fourth Amendment protection); 6-3 (result). Opinion of Court by Rehnquist, joined by O'Connor, Scalia, Kennedy, and Thomas. Concurring opinions by Scalia, joined by Thomas; by Kennedy; and by Breyer (concurring in result, but agreeing with dissent on Fourth Amendment coverage). Dissenting opinion by Ginsburg, joined by Stevens and Souter.

Minnesota v. Mille Lacs Band of Chippewa Indians 119 S. Ct. 1187, 67 USLW 4189 (3-24-99)

Native Americans, treaty rights: Several Bands of Chippewa Indians retain rights guaranteed by an 1837 Treaty "during the pleasure of the President" to hunt, fish, and gather rice on lands ceded to the United States. These usufructuary rights were not eliminated by an 1850 Executive Order, by an 1855 Treaty, or by admission of Minnesota into the Union in 1858. The 1850 Executive Order purported to revoke these hunting, fishing, and gathering "privileges granted temporarily to the Chippewa Indians," but the Order was understood as a "removal" order requiring relocation of the Indians, and as such exceeded the President's authority. Neither the Removal Act nor the Treaty itself authorized the President to order removal of the Indians. The portion of the Executive Order revoking the usufructuary rights is not severable from the invalid removal order because "it is clear that President Taylor intended the 1850 order to stand or fall as a whole." The 1855 Treaty, by which the Indians "relinquish[ed] and convey[ed] . . . any and all right, title, and interest [in] lands," relinquished lands, not usufructuary rights. Minnesota's enabling act does not abrogate the 1837 Treaty, nor does the "equal footing doctrine." Statehood by itself is insufficient to extinguish Indian treaty rights to hunt, fish, and gather, because such treaty rights are still subject to reasonable and non-discriminatory state conservation regulations. The contrary interpretation of the equal footing doctrine in *Ward v. Race Horse* (1896) is rejected.

5-4. Opinion of Court by O'Connor, joined by Stevens, Souter, Ginsburg, and Breyer. Dissenting opinions by Rehnquist, joined by Scalia, Kennedy, and Thomas; and by Thomas.

Mitchell v. United States 119 S. Ct. 1307, 67 USLW 4230 (4-5-99)

Self-incrimination: A guilty plea does not waive the privilege against self-incrimination at the sentencing phase of a federal trial. Incrimination is not complete once guilt has been adjudicated. Rather, a defendant may have a legitimate fear of adverse consequences from testimony at sentencing. The Court has already held that the privilege against self-incrimination applies in a capital sentencing hearing, and there is no reason not to apply the principle to non-capital sentencing hearings as well. A district court's explanation, pursuant to Rule 11, that a defendant who pleads guilty will lose the right to remain silent at trial, does not suggest to a defendant that he could also lose the right to remain silent at sentencing. The rule applicable at trial that no negative inference may be drawn from the defendant's failure to testify applies with equal force at sentencing. The district court may not make an adverse inference, based on the defendant's silence at sentencing, about circumstances and details of the crime that bear on sentencing — in this case the amount of drugs sold by the defendant. The Government retains the burden at the sentencing phase of proving facts relevant to the crime, and may not "enlist the defendant in this process at the expense of the self-incrimination privilege."

9-0 (effect of guilty plea); 5-4 (adverse inference). Opinion of Court by Kennedy, joined by Stevens, Souter, Ginsburg, and Breyer. Opinions concurring in part and dissenting in part by Scalia, joined by Rehnquist, O'Connor, and Thomas; and by Thomas.

Murphy Bros. v. Michetti Pipe Stringing, Inc. 119 S. Ct. 1322, 67 USLW 4238 (4-5-99)

Removal, timing, service of process: The 30-day period established by 28 U.S.C. § 1446(b) for removal of actions from state to federal court does not begin to run until formal service of process, even if the defendant has already received a copy of the complaint. Section 1446(b) provides that notice of removal "shall be filed within thirty days after the receipt by the defendant, through service or otherwise, of a copy of the initial pleading." In this case the plaintiff filed a complaint in an Alabama court and 3 days later faxed a file-stamped copy of the complaint to the defendant; the defendant was not formally served until two weeks later. The defendant's notice of removal, filed 30 days after service of process and 44 days after receipt of the complaint, complied with section 1446(b). Historically, service of process has been the official trigger for responsive action by the party named as a defendant. Nothing in the legislative history of enactment of the modern version of the section indicates that Congress intended to dispense with this historic function. Rather, the accompanying Senate report explained that the measure was intended to correct a problem that could occur in New York and other states, in which the period for removal might end before the defendant obtained access to the complaint. Similar language in Federal Rule of Civil Procedure 81, governing the time allowed a defendant to answer a complaint, has been interpreted to afford the defendant the specified number of days after service of process.

6-3. Opinion of Court by Ginsburg, joined by Stevens, O'Connor, Kennedy, Souter, and Breyer. Dissenting opinion by Rehnquist, joined by Scalia and Thomas.

Murphy v. United Parcel Service 119 S. Ct. 2133, 67 USLW 4549 (6-22-99)

ADA, "regarded as" disabled: An individual fired from his job as a mechanic because of high blood pressure that prevented him from receiving DOT certification to drive a commercial vehicle – an essential function of this particular mechanic's job – is not "regarded as" disabled within the meaning of the ADA definition of "disability." As the Court determined in *Sutton v. United Airlines*, the initial issue of whether the petitioner was "disabled" should be determined with reference to the mitigating measures he employs. A person is "regarded as" disabled if a covered employer believes that the person's actual, nonlimiting impairment substantially limits one or more major life activities. No such showing was made in this case. The petitioner established that he is regarded as unable to perform the job of mechanic only when that job requires driving a commercial motor vehicle, but it is undisputed that he is generally employable as a mechanic. At most, the petitioner is regarded as unable to perform only a particular job – not an entire class or broad range of jobs.

7-2. Opinion of Court by O'Connor, joined by Rehnquist, Scalia, Kennedy, Souter, Thomas, and Ginsburg. Dissenting opinion by Stevens, joined by Breyer.

NASA v. FLRA 119 S. Ct. 1979, 67 USLW 4468 (6-17-99)

Inspector General Act, employee examinations, FSLMRS: An investigator employed in NASA's Office of Inspector General can be considered a "representative" of NASA when examining a NASA employee, and consequently the right to union representation guaranteed by the Federal Service Labor-Management Relations Statute, 5 U.S.C. § 7114(a)(2)(B), applies. By its terms, the provision is not limited to agency investigators representing an "entity" within the agency that collectively bargains with the employee's union. Neither the fact that the relevant language is contained in a larger section addressing collective bargaining rights, nor the fact that the phrase "representative of the agency" is used elsewhere in the statute to refer to management representatives responsible for collective bargaining requires a different reading. Moreover, there is no basis in the history and purpose of the FSLMRS to give § 7114(a)(2)(B) a narrow construction that covers some, but not all, interviews by agency representatives. Nor does the Inspector General Act (IGA) require a limiting construction. Rather, the IGA provides that Inspectors General "shall report to and be under the general supervision of the head of the establishment involved," and also refers to the agency "within which [an IG's] Office is established." Although enforcing § 7114(a)(2)(B) may lessen an Inspector General's ability to maintain the confidentiality of its investigations, the provision "vindicates obvious countervailing federal policies" favoring fair treatment of employees under investigation.

5-4. Opinion of Court by Stevens, joined by Kennedy, Souter, Ginsburg, and Breyer. Dissenting opinion by Thomas, joined by Rehnquist, O'Connor, and Scalia.

National Fed'n of Fed. Employees v. Department of the Interior 119 S. Ct. 1003, 67 USLW 4170 (3-3-99)

Labor, federal employees, midterm bargaining: The Federal Service Labor-Management Relations Statute is ambiguous as to the duty of federal employers to bargain midterm (*i.e.*, while the basic collective bargaining agreement is in effect) over matters not included in the basic agreement. The statute, 5 U.S.C. § 7114(a)(4), simply provides that the federal agency employer and the union representative "shall meet and negotiate in good faith for the purposes of arriving at a collective bargaining agreement." The "arriving at" language is not dispositive, because there is nothing in the circular definition of "collective bargaining agreement" to exclude a midterm agreement. The statutory ambiguity is consistent with the conclusion that Congress delegated to the Federal Labor Relations Authority the power to determine whether, where, and when midterm bargaining is required. The statute also grants the Authority power to determine whether an agency must bargain "endterm" over including in the basic collective bargaining agreement a clause requiring midterm bargaining.

5-4. Opinion of Court by Breyer, joined by Stevens, Kennedy, Souter, and Ginsburg. Dissenting opinion by O'Connor, joined by Rehnquist, and joined in part by Scalia and Thomas.

NCAA v. Smith 119 S. Ct. 924, 67 USLW 4130 (2-23-99)

Sex discrimination, Title IX, scope of coverage: Receipt of dues from member colleges and universities that receive federal funds does not bring the National Collegiate Athletic Association (NCAA) within the scope of Title IX of the Education Amendments of 1972. A private action based on this theory, and challenging application of NCAA rules governing postgraduate eligibility for participation in intercollegiate athletics, cannot be maintained. Title IX prohibits sex discrimination in "any education program or activity receiving Federal financial assistance," and a regulation defines a "recipient" of such assistance as any entity "to whom Federal financial assistance is extended directly or through another recipient." Federal assistance is received "through another recipient" if it is earmarked for such payments, as is the case with a college that enrolls students who receive federal funds earmarked for college expenses. There is no allegation, however, that NCAA member institutions pay their dues with federal funds earmarked for the purpose of paying NCAA dues. Entities such as the NCAA that merely benefit economically from federal assistance are not "recipients" covered by Title IX.

9-0. Opinion for unanimous Court by Ginsburg.

Neder v. United States 119 S. Ct. 1827, 67 USLW 4404 (6-10-99)

Harmless error; fraud statutes, materiality: The district court's error in failing to submit to the jury the issue of materiality in a tax fraud case was "harmless error." The error at issue — a jury instruction that omits an element of the offense — differs markedly from the constitutional violations that have been held to defy harmless-error review. Errors that require reversal affect the framework in which the trial proceeds, and "necessarily render a trial fundamentally unfair." An instruction that omits an element of an offense does not *necessarily* render a criminal trial fundamentally unfair or unreliable. In this case, in which the defendant failed to report over $5 million in income and filed false returns, the evidence supporting materiality was "overwhelming," and the court's failure to submit the materiality issue to the jury was harmless error. Materiality of falsehood is an element of a "scheme or artifice to defraud" under the federal mail fraud, wire fraud, and bank fraud statutes. Under a natural reading of the statutory text itself, materiality would not be an element of the fraud statutes. However, where Congress uses terms that have accumulated a settled meaning under the common law, a court must infer, unless the statute dictates otherwise, that Congress intended to incorporate the established meaning. The well-settled meaning of "fraud" required a misrepresentation or concealment of a material fact. Nothing in the fraud statutes dictates a different conclusion, so it is presumed that Congress intended to incorporate materiality.

6-3 (harmless error); **9-0** (materiality). Opinion of Court by Rehnquist, unanimous on materiality issue, and joined by O'Connor, Kennedy, Thomas, and Breyer on harmless error issue. Concurring opinion by Stevens. Opinion by Scalia, concurring in part and dissenting in part, joined by Souter and Ginsburg.

Nynex Corp. v. Discon, Inc. 119 S. Ct. 493, 67 USLW 4031 (12-14-98)

Antitrust, group boycotts: The rule that group boycotts are illegal *per se* does not apply to a buyer's decision to buy from one seller instead of another, whenever that decision cannot be justified in terms of ordinary competitive objectives. In this case, a purchaser of telephone removal services allegedly switched purchases from the respondent to a competitor because the respondent refused to participate in a scheme to defraud phone service customers. The group boycott *per se* rule is limited to cases involving horizontal agreements among direct competitors. This case does not involve any horizontal agreement, but instead involves a "vertical" agreement between supplier and customer. There is no special feature of this case to distinguish it from precedents limiting the *per se* rule.

9-0. Opinion for unanimous Court by Breyer.

Olmstead v. L.C. 119 S. Ct. 2176, 67 USLW 4567 (6-22-99)

ADA, mentally disabled, community placement: The ADA's general prohibition on discrimination against disabled persons in the provision of public services requires placement of persons with mental disabilities in community settings rather than institutions if the state's treatment professionals have determined that community placement is appropriate, if the transfer is not opposed by the affected individual, and if the placement can be reasonably accommodated, taking into account the resources available to the state. Unjustified institutionalization is properly regarded as discrimination by reason of disability. The Department of Justice regulations requiring public entities to administer services in "the most integrated setting appropriate" are entitled to deference under *Chevron v. NRDC* (1984). Moreover, congressional findings in the ADA explicitly identify unjustified "segregation" of disabled persons as a form of "discrimination."

6-3. Opinion of Court by Ginsburg, joined by Stevens, O'Connor, Souter, and Breyer. Separate part of Ginsburg opinion joined by O'Connor, Souter, and Breyer. Concurring opinions by Stevens; and by Kennedy, joined in part by Breyer. Dissenting opinion by Thomas, joined by Rehnquist and Scalia.

Ortiz v. Fibreboard Corp. 119 S. Ct. 2295, 67 USLW 4632 (6-23-99)

Class actions, asbestos settlement: Applicants for certification of a mandatory settlement class on a limited fund theory under Federal Rule of Civil Procedure 23(b)(1)(B) must show that the settlement fund is limited by more than the agreement of the parties, and will be allocated to claimants belonging within the class by a process addressing any conflicting interests of class members. The record on which the district court in this case rested its class certification did not support these essential premises of mandatory limited fund actions. There is good reason to treat these limited fund characteristics as "presumptively necessary," since the Advisory Committee that developed Rule 23 did not contemplate that the mandatory class action codified in subdivision (b)(1)(B) would be used to aggregate unliquidated tort claims on a limited fund rationale, and since serious constitutional concerns (jury trial and due process rights of absent class members) are implicated. There was no evaluation of the amount of insurance money that would be available to pay claims, and consequently there was no adequate demonstration of the fund's upper limit. There was also inadequate consideration of the inclusiveness of the class and of equity among class members. Several groups, including persons who had previously settled but retained the right to sue again upon development of asbestos-related malignancy, plaintiffs with claims pending at the time of an initial settlement agreement, and "inventory" plaintiffs, were excluded from the class. There was no division of plaintiffs between holders of present and future claims, and thus there was inadequate protection against conflicting interests of counsel. The class also did not accommodate the different interests of plaintiffs whose claims arose while Fibreboard maintained insurance, and those whose claims arose after the insurance was discontinued. Another departure from "limited fund antecedents" is that Fibreboard's net worth was not taken into account in determining the size of the fund.

7-2. Opinion of Court by Souter, joined by Rehnquist, O'Connor, Scalia, Kennedy, Thomas, and Ginsburg. Concurring opinion by Rehnquist, joined by Scalia and Kennedy. Dissenting opinion by Breyer, joined by Stevens.

O'Sullivan v. Boerckel 119 S. Ct. 1728, 67 USLW 4389 (6-7-99)

Habeas corpus, exhaustion of state remedies: Before a federal court may grant habeas relief to a state prisoner, that prisoner must exhaust his remedies in state court, and this required exhaustion includes petitioning a state court of last resort that has discretionary control over its docket. The governing statute, 28 U.S.C. § 2254(c), provides that a habeas petitioner shall not be deemed to have exhausted his state remedies "if he has the right under [state law] to raise, by any available procedure, the question presented." This does not require state prisoners to invoke every possible avenue of state review, but it does require that prisoners give state courts "one full opportunity to resolve any constitutional issues by invoking one complete round of the State's appellate review process." Because the respondent raised three issues in his federal habeas petition that he had not raised in his petition for leave to appeal to the Illinois Supreme Court, and because the time for filing in Illinois had long passed, he procedurally defaulted on those claims.

6-3. Opinion of Court by O'Connor, joined by Rehnquist, Scalia, Kennedy, Souter, and Thomas. Concurring opinion by Souter. Dissenting opinions by Stevens, joined by Ginsburg and Breyer; and by Breyer, joined by Stevens and Ginsburg.

Peguero v. United States 119 S. Ct. 961, 67 USLW 4154 (3-2-99)

***Habeas corpus*, harmless error**: A district court's failure to advise a defendant of his right to appeal his sentence, as required by Federal Rule of Criminal Procedure 32(a)(2), does not provide a basis for *habeas corpus* relief if the defendant was aware of his right to appeal when the trial court failed to give the advice. Because the defendant was aware of his right to appeal, he suffered no prejudice from the trial court's omission.

9-0. Opinion for unanimous Court by Kennedy. Concurring opinion by O'Connor, joined by Stevens, Ginsburg, and Breyer.

Pfaff v. Wells Electronics, Inc. 119 S. Ct. 304, 67 USLW 4009 (11-10-98)

Patents, invention "on sale" more that a year: A product can be "on sale" within the meaning of section 102(b) of the Patent Act of 1952, 35 U.S.C. § 102 (b), if it has been offered for sale, even if it has not yet been reduced to practice. Section 102(b) provides that an "invention" may not be patented if it has been "on sale" for more than one year before the patent application was filed. An "invention" is an inventor's conception rather than a physical embodiment of that idea. It is well settled that an invention may be patented before it is reduced to practice. Two conditions must be satisfied before an invention is "on sale." First, the product must be the subject of a commercial sale. In this case, the product had been offered for sale more than a year prior to patent application. Second, the invention must be ready for patenting. This latter condition may be satisfied in at least two ways — by proof of reduction to practice, or by proof that the inventor had prepared drawings or other descriptions of the invention that were sufficiently specific to enable a person skilled in the art to practice the invention. Here, the second condition was satisfied by drawings that the inventor had provided to a manufacturer before the critical date.

9-0. Opinion for unanimous Court by Stevens.

Reno v. American-Arab Anti-Discrimination Comm. 119 S. Ct. 936, 67 USLW 4133 (2-24-99)

Immigration, deportation, judicial review, selective enforcement: Provisions of the Illegal Immigration Reform and Immigrant Responsibility Act of 1996 (IIRIRA) limiting judicial review apply to certain types of challenges to deportation proceedings that were ongoing at the time of enactment of IIRIRA. The "supposed tension" between 8 U.S.C. § 309(c)(1), which sets a general rule of inapplicability to pending cases, and § 306(c)(1), which provides that §1252(g) applies to pending cases, is resolved by a "narrow reading" of the latter provision. 8 U.S.C. §1252(g) should be read as barring judicial review, prior to a final deportation order, of a limited subset of claims challenging three discrete types of actions by the Attorney General — commencing proceedings, adjudicating cases, or executing removal orders. The instant case, involving a claim that respondents were targeted for deportation because of their affiliation with a politically unpopular group, fits squarely within the first category as a challenge to the commencement of proceedings. The three categories should not be treated as all-encompassing. Nowhere in the U.S. Code is precise and narrow language of this nature used as a shorthand means of imposing a general jurisdictional limitation. Also, there is "good reason" for Congress to insulate these particular actions from judicial review, since each involves a stage at which the Attorney General may exercise nonreviewable discretion to abandon deportation proceedings. The doctrine of constitutional doubt is inapplicable because there is no constitutional right implicated. "As a general matter . . . an alien unlawfully in this country has no constitutional right to assert selective enforcement as a defense against his deportation."

8-1. Opinion of Court by Scalia, joined by Rehnquist, O'Connor, Kennedy, and Thomas, and joined in part by Ginsburg and Breyer. Concurring opinion by Ginsburg, joined in part by Breyer. Concurring opinion by Stevens. Dissenting opinion by Souter.

Richardson v. United States 67 USLW 4381 (6-1-99)

Jury unanimity, "continuing criminal enterprise": A jury in a case brought under 18 U.S.C. § 848, which forbids any person from engaging in a "continuing criminal enterprise," must unanimously agree not only that the defendant committed some "continuing series of violations," but also which specific violations make up that continuing series. It is well settled that a federal jury may convict only if it finds unanimously that the Government has proved each element of an offense. A jury may, however, disagree as to which of several possible means the defendant used to commit an element of the crime. For purposes of section 848, each violation making up a "series of violations" should be considered to be a separate "element" of the offense, and not merely the possible "means" by which the offense was committed. The statute provides that a person is engaged in a continuing criminal enterprise if he violates any provision of the federal drug laws, and if "such violation is a part of a continuing series of violations." Use of the word "violation" suggests that each "violation" amounts to a separate element of the offense that requires jury unanimity. Also, the breadth of possible drug law violations that could comprise a "series" means that, absent a unanimity requirement, there could be wide disagreement among jurors as to just what the defendant did or did not do. Finally, the statute should be construed so as to avoid possible constitutional issues that could be raised under the alternative construction.

6-3. Opinion of Court by Breyer, joined by Rehnquist, Stevens, Scalia, Souter, and Thomas. Dissenting opinion by Kennedy, joined by O'Connor and Ginsburg.

Roberts v. Galen of Virginia, Inc. 119 S. Ct. 685, 67 USLW 4062 (1-13-99)

Emergency Medical Treatment and Active Labor Act: Recovery in an action brought under the Emergency Medical Treatment and Active Labor Act for a hospital's failure to provide necessary stabilizing treatment for an emergency medical condition is not contingent upon proof of improper motive. Section 1395dd(b) of the Act requires hospitals to provide "for such further medical examination and such treatment as may be required to stabilize the medical condition." The provision is not qualified by a requirement of "appropriateness," and cannot "reasonably be read to require an improper motive."

9-0. *Per curiam.*

Ruhrgas AG v. Marathon Oil Co. 119 S. Ct. 1563, 67 USLW 4315 (5-17-99)

Federal courts, priority of jurisdictional issues: There is "no unyielding jurisdictional hierarchy" in cases removed from state to federal court, or in cases originating in federal court. Federal district courts have discretion to dismiss a removed case for lack of personal jurisdiction without reaching the issue of subject matter jurisdiction. The principles that require a court to find subject matter jurisdiction before proceeding to the merits do not necessarily require a set sequencing of jurisdictional issues. The possibility of issue preclusion in subsequent state-court litigation merits consideration, but is not dispositive. In most instances, "both expedition and sensitivity to state courts' coequal stature" should impel the federal court to consider subject matter jurisdiction before personal jurisdiction. However, if the court has a "straightforward" issue of personal jurisdiction that presents "no complex question of state law," and if the alleged defect in subject matter jurisdiction raises a "difficult and novel question," the court does not abuse its discretion by first addressing personal jurisdiction.

9-0. Opinion for unanimous Court by Ginsburg.

Saenz v. Roe 119 S. Ct. 1518, 67 USLW 4291 (5-17-99)

Right to travel, durational residency requirement for welfare: A provision of the California Welfare and Institutions Code limiting new residents, for the first year they live in California, to the level of welfare benefits that they would have received in the state of their prior residence, abridges the right to travel in violation of the Fourteenth Amendment. The right to travel is "firmly embedded in our jurisprudence." A component of the right to travel is the right of a newly arrived citizen to the same privileges and immunities enjoyed by other citizens of that state. Privileges and immunities of citizenship are protected under Article IV by virtue of the new arrival's status as a state citizen, and under the Fourteenth Amendment by virtue of her status as a citizen of the United States. The Court recognized in the *Slaughter-House Cases* in 1873 that the Fourteenth Amendment's Privileges or Immunities Clause guarantees that United States citizens who establish *bona fide* residence in a state are entitled to the same rights as other citizens of that state. Classification based upon the period of residency in California and the location of prior residence penalizes the citizen's right to be treated equally in her new state of residence. Such penalties may not be judged by mere rationality or by an "intermediate" standard of review; instead, the standard must be "no less strict" than the compelling governmental interest test applied in *Shapiro v. Thompson* (1969). The Court in *Shapiro* held that the purpose of deterring welfare applicants from migrating into a state is impermissible. Here, California's professed purpose of saving money is legitimate, but cannot justify its discrimination among equally eligible citizens. Federal approval of such durational residency requirements in the Personal Responsibility and Work Opportunity Reconciliation Act of 1996 cannot resuscitate the constitutionality of California's law. Congress may not authorize the states to violate the Fourteenth Amendment. Article I powers may not be exercised in a manner that violates other specific provisions of the Constitution, and congressional enforcement power under section 5 of the Fourteenth Amendment encompasses no power to restrict, abrogate, or dilute the Amendment's guarantees.

7-2. Opinion of Court by Stevens, joined by O'Connor, Scalia, Kennedy, Souter, Ginsburg, and Breyer. Dissenting opinions by Rehnquist, joined by Thomas; and by Thomas, joined by Rehnquist.

South Central Bell Tel. Co. v. Alabama 119 S. Ct. 1180, 67 USLW 4186 (3-23-99)

Commerce Clause; Taxation, State: Alabama's franchise tax law discriminates against foreign corporations in violation of the Commerce Clause. The law establishes a domestic corporation's tax base as the par value of its capital stock, a value that the corporation may set at whatever level it chooses. The tax base of a foreign corporation, on the other hand, contains balance sheet items that the corporation cannot so manipulate. Denial to foreign corporations of the ability afforded domestic corporations to reduce their tax liability constitutes facial discrimination against interstate commerce and can be upheld only if the State offers sufficient justification. Alabama has not justified the discrimination. The tax is not a "compensatory" tax that offsets the tax burden imposed on domestic corporations. The burdens on foreign and domestic corporations are neither "roughly approximate" nor similar in substance, the one being a tax on the decision to do business in the state, the other being a tax on ownership of a certain form of property. The Eleventh Amendment does not deprive the Supreme Court of appellate jurisdiction over cases such as this arising from state courts. Nor may Alabama apply "*res judicata*" principles to deny relief simply because the same issue had been decided by the Alabama Supreme Court in an earlier case involving different parties.

9-0. Opinion for unanimous Court by Breyer. Concurring opinions by O'Connor and Thomas.

Stewart v. LaGrand 119 S. Ct. 1018, 67 USLW 3557 (3-3-99)

***Habeas corpus*, waiver of challenge to execution by lethal gas**: A convicted murderer who was sentenced to death and who exercised his option under Arizona law to be executed by lethal gas rather than by lethal injection has waived any objection he might have had to the constitutionality of execution by gas. The prisoner in this case also procedurally defaulted by failing to raise this claim on direct appeal after having been sentenced to death by lethal gas prior to the State's adoption of the lethal injection alternative. At the time of the prisoner's direct appeal (1987) there had been sufficient debate about the constitutionality of lethal gas executions that he cannot show cause for his failure to raise the issue on appeal.

8-1. *Per curiam*. Concurring opinion by Souter, joined by Ginsburg and Breyer. Dissenting opinion by Stevens.

Strickler v. Greene 119 S. Ct. 1936, 67 USLW 4477 (6-17-99)

Prosecutorial misconduct; habeas corpus, procedural default: Virginia did not violate the rule derived from *Brady v. Maryland* (1963) that suppression by the prosecution of evidence favorable to an accused violates due process where the evidence is material either to guilt or to punishment. In this case the prosecution withheld an initial statement made to police by a prosecution witness. The statement, much less definite about the defendant's role in the crime than her later testimony, could have been used by the defendant to impeach her credibility. Petitioner's procedural default in not raising this *Brady* claim in state courts is excused by an adequate showing of cause and prejudice; the petitioner had relied on the prosecution's "open file" policy and on assurances that "everything known to the government" had been disclosed. Petitioner could not, however, establish the underlying *Brady* violation. Two of the three components of a violation were established: the evidence was favorable to the accused and was suppressed by the State. The petitioner failed, however, to demonstrate the prejudice necessary to establish "materiality" because he failed to show that there is a reasonable probability that his conviction or sentence would have been different if the materials had been disclosed. Even if the one witness had been "severely impeached," there was other evidence in the record lending "strong support" for the conclusion that the petitioner still would have been convicted and sentenced to death. Moreover, the testimony in question did not relate to the petitioner's eligibility for the death sentence, and was not relied upon by the prosecution in its closing argument during the penalty phase of the trial.

7-2 (*Brady* violation); **9-0** (excusal of procedural default). Opinion of Court by Stevens, joined by Rehnquist, O'Connor, Scalia, Ginsburg, and Breyer, and joined in part by Kennedy, Souter, and Thomas. Opinion by Souter, joined by Kennedy, concurring in part and dissenting in part.

Sutton v. United Airlines 119 S. Ct. 2139, 67 USLW 4537 (6-22-99)

ADA, definition of "disability": The determination of whether an individual is "disabled" for purposes of the Americans with Disabilities Act of 1990 (ADA) should be made with reference to corrective measures that mitigate the individual's impairment, including, for instance, eyeglasses and contact lenses. The ADA defines "disability" as "a physical or mental impairment that substantially limits one or more of [that individual's] major life activities." No agency has been delegated the authority to interpret the term "disability." EEOC guidelines, however, define "major life activities" to include "working," and also provide that individuals are to be evaluated in their hypothetical uncorrected state. This latter EEOC interpretation is "impermissible." The present indicative verb form of the statutory definition ("substantially limits") requires that the individual be presently – not potentially – limited by an impairment. The evaluation as to disability must be individualized, but focus on an uncorrected impairment would require instead that persons be judged as members of a group with similar impairments. Finally, congressional "findings" written into the ADA declare that "some 43,000,000 Americans have one or more physical or mental disabilities." This figure is inconsistent with a definition of disability that would treat all impairments in their uncorrected form; estimates available in 1990 produced a significantly larger number (approximately 160 million) for a nonfunctional "health conditions" approach to defining disability. Because it is included in the ADA's text, the congressional finding "gives content to the ADA's terms, specifically the definition of disability." A second aspect of the statutory definition includes individuals who are "regarded as" having a disability. The petitioners in this case, individuals whose corrected vision was 20/20 or better, were rejected for employment as airline pilots because their uncorrected vision did not meet the airline's minimum requirement of 20/100 uncorrected vision. The ADA allows employers to establish physical criteria for jobs. The fact that petitioners were rejected for employment in one particular job does not establish that the employer regarded them as having an impairment "substantially limiting" their ability to work. The definition requires an allegation that an individual's impairment makes her unable to work in a "broad class of jobs." There are a number of other positions – such as regional pilot and pilot instructor – utilizing petitioners' skills.

7-2. Opinion of Court by O'Connor, joined by Rehnquist, Scalia, Kennedy, Souter, Thomas, and Ginsburg. Concurring opinion by Ginsburg. Dissenting opinions by Stevens, joined by Breyer; and by Breyer.

United States v. Haggar Apparel Co. 119 S. Ct. 1392, 67 USLW 4249 (4-21-99)

Administrative law, deference to agency interpretation: A Customs Service regulation is subject to analysis under principles set forth in *Chevron v. NRDC* (1984). The statute grants importers a partial exemption from customs duties for manufactured articles that are assembled abroad and that have not been enhanced in value "except by being assembled and except by operations incidental to the assembly process." The regulation deems permapressing operations to be an additional step in manufacturing of textiles, and not an incidental part of the assembly process. The regulation is not limited in application to customs officers who classify imported merchandise, but applies to refund suits in the Court of International Trade. "The tariffs do not mean one thing for customs officers and another for importers." Statutes authorizing the Court of International Trade to conduct *de novo* review do not displace the customary *Chevron* deference to agency interpretations. "*De novo* proceedings presume a foundation of law," and deference may be given to the regulations without impairing the court's authority to make factual determinations *de novo* or to apply the regulations to those determinations. The case is remanded for determination of whether the regulation is entitled to deference under application of *Chevron* principles.

9-0; **7-2**. Opinion of Court by Kennedy, unanimous with respect to whether *Chevron* principles apply, and joined by Rehnquist, O'Connor, Scalia, Souter, Thomas, and Breyer on the remand issue. Opinion by Stevens, joined by Ginsburg, concurring in part and dissenting in part.

United States v. Rodriguez-Moreno 119 S. Ct. 1239, 67 USLW 4219 (3-30-99)

Venue, using firearm during crime of violence: Venue in a prosecution for using or carrying a firearm "during and in relation to any crime of violence," in violation of 18 U.S.C. § 924(c)(1), is proper in any district where the crime of violence was committed, even if the firearm was used or carried only in one district. In this case the defendant participated in a kidnaping that began in Texas and continued with transportation of the victim to New Jersey and then to Maryland; in Maryland the defendant used a gun to threaten the victim. Venue was proper in New Jersey even though there was no evidence that the defendant used a gun in New Jersey. Section 924(c)(1) is not a point-in-time offense that can only be committed in the place where the underlying violent crime and the gun use coincide. Rather, where a crime consists of distinct parts that have different localities, the whole may be tried where any part can be proved to have been done. Venue is appropriate for the section 924(c)(1) offense wherever venue is appropriate for the underlying crime of violence.

7-2. Opinion of Court by Thomas, joined by Rehnquist, O'Connor, Kennedy, Souter, Ginsburg, and Breyer. Dissenting opinion by Scalia, joined by Stevens.

United States v. Sun-Diamond Growers 119 S. Ct. 1402, 67 USLW 4265 (4-27-99)

Illegal gratuity statute: The illegal gratuity statute, 18 U.S.C. § 201(c)(1)(A), which prohibits giving "anything of value" to a public official "for or because of any official act performed or to be performed by such public official," requires a showing beyond the mere fact that a gratuity was given because of the recipient's official position. Under the "more natural reading" of this language, an indictment is defective if it does not allege a specific connection between the gratuities and some official act. The provision could have been worded more simply and directly if the aim had been to proscribe all gifts for or because of official position. Broad prohibitions on gift giving found elsewhere in the Code are "more precise and more administrable." Moreover, the Government's position could produce "peculiar results," such as prohibiting a sports team visiting the White House from giving the President a replica jersey, or prohibiting a farmers group before whom the Secretary of Agriculture is speaking from offering him a complimentary lunch in connection with his speech. The illegal gratuity statute is but "one strand of an intricate web of regulations" that includes many "precisely targeted prohibitions." Given this statutory context, the Court will not "expand . . . one piece of the regulatory puzzle so dramatically as to make many other pieces misfits."

9-0. Opinion for unanimous Court by Scalia.

Unum Life Ins. Co. v. Ward 119 S. Ct. 1380, 67 USLW 4243 (4-20-99)

ERISA, preemption: California's "notice-prejudice" rule, under which an insurer may avoid liability for an untimely claim only by establishing that a claimant's delay in filing was prejudicial, is a "law . . . which regulates insurance" within the meaning of ERISA's saving clause, and therefore is not preempted as a law that "relate[s] to any employee benefit plan." The notice-prejudice rule fits a common-sense understanding of insurance regulation. The rule applies to insurance contracts, and is not a general principle applicable outside the insurance context. Moreover, the rule is grounded in policy concerns specific to the insurance industry. Two of the three criteria used to determine whether a state law regulates "the business of insurance" within the meaning of the McCarran-Ferguson Act are also met — the rule serves as "an integral part of the policy relationship between the insurer and the insured," and it is "limited to entities within the insurance industry." California's *Elfstrom* rule, under which the employer could be deemed to be the agent of the insurer (and by application of which the notice in this case would have been timely), is preempted as a law that "relate[s] to [an] employee benefit plan." Deeming the policyholder-employer the agent of the insurer "would have a marked effect on plan administration."

9-0. Opinion for unanimous Court by Ginsburg.

West v. Gibson 119 S. Ct. 1906, 67 USLW 4462 (6-14-99)

Title VII, compensatory damages in administrative proceedings: The Equal Employment Opportunity Commission (EEOC) possesses the authority to require federal agencies to pay compensatory damages when they discriminate in employment in violation of Title VII of the Civil Rights Act of 1964. Section 717(b), added in 1972, grants the EEOC authority to enforce the Act "through appropriate remedies, including reinstatement or hiring of employees with or without back pay." Section 717(c) authorizes an employee or job applicant to "file a civil action." A Compensatory Damages Amendment (CDA) enacted in 1991 authorized award of compensatory damages "[i]n an action brought under section . . . 717." "Read literally," the language of the statutes is consistent with a grant of authority to the EEOC to award compensatory damages. After enactment of the CDA in 1991, award of compensatory damages is a remedy that is "appropriate." The meaning of "appropriate" was not frozen as of 1972; rather, the meaning of the word permits its scope to expand or contract to reflect later changes in the law. Recognizing this authority in the EEOC is consistent with the purposes of the 1972 amendments to encourage administrative resolution of discrimination complaints. While the CDA made no mention of the EEOC, and use of the word "action" often refers to judicial cases and not to administrative proceedings, Congress could have referenced section 717(c) had it desired to limit the remedy to court actions. Conferral of a right to a jury trial (unavailable in an EEOC proceeding) if a complaining party seeks compensatory damages does not preclude a holding that the EEOC may award compensatory damages; the provision merely makes a jury trial available if a complaining party brings a court action under § 717(c). Finally, the provision meets the standard for waiver of sovereign immunity. "[T]he statutory language, taken together with statutory purposes, history, and the absence of any convincing reason for denying the EEOC the relevant power, produce evidence of a waiver that satisfies the [appropriate] standard."

5-4. Opinion of Court by Breyer, joined by Stevens, O'Connor, Souter, and Ginsburg. Dissenting opinion by Kennedy, joined by Rehnquist, Scalia, and Thomas.

Wilson v. Layne 67 USLW 4322 (5-24-99)

Fourth Amendment, media "ride-along", qualified immunity: Police officers violate the Fourth Amendment by bringing members of the media or other third parties into a home during the execution of a warrant if the presence of the third parties in the home was not in aid of the execution of the warrant. Respect for privacy of the home lies at the "core" of the Fourth Amendment; absent exigent circumstances, a warrant is required before officers may enter a home to search or to make an arrest. Moreover, police actions in execution of a warrant must be related to the objectives of the authorized intrusion. In this case the reporters were not present to identify stolen property or otherwise to assist in execution of the warrant, and consequently their presence in the home was not related to the objectives of the authorized intrusion. Generalized interests in furthering law enforcement objectives and publicizing crime-fighting efforts do not suffice to override the right of residential privacy. However, because this right to be free from media intrusion during a search of the home was not "clearly established" at the time of the search in this case, the law enforcement officers (deputy federal marshals and local sheriff's deputies) are entitled to "qualified immunity." A reasonable officer could have believed that it was legal to bring media observers along during the execution of an arrest warrant in the home. At that time (1992) media "ride-alongs" were common, and there were no court decisions holding the practice unlawful. Also, the policy of the U.S. Marshal's Service explicitly contemplated the practice.

9-0 (Fourth Amendment); **8-1** (qualified immunity). Opinion of Court by Rehnquist, unanimous in part, and joined in separate part by O'Connor, Scalia, Kennedy, Souter, Thomas, Ginsburg, and Breyer. Opinion by Stevens concurring in part and dissenting in part.

Wright v. Universal Maritime Service Corp. 119 S. Ct. 391, 67 USLW 4009 (11-16-98)

Labor, arbitration clause, ADA: A generally worded arbitration clause in a collective bargaining agreement, providing only for arbitration of "matters under dispute," does not require a covered employee to use the arbitration procedure for an alleged violation of the Americans with Disabilities Act. The presumption of arbitrability derived from section 301 of the Labor Management Relations Act is inapplicable; that presumption applies only to disputes about the applicability or interpretation of a collective bargaining agreement, and the underlying dispute here involves interpretation of the ADA. A union's waiver of the rights of represented employees to a judicial forum for claims of employment discrimination must be "clear and unmistakable." The collective bargaining agreement in this case does not meet that standard. The arbitration clause is "very general," and the agreement contains no antidiscrimination language, statutory or otherwise. General language to the effect that no provision shall be violative of federal or state law is inadequate to constitute a clear waiver of ADA rights, especially when contrasted with specific language stating that OSHA requirements "shall be binding on both Parties."

9-0. Opinion for unanimous Court by Scalia.

Wyoming v. Houghton 119 S. Ct. 1297, 67 USLW 4225 (4-5-99)

Fourth Amendment, search of auto passenger's belongings: Police officers with probable cause to search a car may search a passenger's personal belongings inside the car if those belongings are capable of concealing the object of the search, even if it is the driver and not the passenger who is under suspicion. The initial step in evaluating the constitutionality of a search is to determine whether the search would have been regarded as unlawful under the common law at the time the Fourth Amendment was adopted. There is a long history that allows officers with probable cause but without a warrant to search for contraband in a vessel, and the same principle has been applied to allow search of containers within motor vehicles. Cases allowing such searches have expressed no qualification based on ownership of the containers. A second inquiry is the reasonableness of the search, and this is determined by balancing the intrusion on individual privacy against the governmental interests at stake. This balancing "must be conducted with an eye to the generality of cases." Passengers "possess a reduced expectation of privacy with regard to the property that they transport in cars," and a search of such property is far less intrusive than a search of the person. On the other hand, the governmental interest in effective law enforcement is "substantial," and the "ready mobility" of cars often makes obtaining a warrant impractical. Also impractical is requiring police officers to determine whether property belongs to the driver or to a passenger, whether the driver and passenger are confederates in crime, and whether the driver may have hidden contraband among a passenger's possessions without the passenger's knowledge.

6-3. Opinion of Court by Scalia, joined by Rehnquist, O'Connor, Kennedy, Thomas, and Breyer. Concurring opinion by Breyer. Dissenting opinion by Stevens, joined by Souter and Ginsburg.

Your Home Visiting Nurse Servs. v. Shalala 119 S. Ct. 930, 67 USLW 4127 (2-23-99)

Medicare Act; Administrative law, judicial review of agency action: A provider of Medicare services has no right to judicial review of a fiscal intermediary's refusal to reopen an annual determination of the amount of reimbursement to which the provider is entitled. The Medicare Act gives a provider the right to an administrative appeal within 180 days of the intermediary's original determination, and the Provider Reimbursement Review Board's decision is subject to review in federal district court. The provider may also, within three years, request the intermediary to reopen the reimbursement determination, and any new decision is subject to review. The regulation says nothing, however, about a refusal to reopen. The Medicare Act authorizes a hearing before the Board if the provider is dissatisfied with an intermediary's "final determination . . . as to the amount" of reimbursement. The Secretary's interpretation of this language to mean that a refusal to reopen is not a "final determination . . . as to the amount," but rather a refusal to make such a determination, is a reasonable interpretation entitled to deference under *Chevron v. NRDC* (1984). These review provisions, authorizing direct appeal and a request for reopening, are not inconsistent with a separate statutory directive that regulations provide for making "suitable" retroactive corrective adjustments.

9-0. Opinion for unanimous Court by Scalia.

Supreme Court
Volume 1 pp. 149-182

SUPREME COURT OPINIONS: OCTOBER 1995 TERM

George Costello
Legislative Attorney
American Law Division

Auciello Iron Works v. NLRB 116 S. Ct. 1754, 64 USLW 4387 (6-3-96)

Labor, disavowal of bargaining agreement: The National Labor Relations Board reasonably concluded that an employer committed an unfair labor practice by disavowing a collective bargaining agreement because of a good-faith doubt, arising from facts known to the employer before its contract offer had been accepted by the union, about the union's majority status at the time the contract was made. In order to help achieve stability in labor-management relations, the Board has adopted a conclusive presumption of majority status during the term of any collective bargaining agreement. This "same need for repose" justified the Board in ruling out an exception for the benefit of an employer with doubts arising from pre-agreement facts. The Board's position generally allows employers to act on their pre-acceptance doubts before contract formation, and the Board could reasonably have concluded that extending the time to act would encourage bad-faith bargaining.

9-0. Opinion for unanimous Court by Souter.

Bailey v. United States 116 S. Ct. 501, 64 USLW 4039 (12-6-95)

Drug trafficking, "use" of a firearm: Evidence of the proximity and accessibility of a firearm to drugs or drug proceeds is not alone sufficient to establish "use" of a firearm within the meaning of 18 U.S.C. § 924(c)(1). That provision penalizes anyone who "uses or carries a firearm" during and in relation to any drug trafficking offense. The Government must show active employment of a firearm to establish "use." The "active employment" interpretation derives from ordinary meaning and dictionary definitions of "use," from statutory context, and from the history of the provision's amendment. Courts normally assume that statutory words have a particular, non-superfluous meaning, and there is no evidence that Congress employed "use" so expansively as to swallow up any significance for "carry." A related provision's distinction between "used" and "intended to be used" reinforces the active employment reading. Also, reliance on accessibility and proximity alone would erase any distinction between "use" and "possession." Therefore, an individual who transported illegal drugs in an automobile with a loaded pistol contained in a bag in the car's trunk did not "use" that firearm in the commission of the offense, nor did an individual "use" a firearm that was found in a locked trunk in a closet in a bedroom from which illegal drugs were retrieved for sale (the companion case of *Robinson v. United States*, 94-7492, consolidated with *Bailey*).

9-0. Opinion for unanimous Court by O'Connor.

Bank One Chicago v. Midwest Bank & Trust 116 S. Ct. 637, 64 USLW 4069 (1-17-96)

Banking, Expedited Funds Availability Act: The Expedited Funds Availability Act provides for federal court jurisdiction not only in suits between customers and banks, but also in suits initiated by one bank against another bank. 12 U.S.C. § 4010(d) vests federal district courts with jurisdiction over "[a]ny action under this section." Subsection (a) provides for a bank's liability to "any person other than another depository institution," and subsection (f) authorizes the Federal Reserve Board to "impose on or allocate among depository institutions the risks of loss and liability." The title of section 4010 ("civil liability") and its drafting history suggest that courts may adjudicate both types of actions. Subsection (f) authorizes the Board to establish rules allocating risk of loss and liability among banks, but does not confer adjudicatory power on the Board. The language "contrasts conspicuously" with statutes in which Congress has given the Board adjudicatory authority. This interpretation allows all check-related claims arising out of the same transaction to be adjudicated in the same forum; the Court "would hesitate" to attribute to Congress a jurisdictional scheme precluding single-forum adjudication.

9-0. Opinion of Court by Ginsburg, joined by all Justices except Scalia, who joined in part. Concurring opinions by Stevens, joined by Breyer; and by Scalia.

Barnett Bank of Marion County v. Nelson 116 S. Ct. 1103, 64 USLW 4161 (3-26-96)

Preemption, banking, insurance: A federal law empowering national banks in small towns to sell insurance (12 U.S.C. § 92) preempts a Florida law prohibiting banks from dealing in insurance. The federal law contains no explicit statement of preemption, but preemption is implicit because the state law stands as an obstacle to the accomplishment of one of the federal law's purposes. The federal law is not limited in application to those situations in which state law also grants permission to engage in the insurance business. The authority conferred on small-town banks is referred to as a "power," and there is no explicit language, as there is in other banking statutes, that exercise of the power is subject to state law. The McCarran-Ferguson Act's special preemption rule, directing courts not to construe federal statutes to preempt state insurance laws unless the federal law "specifically relates to the business of insurance," does not preclude preemption. The stated purpose of this rule is to insure that congressional "silence" not be construed to prevent state regulation of insurance. The federal banking law at issue, however, *does* specifically and explicitly relate to the business of insurance.

9-0. Opinion for unanimous Court by Breyer.

Behrens v. Pelletier 116 S. Ct. 834, 64 USLW 4081 (2-21-96)

Appeals, interlocutory, qualified immunity ruling: A defendant's immediate appeal of an unfavorable qualified-immunity ruling on a motion to dismiss does not deprive the court of appeals of jurisdiction over a second appeal, also based on qualified immunity, following denial of summary judgment. *Mitchell v. Forsyth* (1985), established that a district court's rejection of a claim of qualified immunity at either the dismissal stage or the summary judgment stage is a "final" judgment subject to appeal under 28 U.S.C. § 1291. An unsuccessful appeal from a denial of dismissal cannot make the later denial of a motion for summary judgment any less "final." Also, different issues are presented at the two stages. A motion to dismiss is based on the defendant's conduct as alleged in the complaint, while a motion for summary judgment relies on stipulated evidence.

7-2. Opinion of Court by Scalia, joined by Rehnquist, O'Connor, Kennedy, Souter, Thomas, and Ginsburg. Dissenting opinion by Breyer, joined by Stevens.

Bennis v. Michigan 116 S. Ct. 994, 64 USLW 4124 (3-4-96)

Due Process, forfeiture, innocent owner defense: A Michigan court's order of forfeiture of an automobile, jointly owned by husband and wife, conforms to due process requirements even with no offset for the wife's half interest in the car. The husband had used the car, without his wife's knowledge or consent, to engage in sexual activity with a prostitute. There is "a long and unbroken line of cases hold[ing] that an owner's interest in property may be forfeited by reason of the use to which the property is put even though the owner did not know that it was to be put to such use." The Court's conclusion of 75 years ago is still valid today: these cases "are too firmly fixed in the punitive and remedial jurisprudence of the country to be now displaced." There is no acceptable basis for distinguishing the current situation. Because the forfeiture was consistent with due process and the property was lawfully acquired by means other than eminent domain, the government's seizure of the property does not constitute a "taking" for which compensation is constitutionally compelled.

5-4. Opinion of Court by Rehnquist, joined by O'Connor, Scalia, Thomas, and Ginsburg. Concurring opinions by Thomas and Ginsburg. Dissenting opinions by Stevens, joined by Souter and Breyer; and by Kennedy.

BMW of North America v. Gore 116 S. Ct. 1589, 64 USLW 4335 (5-20-96)

Due Process, punitive damages: Award of $2 million in punitive damages to a consumer fraud plaintiff who sustained actual damages of $4,000 was so "grossly excessive" that it violated the Due Process Clause of the Fourteenth Amendment. An Alabama jury found that the automobile distributor's national policy of not advising dealers and customers of pre-delivery damage to new cars when the cost of repair did not exceed 3% of the suggested retail price constituted "gross, oppressive or malicious" fraud under state law. That same nondisclosure policy is permissible, however, under the laws of about 25 other states. Due process requires fair notice not only of what conduct is unlawful, but also of the severity of the penalty that may be imposed for violation. BMW did not receive "adequate notice" of the magnitude of the sanction that Alabama might impose. Also, application of "three guideposts" leads to the conclusion that the award was grossly excessive. First, the "degree of reprehensibility" was not great, the injury being purely economic, and there being no evidence of bad faith. Second, the punitive damages do not bear a reasonable relationship to actual or potential compensatory damages; a ratio of 500 to 1 in this case is high. Third, the punitive damages are substantially greater than civil or criminal penalties that can be imposed for comparable misconduct.

5-4. Opinion of Court by Stevens, joined by O'Connor, Kennedy, Souter, and Breyer. Concurring opinion by Breyer, joined by O'Connor and Souter. Dissenting opinions by Scalia, joined by Thomas; and by Ginsburg, joined by Rehnquist.

Board of County Comm'rs v. Umbehr 116 S. Ct. 2342, 64 USLW 4682 (6-28-96)

First Amendment, speech, government contractors: Termination or non-renewal of a public contract in retaliation for the contractor's speech on a matter of public concern can violate the First Amendment. The balancing test used to measure the free speech rights of public employees, adjusted to weigh the government's interest as contractor rather than employer, determines whether a First Amendment violation has occurred. The terminated contractor must show that termination was motivated by his speech on a matter of public concern, and the government can establish a valid defense by showing that the contract would have been terminated even without the speech. Government can also prevail by showing that its legitimate interests as contractor, deferentially viewed, outweigh the free speech interests at stake. This case, involving termination of a county's contract with a trash hauler, is remanded so that lower courts can apply the balancing test.

7-2. Opinion of Court by O'Connor, joined by Stevens, Kennedy, Souter, Ginsburg, and Breyer; and joined in part by Rehnquist. Dissenting opinion by Scalia, joined by Thomas.

Brotherhood of Locomotive Eng'rs v. Atchison, Topeka, & Santa Fe R.R. 116 S. Ct. 595, 64 USLW 4045 (1-8-96)

Railway Labor, Hours of Service Act: Time that train employees spend at the end of their shifts waiting for "deadhead" transportation back to the terminal for release from work is "limbo time," not "on duty" time, within the meaning of the Hours of Service Act, 49 U.S.C. § 21103(b). The Act provides that "time spent in deadhead transportation *to* a duty assignment is time on duty, but time spent in deadhead transportation *from* a duty assignment to the place of final release is neither time on duty nor time off duty." This third category of time is known as "limbo time." Although the Act is silent with respect to time spent waiting for transportation at the end of the shift, this time should be treated the same as time spent in transportation. The Act limits the number of hours that train crews may remain on duty, and the purpose of this limitation is to ensure that fatigued employees do not operate trains. Time spent being transported to a duty assignment can contribute to fatigue that may affect performance. Time spent after that performance is completed, whether that time is spent waiting for transportation or whether it is spent while being transported, cannot have that effect. There is a mandatory "off duty" rest time that begins only after on-duty and "limbo" time are completed.

9-0. Opinion for unanimous Court by Kennedy.

Brown v. Pro Football, Inc. 116 S. Ct. 2116, 64 USLW 4554 (6-20-96)

Labor; antitrust: An agreement by several employers to implement, after impasse in collective bargaining, the terms of their last best good-faith wage offer is exempt from challenge under the antitrust laws. The implicit, non-statutory labor exemption from the antitrust laws was developed to limit the authority of an antitrust court to determine labor policy, and to leave with the National Labor Relations Board the primary responsibility for policing the collective bargaining process. The exemption recognizes that some restraints on competition imposed through the collective bargaining process must be shielded from antitrust sanctions. It is appropriate to extend the exemption to the post-impasse actions at issue, and not to limit the exemption to labor-management agreements. Labor law itself regulates post-impasse imposition of a proposed employment term concerning a mandatory subject of bargaining, and multiemployer bargaining should be treated no differently from single-employer bargaining in this respect. Application of antitrust law could "place in jeopardy some of the potentially beneficial labor-related effects that multiemployer bargaining can achieve," since post-impasse discussions and agreements among employers would be subject to antitrust scrutiny.

8-1. Opinion of Court by Breyer, joined by Rehnquist, O'Connor, Scalia, Kennedy, Souter, Thomas, and Ginsburg. Dissenting opinion by Stevens.

Bush v. Vera 116 S. Ct. 1941, 64 USLW 4452 (6-13-96)

Congressional districting, racial gerrymander: Three congressional districts created by Texas law constitute racial gerrymanders that are unconstitutional under the Equal Protection Clause. The district court correctly held that race predominated over legitimate districting considerations, including incumbency, and consequently strict scrutiny applies. None of the three districts is narrowly tailored to serve a compelling state interest. Assuming that compliance with the "results" test of Voting Rights Act § 2 is a compelling state interest, the fact that all three districts are "bizarrely shaped" by racial gerrymandering defeats any claim that the districts were narrowly tailored to serve that interest. Similarly, departure from "sound districting principles" defeats the claim that the districts are narrowly tailored to ameliorate the effects of racial discrimination. Finally, creation of a new District 18 to increase the percentage of the African-American population beyond what it had been in the old district, and beyond what it would have been in that old district under the new census, was not justified by the State's interest in complying with Voting Rights Act § 5's "non-retrogression" principle.

5-4. No opinion of Court. Concurring opinions by O'Connor, joined by Rehnquist and Kennedy; by O'Connor (separately); by Kennedy; and by Thomas, joined by Scalia. Dissenting opinions by Stevens, joined by Ginsburg and Breyer; and by Souter, joined by Ginsburg and Breyer.

Calderon v. Moore 116 S. Ct. 2066, 64 USLW 3836 (6-17-96)

Mootness, order for new trial, appeal by state: California's appeal from an order of a federal district court vacating a conviction and ordering a new trial or release of the defendant was "clearly not moot," and should not have been dismissed as moot. An appeal should be dismissed as moot if the appeals court cannot grant "any effective relief whatever," but even a "partial remedy" is sufficient to avoid mootness. Here a partial remedy was available, since a decision in the State's favor would have relieved the State from the burden of conducting a new trial.

9-0. *Per curiam.*

Carlisle v. United States 116 S. Ct. 1460, 64 USLW 4293 (4-29-96)

Criminal procedure: The federal district court in this case had no authority to grant a post-verdict motion for judgment of acquittal filed one day after the deadline prescribed by Federal Rule of Criminal Procedure 29(c). The rule requires that the motion be made "within 7 days after the jury is discharged or within such further period as the court may fix during the 7-day period," and the court had not during the applicable 7-day period extended the deadline. Rule 45(b), which authorizes validation of some untimely acts, provides that "the court may not extend the time for taking any action under Rule 29." These rules are unambiguous, and afford no basis for the granting of an untimely motion to acquit. It matters not that the motion was accompanied by a claim of legal innocence, that the motion was filed before sentencing, or that the late filing was due to attorney error. The authority of a court under Rule 29(a) "of its own motion" to enter a judgment of acquittal is limited by the provision's caption, "Motion Before Submission to Jury." The inherent supervisory power of federal courts does not include the power to develop rules that circumvent or conflict with the Federal Rules of Criminal Procedure.

7-2. Opinion of Court by Scalia, joined by Rehnquist, O'Connor, Souter, Thomas, Ginsburg, and Breyer. Concurring opinions by Souter; and by Ginsburg, joined by Souter and Breyer. Dissenting opinion by Stevens, joined by Kennedy.

Citizens Bank of Maryland v. Strumpf 116 S. Ct. 286, 64 USLW 4001 (10-31-95)

Bankruptcy, setoff: The bank's "administrative hold" on the respondent's checking account, imposed while the bank sought relief in bankruptcy court from the automatic stay imposed when the respondent had filed under chapter 13 of the Bankruptcy Code, did not constitute a "setoff" within the meaning of 11 U.S.C. § 362(a)(7). That provision imposes an automatic stay of various actions by creditors, including a creditor's "setoff" of any debt that arose before the bankruptcy filing. The respondent had an outstanding balance on a loan from the bank, and the bank asked the bankruptcy court to lift the stay and allow it to set off respondent's checking account balance against the unpaid loan. The administrative hold itself was not a setoff, however. The bank refused to pay only temporarily, pending action by the court, yet a setoff can occur only if there is an intent permanently to settle accounts. The bankruptcy court erred, therefore, in finding the bank in contempt for violating the automatic stay by imposing the administrative hold.

9-0. Opinion for unanimous Court by Scalia.

Colorado Republican Campaign Comm. v. FEC 116 S. Ct. 2309, 64 USLW 4663 (6-26-96)

First Amendment, political party campaign expenditures: The First Amendment bars application of the Party Expenditure Provision of the Federal Election Campaign Act, 2 U.S.C. § 441a(d)(3), to expenditures that the political party makes independently, without coordination with the candidate. That provision limits expenditures by a political party "in connection with the general election campaign of a [congressional] candidate." The expenditures in this case, for a television advertising campaign directed against the other party's likely candidate for the United States Senate, and undertaken before either party had nominated its candidate, were properly considered independent expenditures and not "coordinated" expenditures that must be treated as a campaign contribution.

7-2. No opinion of Court. Opinion announcing Court's judgment by Breyer, joined by O'Connor and Souter. Opinion concurring in part and dissenting in part by Kennedy, joined by Rehnquist and Scalia. Opinion concurring in part and dissenting in part by Thomas, joined in part by Rehnquist and Scalia. Dissenting opinion by Stevens, joined by Ginsburg.

Commissioner v. Lundy 116 S. Ct. 647, 64 USLW 4061 (1-17-96)

Taxation, Federal, refund "look-back" period: The Tax Court may not award a refund of taxes paid more than two years prior to the date on which the Commissioner mailed the taxpayer a notice of deficiency, if, on the date the notice of deficiency was mailed, the taxpayer had not yet filed a tax return for the covered period. Under 26 U.S.C. § 6512(b)(3)(B), the applicable "look-back" period is "the period which would be applicable under section 6511(b)(2)" if a claim for refund had been filed on the date that the notice of deficiency was mailed. Section 6511(b)(2) sets two look-back periods, corresponding to two different scenarios. A taxpayer must make a claim for refund within 3 years from the time the return was filed, "or, if no return was filed by the taxpayer, within 2 years from the time the tax was paid." Here, the taxpayer's wages were withheld in excess of tax liability, and the tax was deemed "paid" on the date due (April 15 of the following year). When the notice of deficiency was mailed more than two years later, the taxpayer still had not filed a return, so the 2-year rather than the 3-year "look-back" was applicable.

7-2. Opinion of Court by O'Connor, joined by Rehnquist, Scalia, Kennedy, Souter, Ginsburg, and Breyer. Dissenting opinions by Stevens, and by Thomas, joined by Stevens.

Cooper v. Oklahoma 116 S. Ct. 1373, 64 USLW 4255 (4-16-96)

Due Process, competency to stand trial: Oklahoma's rule requiring that a criminal defendant prove by clear and convincing evidence his incompetence to stand trial violates due process. It is well established that a criminal trial of an incompetent defendant violates due process, but that a state may place the burden on the defendant to prove his incompetence by a preponderance of the evidence. The additional burden of proving incompetence by clear and convincing evidence, however, allows Oklahoma to try a defendant who is more likely than not incompetent, and thereby threatens the defendant's fundamental right to be tried only while competent. There is little historical support, in English common law or in this country, for requiring the defendant to shoulder the onerous burden of proving incompetence by clear and convincing evidence. The near-uniform application of a standard more protective of a defendant's rights suggests that the heightened standard offends a principle of justice strongly rooted in our peoples' traditions and conscience. The consequences to the defendant of an erroneous finding of competency are "dire," whereas the injury to the State from an erroneous finding of incompetency is "modest."

9-0. Opinion for unanimous Court by Stevens.

Dalton v. Little Rock Family Planning Servs. 116 S. Ct. 1063, 64 USLW 3622 (3-18-96)

Preemption, Hyde Amendment, state abortion funding ban: Lower courts should not have enjoined "in its entirety" Amendment 68 of the Arkansas Constitution, which prohibits use of public funds to pay for an abortion, "except to save the mother's life." The Social Security Act, as amended by the Hyde Amendment, requires that states participating in the Medicaid program fund abortions not only when the mother's life is in danger, but also in cases in which pregnancy resulted from rape or incest. The only conflict, therefore, occurs in cases in which a Medicaid-eligible woman whose pregnancy resulted from rape or incest seeks an abortion not necessary to save her own life. The injunction, which applied "for so long as the State accepts" Medicaid funds, was overbroad in duration as well as scope. The Hyde Amendment is an appropriation limitation, not permanent legislation, and therefore applies for only one fiscal year.

9-0. *Per curiam.*

Degen v. United States 116 S. Ct. 1777, 64 USLW 4413 (6-10-96)

Forfeiture, fugitive disentitlement: A federal district court should not enter judgment against a claimant in a civil forfeiture action simply because he is a fugitive from a related criminal prosecution. Courts have authority, under the fugitive disentitlement doctrine, to dismiss an appeal or a petition for writ of certiorari, but the same reasons do not justify reliance on the doctrine in a civil forfeiture case. There is no risk of delay or frustration in determining the merits of the Government's forfeiture claims, and no danger that the court's judgment will be unenforceable in practice. While a party in a civil forfeiture action is generally entitled to broader discovery rights than is a criminal defendant, the court can manage discovery and other aspects of the litigation so as to avert the possibility of the defendant's using civil discovery to gain an improper advantage in the criminal case. Disentitlement is "too blunt an instrument" for redressing the indignity to the court resulting from the defendant's absence from the criminal proceeding; respect for a court "is eroded, not enhanced, by too free a recourse to rules foreclosing consideration . . . on the merits."

9-0. Opinion for unanimous Court by Kennedy.

Denver Area Educ. Tel. Consortium v. FCC 116 S. Ct. 2374, 64 USLW 4706 (6-28-96)

First Amendment, cable television indecency: Section 10(a) of the Cable Television Consumer Protection and Competition Act of 1992, 47 U.S.C. § 532(h), which permits cable operators to prohibit indecent material on leased access channels, does not violate the First Amendment. Section 10(b) of the law, 47 U.S.C. § 532(j), which requires cable operators to segregate and block indecent programming on leased access channels if they do not prohibit it, does violate the First Amendment. The segregate and block restrictions, which include a requirement that a request for access be in writing, and which allow for up to 30 days' delay in blocking or unblocking a channel, are neither narrowly nor reasonably tailored to serve the government's compelling interest in protecting children from indecent programming. Section 10(c), 47 U.S.C. § 531 note, which permits a cable operator to prevent transmission of "sexually explicit" programming on public access channels, violates the First Amendment.

7-2 (§ 10(a)); **6-3** (§ 10(b)); **5-4** (§10(c)). Opinion of Court by Breyer (with respect to § 10(b) only), joined by Stevens, O'Connor, Kennedy, Souter, and Ginsburg. Other parts of Breyer opinion joined by Stevens, O'Connor, and Souter. Still other parts of Breyer opinion joined by Stevens and Souter. Concurring opinions by Stevens and Souter. Opinions concurring in part and dissenting in part by O'Connor; by Kennedy, joined by Ginsburg; and by Thomas, joined by Rehnquist and Scalia.

Doctor's Associates, Inc. v. Casarotto 116 S. Ct. 1652, 64 USLW 4370 (5-20-96)

Federal Arbitration Act, preemption: A Montana law declaring an arbitration clause unenforceable unless notice that the contract is subject to arbitration appears in underlined capital letters on the first page of the contract is preempted by the Federal Arbitration Act. Section 2 of the FAA declares arbitration clauses valid except "upon such grounds as exist at law or in equity for the revocation of any contract." This means that states may regulate arbitration clauses through application of general contract law principles, but may not invalidate arbitration agreements under state laws applicable only to arbitration provisions. Because Montana's law applies only to arbitration clauses, it is inconsistent with, and preempted by, FAA § 2.

8-1. Opinion of Court by Ginsburg, joined by Rehnquist, Stevens, O'Connor, Scalia, Kennedy, Souter, and Breyer. Dissenting opinion by Thomas.

Exxon Co., U.S.A. v. Sofec, Inc. 116 S. Ct. 1813, 64 USLW 4415 (6-10-96)

Admiralty, negligence, warranty, superseding cause: A plaintiff in admiralty whose actions were the superseding and thus the sole proximate cause of its own injury cannot recover part of its damages from a tortfeasor whose negligence was a cause in fact of the plaintiff's injury, and similarly cannot recover in contract from a party whose breach of warranty was a mere cause in fact of the injury. The proximate cause doctrine and the related superseding cause doctrine are applicable in admiralty. There is no inconsistency in recognizing the superseding cause doctrine and in apportioning damages based upon comparative fault among those tortfeasors whose actions were proximate causes of an injury.

9-0. Opinion for unanimous Court by Thomas.

Felker v. Turpin 116 S. Ct. 2333, 64 USLW 4677 (6-28-96)

Habeas corpus, Supreme Court jurisdiction: Title I of the Antiterrorism and Effective Death Penalty Act of 1996, which limits second or successive habeas corpus petitions in federal courts, does not eliminate the Supreme Court's authority to entertain habeas petitions as original matters pursuant to 28 U.S.C. §§ 2241 and 2254. No provision of the Act mentions the Court's authority to entertain original petitions, and there is no repeal by implication. There is "no plausible argument," therefore, that the Act has deprived the Court of appellate jurisdiction in violation of Art. III, § 2. The Act also does not suspend the writ of habeas corpus in violation of Art. I, § 9, cl. 2. The petition for an original writ of habeas corpus in this case is denied.

9-0. Opinion for unanimous Court by Rehnquist. Concurring opinions by Stevens, joined by Souter and Breyer; and by Souter, joined by Stevens and Breyer.

Field v. Mans 116 S. Ct. 437, 64 USLW 4015 (11-28-95)

Bankruptcy, discharge of debts, fraudulent representation: A creditor need not establish "reasonable reliance" on a debtor's fraudulent representation in order to have a debt excepted from discharge under section 523(a)(2)(A) of the Bankruptcy Code. Instead, the provision incorporates the common law standard of "justifiable reliance," which focuses on the individual's actual understanding rather than on the reasonableness of his reaction. A parallel Code provision applicable to written misrepresentations expressly requires reasonable reliance, but the "negative pregnant" inference derived from the absence of such language in subparagraph (A) is of only minor interpretive aid. More important is the meaning of the language used in subparagraph (A). "Actual fraud" is a term of art that, in the absence of contrary indications, has the common law meaning that was established at the time of enactment. Reference to the Restatement (Second) of Torts, to a leading treatise, and to decisions of state courts establishes that "actual fraud" was understood to require both actual and "justifiable" reliance, but not "reasonable reliance."

7-2. Opinion of Court by Souter, joined by Rehnquist, Stevens, O'Connor, Kennedy, Thomas, and Ginsburg. Concurring opinion by Ginsburg. Dissenting opinion by Breyer, joined by Scalia.

44 Liquormart, Inc. v. Rhode Island 116 S. Ct. 1495, 64 USLW 4313 (5-13-96)

Commercial speech, liquor price advertising: Rhode Island's statutory prohibition against advertisements that provide the public with accurate information about retail prices of alcoholic beverages abridges freedom of speech protected by the First Amendment, and is not shielded from constitutional scrutiny by the Twenty-first Amendment. There is not a "reasonable fit" between the blanket prohibition and the State's goal of reducing alcohol consumption. The Twenty-first Amendment, while it grants states authority over commerce that might otherwise be reserved to the Federal Government, "places no limit whatsoever on other constitutional provisions." *California v. LaRue* (1972) is disavowed to the extent that it relied on the Twenty-first Amendment to uphold a California prohibition on sexually explicit live entertainment in establishments licensed to serve liquor by the drink.

9-0. Opinion of Court by Stevens, joined in part by Scalia, Kennedy, Souter, Thomas, and Ginsburg, and in different part by Scalia, Kennedy, Souter, and Ginsburg. Other portions of Stevens' opinion were joined by Kennedy, Souter, and Ginsburg; by Kennedy, Thomas, and Ginsburg; and by Kennedy and Ginsburg. Concurring opinions by Scalia; by Thomas; and by O'Connor, joined by Rehnquist, Souter, and Breyer.

Fulton Corp. v. Faulkner 116 S. Ct. 848, 64 USLW 4088 (2-21-96)

Commerce Clause, discriminatory state tax: North Carolina's intangibles tax on a fraction of the value of corporate stock owned by North Carolina residents inversely proportional to the corporation's exposure to the State's income tax, violates the "dormant" Commerce Clause. The tax facially discriminates against interstate commerce, and is not a "compensatory tax" designed to make interstate commerce bear a burden already borne by intrastate commerce. The tax meets none of the three criteria for classification as a valid compensatory tax. The State has not identified an intrastate tax for which it may legitimately seek compensation from interstate operations. The general corporate income tax will not suffice for this purpose, and it can be assumed that the State regulates access to its capital markets by means of Blue Sky Laws. It is impossible to satisfy the second criterion by demonstrating that the taxes are roughly equivalent in amount, since there is no evidence of what proportion of the general corporate income tax serves to support the capital market. Finally, it cannot be shown that the taxes fall on substantially equivalent events. *Darnell v. Indiana* (1912) is no longer good law.

9-0. Opinion for unanimous Court by Souter. Concurring opinion by Rehnquist.

Gasperini v. Center for Humanities, Inc. 116 S. Ct. 2211, 64 USLW 4607 (6-24-96)

Seventh Amendment, review of reasonableness of jury verdict: A New York law authorizing appellate courts to review the size of civil jury verdicts and to order new trials when the jury's verdict "deviates materially from what would be reasonable compensation" can be given effect by federal district courts reviewing jury awards in cases based on diversity of citizenship without violating the Seventh Amendment. In diversity actions federal courts apply federal procedural law but must apply state substantive law. New York's law, although it contains a procedural instruction, has a "manifestly substantive" objective. Application of the New York law at the federal appellate level would be "out of sync" with the federal system's allocation of functions between trial and appellate courts. That allocation is "weighted" by the Seventh Amendment's "re-examination" clause, which provides that "no fact tried by a jury, shall be otherwise re-examined in any Court of the United States, than according to the rules of the common law." The principal state and federal interests can be accommodated, however, if the federal district court rather than the appellate court measures the jury award by New York's material deviation standard, and if that application of the standard is then subject to appellate review under the abuse of discretion standard that now governs appeals alleging excessiveness or inadequacy of a jury verdict.

5-4. Opinion of Court by Ginsburg, joined by O'Connor, Kennedy, Souter, and Breyer. Dissenting opinions by Stevens; and by Scalia, joined by Rehnquist and Thomas.

Gray v. Netherland 116 S. Ct. 2074, 64 USLW 4531 (6-20-96)

Habeas corpus, new rule limitation: A *habeas corpus* petitioner's claim that he was denied due process of law because he was not given adequate notice of some of the evidence that the state would use against him in the penalty phase of his trial would, if sustained, necessitate creation of a "new rule," and therefore does not provide a basis upon which he may receive federal *habeas* relief. A criminal defendant has a well-established right to notice of the charges against which he must defend, but notice of the state's evidence is on a different footing. Here, when defendant's counsel learned on the eve of the trial's penalty phase that the state would introduce additional evidence attempting to link the defendant to a crime with which he was not charged, counsel did not seek a continuance, but instead sought exclusion of the evidence. To hold that due process required a continuance whether or not the defendant sought one, or, in the alternative, that evidence must be excluded, would constitute a "new constitutional rule." The case is remanded, however, to consider whether petitioner had presented, on direct appeal or in state *habeas* proceedings, a claim that the state had misrepresented the evidence it intended to present.

5-4. Opinion of Court by Rehnquist, joined by O'Connor, Scalia, Kennedy, and Thomas. Dissenting opinions by Stevens; and by Ginsburg, joined by Stevens, Souter, and Breyer.

Henderson v. United States 116 S. Ct. 1638, 64 USLW 4362 (5-20-96)

Admiralty, service of process: Service of process for an action filed under the Suits in Admiralty Act (SAA) is governed by Rule 4 of the Federal Rules of Civil Procedure, not by section 2 of the SAA, 46 U.S.C. App. § 742. The two provisions are irreconcilable. Rule 4 requires service within 120 days, but allows the court to extend that period, while SAA § 2 requires that service be made "forthwith." Rule 4 supersedes the inconsistent statutory directive. Section 2's process directive is not a "jurisdictional" requirement setting the terms on which the United States waives sovereign immunity, but instead is a rule governing practice and procedure. Under the Rules Enabling Act, 28 U.S.C. § 2072, laws in conflict with rules "shall be of no further force or effect." A rule enacted by Congress, as was Rule 4, supersedes conflicting laws "no less than" a Rule prescribed by the Court.

6-3. Opinion of Court by Ginsburg, joined by Stevens, Scalia, Kennedy, Souter, and Breyer. Concurring opinion by Scalia, joined by Kennedy. Dissenting opinion by Thomas, joined by Rehnquist and O'Connor.

Hercules, Inc. v. United States 116 S. Ct. 981, 64 USLW 4117 (3-4-96)

Government contracts, indemnification, Agent Orange settlements: Chemical manufacturers who produced the defoliant Agent Orange under contracts with the Federal Government are not entitled to indemnification for costs incurred in defending and settling tort claims by Vietnam War veterans alleging injury from use of Agent Orange. The contracts contained no explicit warranties covering indemnification, and none can be implied under the circumstances. When the Government provides specifications directing how a contract is to be performed, it warrants that the contractor will be able to perform the contract satisfactorily by following the specifications. This warranty of specifications does not extend beyond performance of the contract, and hence does not include third-party claims against the contractor. Also, the companies failed to establish existence of an implied-in-fact agreement to indemnify against losses to third parties.

6-2. Opinion of Court by Rehnquist, joined by Scalia, Kennedy, Souter, Thomas, and Ginsburg. Dissenting opinion by Breyer, joined by O'Connor. Stevens did not participate.

Holly Farms Corp. v. NLRB 116 S. Ct. 1396, 64 USLW 4269 (4-23-96)

National Labor Relations Act, "employee": The decision of the NLRB that workers described as "live-haul" crews -- teams of chicken catchers, forklift operators, and truck drivers -- are covered "employees" within the meaning of the National Labor Relations Act, and not exempt "agricultural laborers," is a reasonable interpretation entitled to deference. NLRB appropriations acts tie the definition of "agricultural laborer" to the definition of "agriculture" in the Fair Labor Standards Act. That definition includes work performed "on a farm" as an incident to the raising of poultry. It is clear that the truck drivers do not work "on a farm." Because it is unclear whether the catchers and forklift operators work "on a farm," it is appropriate, under the approach of *Chevron U.S.A. v. NRDC* (1984), for courts to defer to a reasonable administrative interpretation. The live-haul crews are more appropriately tied to the company's slaughtering and processing operations than to the independent farming operations that have contracted to raise chickens for the company. The crews report to work at the company's processing plant, go to the farms to retrieve and load the chickens, and then transport the chickens back to the processing plant. Treating the crews as employees is consistent with longstanding NLRB precedent, and is not inconsistent with Department of Labor interpretations.

9-0, 5-4. Opinion of Court by Ginsburg, joined by Stevens, Kennedy, Souter, and Breyer. Opinion by O'Connor, joined by Rehnquist, Scalia, and Thomas, concurring as to the truck drivers, dissenting as to the chicken catchers and forklift operators.

Jaffee v. Redmond 116 S. Ct. 1923, 64 USLW 4490 (6-13-96)

Evidence, psychotherapist privilege: Confidential communications between a licensed psychotherapist and her patients in the course of diagnosis or treatment are protected from compelled disclosure under Rule 501 of the Federal Rules of Evidence. Rule 501 authorizes federal courts to define new privileges by interpreting common law principles "in the light of reason and experience." All 50 states and the District of Columbia have enacted some form of psychotherapist privilege, and it is appropriate to treat a consistent body of policy determinations by state legislatures as reflecting both reason and experience. In addition, a psychotherapist privilege was among nine privileges recommended by an advisory committee of the Judicial Conference. The privilege serves the public interest by facilitating appropriate mental health care, and, on the other hand, the likely evidentiary benefit that would result from denial of the privilege is "modest." The privilege extends to communications made to licensed social workers "in the course of psychotherapy," as well as to communications with licensed psychiatrists and psychologists. The "vast majority" of states extend the privilege to licensed social workers, whose counseling sessions "serve the same public goals" as those of psychiatrists and psychologists.

7-2. Opinion of Court by Stevens, joined by O'Connor, Kennedy, Souter, Thomas, Ginsburg, and Breyer. Dissenting opinion by Scalia, joined by Rehnquist.

Koon v. United States 116 S. Ct. 2035, 64 USLW 4512 (6-13-96)

Sentencing, departure from Guidelines: In reviewing a district court's decision to depart from the sentencing range set forth in the Sentencing

Guidelines, an appellate court should, for most issues, determine whether the district court abused its discretion, and should not conduct *de novo* review. The Guidelines are designed for a "heartland" of typical cases, and do not adequately take into account cases that are, for one reason or another, unusual. Sentencing courts should determine whether there are circumstances that make a case unusual, and whether the Guidelines and accompanying commentary prohibit, encourage, or discourage departures on the basis of the features that make the case unusual. In this case, involving a downward departure in sentencing of Los Angeles police officers convicted in the nationally publicized beating of suspect Rodney King, the district court was within its discretion in some respects and abused its discretion in other respects. The district court was within its discretion in departing downward because the victim's misconduct "contributed significantly to provoking" the officers' crimes, because of the officers' susceptibility to abuse in prison due to the notoriety of the crimes, and because of the successive state and federal prosecutions. The district court did abuse its discretion, however, in decreasing the sentences because of the effect of the convictions on the officers' future employment possibilities, and because of the low likelihood of the officers' recidivism.

9-0; **8-1** (future employment issue); **6-3** (abuse in prison and successive prosecution issues). Opinion of Court by Kennedy, joined by Rehnquist, O'Connor, Scalia, and Thomas; and joined in part by Stevens, Souter, Ginsburg, and Breyer. Opinion by Stevens concurring in part and dissenting in part. Opinion by Souter, joined by Ginsburg, concurring in part and dissenting in part. Opinion by Breyer, joined by Ginsburg, concurring in part and dissenting in part.

Lane v. Pena 116 S. Ct. 2092, 64 USLW 4541 (6-20-96)

Rehabilitation Act, sovereign immunity: Congress has not fully waived the Federal Government's sovereign immunity against awards of monetary damages for violation of section 504(a) of the Rehabilitation Act, 29 U.S.C. § 794(a). A student dismissed from the United States Merchant Marine Academy because of his disability was entitled to reinstatement, but not monetary damages. Section 504 prohibits discrimination on the basis of disability "under any program or activity conducted by any Executive agency." Section 505(a)(2) provides that remedies available under Title VI of the Civil Rights Act of 1964, including monetary damages, apply also to section 504 violations "by any . . . Federal provider of [financial] assistance." A waiver of sovereign immunity must be unequivocally expressed in statutory text, and any such waiver is strictly construed in favor of the sovereign. The language of section 505 is inadequate to waive sovereign immunity for the broad category of "program[s]" and "activit[ies]" covered by section 504, but instead is limited by its terms to "providers" of financial assistance. The "equalization" amendments of 1986, which abrogated states' Eleventh Amendment immunity from § 504 suits, and which authorized remedies in such actions "to the same extent [as against] any public or private entity other than a State," also did not unambiguously waive the Federal Government's immunity from damages.

7-2. Opinion of Court by O'Connor, joined by Rehnquist, Scalia, Kennedy, Souter, Thomas, and Ginsburg. Dissenting opinion by Stevens, joined by Breyer.

Lawrence v. Chater 116 S. Ct. 604, 64 USLW 3460 (1-8-96)

Supreme Court, standards for vacatur and remand: Under 28 U.S.C. § 2106, which confers authority on the Supreme Court and other federal appellate courts to vacate and remand for "such further proceedings . . . as may be just under the circumstances," the Supreme Court has the power to remand to a lower federal court any case that is properly before the Court in its appellate capacity. An order granting certiorari, vacating the judgment, and remanding the case (a GVR order) is potentially appropriate, subject to the equities of the case, if intervening or recent developments "reveal a reasonable probability that the decision below rests upon a premise that the lower court would reject if given the opportunity for further consideration, and where it appears that such a redetermination may determine the ultimate outcome of the litigation." This principle governs cases involving confessions of error by litigants and cases involving a change in agency interpretation of the governing statute that "is reasonably probably entitled to deference and potentially determinative." *Certainty* that the lower court relied on the changed position or interpretation is not required. It is "important that the meaningful exercise of the Court's appellate docket not be precluded by uncertainty as to what the [lower] court might . . . have relied on," especially given the increase in summary dispositions by the appellate courts. Here, a changed interpretation of the Social Security Act by the Social Security Administration that would result in conferral of benefits denied by the lower courts merits issuance of a GVR order.

7-2. *Per curiam*. Concurring opinion by Rehnquist. Dissenting opinion by Scalia, joined by Thomas.

Leavitt v. Jane L. 116 S. Ct. 2068, 64 USLW 3834 (6-17-96)

Severability, Utah abortion law: The U.S. Court of Appeals for the Tenth Circuit erred in invalidating a provision of Utah's abortion law, regulating abortions after 20 weeks gestational age, on the grounds that it was not severable from another portion of the law, regulating earlier abortions, that had been ruled unconstitutional. The principal issue in severability is whether the legislature would have passed the statute without the unconstitutional section. The Utah Legislature answered this question by including explicit severability language in its abortion code, and the appeals court should not have disregarded this statement of intent.

5-4. *Per curiam*. Dissenting opinion by Stevens, joined by Souter, Ginsburg, and Breyer.

Lewis v. Casey 116 S. Ct. 2174, 64 USLW 4587 (6-24-96)

Prisoners, access to courts: A class action by Arizona prison inmates alleging that the Arizona Department of Corrections furnished inadequate legal assistance and research facilities, thereby depriving inmates of their right of access to the courts, failed to establish the widespread injuries necessary to justify the detailed, system-wide injunction issued by the district court. In order to establish a violation of the access right recognized in *Bounds v. Smith* (1977), an inmate must demonstrate actual injury to that right. It is not enough to allege deficiencies in the prison library or in the prison's legal assistance program; the inmate must go one step further and show that these shortcomings hindered his efforts to pursue a legal claim. In this case the district court identified only two instances of actual injury, and its remedy should have been limited to the deficiencies that produced those injuries. The two instances of injury were "a patently inadequate basis" for finding system-wide violation and for imposition of system-wide relief. Also, the court failed to accord adequate deference to the judgment of corrections authorities in devising a remedy. Instead of turning the matter over to a special master, the court should have ordered the Corrections Department to submit a program remedying constitutional violations.

8-1. Opinion of Court by Scalia, joined by Rehnquist, O'Connor, Kennedy, and Thomas; and joined in part by Souter, Ginsburg, and Breyer. Opinion concurring in part (on inappropriateness of system-wide relief) and dissenting in part (standing-related issues) by Souter, joined by Ginsburg and Breyer. Dissenting opinion by Stevens.

Lewis v. United States 116 S. Ct. 2163, 64 USLW 4581 (6-24-96)

Sixth Amendment, right to jury trial: A defendant who is prosecuted in a single proceeding for multiple petty offenses does not have a constitutional right to a jury trial even if the aggregate of sentences authorized for the offenses exceeds six months. The Sixth Amendment's right to a jury trial extends only to serious offenses, not to petty offenses punishable by six months' imprisonment or less, and the scope of the right does not change just because a defendant faces a potential aggregate prison term in excess of six months for petty offenses charged. The maximum penalty attached to an offense reveals the legislature's judgment about the severity of that offense, and the fact that a defendant may be charged with more than one count of a petty offense does not change that legislative judgment, and does not transform the petty offense into a serious one.

7-2. Opinion of Court by O'Connor, joined by Rehnquist, Scalia, Souter, and Thomas. Concurring opinion by Kennedy, joined by Breyer. Dissenting opinion by Stevens, joined by Ginsburg.

Libretti v. United States 116 S. Ct. 356, 64 USLW 4005 (11-7-95)

Forfeiture, guilty plea, waiver of right to jury: Federal Rule of Criminal Procedure 11(f), which prohibits a district court from entering a judgment on a guilty plea without determining that there is a "factual basis for the plea," does not require the court to determine whether a factual basis exists for a stipulated asset forfeiture embodied in a plea agreement. By its plain language, the rule applies only to "a plea of guilty" and not to the sentence imposed following entry of judgment on the plea; forfeiture is punishment that is part of the sentence. Although Rule 31(e) requires a special jury verdict on the scope of forfeiture, a district court need not advise a defendant that his guilty plea will result in waiver of this Rule 31 right. A defendant must be advised that a guilty plea will constitute a waiver of certain constitutional rights, including the right to a jury determination of guilt, but the Rule 31 right is not such a right. Here the defendant's stipulation to forfeiture of specified assets was an adequate waiver of his Rule 31 right.

8-1. Opinion of Court by O'Connor, joined by Rehnquist and Kennedy, and joined in part by Scalia, Souter, Thomas, Ginsburg, and Breyer. Concurring opinions by Souter and Ginsburg. Dissenting opinion by Stevens.

Lockheed Corp. v. Spink 116 S. Ct. 1783, 64 USLW 4430 (6-10-96)

ERISA, prohibited "transaction": ERISA § 406 does not prohibit an employer from conditioning receipt of early retirement benefits on the employee's agreement to release any employment-related claims against the employer. Section 406 regulates the conduct of plan "fiduciaries" by prohibiting certain "transactions." Lockheed and its plan sponsors were not acting as "fiduciaries" when they altered the terms of their pension plans to offer the early retirement options. As is the case with welfare benefit plans, the amendment of a retirement plan is not an act of plan management or administration that comes within the ambit of fiduciary obligations. Also, the payment of benefits by plan administrators in exchange for performance of some condition by the employee is not a "transaction" that section 406 prohibits fiduciaries from undertaking. Sections of the Omnibus Budget Reconciliation Act of 1986 that amended ERISA and the Age Discrimination in Employment Act to prohibit age-based benefit accrual rules do not apply retroactively.

9-0; **7-2**. Opinion of Court by Thomas, unanimous on the "fiduciary" and OBRA interpretations, and joined by Rehnquist, Stevens, O'Connor, Scalia, Kennedy, and Ginsburg on the "transaction" issue. Opinion by Breyer, joined by Souter, concurring in part and dissenting as to the Court's consideration of the "transaction" issue.

Lonchar v. Thomas 116 S. Ct. 1293, 64 USLW 4245 (4-1-96)

Habeas corpus: If a district court cannot dismiss a habeas corpus petition on the merits before the petitioner's scheduled execution, the court is obligated to address the merits and must issue a stay to prevent the case from becoming moot. The appeals court in this case erred in issuing an order vacating the stay of execution. Federal courts lack authority to dismiss a valid first habeas corpus petition for "equitable reasons" other than reasons listed in federal statutes or in the Federal Habeas Corpus Rules, or well established in Supreme Court precedents. Rule 9(a) directly addresses the factor -- delay -- that led the appeals court to dismiss the petition for equitable reasons, yet the court made no finding of "prejudice" to the State as required by the Rule.

9-0. Opinion of Court by Breyer, joined by Stevens, O'Connor, Souter, and Ginsburg. Concurring opinion by Rehnquist, joined by Scalia, Kennedy, and Thomas.

Lotus Dev. Corp. v. Borland Int'l 116 S. Ct. 804, 64 USLW 4059 (1-16-96)

Copyright, computer program menu: The decision of the United States Court of Appeals for the First Circuit, 49 F.3d 807, holding that a computer program's menu command hierarchy is a "method of operation" excluded from copyright protection by 17 U.S.C. § 102(b), is affirmed by equally divided vote.

4-4. *Per curiam*, Justice Stevens not participating.

Louisiana v. Mississippi 116 S. Ct. 290, 64 USLW 4003 (10-31-95)

States, boundaries: Louisiana's exceptions to the report of a special master on a disputed portion of the Mississippi River boundary between Louisiana and Mississippi are overruled. Stack Island, initially within Mississippi's boundary before the river's main navigational channel shifted to the east of the island and before erosion on the east bank of the island and accretion on the west bank changed the location of the island, remains within Mississippi. The general rule of "thalweg" places a river boundary along the main downstream navigational channel, and provides that the boundary moves as the channel changes. An "island exception" to the general rule, however, provides that a boundary once established on one side of an island remains there, even if the main downstream navigational channel shifts to the island's other side.

9-0. Opinion for unanimous Court by Kennedy.

Loving v. United States 116 S. Ct. 1737, 64 USLW 4390 (6-3-96)

Military justice; Separation of powers: Congress may delegate to the President the authority to limit imposition of capital punishment by prescribing aggravating factors applicable in military trials, and Congress has delegated this authority in a valid manner. Both premeditated murder and felony murder are capital offenses under the Uniform Code of Military Justice (UCMJ), but further refinement of these statutory categories is necessary to their constitutional validity. Authority to prescribe aggravating factors is conferred on the President by the UCMJ, which provides that punishment imposed by a court-martial may not exceed "such limits as the President may prescribe." Congress' power under Art. I, § 8, cl. 14 to "make rules for the government and regulation of the land and naval forces" is not exclusive, but may be shared with the President. Ordinarily, a delegation must contain some "intelligible principle" to guide implementation. In this case, however, the delegation was made to the President in his role as Commander in Chief. "The same limitations on delegation do not apply" if the entity authorized to exercise delegated authority itself possesses independent authority over the subject matter. "Measured cooperation" between the two political branches in areas of shared power vindicates rather than disserves separation-of-powers principles.

9-0. Opinion of Court by Kennedy, joined by Rehnquist, Stevens, Souter, Ginsburg, and Breyer, and joined in part by O'Connor and Scalia. Concurring opinions by Stevens, joined by Souter, Ginsburg, and Breyer; by Scalia, joined by O'Connor; and by Thomas.

Markman v. Westview Instruments, Inc. 116 S. Ct. 1384, 64 USLW 4263 (4-23-96)

Seventh Amendment, jury trial, patent claim: The interpretation of terms in a patent claim is a matter of law reserved entirely for the court. The Seventh Amendment, which preserves the right to trial by jury in suits at common law, does not require that such issues be decided by a jury. Patent infringement cases were tried at law when the Seventh Amendment was adopted, and consequently must be tried by a jury today. For the particular issue of claim construction, however, there is no direct common law antecedent. Support for submitting such issues to the jury likewise cannot be found in more recent precedent. On the other hand, considerations bearing on the sound administration of justice favor resolution by judges. Judges are trained in exegesis, frequently construe written instruments, and consequently are better suited than juries to find the acquired meaning of patent terms.

9-0. Opinion for unanimous Court by Souter.

Matsushita Elec. Indus. Co. v. Epstein 116 S. Ct. 873, 64 USLW 4101 (2-27-96)

Full Faith and Credit, federal court respect for state court judgments: A federal court may not withhold full faith and credit from a state court judgment approving a class-action settlement simply because the settlement releases claims within the exclusive jurisdiction of the federal courts. The Full Faith and Credit Act, 28 U.S.C. § 1738, directs federal courts to treat a state court judgment with the same respect that it would receive in the courts of the rendering state. Neither the fact that the state court judgment was the product of a class action, nor the fact that it incorporated a settlement agreement, undermines initial applicability of § 1738. In this case, Delaware would give preclusive effect to its court's judgment releasing exclusively federal claims, and there is no valid reason why federal courts should refuse to give that judgment preclusive effect. Section 27 of the Securities Exchange Act, which confers exclusive jurisdiction on federal courts over actions arising under that Act, did not implicitly repeal the Full Faith and Credit Act for purposes of state court judgments releasing Exchange Act claims.

7-2 as to judgment reversing lower court. Opinion of Court by Thomas, joined by Rehnquist, O'Connor, Scalia, Kennedy, Souter, and Breyer, and joined in part by Stevens and Ginsburg. Opinion by Stevens concurring in part and dissenting in part. Opinion by Ginsburg concurring in part and dissenting in part, joined by Stevens, and joined in part by Souter.

Medtronic, Inc. v. Lohr 116 S. Ct. 2240, 64 USLW 4625 (6-26-96)

Preemption, Medical Device Amendments: A state common law negligence action against the manufacturer of a heart pacemaker lead is not preempted by the Medical Device Amendments of 1976. That Act prohibits states from adopting or continuing in effect "with respect to a [medical] device" any requirement that is "different from, or in addition to" the applicable federal requirement and that relates to the safety or effectiveness of the device. The pacemaker device at issue had not been subjected to the full-blown pre-market approval process under the Act, but instead, following "pre-market notification" by the manufacturer, had been found by the FDA to be "substantially equivalent" to a device allowed to remain on the market under a grandfathering provision. Given the limited purpose of the "substantial equivalence" exemption and the presumption against preemption, a claim alleging defective design of the product was not preempted. The Act does not prevent states from providing a damages remedy for violation of common law duties that parallel federal requirements. Various claims relating to manufacturing and labeling also are not preempted. FDA regulations reinforce the statute's policy limiting preemption to situations in which a particular state requirement threatens to interfere with a specific federal interest. The state common law requirements were not specifically developed to govern medical devices, and their generality removes them from the category of requirements "with respect" to specific devices.

9-0 (design and damages issues); **5-4** (manufacturing and labeling issues). Opinion of Court by Stevens, joined by Kennedy, Souter, Ginsburg, and Breyer. Separate parts of Stevens opinion joined only by Kennedy, Souter, and Ginsburg. Concurring opinion by Breyer. Opinion concurring in part and dissenting in part by O'Connor, joined by Rehnquist, Scalia, and Thomas.

Meghrig v. KFC Western, Inc. 116 S. Ct. 1251, 64 USLW 4135 (3-19-96)

RCRA, remedies for "imminent endangerment": Section 7002 of the Resource Conservation and Recovery Act, 42 U.S.C. § 6972, does not authorize a private cause of action to recover costs that have already been expended for cleaning up a toxic waste site that no longer poses an endangerment to health or the environment. The section authorizes actions against persons who are contributing, or have contributed, to disposal of solid waste that "may present an imminent and substantial endangerment to health or the environment." This timing restriction quite clearly excludes waste that no longer presents such a danger. Also, the limited remedies available under section 7002 do not encompass recovery of past cleanup costs; the court may restrain any conduct creating an endangerment, or may order the defendant "to take such other action as may be necessary." These RCRA remedies differ markedly from remedies available under the Superfund law, which clearly authorizes recovery of cleanup costs.

9-0. Opinion for unanimous Court by O'Connor.

Melendez v. United States 116 S. Ct. 2057, 64 USLW 4525 (6-17-96)

Sentencing, statutory minimum: A Government motion attesting to the defendant's substantial assistance in a criminal investigation and requesting that the district court depart below the minimum of the applicable sentencing range under the Sentencing Guidelines does not also authorize the court to depart below any applicable statutory minimum sentence. A statute, 18 U.S.C. § 3553(e), authorizes a district court "[u]pon motion of the Government" to impose a sentence below a statutory minimum so as to reflect a defendant's substantial assistance to the prosecution. A policy statement in the Sentencing Guidelines contains similar language authorizing a court to "depart from the guidelines" for the same reason. The policy statement does not create a "unitary motion system." A motion requesting departure from "the guidelines" but not mentioning the statutory minimum sentence is not sufficient to satisfy § 3553(e)'s requirement of a motion requesting departure from a statutory minimum.

9-0; **7-2** (on "unitary motion" issue). Opinion of Court by Thomas, joined by Rehnquist, Scalia, Kennedy, Souter, and Ginsburg, and joined in part by O'Connor and Breyer. Concurring opinions by Souter and by Stevens. Opinion by Breyer, joined by O'Connor, concurring in part and dissenting in part.

Montana v. Egelhoff 116 S. Ct. 2013, 64 USLW 4500 (6-13-96)

Due Process, criminal responsibility, voluntary intoxication: Montana's law providing that voluntary intoxication may not be taken into account in determining the existence of a mental state that is an element of a criminal offense does not violate the Due Process Clause. Defining *mens rea* to eliminate the exculpatory value of voluntary intoxication does not offend a fundamental principle of justice. There is a lengthy common law tradition rejecting intoxication as a defense in criminal actions, and a later exception for crimes involving a "specific intent" has not been so uniformly accepted as to qualify as "fundamental."

5-4. No opinion of Court. Concurring opinions by Scalia, joined by Rehnquist, Kennedy, and Thomas; and by Ginsburg. Dissenting opinions by O'Connor, joined by Stevens, Souter, and Breyer; by Souter; and by Breyer, joined by Stevens.

Morse v. Republican Party of Virginia 116 S. Ct. 1186, 64 USLW 4207 (3-27-96)

Voting Rights Act, fee for Party convention: Section 5 of the Voting Rights Act, which prohibits covered jurisdictions from enforcing new voting qualifications or procedures without first obtaining court approval or preclearance by the Attorney General, applies to selection of delegates to a political party's state nominating convention. The Virginia Republican Party's decision to charge state convention delegates a registration fee, therefore, should have been submitted for preclearance. Section 10 of the Act, which authorizes the Attorney General to bring suit to enjoin enforcement of any poll taxes, creates an implied private right of action.

5-4. No opinion of Court. Opinion by Stevens, joined by Ginsburg. Concurring opinion by Breyer, joined by O'Connor and Souter. Dissenting opinions by Scalia, joined by Thomas; by Kennedy, joined by Rehnquist; and by Thomas, joined by Rehnquist and Scalia, and joined in part by Kennedy.

Neal v. United States 116 S. Ct. 763, 64 USLW 4077 (1-22-96)

Sentencing, drug sale, weight of carrier medium: The revised Sentencing Guideline, under which each dose of LSD on a carrier medium is given a constructive or presumed weight of 0.4 milligrams, does not govern determination of applicability of the mandatory minimum sentence under 21 U.S.C. § 841(b)(1)(A)(v). Rather, a dual system applies for calculating LSD weights. In *Chapman v. United States* (1991), the Court interpreted the mandatory minimum provision to require that the weight of blotter paper used as a carrier medium be added to the weight of the pure drug in determining how much of a "mixture or substance" containing LSD has been sold. The Sentencing Commission had no authority to override the Court's interpretation of the statute, and did not intend to do so. Nor is the Commission's revision of the Guideline a persuasive reason for the Court to change its *Chapman* interpretation. Under the doctrine of *stare decisis*, the Court strongly adheres to its interpretation of a statute. Congress, not the Court, has the responsibility for revising its statutes.

9-0. Opinion for unanimous Court by Kennedy.

NLRB v. Town & Country Electric, Inc. 116 S. Ct. 450, 64 USLW 4022 (11-28-95)

National Labor Relations Act, "employee": The NLRB's determination that a worker can be an "employee" within the definition of the National

Labor Relations Act, 29 U.S.C. § 152(3), even if the worker is paid by a union to help organize the company for which he works, is entitled to deference. The Board's interpretation is consistent with the broad language of the Act's definition ("the term 'employee' shall include any employee") and with ordinary dictionary definitions, and is also consistent with the Act's purposes of protecting employee organizing activities and promoting collective bargaining. Earlier decisions of the Court have given the definition a broad, literal reading. Also, a provision of the Labor Management Relations Act specifically contemplates the possibility that a company's employee might also work for a union.

9-0. Opinion for unanimous Court by Breyer.

Norfolk & Western Ry. v. Hiles 116 S. Ct. 890, 64 USLW 4111 (2-27-96)

Safety Appliance Act: A railroad is not liable under section 2 of the Safety Appliance Act, 49 U.S.C. § 20302(a)(1)(A), for injuries incurred by an employee while trying to straighten a misaligned drawbar. The Act requires that railroads equip cars with couplers that couple automatically by impact, and that can be uncoupled, "without the necessity of men going between the ends of the cars." This duty is not breached when a drawbar becomes misaligned during the ordinary course of railroad operations. Liability under the Act is predicated on failure of coupling equipment to perform as required. Before that liability can arise, couplers must be placed in a position to operate on impact, and this preparation includes proper alignment of drawbars.

9-0. Opinion for unanimous Court by Thomas.

O'Connor v. Consolidated Coin Caterers 116 S. Ct. 1307, 64 USLW 4243 (4-1-96)

Age Discrimination: A plaintiff alleging that he was discharged in violation of the Age Discrimination in Employment Act need not show that he was replaced by someone outside the age group protected by the ADEA. What is needed in order to create a *prima facie* case is evidence to create an inference that an employment decision was based on the illegal criterion of the employee's age. The fact that a replacement (here, 40 years old) is substantially younger than the dismissed employee (here, 56) is a far more reliable indication of illegal discrimination than is the fact that the replacement is not within the protected age group (persons "at least 40").

9-0. Opinion for unanimous Court by Scalia.

O'Hare Truck Service, Inc. v. City of Northlake 116 S. Ct. 2353, 64 USLW 4694 (6-28-96)

First Amendment, political association, government contractors: The principles announced in *Elrod v. Burns* (1976) and *Branti v. Finkel* (1980), protecting most government employees from political affiliation requirements, apply to independent government contractors. *Elrod* and *Branti* established that patronage does not justify the coercion of a person's political beliefs and associations. No justification has been offered for limiting these protections to government employees and denying them to those who perform the government's work outside the formal employment relationship. The petitioner had a cause of action under the First Amendment, therefore, when the city, in retaliation for the petitioner's refusal to make a contribution to the mayor's campaign, and for his support of the mayor's opponent, removed petitioner's company from a list of towing companies offered towing business on a rotating basis

7-2. Opinion of Court by Kennedy, joined by Rehnquist, Stevens, O'Connor, Souter, Ginsburg, and Breyer. Dissenting opinion by Scalia, joined by Thomas.

Ornelas v. United States 116 S. Ct. 1657, 64 USLW 4373 (5-28-96)

Fourth Amendment, appellate review: As a general matter, ultimate determinations of reasonable suspicion for an investigatory stop and probable cause to conduct a warrantless search should be reviewed *de novo* on appeal. The federal appeals court erred in this case in reviewing the district court's decisions only for "clear error." Both the reasonable suspicion and the probable cause determinations involve two-step processes, the first being the finding of facts about the circumstances surrounding the search, and the second being application of the law to the facts. Appellate courts should review a trial court's factual findings only for clear error and should give "due weight" to inferences that the trial court has drawn from those facts, but should review *de novo* the application of law to those facts.

8-1. Opinion of Court by Rehnquist, joined by Stevens, O'Connor, Kennedy, Souter, Thomas, Ginsburg, and Breyer. Dissenting opinion by Scalia.

Peacock v. Thomas 116 S. Ct. 862, 64 USLW 4095 (2-21-96)

Federal courts, ancillary jurisdiction; ERISA: The federal district court lacked jurisdiction over an action by a federal judgment creditor seeking to impose liability for an ERISA money judgment on a "third person," not the judgment debtor, alleged to have conspired to prevent satisfaction of the judgment. The defendant in the second action, an officer of the debtor corporation, had transferred assets of the corporation to other creditors, including himself. Because the second action alleged no violation of ERISA, the court lacked jurisdiction under ERISA to order "appropriate equitable relief" to redress violations. A district court's ancillary jurisdiction is usually limited to factually interdependent claims that are raised in the original action, not in a subsequent action. A court's ancillary jurisdiction to enforce its own judgments may in some circumstances extend to third parties required to assist in protection and enforcement of the judgment, but may not extend to the shifting of liability to third persons.

8-1. Opinion of Court by Thomas, joined by Rehnquist, O'Connor, Scalia, Kennedy, Souter, Ginsburg, and Breyer. Dissenting opinion by Stevens.

Pennsylvania v. Labron 116 S. Ct. 2485, 64 USLW 3863 (7-1-96)

Fourth Amendment, automobile search: Police may conduct a warrantless search of an automobile if the vehicle is "readily mobile and probable cause exists to believe it contains contraband." The Pennsylvania Supreme Court erred, therefore, in holding that both probable cause and "exigent circumstances" must be present to justify a warrantless search of an automobile. Pennsylvania's argument that the U.S. Supreme Court lacked jurisdiction because the state court's judgment rested on an "adequate and independent state ground" is rejected. The adequacy and independence of any state law ground was not clear on the face of the opinion, since state cases cited by the Pennsylvania court relied in part on analysis of the Fourth Amendment, and consequently Pennsylvania law on the subject is "interwoven" with federal law.

7-2. *Per curiam.* Dissenting opinion by Stevens (adequate and independent state ground issue), joined by Ginsburg.

Quackenbush v. Allstate Ins. Co. 116 S. Ct. 1712, 64 USLW 4379 (6-3-96)

Appeals; Abstention: A federal district court's abstention-based order remanding a case to state court is reviewable on appeal. An abstention-based remand is not within the categories of remands made unreviewable by 28 U.S.C. § 1447(d), and it fits within the narrow class of non-final orders that are immediately appealable under 28 U.S.C. § 1291. The order puts the litigants effectively out of court, it conclusively determines an issue that is separate from the merits, and the rights asserted are sufficiently important to warrant an immediate appeal. However, abstention was inappropriate in this case, an action by the California Insurance Commissioner to recover contract and tort damages from the insurance company. The abstention doctrine, under which federal courts may defer in some circumstances to state proceedings, permits federal courts to dismiss or remand cases only if the relief being sought is equitable or otherwise discretionary. While a stay order may be an appropriate means of abstention in some damages actions, a remand order is not.

9-0. Opinion for unanimous Court by O'Connor. Concurring opinions by Scalia and Kennedy.

Richards v. Jefferson County 116 S. Ct. 1761, 64 USLW 4405 (6-10-96)

Due Process, notice, res judicata: Taxpayers who challenged the validity of the county's occupation tax were denied due process by a decision of the Alabama Supreme Court holding them bound by an earlier judgment in a case in which they did not participate and about which they received no notice. Under the circumstances, the taxpayers could not have received adequate representation in the earlier action. The plaintiffs in the earlier action did not sue on behalf of a class, and there is no reason to suppose that the interests of absent taxpayers were adequately protected. This action, challenging the validity of the state's levy of personal funds, was not the type of taxpayer action that is brought on behalf of the public at large to challenge alleged misuse of public funds, and over which states have broad leeway to limit taxpayer standing.

9-0. Opinion for unanimous Court by Stevens.

Romer v. Evans 116 S. Ct. 1620, 64 USLW 4353 (5-20-96)

Equal Protection, denial of protected status to homosexuals: Amendment 2 to the Colorado Constitution, which prohibits all legislative, executive, or judicial action at any level of state or local government if that action is designed to protect homosexuals, violates the Equal Protection Clause of the Fourteenth Amendment. The amendment, adopted by statewide referendum in 1992, does not bear a rational relationship to a legitimate governmental purpose. The breadth of the amendment is so great that it cannot be credited with advancing the State's interest in protecting freedom of association for landlords and employers, and there is no other legitimate governmental interest or discrete purpose at which the amendment is directed. The "unprecedented" singling out of a class of persons for disqualification from legal protection offends the basic principle that government must "remain open on impartial terms to all who seek its assistance." The amendment does not merely deprive homosexuals of special rights and place them in the same position as all other people, but instead imposes a special disability on those persons alone.

6-3. Opinion of Court by Kennedy, joined by Stevens, O'Connor, Souter, Ginsburg, and Breyer. Dissenting opinion by Scalia, joined by Rehnquist and Thomas.

Rutledge v. United States 116 S. Ct. 1241, 64 USLW 4238 (3-27-96)

Double Jeopardy: 21 U.S.C. § 846, prohibiting conspiracy to commit drug offenses, is a lesser included offense of 21 U.S.C. § 848, which prohibits a "continuing criminal enterprise." Section 846 does not require proof of any fact that is not also a part of the continuing criminal enterprise offense, so, under the test set forth in *Blockburger v. United States* (1932), there are not two separate offenses. Although the petitioner was sentenced to two identical life terms, to run concurrently, the sentences nonetheless amounted to multiple punishment because a $50 special assessment was imposed on each conviction. There is no clear evidence that Congress intended to allow multiple punishments.

9-0. Opinion for unanimous Court by Stevens.

Seminole Tribe of Florida v. Florida 116 S. Ct. 1114, 64 USLW 4167 (3-27-96)

Eleventh Amendment, abrogation of states' immunity by Congress: A provision of the Indian Gaming Regulatory Act authorizing an Indian tribe to sue a state in federal court to compel performance of a duty to negotiate in good faith toward the formation of a compact violates the Eleventh Amendment. In exercise of its powers under Article I, Congress may not abrogate states' Eleventh Amendment immunity from suit in federal court. There is no principled basis for distinguishing Congress' power to abrogate state immunity when regulating commerce with Indian tribes from its power to do so when regulating commerce among the states. *Pennsylvania v. Union Gas Co.* (1989), which upheld abrogation in exercise of the power to regulate interstate commerce, is overruled. Congressional authority to abrogate state immunity when legislating pursuant to the Fourteenth Amendment is distinguishable, since the Fourteenth Amendment, adopted after the Eleventh, altered the pre-existing balance between state and federal power achieved by Article III and the Eleventh Amendment. The doctrine of *Ex parte Young* (1908), recognizing that some actions for injunctive relief against state officials are not barred by the Eleventh Amendment, is not available to supplement the "detailed remedial scheme" of the Indian Gaming Regulatory Act.

5-4. Opinion of Court by Rehnquist, joined by O'Connor, Scalia, Kennedy, and Thomas. Dissenting opinions by Stevens; and by Souter, joined by Ginsburg and Breyer.

Shaw v. Hunt 116 S. Ct. 1894, 64 USLW 4437 (6-13-96)

Congressional districting, racial gerrymander: North Carolina's congressional districting law, containing the racially gerrymandered 12th Congressional District as well as another majority-black district, violates the Equal Protection Clause because, under strict scrutiny applicable to racial classifications, creation of the district was not narrowly tailored to serve a compelling state interest. The district is not justified by any of the three interests identified by the State. Remedying racial discrimination may in proper cases justify a government's use of racial classifications, but the district court's finding that the redistricting plan was not actually aimed at ameliorating past discrimination was not clearly erroneous. Creation of District 12 was not necessary to comply with section 5 of the Voting Rights Act, under which the Justice Department had denied preclearance to an earlier plan containing only one majority-black district. The Justice Department's policy of requiring a state to maximize the number of majority-black districts is "insupportable." Assuming arguendo that compliance with section 2 of the Voting Rights Act can be a compelling state interest, and that creation of a second majority-minority district was necessary for compliance with section 2, the creation of District 12 was not narrowly tailored to that end. To establish a § 2 violation, a plaintiff must establish that an under-represented minority group is geographically compact. But District 12 itself, about 160 miles long and in places no wider than the corridor of an interstate highway, is not compact, and hence cannot be an appropriate remedy. Section 2 does not authorize the creation of a majority-minority district in one part of a state to remedy a violation elsewhere in the state. The right protected by § 2 is an individual right, not a group right.

5-4. Opinion of Court by Rehnquist, joined by O'Connor, Scalia, Kennedy, and Thomas. Dissenting opinions by Stevens, joined in part by Ginsburg and Breyer; and by Souter, joined by Ginsburg and Breyer.

Smiley v. Citibank (South Dakota) 116 S. Ct. 1730, 64 USLW 4399 (6-3-96)

Banking; Administrative law: The Comptroller of the Currency's interpretation of section 30 of the National Bank Act of 1864, 12 U.S.C. § 85, as including credit card late payment fees within the meaning of "interest" is reasonable, and is entitled to deference by the courts under principles articulated in *Chevron USA v. NRDC* (1984). There is a presumption that, if Congress vests an agency with authority to implement a statute, Congress also intends for the agency to resolve statutory ambiguity. The agency's resolution need not be the best interpretation of the statute, only a reasonable one. Deference is appropriate in this case even though the Comptroller's interpretation was made more than 100 years after enactment of the statute, and even though the interpretation was prompted by litigation. Section 30, which provides that a national bank may charge its loan customers "interest" at the rate allowed by the state where the bank is located, does not limit the meaning of "interest" to fees that vary according to the amount owed and the length of time that payment is delayed. Legal dictionaries of the enactment era defined "interest" in more general terms, and similarly included a broad meaning for "rate." The fact that the late fee functions as a penalty is not dispositive, since the categories of "interest" and "penalty" are not mutually exclusive.

9-0. Opinion for unanimous Court by Scalia.

Stutson v. United States 116 S. Ct. 600, 64 USLW 3459 (1-8-96)

Vacatur and remand, criminal case: An order granting certiorari, vacating the judgment, and remanding the case (a GVR order) is appropriate in this criminal case through application of the principles announced in *Lawrence v. Chater*, *supra*. Especially in criminal cases involving imprisonment, interests in judicial efficiency and finality must occasionally give way. The petitioner had no appellate review of his conviction, the district court having ruled that his appeal was untimely and not the result of "excusable neglect," and the appellate court having summarily affirmed. Following decisions of six appeals courts interpreting the "excusable neglect" standard differently than the lower courts in this case, the Solicitor General reversed the Government's position in response to the petition for certiorari.

6-3. *Per curiam*. Dissenting opinions by Rehnquist, and by Scalia, joined by Thomas.

Things Remembered, Inc. v. Petrarca 116 S. Ct. 494, 64 USLW 4035 (12-5-95)

Appeals, order remanding case to state court: An order of a federal district court remanding a bankruptcy case to state court on grounds of untimely removal is not reviewable by a federal court of appeals. The general language of 28 U.S.C. § 1447(d), precluding review of any order "remanding a case to the State court from which it was removed," is applicable to bankruptcy cases. Untimely removal is a basis for remand recognized by § 1447. Existence of a separate provision (28 U.S.C. § 1452) authorizing removal of bankruptcy cases, authorizing remands of such cases on equitable grounds, and making such remands unreviewable, does not preclude application of § 1447(d), and it matters not whether the removal was effected pursuant to § 1452. The two provisions can "comfortably coexist in the bankruptcy context."

9-0. Opinion for a unanimous Court by Thomas. Concurring opinions by Kennedy, joined by Ginsburg, and by Ginsburg, joined by Stevens.

Thompson v. Keohane 116 S. Ct. 457, 64 USLW 4027 (11-29-95)

***Miranda* warning, "in custody" determination**: State court determinations that a suspect was not "in custody" for purposes of a *Miranda* warning are not solely "factual issues" that, pursuant to 28 U.S.C. § 2254(d), must be "presumed to be correct" in a federal *habeas corpus* proceeding. "Factual" issues include such things as recitals of events and circumstances and credibility of witnesses. *Miranda* "in-custody" determinations require two discrete inquiries. The first, a factual issue entitled to the presumption of correctness, inquires into the circumstances surrounding the interrogation. The second inquiry -- "whether a reasonable person would have felt that he or she was not at liberty to terminate the interrogation and leave" -- involves application of a legal standard to established facts and presents a mixed question of law and fact qualifying for independent review by federal *habeas* courts.

7-2. Opinion of Court by Ginsburg, joined by Stevens, O'Connor, Scalia, Kennedy, Souter, and Breyer. Dissenting opinion by Thomas, joined by Rehnquist.

Tuggle v. Netherland 116 S. Ct. 283, 64 USLW 3315 (10-30-95)

Death penalty, invalid aggravating factor: The Virginia Supreme Court erred in reinstating a death sentence, following invalidation of one statutory aggravating circumstance, on the sole basis that the jury had found another aggravating circumstance to exist. *Zant v. Stephens* (1983) held that invalidation of one aggravating factor does not necessarily require that a death sentence be set aside. But neither does the existence of a remaining valid aggravating factor always excuse a constitutional error in the admission or exclusion of evidence. The State had committed constitutional error violative of principles set forth in *Ake v. Oklahoma* (1985), by introducing psychiatric testimony that the indigent defendant demonstrated a high degree of future dangerousness, and by not providing the defendant the assistance of an independent psychiatrist. While psychiatric evidence submitted by the defendant would not have affected the jury's finding on the other aggravating factor ("vileness" of the crime), that evidence might have affected the jury's decision, based on all the evidence before it, to impose death rather than life imprisonment.

9-0. *Per curiam*.

United Food & Commercial Workers v. Brown Group 116 S. Ct. 1529, 64 USLW 4330 (5-13-96)

WARN Act, standing to sue: The Worker Adjustment and Retraining Notification Act (WARN Act) authorizes a union to sue for damages on behalf of its members. An employer who violates the Act's notice requirements is liable to aggrieved employees for backpay and benefits, and the Act authorizes "a representative of employees" to sue to enforce that liability. The union has standing to bring such an action on behalf of its members. The third requirement of the three-part test for associational standing -- that neither the claim asserted nor the relief requested requires the participation of individual members in the lawsuit -- is a prudential rule that is not required by Article III of the Constitution. Congress may override this prudential rule by statute, and has done so in the WARN Act.

9-0. Opinion for unanimous Court by Souter.

United States v. Armstrong 116 S. Ct. 1480, 64 USLW 4305 (5-13-96)

Selective prosecution, discovery: A defendant in a federal criminal trial is entitled to discovery on a claim that the prosecuting attorney singled him out for prosecution on the basis of his race only if he can make a threshold showing that the government declined to prosecute similarly situated suspects of other races. Federal Rule of Criminal Procedure 16, which requires the government to allow the defendant access to documents in its possession "which are material to the preparation of the defendant's defense," applies only to preparation of a defense against the government's case-in-chief, and not to the preparation of selective prosecution claims. Courts are properly hesitant to interfere with prosecutorial discretion, and consequently there is a rigorous standard for proof of a selective prosecution claim. There should be "a correspondingly rigorous standard for discovery in aid of such a claim." To obtain discovery, there must be some evidence tending to show the existence of racially discriminatory effects, and this must include some evidence that similarly situated defendants of other races could have been prosecuted but were not.

8-1. Opinion of Court by Rehnquist, joined by O'Connor, Scalia, Kennedy, Souter, Thomas, and Ginsburg. Concurring opinions by Souter, Ginsburg, and Breyer. Dissenting opinion by Stevens.

United States v. IBM Corp. 116 S. Ct. 1793, 64 USLW 4419 (6-10-96)

Export Clause, prohibited federal tax: A federal tax on insurance premiums paid to foreign insurers not subject to the federal income tax, 26 U.S.C. § 4371, violates the Export Clause of the Constitution, Art. I, § 9, cl. 5, as applied to casualty insurance for losses incurred during the shipment of goods from locations within the United States to purchasers abroad. The case is governed by *Thames & Mersey Marine Ins. Co. v. United States* (1915), which held that a federal stamp tax on policies insuring marine risks could not be applied to policies covering export shipments. The Government's request that *Thames & Mersey* be overruled is rejected. The Government did not argue that the insurance policies had a value separate from the value of the exported goods, and principles of *stare decisis* caution against overruling a longstanding precedent on a theory not argued by the parties. There is no need to harmonize Export Clause analysis with that governing the Commerce Clause or the Import-Export Clause (applicable to states). There is a distinction between imposts or duties, to which the Import-Export Clause applies, and taxes, to which the Export Clause applies.

6-2. Opinion of Court by Thomas, joined by Rehnquist, O'Connor, Scalia, Souter, and Breyer. Dissenting opinion by Kennedy, joined by Ginsburg. Stevens did not participate.

United States v. Noland 116 S. Ct. 1524, 64 USLW 4328 (5-13-96)

Bankruptcy, equitable subordination of tax penalty: A bankruptcy court may not, in exercise of its power under 11 U.S.C. § 510(c) to subordinate claims "under principles of equitable subordination," equitably subordinate claims on a categorical basis in derogation of statutory priorities. In this case the bankruptcy court made no finding of misconduct by the government, but nonetheless subordinated an I.R.S. claim for a tax penalty based on its reading of the Bankruptcy Code as reflecting a general preference for compensation of "actual loss claims." This action conflicted with the Code's requirement that a post-petition tax penalty should receive the priority of an administrative expense. Section 510(c) gives bankruptcy courts authority to make equitable exceptions to the general rule when justified by particular facts, but does not confer authority to rewrite the general rule.

9-0. Opinion for unanimous Court by Souter.

United States v. Reorganized CF&I Fabricators 116 S. Ct. 2106, 64 USLW 4548 (6-20-96)

Bankruptcy: The "tax" assessed under 26 U.S.C. § 4971(a) equal to 10% of the amount of an accumulated funding deficiency in pension plans is not entitled to priority under the Bankruptcy Code, 11 U.S.C. § 507(a)(7)(E), as an "excise tax." Instead, the payment is, for bankruptcy purposes, a "penalty," to be dealt with as an ordinary, unsecured claim. The term "excise tax" is not defined in section 507 or elsewhere in the Bankruptcy Code, and there is also no cross-reference to a Tax Code definition. A "functional examination" leads to the conclusion that the exaction is a penalty rather than a tax. The exaction is not merely an enforced contribution for the support of government, but instead functions as punishment for failure to maintain pension funds at required levels. The Bankruptcy Court should not, however, have subordinated the Government's claim under § 4971 to claims of other general, unsecured creditors. Categorical subordination of this general nature is beyond the scope of authority of "equitable subordination" conferred by 11 U.S.C. § 510.

8-1 (penalty/tax issue); **9-0** (equitable subordination issue). Opinion of Court by Souter, joined by Rehnquist, Stevens, O'Connor, Kennedy, Ginsburg, and Breyer; and joined in part by Scalia. Opinion by Thomas concurring in part and dissenting in part.

United States v. Ursery 116 S. Ct. 2135, 64 USLW 4565 (6-24-96)

Forfeiture, Double Jeopardy: Civil forfeitures do not constitute "punishment" for purposes of the Double Jeopardy Clause. There were no successive punishments, and there was no violation of double jeopardy, therefore, when the Government brought a criminal prosecution for drug offenses against a person whose house was the subject of a forfeiture action because it had been used to facilitate the drug offenses (*Ursery*), or when the Government instituted a forfeiture action against the property of persons who had already been convicted of money laundering offenses (the consolidated case of *United States v. $405,089.23*, No. 95-346). The Court long ago drew a distinction, for double jeopardy purposes, between *in rem* civil forfeiture proceedings and *in personam* civil penalties; the former do not implicate the Double Jeopardy Clause, while the latter may. It is clear from the statutes at issue (21 U.S.C. § 881 and 18 U.S.C. § 981) that Congress intended to create civil *in rem* forfeiture authority, and there is little evidence that the forfeiture proceedings are so punitive in form and effect as to render them criminal despite Congress' intent to the contrary.

8-1. Opinion of Court by Rehnquist, joined by O'Connor, Kennedy, Souter, Ginsburg, and Breyer. Concurring opinions by Kennedy; and by Scalia, joined by Thomas. Dissenting opinion by Stevens.

United States v. Virginia 116 S. Ct. 2264, 64 USLW 4638 (6-26-96)

Equal Protection, male-only military college: Virginia's exclusion of women from the educational opportunities provided by Virginia Military Institute (VMI) denies to women the equal protection of the laws. A state must demonstrate "exceedingly persuasive justification" for gender discrimination, and Virginia has failed to do so in this case. Virginia has not demonstrated that VMI's exclusion of women was designed to further a state policy of diversity in educational opportunity. Virginia also failed to establish that VMI's "adversative" approach to character development and leadership training would have to be modified drastically to accommodate women. The State's fears are based on generalizations that fail to recognize that some individual women may have the will and capacity for adversative training. Creation of a separate program for women -- the Virginia Women's Institute for Leadership (VWIL) at Mary Baldwin College -- does not eliminate the constitutional violation. The

VWIL is a "separate and unequal" program that affords women no opportunity to experience the "rigorous military training for which VMI is famed," and that is also inferior in terms of student body, faculty, course offerings, facilities, alumni network, and prestige.

7-1. Opinion of Court by Ginsburg, joined by Stevens, O'Connor, Kennedy, Souter, and Breyer. Concurring opinion by Rehnquist. Dissenting opinion by Scalia. Thomas did not participate.

United States v. Winstar Corp. 116 S. Ct. 2432, 64 USLW 4739 (7-1-96)

Government contracts, breach by Government: The Federal Government breached contracts with purchasers of ailing thrift institutions by implementing provisions of the Financial Institutions Reform, Recovery, and Enforcement Act of 1989 (FIRREA). The purchasers had been induced to purchase ailing thrifts by the Federal Home Loan Bank Board's promise to allow part of the purchase price to be considered as supervisory goodwill and credited toward the capital reserve requirement. FIRREA, however, required exclusion of goodwill and other intangible assets from the definition of "core capital" used in calculating an institution's capital reserve. As a result, two of the three respondent thrifts were seized and liquidated by federal regulators for failure to meet capital requirements, and the other avoided seizure through private recapitalization. The Government has not established a valid defense for its breach of contract. The sovereign acts doctrine, under which "public and general" sovereign acts may excuse the Government from contractual performance, cannot be relied upon in this case, in which the essence of the agreement was the Government's assumption of the risk of regulatory change.

7-2. No opinion of Court. Opinion announcing Court's judgment by Souter, joined by Stevens and Breyer, and joined in part by O'Connor. Concurring opinions by Breyer; and by Scalia, joined by Kennedy and Thomas. Dissenting opinion by Rehnquist, joined in part by Ginsburg.

Varity Corp. v. Howe 116 S. Ct. 1065, 64 USLW 4138 (3-19-96)

ERISA, fiduciary obligations: Beneficiaries of a company's employee welfare benefit plan may sue their plan's administrator under ERISA § 502(a)(3) for breach of fiduciary duty in making deliberate misrepresentations designed to persuade the beneficiaries to switch their employment to an insolvent subsidiary. There was sufficient support for the district court's finding that the plan administrator, also the employer, was acting in a fiduciary capacity when it made the misrepresentations. Deliberate deceptions violate the ERISA-imposed fiduciary obligation to act "solely in the interest of" plan participants and beneficiaries. ERISA § 502(a)(3) authorizes a civil action by individual plan beneficiaries. Although paragraph (2) of the same subsection, which applies to breaches of fiduciary duty, has been interpreted to authorize only plan relief, not individual relief, this limitation does not apply to paragraph (3). Under the subsection's structure, paragraph (3) is a catchall provision that can also apply to breach of fiduciary duty. This interpretation is reinforced by other provisions of the Act, including ERISA's stated policy (§ 2(b)) of providing plan beneficiaries "appropriate remedies" and "ready access" to court.

6-3. Opinion of Court by Breyer, joined by Rehnquist, Stevens, Kennedy, Souter, and Ginsburg. Dissenting opinion by Thomas, joined by O'Connor and Scalia.

Whren v. United States 116 S. Ct. 1769, 64 USLW 4409 (6-10-96)

Fourth Amendment, traffic stop, probable cause: The temporary detention of a motorist who police have probable cause to believe has committed a traffic violation is consistent with the Fourth Amendment even if a reasonable officer would not normally have stopped the motorist to enforce the traffic laws. The fact that the officer may have used a traffic stop as pretext for investigation of other crimes is irrelevant if there was probable cause to believe that a traffic violation had occurred. The existence of probable cause establishes the constitutional reasonableness of traffic stops regardless of the actual motivations of the officers involved, and regardless of whether the officer's conduct deviated materially from customary police practices.

9-0. Opinion for unanimous Court by Scalia.

Wisconsin v. City of New York 116 S. Ct. 1091, 64 USLW 4153 (3-20-96)

Census, apportionment, statistical adjustment: The decision of the Secretary of Commerce not to conduct a post-enumeration survey and statistical adjustment for undercount in the 1990 Census is reasonable, and well within the bounds of discretion conferred by the Constitution and by statute. The Constitution (Art. I, § 2, cl. 3) vests broad discretion in Congress to determine the manner in which the census is to be undertaken, and the Census Act, 13 U.S.C. § 141(a), confers on the Secretary the responsibility to conduct the census "in such form and content as he may determine." The appeals court erred in applying a heightened standard of review derived from cases involving the drawing of congressional district lines within state boundaries. The Secretary's decision not to adjust census figures "need bear only a reasonable relationship to the accomplishment of an actual enumeration of the population, keeping in mind the constitutional purpose of the census" to provide data for apportioning congressional representatives among the states.

9-0. Opinion for unanimous Court by Rehnquist.

Wood v. Bartholomew 116 S. Ct. 7, 64 USLW 3267 (10-10-95)

Due process, *Brady* rule: The prosecution's failure to turn over to the defense the results of a polygraph examination of a key prosecution witness did not constitute a denial of due process within the rule of *Brady v. Maryland* (1963). Evidence is material under *Brady*, and the failure to disclose it justifies setting aside a conviction, only if there exists a reasonable probability that the result would have been different had the evidence been disclosed. No such probability existed in this case. The polygraph results were inadmissible under state law, even for impeachment purposes, and hence did not constitute "evidence." Even without the testimony of the prosecution witness, the case against the defendant was "overwhelming." Also, the defendant's trial counsel testified at the *habeas* proceeding that he did not believe the outcome of the trial would have been different had he known of the polygraph results.

5-0. *Per curiam.* Justices Stevens, Souter, Ginsburg, and Breyer dissented "from summary disposition of this case."

Yamaha Motor Corp. v. Calhoun 116 S. Ct. 619, 64 USLW 4048 (1-9-96)

Appeals; admiralty: Under 28 U.S.C. § 1292(b), which allows federal district courts to certify for interlocutory appeal an order raising a controlling question of law as to which there is substantial ground for difference of opinion, courts of appeals may exercise jurisdiction over any question that is fairly included within the certified order, and need not limit consideration to the controlling question identified by the district court. The federal maritime claim supplied by *Moragne v. States Marine Lines* (1970) does not provide the exclusive remedy in cases involving the death in territorial waters of a "nonseafarer" -- a person who is neither a seaman covered by the Jones Act nor a longshore worker covered by the Longshore and Harbor Workers' Compensation Act. Instead, state remedies are available in a case involving death from a jet ski accident.

9-0. Opinion for unanimous Court by Ginsburg.

Zicherman v. Korean Air Lines 116 S. Ct. 629, 64 USLW 4055 (1-16-96)

Warsaw Convention, Death on the High Seas Act: Who may bring suit under Article 17 of the Warsaw Convention for damages arising out of a plane crash, and what types of damages are compensable in such actions, are questions to be answered by the applicable domestic law of the contracting states. In this case, arising out of the downing of Korean Air Lines Flight 007 in 1983, the parties agree that the law of the United States governs. The applicable law, the Death on the High Seas Act, limits recovery to "pecuniary loss sustained" (46 U.S.C. § 762), and hence does not authorize recovery of loss-of-society damages. Where DOHSA applies, neither state law nor general maritime law can provide a basis for recovery of loss-of-society damages.

9-0. Opinion for unanimous Court by Scalia.

Supreme Court
Volume 1 pp. 183-260

THE LAW OF CHURCH AND STATE: DEVELOPMENTS IN THE SUPREME COURT SINCE 1980

David M. Ackerman
Legislative Attorney
American Law Division

Introduction

The religion clauses of the First Amendment to the Constitution provide that "Congress shall make no law respecting an establishment of religion, or prohibiting the free exercise thereof ...." In modern times the Supreme Court has frequently construed these clauses to create, in Thomas Jefferson's words, a "wall of separation between church and state."[1] But the Court's decisions have often been controversial, and they have repeatedly precipitated vigorous political opposition. The election of Ronald Reagan to the Presidency in 1980 reflected that opposition, in part, and gave impetus to a concerted and ongoing effort to change the Court's church-state jurisprudence.

That effort has, in part, been direct — energetic efforts in 1984 (led by President Reagan) and in the 104th and 105th Congresses to amend the Constitution[2]; repeated

[1] In a letter of January 1, 1802, to the Baptist Association of Danbury, Connecticut, President Jefferson stated as follows:

> Believing with you that religion is a matter which lies solely between man and his God; that he owes account to none other for his faith or his worship; that the legislative powers of the Government reach actions only, and not opinions — I contemplate with sovereign reverence that act of the whole American people which declared that their legislature should "make no law respecting an establishment of religion or prohibiting the free exercise thereof," thus building a wall of separation between church and State.
> Quoted in Everson v. Board of Education, 330 U.S. 1, 16 (1947).

The Court's modern interpretation of these clauses generally dates from the time it incorporated them into the due process clause of the Fourteenth Amendment and held them applicable to the states — Cantwell v. Connecticut, 310 U.S. 296 (1940) (free exercise clause) and Everson v. Board of Education, *supra* (establishment clause).

[2] In 1981 President Reagan became the first President to propose a constitutional amendment on school prayer. *See* S.J.Res. 199 and H.J.Res. 493, 97th Cong., 1st Sess. (1981). In 1984 the Senate Judiciary Committee reported a modified version of that amendment (S.J.Res. 73), and the Senate debated the matter for two and a half weeks. Ultimately, a majority voted in favor of it, 56-44. *See* 130 CONG. REC. 5619 (March 20, 1984). But that vote was 11 votes short of the two-thirds majority necessary for the measure to be adopted. The possibility of amending the Constitution on church-state matters re-emerged in 1995, soon after the Republican takeover of the House and the Senate; and although no formal votes occurred in the 104th Congress, a number of significant developments occurred. Perhaps most

verbal attacks on the Court's separationist constructions of the religion clauses[3]; and a concerted effort by the Solicitors General for Presidents Reagan and Bush, both in cases when the government was a party and as *amicus curiae* when it was not, to persuade the Court to allow government greater freedom of action with respect to religion.[4] But to greater and more long-lasting effect, the election of President Reagan and his successor, President Bush, opened the door to the possibility of changing the Court's church-state jurisprudence by means of the exercise of the Presidential powers of Article II, Section 2, of the Constitution to "nominate and ... appoint ... Judges of the supreme Court."

Presidents Reagan and Bush replaced more than half of the Court during their twelve years in office. Chief Justice Burger (1985) and Justices Stewart (1980), Powell (1986), Brennan (1990), and Marshall (1991) all retired from the Court during this period, and in their stead President Reagan elevated Justice Rehnquist to Chief Justice and appointed Justices O'Connor, Scalia, and Kennedy, while President Bush appointed Justices Souter and Thomas. The new appointees have not entirely fulfilled the expectations of the Presidents who appointed them,[5] but they have fueled the increasing dominance on the Court of what are deemed "conservative" constructions of the law and have precipitated vigorous debates about the meaning of the religion clauses.

During this time the Supreme Court has been a willing, even eager, forum for disputes over the proper relationship between government and religion. From the fall

---

[2](...continued)
important, the constitutional debate in Congress broadened beyond the school prayer issue to include other aspects of the Court's church-state jurisprudence. In the 105th Congress that interest and debate has persisted; and on October 24th, 1997, the Subcommittee on the Constitution of the House Judiciary Committee favorably reported a modified version of a broad-gauge constitutional amendment introduced by Rep. Istook (H.J.Res. 73) to the full committee. For a fuller description of Congressional action, *see* CRS, *School Prayer: The Congressional Response, 1962-1996* (Oct. 16, 1996) (Report 96-846A).

[3] See, *e.g.*, the address by Attorney General Edwin Meese III to the House of Delegates of the American Bar Association (July 9, 1985).

[4] The Solicitors General under Presidents Reagan and Bush repeatedly urged the Court to loosen the constraints of the religion clauses on government action affecting religion since 1980. Of the forty-nine church-state cases decided during their terms, the Solicitor General proffered his views in thirty — sixteen because the United States was a party, fourteen as an amicus curiae. The Solicitors General under President Clinton have filed briefs in two of the five church-state cases that have been reviewed since 1992.

[5] See, *e.g.*, Lee v. Weisman, 505 U.S. 577 (1992), in which the Court reaffirmed its prior school prayer decisions and held that the establishment clause forbids a public secondary school from including prayers by a clergyman in its commencement ceremony. The decision was 5-4, with Justices O'Connor, Kennedy, and Souter — all appointed by Presidents Reagan and Bush — joining Justices Blackmun and Stevens in the majority. Indeed, Justice Souter appears to have become one of the leading separationists on the Court, and Justice O'Connor has generally been a moderate on church-state issues.

of 1980 to the present the Court has handed down 54 decisions[6] in cases raising church-state issues — more than in any prior comparable time period. Its decisions have involved new dimensions of such familiar issues as religious activities in the public schools and direct public aid to sectarian schools. But the Court has also addressed such relatively unexplored matters as the constitutionality of the public display of religious symbols, legislative prayer, indirect aid to sectarian schools, government regulation of minority religious practices, special protection or benefits for religion, and the taxation of religious entities.

The Court has been sharply split in many of these decisions, with the Justices vigorously, and sometimes heatedly, arguing their various viewpoints. More than a quarter of the Court's church-state decisions since 1981 have been by a margin of 5-4 (compared to less than 20 percent for all of the Court's decisions during this period).[7] But the changes in the Court's composition have had a demonstrable effect. On the free exercise clause, in particular, the Court has dramatically altered its interpretation and restricted the scope of the clause as a constraint on government action.[8] And in its most recent Term, the Court for the first time explicitly repudiated a previous establishment clause decision.[9] It has as well, since 1980, rendered an increasing number of decisions that can best be described as accommodationist in both their reasoning and their results.

President Clinton has appointed two Justices to the Supreme Court since he took office in 1993,[10] but those appointments have not reestablished a separationist majority on the Court.[11] The net effect of the changes on the Court since 1980 is that

---

[6] This total obviously is selective in some respects. It includes all decisions involving the establishment or free exercise clauses, all decisions concerning religious discrimination under Title VII of the Civil Rights Act of 1964, selected decisions involving religious speech but decided under the free speech clause, and selected decisions involving interpretation of the tax code. It does not include dismissals of appeals from state court decisions or summary affirmances by an equally divided Court. *See* the Appendix for a listing of the pertinent cases and for a breakdown of how the Justices voted on each case.

[7] These statistics are based on the annual compilations published in the November *Harvard Law Review*. Since the 1981 Term (no statistics on 5-4 decisions were compiled for the 1980 Term), 387 of the Court's 2060 written decisions have been by 5-4 margins — a percentage of 18.8. In contrast, 16 of its 60 church-state decisions (several of its 54 cases involved more than one issue) have been by 5-4 margins — a percentage of 26.6.

[8] Employment Division, Oregon Department of Human Resources v. Smith, 494 U.S. 872 (1990).

[9] Agostini v. Felton, 117 S.Ct. 1997 (1997), overturning Aguilar v. Felton, 473 U.S. 402 (1985) and parts of three other decisions.

[10] He appointed Justice Ruth Bader Ginsburg in 1993 to replace Justice Byron White and Justice Stephen Breyer in 1994 to replace Justice Harry Blackmun.

[11] In the few church-state decisions in which they have participated since their confirmations, both Justice Breyer and Justice Ginsburg appear to be largely separationist in their views; but neither is wholly predictable. Justice Ginsburg was part of a separationist majority in Board of Education of the Kiryas Joel Village School District v. Grumet, 512 U.S.

(continued...)

the Court has become almost evenly split on church-state issues with, perhaps, a slight tilt toward the accommodationist perspective: Justices Stevens, Souter, Ginsburg, and Breyer appear to be largely separationist; Chief Justice Rehnquist and Justices Scalia and Thomas are staunchly accommodationist; and Justices O'Connor and Kennedy frequently lean toward accommodationist conclusions but are less predictable.

In short, the period since 1980 has been a time of sustained ferment on the Court about the law of church and state. That ferment has produced spirited and extensive arguments about the proper relationship of government and religion and the meaning of the religion clauses of the First Amendment, and the Court has handed down a plethora of specific rulings. This report provides an overview of that ferment and of the changes in the Court's church-state jurisprudence. It examines the doctrinal shifts and debates on the free exercise and establishment of religion clauses that have occurred on the Court since Ronald Reagan's election to the Presidency in 1980. It summarizes and examines as well the legal effect of the 54 decisions the Supreme Court has handed down concerning church and state from its October, 1980 Term, through its October, 1996 Term (*i.e.*, October, 1980, through June, 1997). Finally, it concludes with an Appendix listing all of the Court's church-state decisions during this period and the votes of each of the Justices.

"Congress Shall Make No Law ... Prohibiting the Free Exercise [of Religion]": The Constriction of the Strict Scrutiny Standard

(a) From *Thomas* to *Smith*. Most of the political furor over the Court's church-state jurisprudence in the past several decades has stemmed from its decisions concerning religion in the public schools, public aid to sectarian schools, and the display of religious symbols in public places — all of which are essentially establishment clause or free speech issues. But with little public attention, at least until the present decade, the Court has also been struggling with the question of how broadly to interpret the free exercise clause. It has long been settled that the clause

---

[11](...continued)
687 (1994), in which the Court struck down as a violation of the establishment clause a New York statute which permitted a community of Hasidic Jews to create their own public school district and receive public funds for special educational services for the disabled children of their community. She authored or joined separationist dissents in Rosenberger v. The Rector and Visitors of the University of Virginia, 115 S.Ct. 2510 (1995), which held the clause not to bar the University from subsidizing the printing costs of a student religious publication; in Capitol Square Review and Advisory Board v. Pinette, 115 S.Ct. 2440 (1995), which held the clause not to be violated by the display of a cross by the Ku Klux Klan in a public park in front of a State capitol building during the Christmas season;and in Agostini v. Felton, *supra*, which for the first time overturned a prior establishment clause decision by the Court and held the clause not to be violated by the provision of educational services by public school teachers to sectarian schoolchildren on the premises of the sectarian schools. But she joined the majority in City of Boerne v. Flores, 117 S.Ct. 2157 (1997), which held the Religious Freedom Restoration Act unconstitutional. Justice Breyer was not on the Court for the Kiryas Joel decision, but joined Justice Ginsburg in separationist dissents in Rosenberger and in Agostini. In contrast, however, he was part of the majority in Pinette and dissented in Boerne.

protects religious **beliefs** absolutely from governmental interference.[12] The difficult question has been whether, and the extent to which, the clause also protects **religiously motivated conduct or action** from governmental interference.

A century ago the Court construed the free exercise clause to provide **no** protection whatsoever for conduct compelled or motivated by religious beliefs.[13] But that interpretation gradually changed, and in the decades immediately preceding the 1980s, the Court settled on a broad view of the scope of the free exercise clause. In two seminal decisions — *Sherbert v. Verner*[14] and *Wisconsin v. Yoder*[15] — the Court held that religious interests are to be considered of **paramount** importance in the constitutional scheme and that government actions infringing those interests are to be viewed as **highly suspect**. In *Sherbert* the Court held that a state could not, consistent with the free exercise clause, deny unemployment compensation benefits to a person who was fired because she refused to work on her Sabbath. The denial of benefits, the Court said, pressured the claimant to forego her religious practice and thus could be justified only if it served "some compelling state interest," a standard it found the state to be unable to meet.

Similarly, in *Yoder* the Court held the free exercise clause to mandate an exemption for the Old Order Amish from Wisconsin's compulsory education laws. Those laws required all children to attend school until the age of sixteen, but the Amish believed that attendance beyond the eighth grade would expose their children to worldly influences dangerous to their salvation. In holding for the Amish, the Court said that "there are areas of conduct protected by the Free Exercise Clause of the First Amendment and thus beyond the power of the state to control, even under regulations of general applicability."[16]

In these two cases, in other words, the Court held that government action alleged to interfere with religious practices could be constitutional only if it were shown to serve some compelling public interest and to be no more restrictive of religious practices than necessary. Government action burdening religious exercise, in short, was deemed to be subject to a constitutional standard of **strict scrutiny**.

But over the course of the 1980s the Court dramatically altered this construction of the free exercise clause. Two decisions a decade apart encapsulated that process. In the first decision in 1981, *Thomas v. Review Board, Indiana Employment Security Commission*,[17] the Court strongly reaffirmed the broad and sweeping construction it had given the free exercise clause in *Sherbert* and *Yoder*. In *Thomas*, as in *Sherbert*, it held the clause to require a state to grant unemployment compensation benefits to

---

[12] Cantwell v. Connecticut, 310 U.S. 296 (1940).

[13] See, *e.g.*, Reynolds v. United States, 98 U.S. (8 Otto) 145 (1878) (free exercise clause held to be no defense in prosecution of Mormons for bigamy and polygamy).

[14] 374 U.S. 398 (1963).

[15] 406 U.S. 205 (1972).

[16] *Id.* at 220.

[17] 450 U.S. 707 (1981).

an individual who interpreted the Bible to forbid him from accepting work on an armaments production line and who, as a consequence, quit his job. The Court did so even though Thomas's scriptural interpretation was a personal one and was not shared by the religious community to which he belonged (Jehovah's Witnesses) and even though a denial of benefits would have only indirectly burdened his ability to practice his religion.[18] *Thomas*, thus, made crystal clear that governmental actions infringing religiously motivated conduct are to be reviewed by the courts under a standard of strict scrutiny:

> The state may justify an inroad on religious liberty by showing that it is the least restrictive means of achieving some compelling state interest. However, it is still true that "the essence of all that has been said and written on the subject is that only those interests of the highest order ... can overbalance claims to the free exercise of religion."[19]

The decision in *Thomas* was 8-1, with only then-Justice Rehnquist dissenting.

But in a decision in 1990, the Court reached a dramatically different conclusion. In *Employment Division, Oregon Department of Human Resources v. Smith*,[20] the Court held the free exercise clause to provide **no** protection whatever for the use of peyote in the religious ceremonies of the Native American Church. Technically, the issue in the case was identical to that in *Thomas* — the eligibility for unemployment benefits of two individuals who were unemployed because they had been fired from their jobs as drug counselors for using peyote in the religious ceremonies of their church. But the determinative questions in the case were whether the Indians' sacramental use of peyote was illegal under Oregon's controlled substances law and, if so, whether the free exercise clause nonetheless required an exemption from the law for such a religious use. The Oregon Supreme Court construed the State's law to apply to the sacramental use of peyote, and the U.S. Supreme Court held the free

---

[18] A denial of unemployment benefits would not have precluded Thomas from practicing his religion but only made it more expensive to do so. But the Court found this indirect burden to be "substantial":

> Where the state conditions receipt of an important benefit upon conduct proscribed by a religious faith, or where it denies such a benefit because of conduct mandated by religious belief, thereby putting substantial pressure on an adherent to modify his behavior and to violate his beliefs, a burden upon religion exists. While the compulsion may be indirect, the infringement upon free exercise is nonetheless substantial.
>
> Thomas, 450 U.S. at 717-18.

[19] *Id.* at 718, quoting Wisconsin v. Yoder, 406 U.S. 205, 215 (1972).

[20] 494 U.S. 872 (1990).

exercise clause **not** to compel an exemption.[21] Consequently, the Court held Oregon's denial of unemployment benefits to be constitutional.

That holding was not, in itself, surprising and could have been reconciled with the Court's prior jurisprudence. What was unexpected was that on the way to that conclusion a majority of the Court largely abandoned the strict scrutiny test as the standard for free exercise cases. The Court said the compelling public interest test was simply "inapplicable" to the circumstances of this case. The free exercise clause, Justice Scalia wrote for the majority, **never** "relieve[s] an individual of the obligation to comply with a 'valid and neutral law of general applicability.'" To employ the compelling interest test for free exercise purposes, he said, would "court ... anarchy," permit every individual "to become a law unto himself," and create "a private right to ignore generally applicable laws."[22] Religious minorities, he said, need to seek protection for their practices in the political process, not the courts. The fact that "the political process will place at a relative disadvantage those religious practices that are not widely engaged in," he stated, is simply an "unavoidable consequence of democratic government."[23] The margin was 5-4, with the majority formed by the lone dissenter in *Thomas* (Chief Justice Rehnquist), two new appointees to the Court (Justices Scalia and Kennedy), and two who had been in the majority in *Thomas* (Justices White and Stevens).[24]

The Court did not abandon strict scrutiny entirely. Justice Scalia's articulation of the new standard retained strict scrutiny for cases involving state denials of unemployment compensation to persons who become or remain unemployed because of a conflict between their religious beliefs or practices and the requirements of the job — the area in which the strict scrutiny test was first applied in the free exercise area. In addition, his opinion said strict scrutiny was still appropriate for governmental actions that discriminate against religion or deliberately impose special burdens on religion. Finally, Justice Scalia suggested that "hybrid" claims, *i.e.*, those involving a free exercise claim coupled with another constitutional interest such as

---

[21] The case had been before the Court two years previously. But at that time the Oregon Supreme Court had not ruled on whether the state's criminal drug statute applied to the sacramental use of peyote or, if it did, whether that application was compatible with the Oregon Constitution or the free exercise clause. Consequently, the Supreme Court had remanded the case back to the Oregon Supreme Court for consideration of those issues. *See* Employment Division, Department of Human Resources v. Smith, 483 U.S. 660 (1988), *vacating and remanding*, 301 Or. 209, 721 P.2d 445 (1986). In that reconsideration the Oregon Supreme Court held the state's controlled substance statute to apply to those who used peyote in religious ceremonies but held the free exercise clause to immunize such use from prosecution. *See* Smith v. Employment Division, Department of Human Resources, 307 Or. 68, 763 P.2d 146 (1988).

[22] Smith, 494 U.S. at 884-86.

[23] *Id.* at 890.

[24] Although the margin was 5-4 on the disavowal of the strict scrutiny test, the Court divided 6-3 on the merits. Justice O'Connor joined Chief Justice Rehnquist and Justices Scalia, Kennedy, White, and Stevens in ruling the two Indians ineligible for unemployment benefits. But she did so on the grounds Oregon had a compelling interest in regulating the use of drugs, and she dissented vigorously from their disavowal of the strict scrutiny test.

freedom of speech or parental rights, might also be constitutionally entitled to some degree of exemption from neutral, generally applicable laws. But his opinion left it decidedly unclear whether strict scrutiny would apply to such cases, and in any event clearly abandoned strict scrutiny for all non-hybrid cases other than those involving denials of unemployment compensation or deliberate governmental targeting of religion.

The four dissenters sharply criticized the majority's constriction of the strict scrutiny test. Justice O'Connor asserted that Justice Scalia's view "dramatically departs from well-settled First Amendment jurisprudence ..., is incompatible with our Nation's fundamental commitment to individual religious liberty ..., and relegates a serious First Amendment value to the barest level of minimum scrutiny ...." Religious liberty, she said, is a preferred value, and the free exercise clause should be interpreted to bar "encroachment upon this liberty, whether direct or indirect, unless required by clear and compelling governmental interests 'of the highest order.'" Justice Blackmun, joined by Justices Brennan and Marshall, charged that the majority's decision "effectuates a wholesale overturning of settled law concerning the Religion Clauses of our Constitution." It is a "settled and inviolate principle of this Court's First Amendment jurisprudence," he said, that "a state statute that burdens the free exercise of religion ... may stand only if the law in general, and the State's refusal to allow a religious exemption in particular, are justified by a compelling interest that cannot be served by less restrictive means."

In short, in *Smith* the Court re-interpreted the free exercise clause to mean that, in most circumstances, an individual possesses no constitutional right not to comply "with a valid and neutral law of general applicability on the ground that the law proscribes (or prescribes) conduct that his religion prescribes (or proscribes)."[25]

(b) Harbingers of *Smith*. This demise of the strict scrutiny test for most free exercise cases and the consequent subordination of religious conduct to the will of political majorities, although unexpected in *Smith*, had in fact been foreshadowed throughout the decade. In eight free exercise decisions between *Thomas* and *Smith*, the Court had demonstrated increasing discontent with the strict scrutiny test in free exercise cases. Four of those decisions nominally employed the test, but the Court held the government to have met its requirements. In the four other decisions the Court simply held strict scrutiny to be inapplicable in particular contexts.

In *United States v. Lee*,[26] decided within a year of *Thomas*, the Court unanimously held the free exercise clause **not** to exempt an Amish employer from paying the employer's portion of Social Security taxes. The Court noted that the religious beliefs of the Amish specifically oppose support for a public system of social insurance. But it held the employer not to be entitled to an exemption because, it

---

[25] Employment Division v. Smith, *supra*, at 878.

[26] 455 U.S. 252 (1981).

said, "mandatory participation is indispensable to the fiscal vitality of the social security system."[27]

The following Term in *Bob Jones University v. United States*[28] the Court upheld IRS' imposition of a racial nondiscrimination condition on the tax exemption accorded a private college notwithstanding the college's claim that its discriminatory practices were mandated by religious belief. On the free exercise claim the Court applied strict scrutiny but simply asserted in conclusory fashion that "the Government has a fundamental, overriding interest in eradicating racial discrimination in education" and that its interest "substantially outweighs whatever burden denial of tax benefits places on petitioners' exercise of their religious beliefs." The Court's decision on the free exercise issue was again unanimous.[29]

Subsequently, in 1989 the Court in *Hernandez v. Commissioner of Internal Revenue*[30] upheld IRS' denial of a tax deduction to members of the Church of Scientology for payments made for "auditing" and "training" services. The members claimed that these services were central to the practice of their faith and that the payments made for them were "fixed donations" entitled to be treated as charitable contributions under the Internal Revenue Code. But the Court denied the claim, 5-2. The Court said that it doubted that the disallowance of the deduction placed any "substantial burden" on the Scientologists' practice of their religion but that even if it did, the disallowance was justified by the compelling governmental interest in maintaining a uniform tax system, "free of 'myriad exceptions flowing from a wide variety of religious beliefs.'"[31]

Finally, in *Jimmy Swaggart Ministries v. Board of Equalization*[32] in 1990, the Court unanimously upheld the imposition of a general sales and use tax on a religious organization's sale of religious materials. Nominally using the strict scrutiny test, the Court found the imposition of the taxes to violate no religious precept of the religious organization and to impose no burden on religious organizations different from that imposed on other sellers. Although the taxes reduced the amount of money the religious organization had to spend on its religious activities, the Court held that burden to be "not constitutionally significant."

---

[27] *Id.* at 258.

[28] 461 U.S. 574 (1983).

[29] *Id.* at 604. Justice Rehnquist dissented from the Court's holding that the IRS could impose a racial nondiscrimination condition on the grant of tax-exempt status to private schools; but he agreed that if such a condition were imposed, it would not violate the free exercise clause. See *id.* at 622, n. 3 (Rehnquist, J., dissenting).

[30] 490 U.S. 680 (1989).

[31] *Id.* at 687, quoting United States v. Lee, *supra*, at 260.

[32] 493 U.S. 378 (1990).

These four decisions preserved the form, if not the substance, of strict scrutiny. Four other decisions eschewed even the form. In *Goldman v. Weinberger*[33] the Court upheld a military dress code against the free exercise claim of a Jewish psychologist who felt religiously obligated to wear a yarmulke while on duty. An Air Force regulation mandating "uniform dress" and barring the wearing of headgear while indoors had been construed to bar yarmulkes. The Court held the *Sherbert-Yoder-Thomas* test to be inapplicable in the military context and, as a consequence, found the free exercise clause to require no exception for religious apparel. "The military," the Court said, "is ... a specialized society separate from civilian society" and thus "our review of military regulations challenged on First Amendment grounds is far more deferential than constitutional review of similar laws or regulations designed for civilian society." "Courts," it asserted, "must give great deference to the professional judgment of military authorities concerning the relative importance of a particular military interest."[34] So long as the military regulations in question are reasonable and evenhanded, it held, the free exercise clause is not violated. The decision was by a 5-4 margin.[35]

Similarly, in *O'Lone v. Estate of Shabazz*[36] the Court held strict scrutiny not to be applicable in the prison context. The case involved a free exercise challenge by several Muslim prisoners against New Jersey prison regulations that had the effect of preventing their participation in Jumu'ah, a weekly worship service commanded by the Koran. In upholding the regulations, again by a 5-4 margin, the Court asserted that "we take this opportunity to reaffirm our refusal, even where claims are made under the First Amendment, to 'substitute our judgment on ... difficult and sensitive matters of institutional administration' (citation omitted) for the determinations of those charged with the formidable task of running a prison."[37] "To ensure that courts afford appropriate deference to prison officials," it stated, prison regulations need be examined only to determine whether they are "reasonably related to legitimate penological interests" such as security and rehabilitation.[38] Finding the regulations in question to be related to both those interests, the Court denied the prisoners' free exercise claims.

In *Bowen v. Roy*[39] the Court held strict scrutiny to be inappropriate with respect to the government's internal administrative practices that were alleged to burden an individual's religious beliefs and practices. That case involved a challenge by an

---

[33] 475 U.S. 503 (1986).

[34] *Id.* at 506-07. The majority was composed of Chief Justice Burger and Justices Rehnquist, White, Powell, and Stevens.

[35] Congress, it might be noted, responded to this decision by adopting a statute permitting military personnel to wear items of religious apparel while on duty so long as the items are "neat and conservative" and do not "interfere with the performance of the member's military duties." See 10 U.S.C. 774 (1988).

[36] 482 U.S. 342 (1987).

[37] *Id.* at 353, quoting Block v. Rutherford, 468 U.S. 576, 588 (1984).

[38] *Id.* at 349.

[39] 476 U.S. 693 (1986).

Abenaki Indian family to the government's requirements that applicants for benefits under the Aid to Families with Dependent Children program furnish state welfare agencies the Social Security numbers of all members of their household and that the agencies use the numbers in administering their AFDC program.[40] The Indians' interpretation of their religion deemed personal numerical identifiers a "great evil" to be avoided and perceived their use as preventing an individual from exercising control over his life and robbing him of his spirit. The Court, without a majority opinion, remanded the issue concerning the constitutionality of requiring the Indians to provide their Social Security numbers as a condition of receiving assistance back to the lower court to see if it had become moot. But on the issue of the constitutionality of the government using Social Security numbers already in its possession to administer its programs, the Court, by an 8-1 margin, found no free exercise violation.[41] The Court asserted that the claim amounted to an effort "to dictate the conduct of the Government's internal procedures" and a "demand that the Government join in the (Indians') chosen religious practices ...."[42] The claimant's ability to "believe, express, and exercise his religion," the Court held, was simply not impaired by the government's administrative use of a Social Security number.

Finally, the Court held strict scrutiny analysis to be inapplicable with respect to the government's land use decisions in *Lyng v. Northwest Indian Cemetery Protective Association*.[43] The proposed building of a road for logging purposes in a region of a National Forest in California had been challenged on free exercise grounds by several Indian tribes that deemed the region to be sacred and used it for religious ceremonies. But the Court held that "even if we assume that ... the ... road will virtually destroy the Indians' ability to practice their religion, the Constitution simply does not provide a principle that could justify upholding (their) legal claims."[44] The Court said the critical question was whether the government's action directly coerced individuals into violating their religious beliefs or imposed unique disabilities on religious activities, and it held that the road-building plan did not. The road, it found, would only have "incidental effects" that might "make it more difficult to practice certain religions"[45]; and thus, the Court said, the government did not need to demonstrate a compelling justification for the plan. "Whatever may be the exact line between unconstitutional prohibitions on the free exercise of religion and the legitimate conduct by government of its own affairs," the Court stated, "the location

---

[40] The case was brought by an Abenaki Indian who claimed on behalf of his two-year old daughter that a Social Security number would undermine the uniqueness of her person and spirit and prevent her from asserting the control over her life necessary to develop spiritual power. That damage, he claimed, would flow both from obtaining a Social Security number for her and from the use of that number by the state welfare agency.

[41] Only Justice White dissented from this portion of the Court's ruling, saying without further explanation that Thomas and Sherbert "control this case." See Bowen v. Roy, 476 U.S. at 733 (White, J., dissenting).

[42] *Id.* at 700.

[43] 485 U.S. 439 (1988).

[44] *Id.* at 451-52.

[45] *Id.* at 450.

of the line cannot depend on measuring the effects of a governmental action on a religious objector's spiritual development."[46] Again, the margin of decision was 5-4.

Between *Thomas* and *Smith* the Court did employ strict scrutiny to invalidate government action on two occasions, both involving state denials of unemployment compensation to individuals who were unemployed for religious reasons. In *Hobbie v. Unemployment Appeals Commission of Florida*[47] the Court held unconstitutional Florida's denial of unemployment benefits to a person who had been fired from her retail sales job because she had joined the Seventh Day Adventist Church and was no longer available for work on her Sabbath, which ran from sundown Friday to sundown Saturday. In an 8-1 decision, the Court held this case to be controlled by *Sherbert* and *Thomas* and thus subject to strict scrutiny. Finding no significant differences between those cases and this one, it reiterated that "the State may not force an employee 'to choose between following the precepts of her religion and forfeiting benefits, ... and abandoning one of the precepts of her religion in order to accept work.'"[48]

Similarly, in *Frazee v. Illinois Department of Employment Security*[49] the Court unanimously held unconstitutional Illinois' denial of unemployment benefits to an individual who refused a job that would have involved working on Sunday, his Sabbath. The allegedly unique fact of the case was that Frazee belonged to no organized religious sect or church and his refusal to work, thus, was based on his personal beliefs as a Christian and not on the tenets or teachings of any established religious body. But the Court found this fact not to distinguish the case from *Sherbert*, *Thomas*, and *Hobbie*. In every one of those cases, it said, the claimant was "forced to choose between fidelity to religious belief and ... employment."[50] Finding no compelling justification for Illinois' denial of benefits, the Court held it unconstitutional.

In sum, it is clear that since 1980 the Court has substantially restricted the scope of the free exercise clause. At the beginning of the decade *Thomas*, building on the foundation of *Sherbert* and *Yoder*, seemed to command that the government accommodate minority religious practices in all but the most compelling countervailing circumstances. But after *Goldman, Shabazz, Roy, Lyng*, and *Smith*, that can no longer be said to be the case. Those decisions redressed the balance between religious interests and governmental interests and resurrected the standard of review for free exercise cases that the Court frequently used prior to its 1963 decision in *Sherbert v. Verner, supra.* That standard is essentially one of **formal neutrality**. Except in the narrow category of eligibility for governmental benefits and the ill-defined area of "hybrid" claims, the free exercise clause means only that government must regulate religious practices in a neutral, evenhanded manner. The

---

[46] *Id.* at 451.

[47] 480 U.S. 136 (1987).

[48] *Id.* at 146, quoting Sherbert v. Verner, *supra*, at 404.

[49] 489 U.S. 829 (1989).

[50] *Id.* at 1516, quoting Hobbie, *supra*, at 144.

clause no longer compels the government to exempt particular religious practices from the reach of its statutes and accommodate religious needs in its actions. By the beginning of the 1990s, then-Justice Rehnquist's dissent in *Thomas* had become the Court's standard for most free exercise cases:

> Where ... a State has enacted a general statute, the purpose and effect of which is to advance the State's secular goals, the Free Exercise Clause does not ... require the State to conform that statute to the dictates of religious conscience of any group.[51]

(c) The Aftermath of *Smith*.

(1) Lukumi Babalu Aye. Since the *Smith* decision in 1990, the Court has considered only one other free exercise case, and in that case it used *Smith's* framework of analysis but still found strict scrutiny to be applicable. In *Church of the Lukumi Babalu Aye, Inc. v. City of Hialeah*[52] the Court held unconstitutional a city's ordinances prohibiting the ritual sacrifice of animals. The case arose when the Church of the Lukumi Babalu Aye, Inc., sought to bring the practices of the Santeria religion into the open by establishing a church and cultural center in Hialeah, Florida. The Santeria faith has no centralized authority or written tenets but centers on the performance of certain rituals and ceremonies for such life events as birth, marriage, sickness, and death. These rituals often involve the sacrifice of goats, fowl, sheep, and/or turtles by means of cutting their carotid arteries and previously had been performed in private homes with only limited public awareness. When the proposal to establish a Santeria church and cultural center in Hialeah became public, these practices aroused vehement public antipathy. The City Council responded by adopting a series of resolutions and ordinances condemning Santeria's practices and making various aspects of the Santeria sacrifice ritual illegal.

The Supreme Court held Hialeah's ordinances to violate the free exercise clause, 9-0. The Court noted that under *Smith* "a law that is neutral and of general applicability need not be justified by a compelling governmental interest even if the law has the incidental effect of burdening a particular religious practice."[53] But it found Hialeah's ordinances to be neither neutral nor of general applicability, because they prohibited the killing of animals only for religious reasons. Killing for secular reasons — hunting, pest control, euthanasia, *etc.* — was not affected. As a consequence, Justice Kennedy concluded for the Court, "the ordinances had as their object the suppression of religion,"[54] and strict scrutiny of the ordinances was still appropriate under the *Smith* framework of analysis. Finding that Hialeah failed to show either that the ordinances served any compelling governmental interests or that they were drawn in narrow terms to accomplish their objectives, Justice Kennedy concluded for the Court that the ordinances violated the free exercise clause:

---

[51] Thomas v. Review Board, Indiana Employment Security Division, 450 U.S. at 723 (Rehnquist, J., dissenting).

[52] 508 U.S. 520 (1993).

[53] *Id.* at 2226.

[54] *Id.* at 2231.

> Legislators may not devise mechanisms, overt or disguised, designed to persecute or oppress a religion or its practice. The laws here in question were enacted contrary to these constitutional principles, and they are void.[55]

Thus, *Babalu Aye* made clear that, notwithstanding the Court's relaxation of the free exercise clause in *Smith*, government still cannot single out particular religious practices for special burdens not imposed on analogous secular conduct. The free exercise clause, as construed in *Smith*, may not mandate any exemptions for religious practices from burdensome or even prohibitory laws, but it does mandate that such laws be neutral and generally applicable.

(2) RFRA and City of Boerne. The apparent abandonment of strict scrutiny in *Smith* aroused widespread concern in the religious community and elsewhere and led Congress, after three years of consideration, to enact the "Religious Freedom Restoration Act" (RFRA).[56] Purportedly leaving *Smith* intact as the constitutional standard for free exercise cases, RFRA mandated the strict scrutiny test as a **statutory** standard governing the interaction of government and religious exercise. As enacted, it provided that a statute or regulation of general applicability could lawfully burden a person's exercise of religion only if it were shown to be "essential to further a compelling governmental interest and (to be) the least restrictive means of furthering that compelling governmental interest." RFRA made the standard applicable to governmental action at every level of government — federal, state, and local — and allowed aggrieved persons to bring suit if they believed their free exercise of religion had been restricted by government in violation of the statutory strict scrutiny standard.

However, in 1997 the Supreme Court held RFRA to be unconstitutional as applied to the states. In *City of Boerne, Texas v. Flores*[57] the Court held, 6-3, that Congress lacks the constitutional power to impose such a sweeping requirement on the states. In enacting RFRA Congress had relied, in part, on its power under § 5 of the Fourteenth Amendment to enact "appropriate legislation" to enforce the substantive protections of the Amendment, including the religious liberty protections incorporated in the due process clause. But the Court said that RFRA exceeded Congress' power under §5. In imposing a strict scrutiny standard for free exercise claims, it stated, Congress altered the meaning of the free exercise clause as determined by the Court, and "[l]egislation which alters the meaning of the Free Exercise Clause cannot be said to be enforcing the Clause."

Moreover, the Court asserted, RFRA constituted "a considerable ... intrusion into the States' traditional prerogatives and general authority to regulate for the health and welfare of their citizens." In enacting RFRA, it noted, Congress had failed to develop a legislative record that showed extensive denials of religious liberty. Yet RFRA was so broad, the Court said, that it intruded "at every level of government, displacing laws and prohibiting official actions of almost every description and

---

[55] *Id.* at 2234.

[56] P.L. 103-41, 103d Cong., 1st Sess. (Nov. 16, 1993); 42 U.S.C.A. 2000bb *et seq.*

[57] 117 S.Ct. 2157 (1997).

regardless of subject matter." As a consequence, the Court concluded, RFRA "reflects a lack of proportionality or congruence between the means adopted and the legitimate end to be achieved ... and contradicts vital principles necessary to maintain separation of powers and the federal balance."

The Clinton Administration, it might be noted, maintains that RFRA remains valid for the federal government, because for that application Congress did not rely on § 5 of the Fourteenth Amendment. That issue remains in litigation.

(d) Conclusion. Both *Babalu Aye* and *City of Boerne* illustrate that the ferment on the Court over the free exercise clause has not been ended by *Smith*. In *Babalu Aye* Justices Blackmun, O'Connor, and Souter, although joining in the Court's judgment in the case, all criticized its use of the *Smith* rule. Justice Souter argued that the *Smith* rule reflects a particularly narrow conception of neutrality. "A law that is religion neutral on its face or in its purpose," he said, "may lack neutrality in its effect by forbidding something that religion requires or requiring something that religion forbids." Thus, he argued, the "formal" neutrality reflected in the *Smith* rule, which only bars laws which intentionally discriminate against religion, needs to be supplemented with "substantive" neutrality, which would "generally require government to accommodate religious differences by exempting religious practices from formally neutral laws." He said as well that *Smith* is "in tension with" the Court's prior free exercise decisions and with the historical evidence of the original intent of the free exercise clause. In a proper case, he said, the Court should "re-examine the rule *Smith* declared." Justices Blackmun and O'Connor reiterated the view they articulated in their opinions in *Smith* that "*Smith* was wrongly decided." Similarly, in *City of Boerne* Justices O'Connor and Breyer (Blackmun's replacement) argued that the case should have been used as a vehicle for overturning *Smith*, and Justice Souter contended that there should at least have been briefing and argument on the merits of *Smith* before the Court addressed the question of Congress' authority under § 5 of the Fourteenth Amendment.

Nonetheless, the central fact remains: Since 1980 the Supreme Court has substantially restricted the constitutional protection afforded religious practices by the free exercise clause. As a matter of constitutional law, *Smith* reigns. Intentional discrimination against religious practices violates the free exercise clause, but not inadvertent discrimination that results from the application of statutes and regulations of general applicability. Moreover, Congress' power to alter the effects of that decision by means other than a constitutional amendment has been cast in substantial doubt, at least with respect to the states.

"Congress Shall Make No Law Respecting an Establishment of Religion...": *Lemon* and the Lessons of History

The debates among the Justices about the free exercise clause in the period since 1980 have been, at least until *Smith*, relatively sedate. But that has not been the case with the establishment clause. On the construction of that clause the Justices have disagreed vigorously and, at times, testily. The Court has not yet altered its interpretation of the establishment clause as dramatically as it has the construction of the free exercise clause, but the changing composition of the Court has still had a substantial impact. Since 1980 the Court has rendered a number of decisions that are accommodationist in nature; it has modified the *Lemon* test of constitutionality under the clause and used it less consistently than before; its reasoning has increasingly departed from that used in its prior interpretations of the clause; and in 1997, for the first time, it overturned a prior establishment clause decision.

The arguments on the Court have ranged over virtually every aspect of its establishment clause jurisprudence. In part the criticism of its past decisions has been wholesale in nature. Various Justices have termed the Court's establishment clause jurisprudence "embarrassing,"[58] "unprincipled,"[59] "in hopeless disarray,"[60] and as manifesting an "unjustified hostility toward religion."[61] But four aspects of the separationist interpretation of the establishment clause have been particular focal points for criticism and debate: (1) the Court's repeated use of Jefferson's phrase "wall of separation between church and state" as a metaphor for the meaning of the establishment clause; (2) its reliance on European and colonial history in interpreting the clause; (3) its development and application of what is known as the tripartite, or *Lemon*, test; and (4) its understanding of the original intent of the first Congress in formulating the establishment clause. All of these aspects have been interwoven in the Court's establishment clause jurisprudence, and all are critical to any reinterpretation.

(a) The Separationist Understanding. In the seminal decisions of the Court's modern establishment clause jurisprudence, the Court rooted its interpretation of the clause in the history of the American colonies and of the colonists' European forebears. The First Amendment "is at once," the Court said in 1947, "the refined product and the terse summation of that history."[62] The Court cited in particular the "turmoil, civil strife, and persecutions" that had been endemic in Europe in the centuries preceding and contemporaneous with the colonization of America as various religious sects allied themselves with government to establish their supremacy[63]:

> With the power of government supporting them, at various times and places, Catholics had persecuted Protestants, Protestants had persecuted Catholics, Protestant sects had persecuted other Protestant sects, Catholics of one shade of belief had persecuted Catholics of another shade of belief, and all of these had from time to time persecuted Jews. In efforts to force loyalty to whatever religious group happened to be on top and in league with the government of a particular

---

[58] Edwards v. Aguillard, 482 U.S. 578, 639 (1987) (Scalia, J., dissenting).

[59] Wallace v. Jaffree, 472 U.S. 38, 113 (1985) (Rehnquist, J., dissenting).

[60] Rosenberger v. The Rector and Visitors of the University of Virginia, *supra* (Thomas, J., concurring).

[61] County of Allegheny v. American Civil Liberties Union, Greater Pittsburgh Chapter, 492 U.S. 573, 655 (1989) (Kennedy, J., dissenting).

[62] Everson v. Board of Education, 330 U.S. 1, 33 (1947) (Rutledge, J., dissenting).

[63] *Id.* at 8 (opinion of the Court)..

time and place, men and women had been fined, cast in jail, cruelly tortured, and killed.[64]

Many of the early settlers came to America, the Court said, to "escape the bondage which compelled them to support and attend government-favored churches."[65] Although they often engaged in the same practices themselves, the Court observed that over time the colonists gradually developed a "feeling of abhorrence" about such practices and by the time of the Revolution had begun to disestablish the unions of church and state that existed.

In these early decisions the Court stressed as "particularly relevant" to the meaning of the First Amendment the experience of Virginia, which, after a momentous struggle, disestablished the Anglican Church in 1785 and adopted Jefferson's "Bill for Religious Liberty." Virginia, it said, "provided a great stimulus and able leadership" for the view that "individual religious liberty could be achieved best under a government which was stripped of all power to tax, to support, or otherwise to assist any or all religions, or to interfere with the beliefs of any religious individual or group."[66] Virginia's experience, the Court said, "best reflect[ed] the long and intensive struggle for religious freedom in America."[67] Indeed, so instructive was Virginia's example, the Court declared, that "the provisions of the First Amendment ... had the same objective and were intended to provide the same protection against governmental intrusion on religious liberty as the Virginia statute."[68]

As part of this emphasis, the Court also stressed the importance of the views of James Madison and Thomas Jefferson to the interpretation of the First Amendment. Both had played leading roles in disestablishing the Anglican church in Virginia: Madison was the author of the "Memorial and Remonstrance Against Religious Assessments" in 1784 that articulated numerous arguments against taxation for the benefit of religious institutions; and Jefferson was the author of the "Virginia Bill for Religious Liberty" that ultimately was enacted in 1785.[69] Madison also was a primary architect of the Bill of Rights in the First Congress. Indeed, so central was his role in the latter process, one Justice said, that the establishment clause "is the compact and exact summation of its author's views formed during his long struggle for religious freedom"[70]:

> All the great instruments of the Virginia struggle for religious liberty thus became warp and woof of our constitutional tradition, not simply by the course of history, but by the

---

[64] *Id.*, at 9.

[65] *Id.*

[66] *Id.* at 11.

[67] McGowan v. Maryland, 366 U.S. 420, 437 (1961).

[68] *Id.* at 13.

[69] *Id.*; Engel v. Vitale, 370 U.S. 421, 427-28 (1962). See also McGowan v. Maryland, 366 U.S. 420, 437-440 (1961).

[70] Everson v. Board of Education, 330 U.S. at 31 (Rutledge, J., dissenting).

> common unifying force of Madison's life, thought and sponsorship. He epitomized the whole of that tradition in the Amendment's compact, but nonetheless comprehensive, phrasing.[71]

This history and the debates in the First Congress on what became the First Amendment, the Court said, showed that the establishment clause was intended to do more than prohibit direct government compulsion or coercion in matters of religion. It identified two broad purposes underlying the clause:

> Its first and most immediate purpose rested on the belief that a union of government and religion tends to destroy government and to degrade religion. The history of governmentally established religion, both in England and in this country, showed that whenever government had allied itself with one particular form of religion, the inevitable result had been that it had incurred the hatred, disrespect and even contempt of those who held contrary beliefs. That same history showed that many people had lost their respect for any religion that had relied upon the support of government to spread its faith. The Establishment Clause thus stands as an expression of principle on the part of the Founders of our Constitution that religion is too personal, too sacred, too holy, to permit its "unhallowed perversion" by a civil magistrate.
>
> Another purpose of the Establishment Clause rested upon an awareness of the historical fact that governmentally established religions and religious persecutions go hand in hand .... It was in large part to get completely away from this sort of systematic religious persecution that the Founders brought into being our Nation, our Constitution, and our Bill of Rights with its prohibition against any governmental establishment of religion.[72]

Thus, the Court concluded that the establishment clause, "in its final form, did not simply bar a congressional enactment *establishing a church*; it forbade all laws *respecting an establishment of religion* .... [T]he First and Fourteenth Amendment afford protection against religious establishment far more extensive than merely to forbid a national or state church."[73] In the classic statement of the separationist understanding, Justice Black stated for the Court:

> The "establishment of religion" clause of the First Amendment means at least this: Neither a state nor the Federal Government can set up a church. Neither can pass laws which aid one religion, aid all religions, or prefer one religion over another. Neither can force nor influence a person to go to or to remain away from church against his will or force him to profess a belief or disbelief in any religion. No person can be punished for entertaining or professing religious beliefs or disbeliefs, for church attendance or non-attendance. No tax in any amount, large or small, can be levied to support any religious activities or institutions, whatever they may be called, or whatever form they may adopt to teach or practice religion .... In the

---

[71] *Id.* at 39.

[72] Engel v. Vitale, 370 U.S. at 431-33.

[73] McGowan v. Maryland, *supra*, at 441-42.

> words of Jefferson, the clause against establishment of religion by law was intended to erect "a wall of separation between church and State."[74]

Initially, every member of the Court joined in this separationist reading of the historical underpinnings and consequent broad scope of the establishment clause.[75]

The tripartite test developed more slowly. Not until *Abington School District v. Schempp*[76] in 1963 did the Court first distill a test to help it ferret out establishment clause violations. In that case it stated that to pass muster under the clause governmental action had to have "a secular legislative purpose and a primary effect that neither advances nor inhibits religion."[77] Subsequently, in *Walz v. Tax Commission of New York*[78] in 1970 the Court articulated a requirement that government action not precipitate excessive entanglement between government and religion. Finally, in *Lemon v. Kurtzman*[79] in 1971 the tripartite test gained its full articulation:

> First, the statute must have a secular legislative purpose; second, its principal or primary effect must be one that neither advances nor inhibits religion ...; finally, the statute must not foster "an excessive entanglement with religion."

The Court further held that a statute or governmental action had to satisfy every prong of the tripartite test. Although often stating that the test was merely a "guideline" or "signpost," the Court used the test in every establishment clause case but one between its inception and 1991[80]; and after a lapse of several years, the Court

---

[74] Everson v. Board of Education, 330 U.S. at 15-16. Jefferson had created his "wall of separation" metaphor in 1802. *See* n. 1.

[75] Dissenting from the result but not the historical reasoning of the majority in Everson, 330 U.S. 1 (1947), Justice Rutledge asserted for himself and three other dissenters the following understanding of the establishment clause:

> Not simply an established church, but any law respecting an establishment of religion is forbidden. ...The Amendment's purpose was not to strike merely at the official establishment of a single sect, creed or religion, outlawing only a formal relation such as had prevailed in England and some of the colonies. Necessarily it was to uproot all such relationships. But the object was broader than separating church and state in this narrow sense. It was to create a complete and permanent separation of the spheres of religious activity and civil authority by comprehensively forbidding every form of public aid or support for religion.
> 330 U.S. at 31-32 (Rutledge, J., dissenting).

[76] 374 U.S. 203 (1963).

[77] *Id.* at 222.

[78] 397 U.S. 664 (1970).

[79] 403 U.S. 602, 612-13 (1971).

[80] See Marsh v. Chambers, 463 U.S. 783 (1983) (upholding the constitutionality of legislative prayers). Larson v. Valente, 456 U.S. 228 (1983) is also sometimes cited as a case that did not use the *Lemon* standard, because the Court primarily relied on a strict scrutiny

(continued...)

used it anew in its most recent establishment clause decision, albeit in modified form.[81]

(b) The Critique. Notwithstanding the initial unanimity of the Court's historical analysis and its almost unfailing recourse to the tripartite test (at least prior to 1991), every aspect of the separationist understanding of the establishment clause has come under persistent criticism. Indeed, the Court's interpretation of history and use of Jefferson's phrase "wall of separation" as a metaphor for the establishment clause was criticized by Justice Reed as early as 1948,[82] and Justice White raised questions about the excessive entanglement prong of the tripartite test in the very case in which the test was first fully articulated.[83] But during the 1980s criticism of the history relied upon by the Court, the "wall of separation" metaphor, the tripartite test, and the Court's understanding of the original intent of the establishment clause crescendoed. During this time Chief Justices Burger and Rehnquist and Justices White, Kennedy, and Thomas all attacked the historical justifications for a separationist construction of the establishment clause. The tripartite test, in turn, was attacked in part or in whole by Chief Justice Rehnquist and Justices White, O'Connor, Scalia, Kennedy, and Thomas.

---

[80](...continued)
test in striking down a charitable solicitations statute as religiously discriminatory. But that contention is not wholly correct, because the Court also used the entanglement prong of the tripartite test. In church-state cases subsequent to 1991 the Court has used (1) a coercion test (*see* Lee v. Weisman, 505 U.S. 577 (1992) (holding the inclusion of prayers by a clergyman in a public school commencement ceremony to be unconstitutional)); (2) a neutrality test (*see* Zobrest v. Catalina Foothills School District, 509 U.S. 1 (1993) (upholding the provision of a sign language interpreter to a deaf student attending a Catholic high school); Board of Education of the Kiryas Joel Village School District v. Grumet, 512 U.S. 687 (1994) (striking down a state statute creating a special education school district for a single religious group); and Rosenberger v. The Rector and Visitors of the University of Virginia, 515 U.S. 819 (1995) (upholding the funding of a student religious publication out of a student activities fund)); or (3) used a modified version of the *Lemon* test (*see* Capitol Square Review and Advisory Board v. Pinette, 515 U.S. 753 (1995) (using an endorsement version of the *Lemon* test in upholding the private display of a cross at Christmastime in a public square in front of a State Capitol building) and Agostini v. Felton, 117 S.Ct. 1997 (1997) (submerging the entanglement prong of the *Lemon* test into the primary effect prong in upholding as constitutional the provision by public school teachers of remedial educational services to sectarian schoolchildren on the premises of the sectarian schools)).

[81] Agostini v. Felton, 117 S.Ct. 1997 (1997). In this decision the Court held excessive entanglement not to be a separate element of the tripartite test but a part of the primary effect inquiry.

[82] McCollum v. Board of Education, 333 U.S. 203, 244-48 (1948) (Reed, J., dissenting). Of the "wall of separation" metaphor, Justice Reed said that "[a] rule of law should not be drawn from a figure of speech." *Id.* at 247.

[83] Lemon v. Kurtzman, 403 U.S. at 661-671 (White, J., dissenting).

The critiques have been voiced in both majority decisions and concurring and dissenting opinions. In 1983 in *Marsh v. Chambers*,[84] for instance, a majority of the Court emphasized other aspects of American history in upholding as constitutional the practice of legislatures opening their daily sessions with prayer by a paid chaplain, 6-3. Chief Justice Burger, writing for the Court, ignored the history of religious conflict in Europe and the colonies and stressed instead the ubiquity of the practice of legislative prayer from colonial times forward. He also cited as critically important the fact that the First Congress authorized the appointment of paid chaplains for itself within three days of agreeing on the language of the Bill of Rights and that James Madison served on the House committee to decide how chaplains should be chosen and voted for the bill authorizing the payment of the chaplains. Eschewing any reference to, or use of, the tripartite test in deciding the case, the Chief Justice concluded that legislative prayer "has become part of the fabric of our society ... [and] is simply a tolerable acknowledgment of beliefs widely held among the people of this country."[85]

One year later in *Lynch v. Donnelly*[86] a narrower majority of the Court expanded on that accommodationist emphasis in upholding a city's inclusion of a creche in a Christmas display that included such other items as a Santa Claus house, reindeer, Santa's sleigh, colored lights, and a banner proclaiming "Season's Greetings." Chief Justice Burger, again writing for the Court, this time used the tripartite test but stressed that the Court was not "confined to any single test or criterion in this sensitive area."[87] More significantly, the Chief Justice emphasized what he called "an unbroken history of official acknowledgment by all three branches of government of the role of religion in American life from at least 1789."[88] Official invocations of Divine guidance, proclamations of days of thanksgiving and prayer, legislative chaplains, the national motto "In God We Trust" on the nation's currency, the phrase "one nation under God" in the Pledge of Allegiance, the designation of Thanksgiving and Christmas as national holidays, the invocation "God save the United States and this Honorable Court" at the opening of judicial sessions, the display of religious paintings in public art galleries — all illustrated the principle, the Chief Justice asserted, that the Constitution does not require "complete separation of church and state ... [but] affirmatively mandates accommodation ... of all religions, and forbids hostility toward any."[89] The metaphor "wall of separation," the Chief Justice stated, fails to give "a wholly accurate description of the practical aspects of the relationship that in fact exists between church and state."[90] The decision was 5-4.

---

[84] 463 U.S. 783 (1983).

[85] Marsh v. Chambers, 463 U.S. at 792.

[86] 465 U.S. 668 (1984).

[87] *Id.* at 679.

[88] *Id.* at 674.

[89] *Id.* at 673.

[90] *Id.*

Dissenting in *Wallace v. Jaffree*[91] in 1985, Justice Rehnquist — soon to be elevated to Chief Justice — authored the most searing and comprehensive critique of the Court's separationist construction of the establishment clause. He condemned the Court's use of Jefferson's phrase "wall of separation" as a metaphor for the establishment clause as "misleading," "useless," a "mischievous diversion," and a "metaphor based on bad history."[92] Jefferson, Justice Rehnquist noted, did not even play a direct role in the adoption of the Bill of Rights, as he was in France at the time as the American ambassador. Madison, he agreed, was "undoubtedly the most important architect ... of the Bill of Rights"; but the records of the First Congress, Justice Rehnquist claimed, demonstrated that Madison's role in the drafting and adoption of the language of the religion clauses was not that of "an advocate of incorporating the Virginia Statute of Religious Liberty into the United States Constitution" but of "an advocate of sensible legislative compromise."[93] Based on the records of the debate, it is "indisputable," Justice Rehnquist asserted, that Madison saw the establishment clause "as designed to prohibit the establishment of a national religion, and perhaps to prevent discrimination among sects. He did not see it as requiring neutrality on the part of government between religion and irreligion."[94] The contrary view set forth by the Court in *Everson v. Board of Education, supra*, he asserted, was "totally incorrect."[95]

Justice Rehnquist further noted that the First Congress re-enacted the Northwest Ordinance of 1787, which provided land grants in the designated territories for both sectarian and public schools, and adopted a resolution calling on the President to designate a "day of public thanksgiving and prayer." Moreover, he said, in the nineteenth century Congress routinely appropriated money to support sectarian Indian education by religious organizations, and the eminent constitutional authorities Joseph Story and Thomas Cooley both asserted that the religion clauses permitted nondiscriminatory governmental assistance to religion. Agreeing with the separationists' view that "[t]he true meaning of the Establishment Clause can only be seen in its history,"[96] Justice Rehnquist, nonetheless, concluded that prior to the Court's modern attempts to construe the establishment clause the clause had a "well-accepted meaning: it forbade establishment of a national religion, and forbade preference among religious sects or denominations.... [It] did not require government neutrality between religion and irreligion nor did it prohibit the Federal Government

---

[91] 472 U.S. 38 (1985). Justice Rehnquist's critique of the Court's use of history was largely informed by the analysis set forth in ROBERT L. CORD, SEPARATION OF CHURCH AND STATE: HISTORICAL FACT AND CURRENT FICTION (1982).

[92] *Id.* at 92, 107.

[93] *Id.* at 98.

[94] *Id.*

[95] *Id.*, at 99.

[96] *Id.* at 113.

from providing nondiscriminatory aid to religion."[97] The wall of separation metaphor, he said, "should be frankly and explicitly abandoned."[98]

With respect to the tripartite test, Justice Rehnquist charged that it "has no basis in the history of the amendment it seeks to interpret, is difficult to apply, and yields unprincipled results ...."[99] The secular purpose prong, he said, "has proven mercurial in application,"[100] because it is not clear whether it prohibits all aid to sectarian institutions or only that which is accompanied by a stated purpose to aid religion. The entanglement prong, he asserted, had become "divorced" from its use in a historical context in *Walz* and, when joined with the primary effect prong, had created a "Catch-22" in school aid cases: the effect test required such government aid to be "closely watched lest it be put to sectarian use," but the entanglement test rendered aid unconstitutional precisely because it is closely watched. Finally, he claimed, the tripartite test "has caused this Court to fracture into unworkable plurality opinions," has yielded "unprincipled results," and "has produced only consistent unpredictability."[101]

Justice White, in a separate dissent in *Wallace*, expressed appreciation for Justice Rehnquist's explication of the history of the religion clauses and, as he had even in the 1970s,[102] called for "a basic reconsideration of our precedents."[103]

In *Edwards v. Aguillard*[104] in 1987, Justice Scalia, appointed to the Court in 1986, began to articulate what has become a steady drumbeat of derision about the Court's establishment clause jurisprudence. In that case the Court held unconstitutional a Louisiana statute that mandated that creationism be taught along with evolution in the public schools on the grounds the statute was intended to endorse and promote a particular religious doctrine. Justice Scalia dissented from that conclusion and condemned the Court's establishment clause jurisprudence as "embarrassing."[105] More particularly, he asserted that the Court's application of the purpose prong of the tripartite test had "made such a maze of the Establishment Clause that even the most conscientious governmental officials can only guess what motives will be held unconstitutional." The purpose test, he charged, "exacerbates the tension between the Free Exercise and Establishment Clauses, has no basis in the language or history of the Amendment, and ... has wonderfully flexible

---

[97] *Id.* at 106.

[98] *Id.* at 107.

[99] *Id.* at 112.

[100] *Id.* at 108.

[101] *Id.* at 110, 112.

[102] See, *e.g.*, Committee for Public Education v. Nyquist, 413 U.S. 756, 813 (1973) (White, J., dissenting).

[103] Wallace v. Jaffree, 472 U.S. at 90-91 (White, J., dissenting).

[104] 482 U.S. 578 (1987).

[105] *Id.* at 639 (Scalia, J., dissenting).

consequences."[106] More generally, he has "bemoaned the strange Establishment Clause geometry of crooked lines and wavering shapes [*Lemon's*] intermittent use has produced," and has likened the test to "some ghoul in a late-night horror movie that repeatedly sits up in its grave and shuffles abroad, after being repeatedly killed and buried ..., frightening the little children and ... attorneys ...."[107]

In 1989 in *County of Allegheny v. American Civil Liberties Union, Greater Pittsburgh Chapter*[108] Justice Kennedy, appointed to the Court in 1988, suggested that "substantial revision of our Establishment Clause doctrine may be in order."[109] In that case the Court held unconstitutional the display of a creche by itself in a county courthouse but found constitutional the display of a Christmas tree and a menorah in front of a city-county building during the Christmas and Chanukah seasons. Justice Kennedy argued in partial dissent that the Court's holding with respect to the creche display "reflects an unjustified hostility toward religion, a hostility inconsistent with our history and our precedents."[110] "Government policies of accommodation, acknowledgment, and support for religion," he said, "are an accepted part of our political and cultural heritage."[111] Thus, he charged, any interpretation of the establishment clause that invalidates "historical practices" and "longstanding traditions" of government acknowledgment and accommodation of religion can not be legitimate. The establishment clause, he said, ought to be construed to mean only that "government may not coerce anyone to support or participate in any religion or its exercise; and it may not, in the guise of avoiding hostility or callous indifference, give direct benefits to religion in such a degree that it in fact 'establishes a [state] religion or religious faith, or tends to do so.'"[112]

Finally, Justice Thomas, in a concurring opinion in *Rosenberger v. Rector and Visitors of the University of Virginia*[113] took sharp issue with the separationist view that the establishment clause bars nondiscriminatory assistance to religion. Terming the Court's establishment clause jurisprudence to be "in hopeless disarray," he said that Virginia's controversy over assessments in 1785 and Madison's "Memorial and Remonstrance" had nothing to do with a subsidy available to both religious and nonreligious entities. Instead, he contended, it concerned only the support of ministers and teachers of religion. Thus, he argued, that incident, as well as Madison's actions in bringing about a Bill of Rights, cannot be used to support the "extreme view that the government must discriminate against religious adherents by

---

[106] *Id.* at 640.

[107] Lamb's Chapel v. Center Moriches School District, 508 U.S. 384, 403 (1993) (Scalia, J., concurring in the judgment).

[108] 492 U.S. 573 (1989).

[109] *Id.* at 655, 656 (Kennedy, J., concurring in part and dissenting in part).

[110] *Id.* at 655.

[111] *Id.* at 657.

[112] *Id. at* 659, quoting Lynch v. Donnelly, *supra*, at 678.

[113] 515 U.S. 819, 852 (1995) (Thomas, J., concurring).

excluding them from more generally available financial subsidies."[114] Moreover, he asserted, government in the early years of the Republic provided a number of supports for religion — Congress hired a chaplain; religious properties were exempted from property taxes; the Northwest Ordinance of 1787 provided land grants for the benefit of schools, many of which were sectarian; and copyright protections included religious authors and publications. He concluded:

> Thus, history provides an answer for the constitutional question posed by this case .... [There is] no evidence that the Framers intended to disable religious entities from participating on neutral terms in evenhanded government programs. The evidence that does exist points in the opposite direction ....[115]

(c) The Response. These criticisms of the Court's broad interpretation of the establishment clause, of course, have not gone without rejoinder. In further support of the "wall of separation" construction, for instance, Justice Brennan cited the historical facts that the Constitution broke with the common practice of the day in not invoking the name of God, that Madison subsequently recanted his views regarding the constitutionality of legislative chaplains and prayers, and that Presidents Jefferson and Jackson refused on establishment clause grounds to proclaim national days of thanksgiving or fasting.[116] He also argued that the acts of the First Congress cannot alone serve as an authoritative guide to the meaning of the establishment clause, because the views of the states that ratified the Bill of Rights also have to be considered.[117] More generally, he argued that "to be truly faithful to the Framers, 'our use of the history of their time must limit itself to broad purposes, not specific practices,'" lest their work be treated as "static and lifeless."[118]

In addition, Justices Blackmun, O'Connor, Brennan, Marshall, and Stevens all have stressed that the people of the United States are now religiously diverse and thus that even if "in the early days of the Republic [the religion clauses] were understood to protect only the diversity within Christianity ..., today they are recognized as guaranteeing religious liberty and equality to 'the infidel, the atheist, or the adherent of a non-Christian faith such as Islam or Judaism.'"[119]

In response to the argument that the establishment clause was intended to allow nondiscriminatory government assistance to religion, Justice Stevens, Brennan, and Marshall have contended that the religious establishments in the six states still retaining them at the time of the Bill of Rights were not limited to a single church but were multiple in nature, *i.e.*, public aid was provided on a nondiscriminatory basis to

---

[114] *Id.* at 857.

[115] *Id.* at 863.

[116] Marsh v. Chambers, 465 U.S. at 807 (Brennan, J., dissenting).

[117] *Id.* at 815-16.

[118] *Id.* at 816, quoting Abington School District v. Schempp, 374 U.S. at 241 (Brennan, J., concurring).

[119] *See* Wallace v. Jaffree, *supra*, at 52, and Allegheny County v. Greater Pittsburgh ACLU, 492 U.S. at 590.

all Christian churches or to all Protestant churches.. Thus, they asserted, the prohibition of the establishment clause was understood by its authors to preclude not just a single established church but multiple establishments as well, *i.e.*, it was intended to prohibit nondiscriminatory aid to all religions.[120] That intent, they claimed, was clearly shown by the evolution in the wording of the religion clauses during their consideration in the First Congress.

Following his appointment to the Court in 1990, Justice Souter, joined by Justices O'Connor and Stevens, argued this view as well. In a concurring opinion in *Lee v. Weisman*, *supra*, Justice Souter examined in detail the debates of the First Congress on what became the religion clauses and concluded:

> The House rejected the Select Committee's version, which arguably ensured only that "no religion" enjoyed an official preference over others, and deliberately chose instead a prohibition extending to laws establishing "religion" in general. The sequence of the Senate's treatment of this House proposal, and the House's response to the Senate, confirm that the Framers meant the Establishment Clause's prohibition to encompass nonpreferential aid to religion .... What is remarkable is that, unlike the earliest House drafts or the final Senate proposal, the prevailing language in not limited to laws respecting an establishment of "a religion," "a national religion," "one religious sect," or specific "articles of faith. The Framers repeatedly considered and deliberately rejected such narrow language and instead extended their prohibition to state support for "religion" in general.[121]

He concluded as well that the language of the establishment clause prohibits more than just governmental coercion of religious belief or of support for religion. The free exercise clause, he noted, also prohibits such coercion and, thus, "a literal application of the coercion test would render the Establishment Clause a virtual nullity."[122]

Justice Blackmun in the opinion of the Court in *Allegheny County v. ACLU, Pittsburgh Chapter* termed the charge of "hostility" to religion leveled against the separationist construction of the establishment clause to be both "offensive" and "absurd":

> Justice Kennedy apparently has misperceived a respect for religious pluralism, a respect commanded by the Constitution, as hostility or indifference to religion. No misperception could be more antithetical to the values embodied in the Establishment Clause .... A secular state ... is not the same as an atheistic or antireligious state. A secular state establishes neither atheism nor religion as its official creed .... It follows directly from the Constitution's proscription against

---

[120] Allegheny County v. Greater Pittsburgh ACLU, *supra*, at 646-47 (Stevens, J., concurring in part and dissenting in part). In so doing Justice Stevens generally followed the historical analysis set forth in LEONARD LEVY, THE ESTABLISHMENT CLAUSE: RELIGION AND THE FIRST AMENDMENT (1986).

[121] Lee v. Weisman, 505 U.S. at 609, 613-15 (Souter, J., concurring).

[122] *Id.* at 618-26.

> government affiliation with religious beliefs or institutions that there is no orthodoxy on religious matters in the secular state.[123]

Thus, he asserted, denying government the power to display a creche on public property at Christmastime "does not represent a hostility or indifference to religion but, instead, the respect for religious diversity that the Constitution requires."[124] "The Constitution," he said, "mandates that the government remain secular, rather than affiliate itself with religious beliefs or institutions, precisely in order to avoid discriminating among citizens on the basis of their religious faiths."[125]

More recently, in an opinion joined by Justices Stevens, Ginsburg, and Breyer, Justice Souter in a dissenting opinion in *Rosenberger v. The Rector and Visitors of the University of Virginia* recapitulated the separationist understanding of the historical underpinnings of the establishment clause and reiterated as well the authority of Madison and Jefferson on its meaning. In response to Justice Thomas' interpretation of Madison's views, he said that "nowhere in the Remonstrance ... did Madison advance the view that Virginia should be able to provide financial support for religion as part of a generally available subsidy program" and noted as well that the outgrowth of the Remonstrance "was not such a bill [but Jefferson'] Bill for Establishing Religious Freedom, which ... proscribed the use of tax dollars for religious purposes."[126] Of the contention that the acts of Congress showed that the establishment clause allows nondiscriminatory aid, Justice Souter rejoined that "individual acts of Congress, especially when they are few and far between, scarcely serve as an authoritative guide to the meaning of the Religion Clauses ... [and are] no more dispositive than the Alien and Sedition Acts in interpreting the First Amendment."[127]

(d) Establishment Clause Tests. The development and criticisms of the *Lemon* tripartite test have been summarized above. That debate is still ongoing but it should be noted that the debate has had two specific consequences to date. First, *Lemon* is no longer the sole test the Court uses. Although it has not been entirely abandoned, in a number of recent decisions the Court has eschewed use of the *Lemon* test entirely.[128] Secondly, in its most recent decision the Court modified the test to a two-prong rather than a tripartite test:

> ...[T]he factors we use to assess whether an entanglement is "excessive" are similar to the factors we use to examine "effect." That is, to assess entanglement,

---

[123] County of Allegheny v. ACLU, Greater Pittsburgh Chapter, 492 U.S. at 610-11.

[124] *Id.* at 613.

[125] *Id.* at 610.

[126] Rosenberger v. Rector and Board of Visitors of the University of Virginia, 515 U.S. 819, 869-71 (1995), n. 1 (Souter, J., dissenting).

[127] *Id.* at 872, n. 2.

[128] *See* Lee v. Weisman, 505 U.S. 577 (1992); Zobrest v. Catalina Foothills School District, 509 U.S. 1 (1993); Board of Education of the Kiryas Joel Village School District v. Grumet, 512 U.S. 687 (1994); and Rosenberger v. The Rector and Visitors of the University of Virginia, 515 U.S. 819 (1995).

> we have looked to "the character and purposes of the institutions that are benefited, the nature of the aid that the State provides, and the resulting relationship between the government and religious authority .... Similarly, we have assessed a law's "effect" by examining the character of the institutions benefited (*e.g.*, whether the religious institutions were "predominantly religious") ... and the nature of the aid that the State provided (*e.g.*, whether it was neutral and nonideological) .... Thus, it is simplest to recognize why entanglement is significant and treat it — as we did in *Walz* — as an aspect of the inquiry into a statute's effect.[129]

In addition, the debate about the appropriate test to implement the establishment clause has given rise to three alternatives to *Lemon* — the endorsement test, the coercion test, and the neutrality test. Each of these has also been subject to dispute.

(1) Endorsement test. Justice O'Connor, appointed to the Court in 1981, authored a concurring opinion in *Lynch v. Donnelly* to suggest not a rejection but a "clarification" of the *Lemon* test.[130] The essential meaning of the establishment clause, she asserted, is that it "prohibits government from making adherence to a religion relevant in any way to a person's standing in the political community." Thus, she said, the clause is violated when government becomes excessively entangled with religious institutions, because that may threaten the independence of such institutions, give favored institutions access to governmental powers or benefits not fully available to nonadherents of the favored religion, and create "political constituencies defined along religious lines." More importantly, she said, the clause is violated by "government endorsement or disapproval of religion":

> Endorsement sends a message to nonadherents that they are outsiders, not full members of the political community, and an accompanying message to adherents that they are insiders, favored members of the political community. Disapproval sends the opposite message.[131]

Thus, the secular purpose prong of the tripartite test, she averred, should be construed to ask whether "government's actual purpose is to endorse or disapprove of religion."[132] The primary effect prong, in turn, should be construed to ask "whether, irrespective of purpose, the practice under review in fact conveys a message of endorsement or disapproval." The entanglement prong, she asserted, should be limited to institutional entanglement, not political entanglement.[133]

---

[129] Agostini v. Felton, 117 S.Ct. at 2015 (1977).

[130] Lynch v. Donnelly, 465 U.S. at 687 (O'Connor, J., concurring).

[131] Lynch v. Donnelly, 465 U.S. at 688.

[132] *Id.* at 690.

[133] Subsequently, it should be noted, a majority of the Court, in a decision authored by Justice O'Connor, eliminated excessive institutional entanglement as a separate criterion of an establishment clause violation. *See* Agostini v. Felton, 117 S.Ct. 1997 (1997).

The Court has employed this revision of the *Lemon* test in several cases.[134] But in *County of Allegheny v. ACLU, Pittsburgh Chapter, supra,* Justice Kennedy termed Justice O'Connor's endorsement test an "unwelcome addition to our tangled Establishment Clause jurisprudence" and said it was "flawed in its fundamentals and unworkable in practice." The test, he charged, would invalidate "scores of traditional practices recognizing the place religion holds in our culture," would "trivialize constitutional adjudication," and would require the Court to "sit as a national theology board" and decide "what every religious symbol means."[135] Justice Scalia in *Capitol Square Review and Advisory Board v. Pinette, supra,* said that in the context of the display of religious symbols the endorsement principle requires officials to "guess" when they might be perceived to be advocating a religious viewpoint and forces them "to weigh a host of imponderables." The endorsement test, he said, provides "no standard whatsoever" for determining when the establishment clause is violated and creates a "minefield" for public officials.

(2) Coercion test. Justice Kennedy, appointed to the Court in 1987, has proffered coercion as the touchstone of an establishment clause violation (although, perhaps, not the only indication of a violation). In *Lee v. Weisman, supra,* Justice Kennedy opined for the Court that "at a minimum, the Constitution guarantees that government may not coerce anyone to support or participate in religion or its exercise, or otherwise act in a way which 'establishes a [state] religion, or religious faith, or tends to do so."[136] Justice O'Connor has criticized the coercion aspect of this test as failing "to take account of the numerous more subtle ways that government can show favoritism to particular beliefs or convey a message of disapproval to others" and thus as failing to "adequately protect the religious liberty or respect the religious diversity of the members of our pluralistic political community." Moreover, she has said, to make coercion the touchstone of an establishment clause violation "would make the Free Exercise Clause a redundancy."[137] Justice Souter, as noted above, has made a similar criticism of the coercion test, contending that it would make the establishment clause a "virtual nullity."

(3) Neutrality test. The concept of neutrality has been a continuing component of the Court's establishment clause jurisprudence. In its first establishment clause decision of the modern era, the Court used that principle to uphold a public subsidy of the costs of transporting children to and from school, including parochial school, stating

---

[134] See Wallace v. Jaffree, 472 U.S. 38 (1985); Grand Rapids School District v. Ball, 473 U.S. 373 (1985); County of Allegheny v. American Civil Liberties Union Greater Pittsburgh Chapter, 492 U.S. 573 (1989); and Capitol Square Review and Advisory Board v. Pinette, 63 U.S.L.W. 4684 (1995).

[135] County of Allegheny v. ACLU, Pittsburgh Chapter, 492 U.S. at 3134 (Kennedy, J., concurring in part and dissenting in part).

[136] Quoting Lynch v. Donnelly, *supra*, at 678.

[137] *Id.* at 3117 (O'Connor, J., concurring in part and concurring in the judgment).

> [t]he First Amendment ... requires the state to be neutral in its relations with groups of religious believers and non-believers; it does not require the state to be their adversary.[138]

In the *Lemon* test the neutrality principle finds expression in the second prong, which requires government action affecting religion to have a primary effect that neither advances nor inhibits religion.

In some areas, such as private religious expression, the Justices concur in their understanding of neutrality.[139] But the principle can have a different meaning for separationists and accommodationists. Thus, depending on which wing of the Court is wielding it, the principle has at various times been described by the Court as one of "benevolent neutrality"[140] and at other times as one of "strict neutrality."[141] Differences emerge most visibly with respect to the inclusion of religious organizations in governmental aid programs. In the separationist construction government must be neutral not only between religions but also between religion and irreligion. From this perspective religious neutrality means not only that government cannot favor one faith over another but also that it cannot provide nondiscriminatory aid to religion generally or otherwise give religion preference over its nonreligious counterparts.[142] Moreover, even in a nondiscriminatory aid program, public aid cannot be used for religious activities or religious proselytizing. This understanding

---

[138] Everson v. Board of Education, 330 U.S. 1, 18 (1947).

[139] *See, e.g.*, Widmar v. Vincent, 454 U.S. 263 (1981) (equal access to university facilities for student religious groups); Board of Education of Westside Community Schools v. Mergens, 496 U.S. 226 (1990) (equal access to secondary school facilities for noncurricular student religious groups); and Capitol Square Review and Advisory Board v. Pinette, 515 U.S. 753 (1995) (display of religious symbols in a public park).

[140] In upholding the tax exemption accorded property owned by religious and other nonprofit organizations in Walz v. Tax Commission of New York, 397 U.S. 664, 669 (1970) the Court asserted:

> The general principle deducible from the First Amendment and all that has been said by this Court is this: that we will not tolerate either governmentally established religion or governmental interference with religion. Short of those expressly proscribed governmental acts there is room for play in the joints productive of a benevolent neutrality which will permit religious exercise to exist without sponsorship and without interference.

[141] In holding state sponsorship of Bible reading and unison prayer in the public schools unconstitutional in Abington School District v. Schempp, 374 U.S. 203, 225 (1963), the Court stated:

> They are religious exercises, required by the States in violation of the command of the First Amendment that the Government maintain strict neutrality, neither aiding nor opposing religion.

[142] *See, e.g.*, City of Grand Rapids v. Ball, 473 U.S. 373 (1985) (striking down a supplemental education program benefiting private schools, most of which were sectarian) and Texas Monthly, Inc. v. Bullock, 489 U.S. 1 (1989) (striking down an exemption of religious books and periodicals from a state sales and use tax).

of the neutrality required by the establishment clause is rejected by accommodationists. Then-Justice Rehnquist contended in *Wallace v. Jaffree*[143] that the original meaning of the establishment clause "forbade establishment of a national church, and forbade preference among religious sects or denominations .... [I]t did not require government neutrality between religion and irreligion nor did it prohibit the Federal Government from providing nondiscriminatory aid to religion." In this view religious organizations should be eligible to participate in public aid programs without giving up their religiosity.

(e) Conclusion. In sum, then, the period since 1980 has witnessed profound discontent by a number of Justices with the historical justifications previously used by the Court for its interpretation of the establishment clause, the "wall of separation" metaphor, and the tripartite *Lemon* test. All of the Justices continue to agree that the meaning and scope of the clause are informed by history, but they sharply disagree on what history is most relevant.

The critique of the separationist understanding of the establishment clause has had a substantial effect, albeit not one as sweeping as the alteration of the interpretation of the free exercise clause. Since 1980 the Court has rendered a number of decisions that are best described as accommodationist in nature (*see infra*); the metaphor "wall of separation" has not been used in a majority opinion by the Court since 1984[144]; the *Lemon* test has been supplemented and often replaced by other tests such as endorsement, coercion, and neutrality; and the entanglement prong of the *Lemon* test has been eliminated as a separate test. Moreover, in its most recent decision the Court for the first time overturned a prior establishment clause decision.[145]

The pace of disputes about the establishment clause on the Court has slowed in recent years, as it has taken fewer such cases than during the decade of the 1980s and the early part of the 1990s. But the intensity of the debate persists and can be expected to persist for some years to come. From virtual unanimity fifty years ago on a separationist understanding of the establishment clause, the Court has become narrowly divided, with perhaps a slight leaning toward an accommodationist view.

Particular Issues

The tumult on the Court over the meaning of the religion clauses has meant that it has faced few easy cases in this area since 1980. As noted earlier, more than a quarter of its decisions during this time have been by a 5-4 margin, and concurring

---

[143] 472 U.S. 38, 106 (Rehnquist, J., dissenting).

[144] Lynch v. Donnelly, 465 U.S. 668 (1984).

[145] In Agostini v. Felton, 117 S.Ct. 1997 (1997), the Court upheld as constitutional the provision of remedial educational services by public school teachers to private schoolchildren on the premises of sectarian schools. In the process the Court overturned Aguilar v. Felton, 473 U.S. 402 (1985) and parts of School District of the City of Grand Rapids v. Ball, 473 U.S. 373 (1985) and Meek v. Pittenger, 421 U.S. 349 (1975), and Wolman v. Walter, 433 U.S. 229 (1977).

and dissenting opinions have abounded (*see* Appendix). The Court's narrowing of the scope of the free exercise clause has been recounted above, and that discussion of the fourteen free exercise decisions rendered by the Court since 1980 (with the exception of the tax cases) will not be repeated here. With respect to the establishment clause, the Court in its decisions since 1980 has:

(a) reaffirmed its past decisions prohibiting government promotion or sponsorship of religious exercises in the public schools, established the constitutional parameters for silent meditation, and held equal access policies for student religious groups at the college and secondary school levels to be constitutional;

(b) expanded the scope of permissible government accommodation of, and overt support for, religious speech in the public square;

(c) reaffirmed some of its precedents concerning direct public aid to sectarian schools and religious social welfare organizations but overturned a line of cases that had prohibited public school teachers from providing educational services to sectarian schoolchildren on the premises of their sectarian schools;

(d) broken new ground with respect to indirect assistance to religious enterprises and activities;

(e) set limits on the extent to which government can provide special benefits and protections for religious practices and organizations;

(f) accorded government substantial discretion to impose general taxes on religious entities and individuals;

(g) generally found no constitutional problem in the application of governmental regulations to religious organizations; and

(h) refused to broaden the doctrine of standing to permit wider challenges to the provision of public benefits to religious organizations.

This section summarizes the Court's decisions in each of these areas and examines their effect on its church-state jurisprudence.

(a) Religion in the Public Schools. Perhaps the most controversial area of the Court's church-state jurisprudence has been its decisions concerning religion in the public schools. Over the last four decades its decisions in this area have precipitated hundreds of proposals for constitutional amendments, recurrent Congressional debates, and passionate public disputes. Few issues in American public life have been as persistent or as contentious. But in six decisions and two summary affirmances since 1980 the Court has made clear the continuing vitality of its precedents in this area. Yet it has also broken new ground by making explicit a constitutional distinction between the **sponsorship** of religious activities in the schools by government and the conduct of such activities by students **at their own initiative**.

In five decisions prior to the beginning of the decade the Court had construed the establishment clause to prohibit government from sponsoring or promoting religious activities or doctrines in the public schools. Struck down by the Court had been state sponsorship of regular devotional activities such as prayer and Bible reading,[146] privately sponsored religious instruction on public school premises during the school day,[147] and state prohibitions on the teaching of evolution.[148] "A State cannot consistently with the First and Fourteenth Amendments," the Court had said, "utilize its public school system to aid any or all religious faiths or sects in the dissemination of their doctrines and ideals."[149]

On the other hand, the Court had prior to 1980 found the establishment clause **not** to be violated by a released time program that permitted public school children to repair to nearby religious centers during the school day for purposes of receiving religious instruction from private teachers.[150] It had in *dicta* affirmed the constitutionality of the public schools teaching **about** religion. And it had in two cases held the free speech and free exercise clauses to mandate exemptions for religious reasons from the otherwise compulsory practices of saluting the flag and attending school until the age of sixteen.[151] In the public schools, the Court had said, "[t]he First Amendment mandates government neutrality between religion and religion, and between religion and nonreligion."[152]

All of these precedents have remained intact since 1980. The Court has reaffirmed its school prayer and curriculum decisions and extended them to commencement prayer, displays of the Ten Commandments, and the teaching of creationism. But it has also found broad constitutional protection for private religious speech in decisions concerning moments of silence and equal access policies for student religious groups at the secondary school and college levels and for student religious publications in a university setting.

(1) Government sponsorship of religion. In two decisions since 1980 the Court summarily affirmed lower court decisions which struck down state laws and practices that permitted teachers to open the school day with prayers composed by themselves or by the state legislature.[153] In a third decision the Court in *Lee v. Weisman*[154] held

---

[146] Engel v. Vitale, 370 U.S. 421 (1962); Abington School District v. Schempp, 374 U.S. 203 (1963); and Chamberlin v. Dade County Board of Public Instruction, 377 U.S. 402 (1964).

[147] McCollum v. Board of Education, 333 U.S. 203 (1948).

[148] Epperson v. Arkansas, 393 U.S. 97 (1968).

[149] McCollum v. Board of Education, 333 U.S. at 211.

[150] Zorach v. Clauson, 343 U.S. 306 (1952).

[151] See West Virginia Board of Education v. Barnette, 319 U.S. 624 (1943), and Wisconsin v. Yoder, 406 U.S. 205 (1972), respectively.

[152] Epperson v. Arkansas, 393 U.S. at 103-04.

[153] Karen B. v. Treen, 455 U.S. 913 (1982), *aff'g mem.*, 653 F.2d 897 (5th Cir. 1981) (affirming a lower federal court decision holding unconstitutional a Louisiana statute and a local school board's implementing regulation which permitted teachers to ask for student volunteers to offer a prayer at the beginning of each school day and, if no student volunteered,

(continued...)

unconstitutional, 5-4, a local school district's policy of permitting clergy to offer invocations and benedictions at graduation ceremonies.

The two summary affirmances, of course, involved no written opinions. In *Weisman* Justice Kennedy, writing for the Court, eschewed use of the *Lemon* test and employed instead the principle that "at a minimum, the Constitution guarantees that government may not coerce anyone to support or participate in religion or its exercise ...."[155] "The injury caused by the government's action" in this instance, he said, "is that the State, in a school setting, in effect required participation in a religious exercise."[156] But "[t]he First Amendment's Religion Clauses," he asserted, "mean that religious beliefs and religious expression are too precious to be either proscribed or prescribed by the State."[157] Rejecting the notion that government could sponsor the rabbi's prayer as a form of "civic" religion in the schools, he said "[t]he Constitution forbids the State to exact religious conformity from a student as the price of attending her own high school graduation."[158]

In two additional cases the Court held unconstitutional state statutes mandating the display of the Ten Commandments on the walls of the public schools and the teaching of creationism. In *Stone v. Graham*[159] the Court struck down, 5-4, a Kentucky statute which required that a copy of the Ten Commandments, purchased with private funds, be posted on the wall of each public classroom in the state. Notwithstanding contrary declarations by the state legislature, the Court found the Ten Commandments to be "undeniably a sacred text" and the "pre-eminent purpose" of the posting requirement to be "plainly religious in nature." As a consequence, it held the posting requirement to be in violation of the first prong of the *Lemon* test and a violation of the establishment clause.

---

[153](...continued)
to offer a prayer themselves) and Wallace v. Jaffree, 466 U.S. 924 (1984), *aff'g mem.*, 705 F.2d 1526 (11th Cir. 1983) (affirming that part of a lower federal court decision holding unconstitutional an Alabama statute which permitted teachers to pray, to lead willing students in prayer, or to lead willing students in the following prayer set forth in the statute:

> Almighty God, You alone are our God. We acknowledge You as the Creator and Supreme Judge of the World. May Your justice, Your truth, and Your peace abound this day in the hearts of our government, in the sanctity of our homes and in the classrooms of our schools. In the name of our Lord. Amen.

[154] 505 U.S. 577 (1992).

[155] *Id.* at 2655.

[156] *Id.* at 2659.

[157] *Id.* at 2656.

[158] *Id.* at 2660.

[159] 449 U.S. 39 (1980) (*per curiam*).

In *Edwards v. Aguillard*[160] the Court reaffirmed and extended its previous ruling in *Epperson v. Arkansas*[161] which had held unconstitutional a state's ban on the teaching of evolution in the public schools. *Aguillard* involved a Louisiana statute that, instead of barring the teaching of evolution, required teachers to give "balanced treatment" to evolution and creationism, *i.e.*, to teach both doctrines. Like the statute involved in *Epperson*, the Court held this statute to violate the purpose prong of the tripartite test, 7-2. In enacting the statute, Justice Brennan wrote for the Court, "the pre-eminent purpose of the Louisiana legislature was clearly to advance the religious viewpoint that a supernatural being created mankind." Noting the "historic and contemporaneous antagonisms between the teachings of certain religious denominations and the teaching of evolution," he concluded that it was not "happenstance that the legislature required the teaching of a theory which coincided with [a] religious view."[162] The purpose of the Act, the Court found, was "to endorse a particular religious doctrine"; as a consequence, it held that the Act violated the establishment clause. Thus, unless creationism can gain acceptance in the scientific community as a scientific theory, *Aguillard* appears to close the constitutional door on further efforts to excise or rebut the teaching of evolution in the public schools.

(2) Private religious expression. In four other decisions since 1980 involving religion in the public schools, however, the Court broke new constitutional ground. In each case it affirmed the constitutionality of private religious expression, and in one case even upheld the public subsidy of religious expression.

In *Wallace v. Jaffree*[163] the Court for the first time addressed the constitutionality of provisions mandating moments of silence at the beginning of each school day.[164] Again relying on the first prong of the *Lemon* test, the Court in *Wallace* struck down an Alabama statute mandating a daily moment of silence in the public schools for purposes of "meditation or voluntary prayer" on the grounds it had been adopted with an illegitimate legislative purpose. By a 6-3 margin the Court found that the Alabama legislature had enacted the statute in question "for the sole purpose of expressing the State's endorsement of prayer activities for one minute at the beginning of each school day." Another statute previously adopted by Alabama, Justice Stevens noted for the Court, already provided for a moment of silence at the beginning of each school day for purposes of meditation. The legislative history of the addition of the phrase "or voluntary prayer" in the later statute, the Court concluded, clearly showed that the statute was intended to serve no secular purpose and was of a "wholly religious character."[165] Justice Stevens stressed, however, that the Court was not holding all moment of silence provisions to be unconstitutional:

---

[160] 482 U.S. 578 (1987).

[161] 393 U.S. 97 (1968).

[162] *Id.* at 591-92.

[163] 472 U.S. 38 (1985).

[164] Justice Brennan had previously opined that a moment of silence at the beginning of the school day would be constitutional. See Abington School District v. Schempp, 374 U.S. at 280-81 (Brennan, J., concurring).

[165] Wallace v. Jaffree, 472 U.S. at 58.

> The legislative intent to return prayer to the public schools is, of course, quite different from merely protecting every student's right to engage in voluntary prayer during an appropriate moment of silence during the schoolday. The 1978 statute already protected that right ....[166]

Thus, it appears likely that statutes or regulations mandating a moment of silence can pass constitutional muster, provided that they are not adopted for the purpose of promoting prayer and are not implemented to give governmental encouragement or preference to prayer.[167]

In two other decisions the Court construed the First Amendment to require or, at least, to permit public universities and public secondary schools to allow student-initiated religious groups to use school facilities during the school day. In *Widmar v. Vincent*[168] the Court held, 8-1, that the freedom of speech clause of the First Amendment bars a public university which permits some student groups to meet in its facilities from denying such use to student groups wanting to engage in religious worship and discussion. Once a university opens its facilities for use by student organizations, Justice Powell wrote for the Court, it may not "enforce a content-based exclusion of religious speech" unless there is a compelling public purpose to be served. The University argued that conformance with the establishment clause and with Missouri's history of strict church-state separation constituted sufficient justification for its ban. But the Court disagreed. Permitting student groups to use campus facilities for religious purposes, it said, would neither place the imprimatur of University sponsorship on any sectarian belief or practice nor single out religious groups for special benefits. Thus, the Court held, the University's "exclusionary policy violates the fundamental principle that a state regulation of speech should be content-neutral ...."[169]

Before and after *Widmar* the same constitutional question arose in the context of student-initiated religious groups in public **secondary** schools. All but one of the state and lower federal courts that examined that question held permission for such groups to meet on the premises of public secondary schools to violate the establishment clause.[170] Congress, however, found the courts' reasoning unpersuasive

---

[166] 472 U.S. at 59. See also the concurring opinions of Justices Powell and O'Connor, *id.*, at 62 and 67, respectively.

[167] A subsequent attempt to obtain clarification from the Court on what kind of moment of silence statute might pass constitutional muster foundered when the Court found that the parties who brought the case to it had no standing to do so. See May v. Cooperman, 572 F.Supp. 1561 (D. N.J. 1983), *aff'd*, 780 F.2d 240 (3d Cir. 1985), *appeal dismissed for want of jurisdiction*, 484 U.S. 72 (1987).

[168] 454 U.S. 263 (1981).

[169] *Id.* at 277.

[170] See Brandon v. Board of Education of the Guilderland Central School District, 635 F.2d 971 (1st Cir. 1980), *cert. den.*, 454 U.S. 1123 (1981); Lubbock Civil Liberties Union v. Lubbock Independent School District, 659 F.2d 1038 (5th Cir. 1982), *cert. den.*, 459 U.S. 1156 (1983); Bell v. Little Axe Independent School District, 766 F.2d 1391 (10th Cir. 1985);

(continued...)

and in 1984, after a vigorous debate, created a **statutory** right at the public secondary school level that replicated the constitutional right at universities articulated in *Widmar*. The Equal Access Act[171] bars public secondary schools that receive federal assistance and that have a limited open forum from discriminating against any student group wishing to meet on the basis of the religious, political, philosophical, or other content of the speech at such meetings. The Act defines "limited open forum" to mean the "opportunity for one or more noncurriculum related student groups to meet on school premises during noninstructional time."

In *Board of Education of Westside Community Schools v. Mergens*[172] the Court held the Equal Access Act to be constitutional, 8-1. The Court construed the Act broadly as a remedy against "perceived widespread discrimination against religious speech in public schools" and said it applied any time a school permitted even one noncurriculum related student group to meet. The Court further found the Act not to promote religion or to place the imprimatur of government on the religious speech that would occur at such meetings. Justice O'Connor, joined by three other Justices,[173] stressed that

> [t]here is a crucial difference between *government* speech endorsing religion and *private* speech endorsing religion. We think that secondary school students are mature enough and are likely to understand that a school does not endorse or support student speech that it merely permits on a nondiscriminatory basis.[174]

Justices Brennan and Marshall agreed with that reasoning but said that Westside needed to take additional steps to make clear that its recognition of a student Bible club did not constitute an endorsement of their views. However, Justices Scalia and Kennedy emphasized the absence of any coercive effect in permitting such meetings to occur. Despite these differing approaches to the issue, the decision clearly ratified the extension of the reasoning of *Widmar* to the public secondary school setting.

Finally, in *Rosenberger v. The Rector and Visitors of the University of Virginia*[175] the Court held, 5-4, that when a public university creates a forum for the expression of student opinions, it cannot exclude student religious opinions. In this instance the University of Virginia fostered the creation of publications by student organizations by paying their printing bills out of the student activities fund (SAF). However, it excluded religious publications, among others, from the subsidy, arguing

---

170(...continued)
Johnson v. Huntington Beach Union High School District, 137 Cal.Rptr. 43, 68 Cal.App.3d 1 (Ct. App.), *cert. den.*, 434 U.S. 877 (1977); and Trietley v. Board of Education of the City of Buffalo, 65 A.D.2d 1, 409 N.Y.S.2d 912 (App. Div. 1978). *Contra* Bender v. Williamsport Area School District, 563 F.Supp. 697 (M.D. Pa. 1983), *reversed*, 741 F.2d 538 (3d Cir.), *vacated for want of jurisdiction*, 475 U.S. 534 (1986).

171 20 U.S.C. 4071-74 (1988).

172 496 U.S. 226 (1990).

173 Chief Justice Rehnquist and Justices White and Blackmun.

174 496 U.S. at 242.

175 515 U.S. 819 (1995).

that the establishment clause prohibits the funding of such a religious activity. But the Court rejected the argument. It held the object of the SAF to be "to open a forum for speech" and the University's exclusion of the religious publication, as a consequence, to constitute viewpoint discrimination violative of the free speech clause of the First Amendment. The SAF was not a tax used to support a church, the Court said, but essentially amounted to a religiously neutral fund to promote private student speech. The Court said the University's policy of exclusion itself threatened to violate the establishment clause because the University would then have to scrutinize every publication and determine when its religious content was too great. Justice O'Connor, the decisive vote in the case, stressed in a concurring opinion the factors that the publications were genuinely independent of the University, that the payments were made not directly to the sponsoring student organizations but to the printer, that numerous publications were subsidized, and that students could, at least hypothetically, seek a refund for any portion of their fees used for speech with which they disagreed. These factors convinced her, she said, that "providing ... assistance in this case would not carry the danger of impermissible use of public funds to endorse Wide Awake's religious message."

In short, since 1980 the Court has reaffirmed that the establishment clause prohibits government from promoting religious faith in the public schools. But it has also made clear that students possess both constitutional and statutory rights to engage in religious activity which they initiate themselves on public school premises and that the establishment clause does not trump the free speech clause with respect to religious speech in a public forum created by a university.

(b) Religion in the Public Square. Prior to 1980 the Court had rendered several decisions involving religious expression in settings other than the public schools. In a series of cases in the 1940s largely involving the Jehovah's Witnesses, the Court established that the free speech clause of the First Amendment provides broad protection for religious solicitation and proselytizing. Held unconstitutional were ordinances and policies that gave local officials unfettered discretion to grant or deny permits to speak in public parks,[176] taxed the sale of religious literature by itinerant evangelists[177] and resident booksellers,[178] and barred the door-to-door distribution of religious handbills.[179] The Court did affirm the legitimacy of neutral time, place, and manner restrictions on speech in public places where the restrictions were genuinely unrelated to the content of the speech involved.[180] And it affirmed as well the legitimacy of restrictions on the use of children in religious solicitations under

---

[176] Cantwell v. Connecticut, 310 U.S. 296 (1941); Niemotko v. Maryland, 340 U.S. 268 (1951); Kunz v. New York, 340 U.S. 290 (1951).

[177] Jones v. Opelika, 319 U.S. 103 (1943); Murdock v. Pennsylvania, 319 U.S. 105 (1943).

[178] Follett v. McCormick, 321 U.S. 573 (1944).

[179] Martin v. Struthers, 319 U.S. 141 (1943).

[180] Fowler v. Rhode Island, 345 U.S. 67 (1953); Poulos v. New Hampshire, 345 U.S. 395 (1953).

a state's labor laws.[181] But it generally established the principle that government is constitutionally barred from restricting speech in public places, whether religious or nonreligious, because of its content.

In these and other cases, the Court also developed the notion of the "public forum," *i.e.*, that certain sites are by their nature and history particularly appropriate for speech activities.[182] It also posited that not all public properties are public forums: "The crucial question is whether the manner of expression is basically compatible with the normal activity of a particular place at a particular time."[183]

Since 1980 the Court has elaborated on its public forum doctrine and made clear that in traditional or designated public fora, government cannot censor speech because of its content without compelling reason. In nonpublic fora, however, government has greater latitude: it can impose regulations that are reasonable so long as the regulations are "not an effort to suppress expression merely because public officials oppose the speaker's view."[184] The Court has applied this framework of analysis in four cases relating to religious speech and solication in such public fora as a state fair, an aiport terminal, and a school auditorium. It has also, in three cases, attempted for the first time to delineate what government can and cannot do with respect to the public display of religious symbols. Finally, in a case of first impression, it resolved the constitutionality of government sponsorship of religious speech in the form of the legislative chaplaincy.

(1) Government regulation of religious speech and solicitation. In four decisions since 1980 the Court has affirmed that in places that traditionally or in practice are devoted to expression, government may not prohibit or censor religious speech without compelling reason or under regulations that are not viewpoint neutral. But it has also reaffirmed that government can impose reasonable time, place, and manner restrictions. In addition, it has held that in regulating charitable solicitations, government must act in an evenhanded manner, *i.e.*, it cannot favor some religious solicitations over others.

---

[181] Prince v. Massachusetts, 321 U.S. 158 (1944).

[182] Justice Roberts described the concept in Hague v. CIO, 307 U.S. 496, 515 (1939) (concurring):

> Wherever the title of streets and parks may rest, they have immemorially been held in trust for the use of the public and, time out of mind, have been used for purposes of assembly, communicating thoughts between citizens, and discussing public questions.

See also Schneider v. State, 308 U.S. 147 (1939).

[183] Grayned v. City of Rockford, 408 U.S. 104, 116 (1972).

[184] Perry Education Association v. Perry Local Educators' Association, 460 U.S. 37, 46 (1983).

Heffron v. International Society for Krishna Consciousness, Inc. (ISKCON)[185] involved a state regulation imposed on the distribution and sale of literature and the solicitation of donations at the Minnesota State Fair. The regulation required such activities to be done only from fixed locations, *i.e.*, pre-assigned rented booths. ISKCON claimed that its religious ritual of Sankirtan requires the faithful to go into public places to distribute or sell religious literature and to solicit donations to support the Krishna religion. But the Court unanimously held Minnesota's "booth rule" to be constitutional with respect to the sale of literature and the solicitation of donations, and by a 5-4 margin upheld it as well with respect to the distribution of literature. The Fair, the Court said, was a limited public forum, and the regulation was a reasonable time, place, and manner restriction. It was applied in a nondiscriminatory manner; was unrelated to the content or the subject matter of the speech involved; did not vest arbitrary discretion in any governmental authority; served the "substantial state interest" of ensuring the orderly movement of the crowds attending the Fair and of avoiding congestion; and left ISKCON and other organizations at the Fair ample opportunity to engage in protected speech.

In *Board of Airport Commissioners of the City of Los Angeles v. Jews for Jesus, Inc.*,[186] in contrast, the Court unanimously struck down a regulation that banned **all** First Amendment activities in the Central Terminal Area of Los Angeles International Airport. The regulation had been applied to bar a minister of the Gospel for Jews for Jesus from distributing free religious literature on a pedestrian walkway in the Airport. The Court, without deciding whether the Terminal constituted a traditional public forum, a limited public forum, or a nonpublic forum, held the regulation to be overbroad and facially unconstitutional. By its terms, Justice O'Connor wrote for the Court, the regulation created "a virtual 'First Amendment Free Zone'" at the Airport. It was not limited to expressive activity that might be disruptive or create congestion, but prohibited "even talking and reading, or the wearing of campaign buttons or symbolic clothing." "No conceivable governmental interest," she stated, "could justify such an absolute prohibition of speech."[187]

In *International Society for Krishna Consciousness, Inc. v. Lee*[188] the Court did reach the question of whether public airport terminals are traditional or designated public fora for free speech purposes, and it held that they are not. As a consequence, the Court held that the airport authority in this instance needed only a rational basis for its regulations. Thus, it held, 6-3, that the authority could constitutionally ban the solicitation of funds in the terminals, because it was reasonable to surmise that the in-person solicitation of funds would be disruptive, pose risks of duress and fraud, and foster congestion. But a different majority of the Justices held, 5-4, that the airport authority could **not** prohibit religious groups from distributing literature in the airport terminals. Justices Kennedy, Blackmun, Stevens, and Souter asserted that the terminals were public fora and that the ban on literature distribution was unconstitutional because it was "not drawn in narrow terms" and did not leave open

---

[185] 452 U.S. 640 (1981).

[186] 482 U.S. 569 (1987).

[187] *Id.* at 575.

[188] 506 U.S. 805 (1992).

"ample alternative channels of communication." However, Justice O'Connor, casting the deciding vote, reasoned that the terminals were not public fora but that leafletting was inherently less disruptive than solicitation and was compatible with the "multipurpose environment of the ... airports."

In *Lamb's Chapel v. Center Moriches School District*[189] the Court unanimously held unconstitutional a school's refusal to permit a religious group to use its school auditorium during non-instructional hours to show a film on family life. The Court noted that the school district generally permitted its schools to be used for social, civic, and recreational purposes after school hours, and concluded that to deny a group the right to use the facilities simply because it was religious discriminated on the basis of viewpoint in violation of the free speech clause. "[T]he government violates the First Amendment," the Court quoted from another case,[190] "when it denies access to a speaker solely to suppress the point of view he espouses on an otherwise includible subject." The school district claimed it denied permission to avoid violating the establishment clause, but the Court rejected that claim. In light of the facts that there was no school sponsorship involved, that the event would have been open to the public, that it would not have taken place during school hours, and that the school property was repeatedly used by a wide variety of private organizations, the Court said, "there was no realistic danger that the community would think that the District was endorsing religion or any particular creed, and any benefit to religion or to the Church would have been no more than incidental."[191]

Finally, in *Larson v. Valente*[192] the Court made clear that government cannot favor some religious organizations and disfavor others in regulating solicitations for contributions. A Minnesota statute required charitable organizations to register and file annual reports with the state as a condition of soliciting funds within the state but exempted religious organizations from these requirements if they received more than 50 percent of their contributions from their own members. The Court, stating that "[t]he clearest command of the Establishment Clause is that one religious denomination cannot be officially preferred over another,"[193] held this 50 percent rule to constitute a denominational preference. The statute, Justice Brennan asserted for the Court, distinguished between well-established churches supported largely by their own members and new religious organizations that for practical or policy reasons sought support from the public at large. Because the statute involved such a preference, the Court analyzed its constitutionality not only under the tripartite test but under a strict scrutiny test. The tripartite test was violated, Justice Brennan wrote, because the measure involved "religious gerrymandering" by the legislature. The legislative debate on the measure, he said, showed an intent that certain religions were to be favored, others disfavored. In addition, the Court held the measure to

---

[189] 508 U.S. 384 (1993).

[190] Cornelius v. NAACP Legal Defense and Education Fund, Inc., 473 U.S. 788, 806 (1985).

[191] Lamb's Chapel v. Center Moriches School District, *supra*, at 397.

[192] 456 U.S. 228 (1982).

[193] *Id.* at 244.

violate the strict scrutiny test. The protection of the state's citizens from abusive practices in the solicitation of funds for charity, Justice Brennan wrote, constituted a sufficiently compelling governmental interest under the strict scrutiny test, but the means chosen to effectuate that interest were not "closely fitted" to that purpose. Nothing validated the assumptions that organizations receiving more than 50 percent of their funds from their own members would be closely supervised by those members, that such membership control was an adequate safeguard against abusive or fraudulent solicitations of the public, or that the need for public disclosure rises in proportion to the percentage of nonmember contributions. Thus, the Court held, the measure failed to meet the requirements of the strict scrutiny test. The decision was by a 5-4 margin.

(2) Display of religious symbols. None of the decisions recounted in the preceding subsection was particularly surprising. But since 1980 the Court has broken new ground in addressing the constitutional parameters governing the display of religious symbols on public property. In two decisions the Court held that government cannot itself display or give preference to the display by others of particular religious symbols but that it can include religious symbols in generally secular holiday displays. In a third decision the Court made clear that private sponsors of religious symbols have a constitutional right to display the symbols in traditional public fora, so long as the circumstances of the display do not connote governmental endorsement.

In *Lynch v. Donnelly*[194] the issue was the constitutionality of a municipality's inclusion of a creche as part of a seasonal Christmas display in a local park. The display included not only the creche but also such items as a "talking" wishing well, a Santa's house, a small village, candy-striped poles, a grouping of carolers and musicians, reindeer pulling Santa's sleigh, hundreds of colored lights, and a large banner reading "Season's Greetings." All of the items in the display, including the creche, had been purchased by the city and were maintained and erected each year by city workers. In a 5-4 decision holding the inclusion of the creche in the display to be constitutional, the Court said the critical fact was that there was "an unbroken history of official acknowledgment by all three branches of government of the role of religion in American life ...." Such items as the designation of Thanksgiving and Christmas as national holidays, the hiring of chaplains by the Congress, the designation of the phrase "In God We Trust" as the nation's motto and its inscription on our coins and currency, the annual National Day of Prayer, the display of religious paintings in public museums — all gave evidence, Chief Justice Burger wrote for the Court, of government's "accommodation of all faiths and all forms of religious expression and hostility toward none." The creche, he said, was simply another permissible accommodation. In the context of the Christmas season, he stated, the creche was an essentially "passive" symbol that promoted Christianity or religion generally no more than numerous other instances of government acknowledgment of religion. Although the creche had religious significance, he concluded, its essential purpose in the display was simply to "depict the historical origins of this traditional event long recognized as a National Holiday."

---

[194] 465 U.S. 668 (1984).

Similarly, the Court in *County of Allegheny v. American Civil Liberties Union, Greater Pittsburgh Chapter*[195] upheld as constitutional Pittsburgh's display of a large Christmas tree, an 18-foot high menorah, and a sign designating the display to be a "Salute to Liberty" in front of the City-County Building during the Christmas season. The case produced numerous concurrences and dissents, and on this issue there was no majority opinion. But Justice Kennedy, for four members of the Court,[196] reiterated the *Lynch* rationale that the tree and menorah were "purely passive symbols of religious holidays" and that by using them the City simply acknowledged "the historical background and the religious as well as secular nature of the Chanukah and Christmas holidays." The display, he asserted, did not use "the government's power to coerce ... to further the interests of Christianity or Judaism in any way." Justices Blackmun and O'Connor concurred in separate opinions that this display was constitutional on the grounds that the display as a whole did not convey a government endorsement of either Christianity or Judaism but instead communicated a message of "pluralism and freedom of belief."

But in *County of Allegheny* the Court also, in a bitterly disputed holding, held unconstitutional a county's display of a creche by itself on the grand staircase of the County Courthouse during the Christmas season. The creche bore an angel at its crest proclaiming "Gloria in Excelsis Deo!" and was erected each year by a private Catholic men's organization. The county decorated the area around the creche each year with poinsettias, evergreen trees, and Christmas wreaths, and invited choirs to participate in a daily program of Christmas carols performed with the creche in the foreground. Justice Blackmun, writing for the Court on this issue, employed Justice O'Connor's endorsement test as the applicable principle in the case and found that the creche communicated an "indisputably religious" message. Moreover, he said, "unlike in *Lynch*, nothing in the context of the display detracts from the creche's religious message." Its display by itself in the "main" and "most beautiful part" of the building that was the seat of county government, he stated, sent "an unmistakable message that [the government] supports and promotes the Christian praise to God that is the creche's religious message." By endorsing a "patently Christian message," he concluded, the display violated the establishment clause.

The third case in this area involved the display of a private religious symbol in a public park adjacent to an important government building. The Ku Klux Klan sought to erect a cross in the public square in front of Ohio's State Capitol Building during the Christmas season but had been rebuffed for the alleged reason its placement in that location would communicate a governmental endorsement of religion. But in *Capitol Square Review and Advisory Board v. Pinette*[197] the Court, by a 7-2 margin held the public square to be a public forum traditionally available for all kinds of expression and held the establishment clause not to justify the state's prohibition on the erection of the cross. Government can censor speech in a traditional public forum only if it has a compelling reason for doing so, Justice Scalia wrote for the Court, but the establishment clause is not such a reason in this context.

---

[195] 492 U.S. 573 (1989).

[196] Chief Justice Rehnquist and Justices White, Scalia, and Kennedy.

[197] 515 U.S. 753 (1995).

"(O)ur precedent," he stated, "establishes that private religious speech, far from being a First Amendment orphan, is as fully protected under the Free Speech Clause as secular private expression." Five Justices further examined whether the placement of the cross in proximity to the State Capitol might communicate a governmental endorsement of religion but, given the history of the square's use for expressive purposes and the presence of a sign disclaiming governmental endorsement, concluded that it would not.

In sum, these cases confirm that the establishment clause permits government to include a religious symbol in a predominantly secular holiday display but also that the clause prohibits government from displaying, or permitting others to display, quintessential religious symbols by themselves at governmental sites that are not public forums. The cases further establish that in forums that are traditional sites of free expression, the display of religious symbols by private parties is fully protected by the free speech clause unless the circumstances communicate a message of governmental endorsement of religion to a reasonable observer. But these principles are tenuous. These three cases have been among the most bitterly disputed establishment clause decisions on the Court, and as a consequence, it seems possible that the issue of the constitutional parameters governing the display of religious symbols might be revisited by the Court in the future.

(3) Legislative chaplaincies. Despite the long history of chaplains and prayers in legislative assemblies, the Court did not have occasion to address the constitutionality of the practice until 1983. In *Marsh v. Chambers*[198] the Court, by a 6-3 margin, held a legislative chaplaincy sponsored and funded by the state of Nebraska not to violate the establishment clause. As previously noted, in deciding this case the Court for the first time eschewed use of the tripartite test, relying instead on two aspects of the history of the practice. Stating that "[t]he opening of sessions of legislative and other public bodies with prayer is deeply embedded in the history and tradition of this country,"[199] the Court first observed that legislative sessions had been opened with prayer for more than two centuries on the national level and more than a century in Nebraska. But secondly, and more importantly, the Court relied upon the acts of the First Congress in concluding that the establishment clause does not proscribe legislative prayer: Only three days prior to giving final approval to the Bill of Rights, Chief Justice Burger wrote for the Court, both houses of the First Congress authorized the appointment of paid chaplains. Thus, he concluded, "clearly the men who wrote the First Amendment did not view paid legislative chaplains and opening prayers as a violation of that Amendment."[200] "To invoke Divine guidance on a public body entrusted with making the laws ...," the Court found, "is simply a tolerable acknowledgment of beliefs widely held among the people of this country."[201]

(c) Public Aid to Religious Organizations. Among the establishment clause issues that have stirred passionate political and legal controversy, the constitutionality

---

[198] 463 U.S. 783 (1983).

[199] *Id.* at 786.

[200] *Id.* at 788.

[201] *Id.* at 792.

of public aid to religious organizations has been the subject of more Supreme Court decisions than any other. Yet the issue persists, and it is one area in which a loosened construction of the establishment clause could have profound effects. That reinterpretation seems to be occurring, at least to some extent. The Court's eight decisions in this area since 1980 have expanded the extent to which government can assist religious enterprises; and, in its most recent decision, the Court for the first time overturned a line of cases that had limited a particular form of such aid.

Prior to the 1980s the Court had construed the establishment clause to impose substantial, although not absolute, constraints on public aid to religious institutions. **Direct** public aid, the Court had said, must be limited to "secular, neutral, and nonideological purposes."[202] Direct support could be provided to the **secular** programs and services sponsored or provided by religious organizations but not to such organizations' **religious** activities or proselytizing. As a consequence, the Court struck down numerous aid programs benefitting sectarian elementary and secondary schools, because the Court found these institutions to be "pervasively sectarian," *i.e.*, so permeated by a religious purpose and character that their secular functions and religious functions were "inextricably intertwined." Under the tripartite *Lemon* test direct aid to such institutions was found either to have an inevitable effect of advancing religion or, if the government attempted to limit the aid to secular use only, to result in the excessive entanglement of government and the assisted institutions as the government monitored the institutions' use of the aid received to be sure the secular use limitation was honored.[203] On the other hand, the Court had found direct public aid to religious institutions that were **not** pervasively sectarian, such as religious hospitals and colleges, to be constitutionally permissible. The Court's rationale was that such institutions were essentially secular in nature and thus the public aid resulted neither in the advancement of religion nor in excessive entanglement between government and the assisted institutions.[204]

Indirect aid benefitting sectarian elementary and secondary schools had also been held unconstitutional by the Court prior to the 1980s.[205] Programs providing both tax benefits and tuition grants were held unconstitutional by the Court because they were designed to benefit only the parents of private schoolchildren and most of the institutions that ultimately benefited from the assistance were pervasively sectarian.[206] Significantly, however, the Court in these cases specifically reserved the question of the constitutionality of "public assistance ... made available generally

---

[202] Committee for Public Education v. Nyquist, 413 U.S. 756, 780 (1973).

[203] *Id.*; Lemon v. Kurtzman, 403 U.S. 602 (1971); Meek v. Pittenger, 421 U.S. 349 (1975); Wolman v. Walter, 433 U.S. 229 (1977).

[204] Bradfield v. Roberts, 175 U.S. 291 (1899); Tilton v. Richardson, 403 U.S. 672 (1971); Roemer v. Maryland Board of Public Works, 426 U.S. 736 (1976).

[205] Committee for Public Education v. Nyquist, *supra*; Sloan v. Lemon, 413 U.S. 826 (1973).

[206] *Id.*

without regard to the sectarian-nonsectarian or public-nonpublic nature of the institution benefitted."[207]

The Court's decisions since 1980 have continued to affirm that government cannot provide assistance directly to pervasively sectarian enterprises but that it can subsidize social welfare programs operated by religious organizations that are not pervasively sectarian. Moreover, it has broken new ground in holding constitutional tuition grant, tax benefit, and education assistance programs that indirectly provide economic benefits to pervasively sectarian schools but that have been "made available without regard to the sectarian-nonsectarian or public-nonpublic nature of the institution benefitted." Finally, the Court overturned a series of prior establishment clause decisions and held it to be constitutional for public school teachers to provide remedial educational services to sectarian school children on the premises of the schools they attended.

(1) Direct assistance programs. In *School District of the City of Grand Rapids v. Ball*[208] and *Aguilar v. Felton*[209] the Court initially held unconstitutional programs in which public school districts sent public school teachers into private sectarian schools to provide remedial and/or enrichment instruction to eligible children attending those schools. But twelve years later in *Agostini v. Felton*[210] the Court overturned *Aguilar* and this part of *Ball,* as well as the related parts of the earlier decisions of *Meek v. Pittenger*[211] and *Wolman v. Walter.*[212] As a result, it is once again constitutionally permissible for public school teachers to provide remedial and enrichment educational services to sectarian school children on the premises of the schools they attend.

The program in *Ball* was locally funded, but *Aguilar* involved New York City's implementation of the federal Title I program for educationally disadvantaged children.[213] In both programs the teachers were public school employees, the services were provided on the premises of the private schools, and the schools involved were almost all pervasively sectarian. But New York City's program included as well an extensive system of controls, including on-site monitoring, to ensure that the teachers did not engage in religious activities or religious instruction.

The Court, by identical margins of 5-4, struck down the Grand Rapids program on the grounds it had a primary effect of advancing religion and the New York City program for the reason it precipitated excessive entanglement between church and state. The establishment clause, Justice Brennan wrote for the Court, "absolutely prohibit[s] government-financed or government-sponsored indoctrination into the

---

[207] Committee for Public Education v. Nyquist, 413 U.S. at 783, n. 38.

[208] 473 U.S. 373 (1985).

[209] 473 U.S. 402 (1985).

[210] 117 S.Ct. 1997 (1997).

[211] 421 U.S. 349 (1975).

[212] 433 U.S. 229 (1977).

[213] 20 U.S.C. 3801 et seq. (1988).

beliefs of a particular religious faith."[214] The Grand Rapids program, he said, posed "a substantial risk of state-sponsored indoctrination" in three ways. The pervasively religious nature of the schools, he asserted, might cause the teachers "to conform their instruction to the environment in which they teach"[215]; the program created a "symbolic union of government and religion" that conveyed a message of government endorsement of the religious faith of the aided institutions; and the program subsidized the religious functions of the aided schools "by taking over a substantial portion of their responsibility for teaching secular subjects."[216] New York City argued in *Aguilar* that its system of controls ensured that its Title I program did not have these unconstitutional effects. But without addressing that issue, the Court held that the system of monitoring and controls itself unconstitutionally entangled the city with the religious schools. Justice Brennan, again writing for the Court, said the "detailed monitoring and close administrative contact" involved in the City's program violated an underlying objective of the establishment clause "to prevent, as far as possible, the intrusion of either [church or state] into the precincts of the other."[217] Notwithstanding the worthwhile social purpose of the program, he said, it created the specter of government agents prowling the halls of religious schools to ward off the "infiltration of religious thought."

Subsequently, a majority of the Justices on the Court expressed a desire to overturn these decisions,[218] and in 1997 in *Agostini v. Felton, supra,* the Court did so, along with its earlier rulings on similar programs in *Meek v. Pittenger, supra,* and *Wolman v. Walter, supra*. Each of the assumptions on which those decisions had been based, Justice O'Connor wrote for the Court, had been "undermined" by more recent decisions. In *Zobrest v. Catalina Foothills School District,*[219] she said, the Court repudiated the notion that the placement of public employees on parochial school grounds inevitably leads to religious indoctrination as well as the assumption that such a placement creates an "impermissible symbolic link" between government and religion. In *Zobrest* and *Witters v. Washington Department of Services for the Blind,*[220] she asserted, the Court rejected the notion that "all government aid that directly aids the educational function of religious schools" is unconstitutional. Finally, she said, absent the assumption that public teachers in a sectarian school necessarily pose a serious risk of inculcating religion, "the assumption that *pervasive* monitoring of [such] teachers is required" is also no longer valid. Thus, she concluded, the constitutionality of the programs should be evaluated under the criterion of neutrality, *i.e.*, whether "aid is allocated on the basis of neutral, secular criteria that neither favor nor disfavor religion, and is made available to both religious and secular beneficiaries

---

[214] 473 U.S. at 385.

[215] *Id.* at 388.

[216] *Id.* at 397.

[217] 473 U.S. at 413.

[218] *See* the concurring opinions of Justices O'Connor and Kennedy and the dissenting opinion of Justice Scalia, joined by Chief Justice Rehnquist and Justice Thomas, in Board of Education of the Kiryas Joel Village School District v. Grumet, 512 U.S. 687 (1994).

[219] 509 U.S. 1 (1993).

[220] 474 U.S. 481 (1986).

on a nondiscriminatory basis." Finding the Title I program to meet that test, she stated, "accordingly, we must acknowledge that *Aguilar*, as well as the portion of *Ball* addressing Grand Rapids' Shared Time program, are no longer good law."[221]

Grand Rapids had also held a second program funded and operated by the city to be unconstitutional, and that ruling was not disturbed by the *Agostini* decision. In that program (the Community Education program) the city paid parochial school teachers to provide an array of before and after school programs to the students who attended their schools and imposed no restrictions regarding religious content. The Court found the program to constitute aid to the institution rather than to the students and held it to "inescapably [have] the primary effect of providing a direct and substantial advancement of the sectarian enterprise."

At the college level the Court, by a 5-4 margin, held in *Rosenberger v. The Rector and Visitors of the University of Virginia*[222] that when a public university creates a forum for the expression of student opinions, it cannot exclude student religious opinions. In this instance the University of Virginia fostered the creation of publications by student organizations by paying their printing bills out of the student activities fund (SAF). However, it excluded religious publications, among others, from the subsidy, arguing that the establishment clause prohibits the funding of such a religious activity. But the Court rejected the argument. It held the object of the SAF to be "to open a forum for speech" and the University's exclusion of the religious publication, as a consequence, to constitute viewpoint discrimination violative of the free speech clause of the First Amendment. The SAF was not a tax used to support a church, the Court said, but essentially amounted to a religiously neutral fund to promote private student speech. The Court said the University's policy of exclusion itself threatened to violate the establishment clause because the University would then have to scrutinize every publication and determine when its religious content was too great. Justice O'Connor, the decisive vote in the case, stressed in a concurring opinion the factors that the publications were genuinely independent of the University, that the payments were made not directly to the sponsoring student organizations but to the printer, that numerous publications were subsidized, and that students could, at least hypothetically, seek a refund for any portion of their fees used for speech with which they disagreed. These factors convinced her, she said, that "providing ... assistance in this case would not carry the danger of impermissible use of public funds to endorse Wide Awake's religious message."

Finally, outside the school context the Court in *Bowen v. Kendrick*[223] upheld as facially constitutional, 5-4, provisions of the Adolescent Family Life Act[224] (AFLA) which permitted grants for pregnancy prevention and care services to adolescents to

---

[221] For a fuller exposition of these cases and their consequences and implications for the Title I program, *see* CRS, *The Implications of Agostini v. Felton for the Provision of Title I Assistance to Nonpublic School Children* (Sept. 9, 1997) (Report No. 97-848).

[222] 515 U.S. 819 (1995).

[223] 487 U.S. 589 (1988).

[224] 42 U.S.C. 300z et seq. (1988).

be made to religious organizations and which mandated that all grantees devise ways of involving other organizations, including religious ones, in the delivery of such services. The Court applied the same principles under the tripartite test as it had in past school aid cases and held the establishment clause not to automatically foreclose all religious organizations from participating in a publicly funded program such as AFLA. Chief Justice Rehnquist, writing for the Court, reiterated that direct public grants cannot be given to pervasively sectarian organizations or otherwise used for religious purposes, but he rejected the contention that "no grants whatsoever can be given under the statute to religious organizations."[225] Although holding the statute facially constitutional, the Court remanded the case back to the district court for further fact-finding on whether particular grantees might have been pervasively sectarian and whether particular grants might have been used for religious purposes.[226]

(2) Indirect assistance programs. In three other decisions involving sectarian elementary and secondary schools, however, the Court has, since 1980, opened the constitutional door to indirect subsidies. In *Mueller v. Allen,*[227] *Witters v. Washington Department of Services for the Blind,*[228] and *Zobrest v. Catalina Foothills School District,*[229] the Court upheld the provision of various forms of educational assistance to individuals on the grounds they possessed a genuinely free choice about whether to use the assistance at sectarian or nonsectarian schools. *Mueller* involved a Minnesota program permitting taxpayers to deduct from their gross income, up to a pre-set maximum, the expenses incurred in sending their children to elementary or secondary school. The deduction could be taken regardless of whether the children attended public or private school and applied to such expenses as tuition, textbooks, fees, and transportation. Then-Justice Rehnquist, writing for the Court, stressed that, in contrast to the earlier indirect assistance programs struck down by the Court,[230] the Minnesota deduction was "available for educational expenses incurred by *all* parents, including those whose children attend public schools and those whose children attend nonsectarian private schools or sectarian private schools."[231] "[A] program ... that neutrally provides state assistance to a broad spectrum of citizens," he concluded, "is not readily subject to challenge under the Establishment Clause." He stressed as well that the assistance was extended to parents rather than directly to sectarian schools, because "[w]here ... aid to parochial schools is available only as a result of decisions

---

[225] 487 U.S. at 611.

[226] Subsequently the parties entered into a settlement agreement and the case was dismissed. *See Kendrick v. Sullivan*, Civil Action No. 83-3175 (D.D.C. Jan. 19, 1993) (order granting joint motion to dismiss with prejudice).

[227] 463 U.S. 388 (1983).

[228] 474 U.S. 481 (1986).

[229] 509 U.S. 1 (1993).

[230] Committee for Public Education v. Nyquist, 413 U.S. 356 (1973) and Sloan v. Lemon, 413 U.S. 388 (1973).

[231] 463 U.S. at 397.

of individual parents no 'imprimatur of state approval' can be deemed to have been conferred on any particular religion, or on religion generally."[232]

The Court's decision in *Mueller* was 5-4. But in *Witters v. Washington Department of Services for the Blind* the Court was unanimous in upholding as constitutional a state vocational rehabilitation grant to a blind person who wanted to use the grant to train for a religious ministry. Justice Marshall, who had dissented in *Mueller*, made no reference to *Mueller* in his opinion for the Court. But he emphasized, as had *Mueller*, that "[a]ny aid provided under Washington's program that ultimately flows to religious institutions does so only as a result of the genuinely independent and private choices of aid recipients."[233] "[T]he fact that aid goes to individuals," he said, "means that the decision to support religious education is made by the individual, not by the State."[234]

In *Zobrest v. Catalina Foothills School District* the Court was again sharply divided, 5-4. The case involved the provision of a sign language interpreter pursuant to the Individuals with Disabilities Education Act (IDEA)[235] to a deaf high school student who wanted to attend a Catholic school. Using the reasoning of *Mueller* and *Witters*, the Court held the assistance not to violate the establishment clause. "The service at issue in this case," the Court said, "is part of a general government program that distributes benefits neutrally to any child qualifying as 'handicapped' under the IDEA, without regard to the 'sectarian-nonsectarian, or public-nonpublic nature' of the school the child attends." Thus, it asserted, the presence of a sign-language interpreter in a sectarian school is the result not of state decision-making but stems from the "private decision of individual parents." The provision of "a neutral service on the premises of a sectarian school as part of a general program that 'is in no way skewed towards religion,'" the Court concluded, "does not offend the Establishment Clause."

Mueller and *Witters*, it should be noted, did not overturn the Court's earlier decisions holding unconstitutional indirect aid to a universe of private elementary and secondary schools that was predominantly sectarian. As noted above,[236] *Committee for Public Education v. Nyquist* and *Sloan v. Lemon* had specifically reserved the question addressed in *Mueller* and *Witters*, *i.e.*, the constitutionality of assistance made available without regard to the sectarian-nonsectarian or public-nonpublic nature of the institutions ultimately benefitted. The critical distinction between *Nyquist* and *Sloan*, on the one hand, and *Mueller* and *Witters*, on the other, remains whether the initial beneficiaries of the government's assistance possess a genuinely

---

[232] *Id.* at 399.

[233] 474 U.S. at 487.

[234] *Id.* at 488. It might be noted that although Witters won this constitutional battle, he eventually lost the war. The Washington Supreme Court held the Washington Constitution to prohibit the use of a vocational rehabilitation grant for religious training. See Witters v. Washington Department of Services for the Blind, 112 Wash.2d 363, 771 P.2d 1119, cert. den., 493 U.S. 850 (1989).

[235] 20 U.S.C. 1400 *et seq.*

[236] *See* p. 46.

free choice about whether to use the assistance at a sectarian or nonsectarian institution. If the government has shaped that decision by limiting the universe of choice to institutions that are predominantly sectarian, the assistance, even though indirect, will likely be found unconstitutional. If the universe of choice is genuinely unfettered, however, the assistance will likely be upheld, even though sectarian institutions may receive some, or even substantial, economic benefit from it.

In sum, then, the Court since 1980 has validated a broader range of both direct and indirect assistance than was thought to be constitutionally permissible prior to 1980.

(d) Governmental Solicitude for Religion. The Court's dimunition of the protection afforded religious practices by the free exercise of religion clause has been detailed in the first section above, and will not be reiterated here. As noted there, except with respect to eligibility for unemployment benefits when there is a conflict between the requirements of a job and an individual's religious precepts, an as-yet undefined area of "hybrid" claims, and government actions that specifically target religion, the Court's decisions on free exercise since 1980 seem to mean that the free exercise clause interposes no barrier to governmental restriction of religious practices through evenhanded regulations.

But seven cases during the 1980s concerned a related dimension of the religion clauses, *i.e.*, deliberate government efforts to **protect** individual and institutional religious practices. If the free exercise clause does not mandate special protection for religious practices, may government nonetheless give religion special privileges or require private entities in society to accommodate religious practices? In its seven decisions the Court upheld government policies that prohibit employers from discriminating on religious grounds as well as policies that exempt religious employers from such prohibitions. But the Court also made clear that government cannot, in the guise of protecting religion, give religious practices an absolute preference over other individual and societal concerns; nor may it give particular religious groups special accommodations that may not be available to others in similar circumstances.

Four cases, in particular, illuminated the limits on what government can do to protect religion. In *Larkin v. Grendel's Den*[237] the Court held unconstitutional, 8-1, a Massachusetts statute that gave churches a veto power over the issuance of liquor licenses to nearby enterprises. The statute provided that liquor licenses could not be issued for enterprises located within 500 feet of a church or school "if the governing body of such church or school files written objection thereto." In this particular case a church near Harvard Square in Cambridge had objected to the issuance of a liquor license to an adjacent restaurant; and the Cambridge License Commission had, in conformity with the statute, denied the restaurant's application, despite the fact that 25 establishments within 500 feet of the church already were so licensed. Chief Justice Burger, writing for the Court, conceded that the state had a valid secular interest in using its zoning powers to "protect spiritual, cultural, and educational centers from the 'hurly-burly' associated with liquor outlets." But the means used in this instance, he said, "enmeshe[d] churches in the exercise of substantial

---

[237] 459 U.S. 116 (1982).

governmental powers contrary to our consistent interpretation of the Establishment Clause." The "core rationale" of the establishment clause, he said, was to prevent "the fusion of governmental and religious functions." But the statute in this case symbolically joined church and state in a joint exercise of legislative authority, failed to require that churches exercise their veto power in a religiously neutral way, permitted religious institutions to exercise important discretionary governmental powers, and created the danger of political fragmentation along religious lines. For those reasons, he concluded, the statute breached the figurative "wall of separation" that insulates religion and government from each other.

Similarly, in *Estate of Thornton v. Caldor, Inc.*[238] the Court struck down, 8-1, a Connecticut statute which gave every employee an absolute right not to work on whatever day of the week the employee designated as the Sabbath. Chief Justice Burger, writing for the Court, said that the statute "imposes on employers and employees an absolute duty to conform their business practices to the particular religious practices of the employee" and "commands that Sabbath religious concerns automatically control over all secular interests at the workplace." Because of the absolute nature of that preference, he concluded, the statute had a primary effect of advancing the religious practice of Sabbath observance in violation of the establishment clause.

Again, in *Texas Monthly, Inc. v. Bullock*[239] the Court struck down, 6-3, a Texas statute that exempted only publications published or distributed by a religious faith and advancing the tenets of that faith from the state's sales tax. Although none of the four opinions issued on the matter had the support of a majority of the Court, five of the Justices held the establishment clause to forbid such an exclusive preference for religious publications. Justices Brennan, Marshall, and Stevens found the narrowness of the exemption to constitute "state sponsorship of religious belief" and to be "a blatant endorsement of religion." Justices Blackmun and O'Connor said that "by confining the tax exemption exclusively to the sale of religious publications, Texas engaged in preferential support for the communication of religious messages." Such a statutory preference, they said, was "constitutionally intolerable."

Finally, in *Board of Education of the Kiryas Joel Village School District v. Grumet*[240] the Court held unconstitutional a New York statute which sought to accommodate the special education needs of children belonging to the Satmar Hasidic sect by creating a public education district whose boundaries coincided with the boundaries of the village inhabited by the sect. The Satmar had refused to send their special needs children to sites outside the village because of the "panic, fear, and trauma" that resulted from leaving their insular community and associating with people "whose ways were so different." So the New York legislature adopted a special statute creating a public school district with boundaries identical to the Satmar village in order to make them eligible for special education funds to subsidize services for their special needs children within the village. But the Supreme Court said, 6-3,

---

[238] 472 U.S. 703 (1985).

[239] 489 U.S. 1 (1989).

[240] 512 U.S. 687 (1994).

that the statute "crosses the line from permissible accommodation to impermissible establishment" and "violates the test of neutrality." There was no assurance, Justice Souter wrote for the Court, that a similar group would be similarly treated in the future. The constitutional vice of the statute, he said, was that it "single(d) out a particular religious sect for special treatment" and delegated a significant governmental power "to an electorate defined by common religious belief and practice, in a manner that fails to foreclose religious favoritism."

But in *Corporation of the Presiding Bishop of the Church of Jesus Christ of Latter-Day Saints v. Amos*[241] the Court unanimously upheld the exemption of religious institutions from the religious nondiscrimination in employment requirements of Title VII of the Civil Rights Act of 1964. Title VII prohibits most public and private employers from discriminating in their employment practices on the grounds of race, color, national origin, sex, and religion.[242] Section 702 of that statute, however, exempts religious institutions from the religious nondiscrimination requirement, *i.e.*, such institutions can discriminate in their employment practices on religious grounds, although not on the other prohibited grounds.[243] In this case an employee dismissed for religious reasons from a job with a nonprofit health facility run by the Mormon Church challenged the constitutionality of the exemption. But the Court held it to be permissible for government "to alleviate significant governmental interference with the ability of religious organizations to define and carry out their religious missions." Even though the exemption applied to all the activities of religious organizations and not just their religious ones, and even though it applied only to religious organizations, Justice White wrote for the Court, it met the requirements of the tripartite test.

Two other cases involving religious discrimination in employment were resolved on statutory grounds. In *Ansonia Board of Education v. Philbrook*[244] the Court construed the reasonable accommodation requirement of Title VII not to require an employer to accede to an employee's preferred accommodation but simply to require a proffer of a "reasonable resolution of the conflict." To effectuate its ban on religious discrimination in employment, Title VII requires employers to "reasonably accommodate" their employees' religious observances and practices unless to do so causes "undue hardship on the conduct of the employer's business."[245] At issue in this case was whether the employer had to accept an employee's preferred accommodation unless it could show that the accommodation would impose an undue hardship. The Court held that it did not, 7-2. "By its very terms," Chief Justice Rehnquist wrote for the Court, "the statute directs that any reasonable

---

241 483 U.S. 327 (1987).

242 42 U.S.C. 2000e *et seq.*

243 *Id.* § 2000e-1.

244 479 U.S. 60 (1986).

245 42 U.S.C. 2000e(j) (1988).

accommodation by the employer is sufficient to meet its accommodation obligation."[246]

Finally, in *Shaare Tefila Congregation v. Cobb*[247] the Court unanimously construed a federal statute to permit a Jewish congregation to seek civil damages from persons who had desecrated its synagogue with anti-Semitic slogans, phrases, and symbols. The statute in question, adopted shortly after the Civil War, guarantees all citizens "the same right ... as is enjoyed by white citizens ... to inherit, purchase, lease, sell, hold, and convey real and personal property"[248] and has been construed by the Court to prohibit private racially motivated interference with property rights.[249] Although Jews today are not considered a distinct race, Justice White concluded for the Court that they are within the protection of the statute, because at the time the statute was adopted "Jews and Arabs were among the peoples then considered to be distinct races." Thus, he said, Jews can bring suit for civil damages under Section 1982 against persons who interfere with their property rights and are motivated by racial animus against Jews.

(e) Taxation of Religious Entities. A number of cases since 1980 have concerned the constitutionality of various taxes imposed on religious organizations and individuals, and in its decisions the Court has made clear that government possesses substantial discretion in this area of the law. The Court previously had made few forays into this subject. In the 1940s cases of *Murdock v. Pennsylvania*[250] and *Follett v. McCormick*[251] the Court had struck down as unconstitutional the imposition of license and occupation taxes on itinerant evangelists. The Court found such taxes to operate as a prior restraint on religious proselytizing and thus to "tend to suppress" such evangelizing, in violation of the First Amendment. Moreover, in 1970 in *Walz v. Tax Commission of New York*[252] the Court upheld as constitutional a property tax exemption afforded by New York City to religious organizations, 8-1. Without quite saying that the exemption was constitutionally mandated, the Court emphasized that the tax exemption of churches from property taxes created a lesser degree of government entanglement with religion than would the contrary policy. While a direct money subsidy might precipitate "a relationship pregnant with involvement and ... encompass sustained and detailed administrative relationships for enforcement of statutory and administrative standards," the Court said, a tax exemption simply means that government "abstains from demanding that the church support the state."[253] The Court also stressed that the exemption was available not just to religious organizations but also to property owned by hospitals, libraries,

---

[246] 479 U.S. at 68.

[247] 481 U.S. 615 (1987).

[248] 42 U.S.C. 1981 (1988).

[249] Jones v. Alfred H. Mayer Co., 392 U.S. 409 (1968).

[250] 319 U.S. 105 (1943).

[251] 321 U.S. 573 (1944).

[252] 397 U.S. 664 (1970).

[253] *Id.* at 673.

playgrounds, scientific, professional, historical and patriotic groups, and that the tax exemption of churches has been part of our national life since colonial times. It concluded that "if tax exemption can be seen as th[e] first step toward "establishment" of religion ..., the second step has been long in coming."[254]

In its more recent decisions the Court, while generally reaffirming these precedents, has not erected any other constitutional barriers to the imposition of general taxes on religious individuals and organizations. In *United States v. Lee*[255] the Court unanimously upheld the imposition of the employer's portion of the Social Security tax on an Amish employer, notwithstanding the Amish' specific religious belief against contributing to a public social insurance system. Congress had by statute exempted self-employed Amish from paying such taxes,[256] but the Court still held the extension of the exemption to Amish employers holding such beliefs not to be constitutionally mandated. "The tax imposed on employers to support the social security system," the Court said, "must be uniformly applicable to all, except as Congress provides explicitly otherwise."[257]

Similarly, in *Bob Jones University v. United States*[258] the Court upheld the IRS' revocation of the income tax exemption of a religious university that, on the basis of its religious beliefs, discriminated on the basis of race. The government has a "fundamental, overriding interest in eradicating racial discrimination in education," the Court stated, and that interest "substantially outweighs whatever burden denial of tax benefits places on petitioners' exercise of their religious beliefs."[259]

Again, in *The Jimmy Swaggart Ministries v. Board of Equalization of California*[260] the Court upheld California's imposition of general sales and use taxes on a religious organization's direct and mail order sales of religious literature. The Ministries argued that the taxes unduly burdened its ability to carry out its religious ministry and created excessive administrative entanglement between government and itself. But the Court asserted that the taxes were imposed neutrally on all retail sales and did not single out religious activity for special and burdensome treatment. It further asserted that any administrative burden involved in collecting and remitting the taxes was not "constitutionally significant."

---

[254] *Id.* at 676.

[255] 455 U.S. 252 (1981).

[256] 26 U.S.C. 1402(g) (1988).

[257] 455 U.S. at 260.

[258] 461 U.S. 574 (1983).

[259] *Id.* at 574. Then-Justice Rehnquist dissented from the Court's ruling that the IRS properly imposed a racial nondiscrimination condition on the tax exemption of private schools but agreed that such a condition did not infringe the schools' free exercise rights. See *id.* at 622, n. 3.

[260] 493 U.S. 378 (1990).

And in *Hernandez v. Commissioner of Internal Revenue*[261] the Court upheld as constitutional IRS' denial of a charitable tax deduction to members of the Church of Scientology for payments they had made for the Church "sacraments" of auditing and training. The charitable deduction, the Court said, was only available for genuine gifts, not for "payments made in return for goods or services" such as the payments for auditing and training. It said the tax code provision was neutral on its face, was not "born of animus to religion in general or Scientology in particular," did not have a primary effect of either advancing or inhibiting religion, and required only "routine regulatory interaction" between government and religious organizations.

Moreover, while finding no constitutional barriers to the imposition of taxes on religious organizations and individuals, the Court in one decision found the establishment clause to bar an exemption from taxation for a religious entity. In *Texas v. Bullock*[262] the Court held unconstitutional, 6-3, a Texas statute that exempted from the state's sales and use taxes only those periodicals and books that promoted the teachings of a religious faith. Although the Justices articulated several different rationales for this conclusion, a majority appeared to agree that the establishment clause means "not only that government may not be overtly hostile to religion but also that it may not place its prestige, coercive authority, or resources behind a single religious faith or behind religious belief in general, compelling nonadherents to support the practices or proselytizing of favored religious organizations and conveying the message that those who do not contribute gladly are less than full members of the community."[263] To avoid the establishment clause flaw of appearing to sponsor or give preferential support to religious belief, a majority held, a tax benefit cannot be confined just to religious organizations but must flow to a broad class of beneficiaries.

Three other tax cases the Court resolved on statutory grounds without addressing any constitutional issues. Two involved the Federal Unemployment Tax Act (FUTA),[264] which requires employers to contribute to state unemployment insurance funds; and both involved a provision of the Act which exempts from coverage "(A) a church or convention or association of churches, or (B) an organization which is operated primarily for religious purposes and which is operated, supervised, controlled, or principally supported by a church or convention or association of churches."[265] The Secretary of Labor construed the legislative history of recent amendments to FUTA to mean that church-related primary and secondary schools were no longer exempted from FUTA by that provision and thus were subject to the FUTA tax. But in *St. Martin Evangelical Lutheran Church v. South Dakota*[266] the Court held that construction of the Act and its legislative history to be invalid. "The only reasonable construction of 26 U.S.C. §3309(b)(1)," the Court stated, "is

---

[261] 490 U.S. 680 (1989).

[262] 489 U.S. 1 (1989).

[263] *Id.* at 9.

[264] 26 U.S.C. 3301-3311 (1988).

[265] 26 U.S.C. 3309(b) (1988).

[266] 451 U.S. 772 (1981).

one that exempts petitioners' church-run schools, and others similarly operated, from mandatory state coverage."[267] Subsequently, in *California v. Grace Brethren Church*[268] the Court refused to reach the question of whether the imposition of FUTA taxes on religious schools **not** affiliated with any church violated the establishment clause, for the reason that the federal district court lacked jurisdiction to decide that issue. The Court held that the Tax Injunction Act,[269] which generally bars the federal courts from enjoining the collection of state taxes where "a plain, speedy, and efficient remedy may be had in the courts of such State," applied to the case, and that therefore the lower court should not have reached the constitutional issue.

Finally, in *Davis v. United States*[270] the Court unanimously construed the tax code not to permit the parents of two Mormon missionaries to deduct the support they provided their sons to enable them to serve as missionaries. The parents argued that their support constituted either charitable contributions in themselves or unreimbursed expenditures incurred in the course of their sons' contributions of services to the Mormon Church and thus should be deductible under § 170 of the Internal Revenue Code.[271] But the Court held that their support did not constitute a charitable contribution, because it was not given in any legally enforceable way for the benefit of the Church, and that they could not claim a deduction for expenses incurred in the course of a third party's contribution of services.

(f) Other Decisions. Of the remaining five church-state decisions by the Court since 1980, only one was decided on the merits. In that case, *Tony and Susan Alamo Foundation v. Secretary of Labor*,[272] the Court unanimously upheld as constitutional the application of the minimum wage and overtime provisions of the Fair Labor Standards Act[273] to employees who worked in various commercial enterprises operated by a religious organization. The Court found no exception in the Act for the commercial activities of religious or other nonprofit organizations and held the application of the FLSA to be "fully consistent with the requirements of the First Amendment." Application of the FLSA neither infringed on the employees' religious convictions that they should not be paid wages for their work, the Court said, nor did its recordkeeping requirements foster any excessive entanglement. "[T]he routine and factual inquiries required by §211(c) bear no resemblance," the Court stated, "to the kind of government surveillance the Court has previously held to pose an intolerable risk of government entanglement with religion."[274]

---

[267] *Id.* at 781.

[268] 457 U.S. 393 (1982).

[269] 28 U.S.C. 1341 (1988).

[270] 495 U.S. 472 (1990).

[271] 26 U.S.C. 170 (1988).

[272] 471 U.S. 290 (1985).

[273] 29 U.S.C. 201 et seq. (1988).

[274] 471 U.S. at 305.

Two of the other cases were decided on standing grounds. In a critically important decision for the Catholic Church, the Court in *United States Catholic Conference v. Abortion Rights Mobilization, Inc.*[275] held that two institutions of the Church that had been held in civil contempt for refusing to comply with discovery orders in a suit challenging their tax-exempt status could, even though they were non-parties to the suit, challenge the plaintiffs' standing to institute the suit. Originally filed in 1981, the suit sought an injunction directing the IRS to revoke the tax exempt status of the United States Catholic Conference and the National Conference of Catholic Bishops on the grounds their political activities with respect to abortion violated § 501(c)(3) of the Internal Revenue Code.[276] The two bodies had been held in civil contempt by the district court when they refused to comply with subpoenas from ARM seeking evidence of their activities regarding abortion, and the lower courts had refused to allow them to challenge ARM's standing to institute the suit in contesting the contempt citation. The Supreme Court reversed and held, 8-1, that they could do so, stating that "the subpoena power of a court cannot be more extensive than its jurisdiction." (On remand, a federal appellate court brought this threat to the tax-exempt status of the Catholic Church to an end by holding that ARM did not have standing and dismissing the suit.[277])

In *Valley Forge Christian College v. Americans United for Separation of Church and State*[278] the Court refused, 5-4, to broaden the doctrine of standing to permit the disposition of surplus government property to a sectarian institution to be challenged on establishment clause grounds. The transaction of concern in this case was the disposition by the Department of Education of land and buildings worth more than a half million dollars to an avowedly sectarian college, without charge. The Court had previously held that taxpayers have standing to challenge exercises of Congressional power under the taxing and spending clause of Article I, § 8, of the Constitution that allegedly violate the establishment clause.[279] But in this case it described that exception to the general rule against taxpayer suits as a narrow one and said it did not apply in this instance, because the action in question was an executive one rather than a Congressional one and because the authorizing legislation was an exercise of Congress' power under the property clause of Article IV of the Constitution rather than of the taxing and spending power of Article I.

The final two cases both involved civil rights but were dismissed for jurisdictional reasons. In *Ohio Civil Rights Commission v. Dayton Christian Schools,*

---

[275] 487 U.S. 72 (1988).

[276] 26 U.S.C. 501(c)(3) exempts from taxation groups "organized and operated exclusively for religious, charitable,...or educational purposes, ...no substantial part of the activities of which is carrying on propaganda, or otherwise attempting, to influence legislation..., and which does not participate in, or intervene in..., any political campaign on behalf of any candidate for public office."

[277] Abortion Rights Mobilization, Inc. v. United States Catholic Conference, 885 F.2d 1020 (2d Cir., 1989), *cert. den.*, 495 U.S. 918 (1990).

[278] 454 U.S. 464 (1982).

[279] Flast v. Cohen, 392 U.S. 83 (1968).

Inc.[280] the Court unanimously held that the federal courts could not adjudicate a conflict between a state civil rights statute and a private school's religious belief and practice prior to the resolution of that conflict by the state civil rights agency. At issue was a conflict between the sex nondiscrimination requirements of an Ohio statute[281] and the nonrenewal by a private Christian school of the contract of a teacher who had become pregnant, pursuant to the school's religious belief that mothers of preschool children should remain at home. A lower federal appellate court had enjoined the investigation and resolution of the matter by the Ohio Civil Rights Commission on the grounds that the Commission's efforts would violate the First Amendment. But the Supreme Court held that the lower courts should have abstained from deciding that issue. *Younger v. Harris*,[282] the Court said, established the rule that federal courts should not enjoin pending state proceedings except in "extraordinary circumstances," both as a matter of comity and out of a "proper respect for the fundamental role of States in our federal system." The school would have ample opportunity to air its constitutional concerns, the Court said, in the judicial review of the Commission's decisions authorized by the Ohio statute.

Finally, in *Equal Employment Opportunity Commission v. Arabian American Oil Company*[283] the Court held that the employment nondiscrimination requirements of Title VII of the Civil Rights Act of 1964 do not apply to United States employers outside the United States. A naturalized U.S. citizen claimed that he had been fired by the Arabian American Oil Company in Saudi Arabia for reasons of race, religion, and national origin, in violation of Title VII. But the Court held that Title VII could apply extraterritorially only if Congress had affirmatively expressed its intention that it do so, and it found the evidence that Congress had so intended "insufficient." As a consequence, it affirmed the lower courts' rulings dismissing the case for lack of jurisdiction.

Conclusion

In his *Memorial and Remonstrance Against Religious Assessments*, James Madison in 1785 warned of the danger that lurked if questions of liberty became "entangled ... in precedents."[284] Yet in the modern United States, where the expansive claims and powers of government conflict virtually daily with the requirements and expectations of one or another religious faith, that is exactly what has happened. The religion clauses, perhaps inevitably, have become the subject of hundreds of judicial precedents.

---

[280] 477 U.S. 619 (1986).

[281] Ohio Rev. Code Ann. 4112.01(A) (Supp. 1985).

[282] 401 U.S. 37 (1971).

[283] 499 U.S. 244 (1991).

[284] Madison, James, Memorial and Remonstrance Against Religious Assessments, par. 3, reprinted as an Appendix to Everson v. Board of Education, 330 U.S. at 63.

Whether that fact poses a danger to religious liberty is a matter of opinion. What is clear is that on the Supreme Court the struggle over the meaning and scope of the religion clauses has become both persistent and intense. On the one hand stands the view that "a union of government and religion tends to destroy government and to degrade religion,"[285] and that a "wall of separation" best serves the interests of both. On the other hand stands the perspective that the relationship of government and religion should be predominantly a legislative matter rather than one subject to sweeping constitutional constraints and that government should be able, in a neutral and nondiscriminatory manner, both to regulate religious practices and to accommodate and even assist religious groups. Since 1980 the latter perspective has come to predominate with respect to the free exercise clause, and it has made substantial inroads with respect to the Court's establishment clause jurisprudence as well.

It seems certain that the ferment on the Court over the religion clauses will persist for some time. Only two of the Justices that sat on the Court at the beginning of the 1980s remain — Chief Justice Rehnquist and Justice Stevens, and they are polar opposites on the interpretation of the religion clauses. But the new Justices, like their predecessors, either have, or are developing, strong views on the meaning of the clauses. The debate seems certain to continue, and likely with vigor.

---

[285] Engel v. Vitale, 370 U.S. at 431.

Appendix
Supreme Court Decisions on Church and State, 1980-1997

Legend: *C—constitutional* *(m)—authored majority opinion*
U—unconstitutional *(d)—authored dissenting opinion*
(c)—authored concurring opinion

Case Name	Stewart	Burger	Powell	Brennan	Marshall	White	Blackmun	Rehnquist	Steven
1980 TERM									
Stone v. Graham, 449 U.S. 39 (1980) (*per curiam*)	C	—	U	U	U	U	—	C	U
Thomas v. Review Board of the Indiana Employment Security Division, 450 U.S. 707 (1981)	U	U (m)	U	U	U	U	U (c)	C (d)	U

Case Name	Stewart	Burger	Powell	Brennan	Marshall	White	Blackmun	Rehnquist	Stevens
1980 TERM (cont.)									
St. Martin Evangelical Lutheran Church v. South Dakota, 451 U.S. 772 (1981)	Exempt from FUTA taxes	Exempt	Exempt	Exempt	Exempt	Exempt	Exempt (m)	Exempt	Exempt (c)
Heffron v. ISKCON, 452 U.S. 640 (1981) booths/distribution of literature	C C	C C	C C	C (c) U (d)	C U	C (m) C (m)	C (c) U (d)	C C	C U

Case Name	Burger	Powell	Brennan	Marshall	White	Blackmun	Rehnquist	Stevens	O'Connor
1981 TERM									
Widmar v. Vincent, 454 U.S. 263 (1981)	U	U (m)	U	U	C (d)	U	U	U (c)	U
Valley Forge Christian College v. Americans United, 454 U.S. 464 (1981)	No standing	No standing	Standing (d)	Standing	No standing	Standing	No standing (m)	Standing (d)	No standing
Karen B. v. Treen, 455 U.S. 913 (1982), *aff'g mem.*, 653 F.2d 897 (5th Cir. 1981)	U	U	U	U	U	U	U	U	U
United States v. Lee, 455 U.S. 252 (1981)	C (m)	C	C	C	C	C	C	C (c)	C

Case Name	Burger	Powell	Brennan	Marshall	White	Blackmun	Rehnquist	Stevens	O'Connor
1981 TERM (cont.)									
Larson v. Valente, 456 U.S. 228 (1982)	C	U	U (m)	U	C (d)	U	C (d)	U (c)	C
California v. Grace Brethren Church, 457 U.S. 393 (1982)	No fed. jur.	No fed. juris.	No fed. juris.	No fed. juris.	No fed. juris.	Fed. juris.	No fed. juris.	Fed. juris. (d)	No fed. juris. (m)
1982 TERM									
Larkin v. Grendel's Den, 459 U.S. 116 (1982)	U (m)	U	U	U	U	U	C (d)	U	U
Bob Jones University v. United States, 461 U.S. 574 (1983)	C (m)	C (c)	C	C	C	C	C (d)	C	C

Case Name	Burger	Powell	Brennan	Marshall	White	Blackmun	Rehnquist	Stevens	O'Connor
1982 TERM (cont.)									
Mueller v. Allen, 463 U.S. 388 (1983)	C	C	U	U (d)	C	U	C (m)	U	C
Marsh v. Chambers, 463 U.S. 783 (1983)	C (m)	C	U (d)	U	C	C	C	U (d)	C
1983 TERM									
Lynch v. Donnelly, 465 U.S. 668 (1984)	C (m)	C	U (d)	U	C	U (d)	C	U	C (c)
Wallace v. Jaffree, 466 U.S. 924 (1984), *aff'g mem.*, 705 F.2d 1526 (11th Cir. 1983)	U	U	U	U	U	U	U	U	U

Case Name	Burger	Powell	Brennan	Marshall	White	Blackmun	Rehnquist	Stevens	O'Connor
1984 TERM (cont.)									
Aguilar v. Felton, 473 U.S. 402 (1985)	C (d)	U (c)	U (m)	U	C (d)	U	C (d)	U	C (d)
1985 TERM									
Witters v. Washington Department of Services for the Blind, 474 U.S. 481 (1986)	C	C (c)	C	C (m)	C (c)	C	C	C	C (c)
Goldman v. Weinberger, 475 U.S. 503 (1986)	C	C	U (d)	U	C	U (d)	C (m)	C (c)	U (d)
Bowen v. Roy, 476 U.S. 693 (1986)	C (m)	C	C	C	U (d)	C (c)	C	C (c)	C (c/d)

Case Name	Burger	Powell	Brennan	Marshall	White	Blackmun	Rehnquist	Stevens	O'Connor
1984 TERM									
Tony and Susan Alamo Foundation v. Secretary of Labor, 471 U.S. 290 (1985)	C	C	C	C	C (m)	C	C	C	C
Wallace v. Jaffree, 472 U.S. 38 (1985)	C (d)	U (c)	U	U	C (d)	U	C (d)	U (m)	U (c)
Estate of Thornton v. Caldor, Inc., 472 U.S. 703 (1985)	U (m)	U	U	U	U	U	C	U	U (c)
School District of the City of Grand Rapids v. Ball, 473 U.S. 373 (1985) (community education/ shared time)	U (c) C (d)	U U	U (m) U (m)	U U	C (d) C (d)	U U	C (d) C (d)	U U	U (c) C (d)

Case Name	Burger	Powell	Brennan	Marshall	White	Blackmun	Rehnquist	Stevens	O'Connor
1985 TERM (cont.)									
Ohio Civil Rights Commission v. Dayton Christian Schools, 477 U.S. 619 (1986)	Fed. ct. should have abstained	ditto	ditto	ditto	ditto	ditto	ditto (m)	ditto (c)	ditto

Case Name	Powell	Brennan	Marshall	White	Blackmun	Rehnquist	Stevens	O'Connor	Scalia
1986 TERM									
Ansonia Board of Education v. Philbrook, 479 U.S. 60 (1986)	Need not select employee's preferred accommodation	ditto	ditto (c/d)	ditto	ditto	ditto (m)	ditto (c/d)	ditto	ditto
Hobbie v. Unemployment Appeals Commission of Florida, 480 U.S. 136 (1987)	U (c)	U (m)	U	U	U	C (d)	U (c)	U	U
Shaare Tefila Congregation v. Cobb, 481 U.S. 615 (1987)	Can sue for desecration of synagogue	ditto	ditto	ditto (m)	ditto	ditto	ditto	ditto	ditto
O'Lone v. Estate of Shabazz, 482 U.S. 342 (1987)	C	U (d)	U	C	U	C (m)	U	C	C

Case Name	Powell	Brennan	Marshall	White	Blackmun	Rehnquist	Stevens	O'Connor	Scalia
1986 TERM (cont.)									
Board of Airport Commissioners of City of Los Angeles v. Jews for Jesus, 482 U.S. 569 (1987)	U	U	U	U (c)	U	U	U	U (m)	U
Edwards v. Aguillard, 482 U.S. 578 (1987)	U (c)	U (m)	U	U (c)	U	C	U	U	C (d)
Corporation of the Presiding Bishop of the Church of Jesus Christ of Latter Day Saints v. Amos, 483 U.S. 327 (1987)	C	C (c)	C	C (m)	C (c)	C	C	C (c)	C

Case Name	Brennan	Marshall	White	Blackmun	Rehnquist	Stevens	O'Connor	Scalia	Kennedy
1987 TERM									
Lyng v. Northwest Indian Cemetery Protective Association, 485 U.S. 439 (1988)	U (d)	U	C	U	C	C	C (m)	C	
United States Catholic Conference v. Abortion Rights Mobilization, 487 U.S. 72 (1988)	USCC can challenge ARM's standing	Cannot challenge (d)	Can challenge	Can challenge	Can challenge	Can challenge	Can challenge	Can challenge	Can challenge (m)
Bowen v. Kendrick, 487 U.S. 589 (1988)	U	U	C	U (d)	C (m)	U	C (c)	C	C (c)

Case Name	Brennan	Marshall	White	Blackmun	Rehnquist	Stevens	O'Connor	Scalia	Kennedy
1988 TERM									
Texas Monthly, Inc. v. Bullock, 489 U.S. 1 (1989)	U (c)	U	U (c)	U (c)	C	U	U	C (d)	C
Frazee v. Illinois Department of Employment Security, 489 U.S. 829 (1989)	U	U	U (m)	U	U	U	U	U	U
Hernandez v. Commissioner of Internal Revenue, 490 U.S. 680 (1989)	—	C (m)	C	C	C	C	U (d)	U	—
County of Allegheny v. ACLU Greater Pittsburgh Chapter, 492 U.S. 573 (1989) creche/ menorah and Christmas tree	U (c) U (d)	U U	C C	U (m) C (c)	C C	U (c) U (d)	U (c) C (c)	C C	C (d) C (c)

Case Name	Brennan	Marshall	White	Blackmun	Rehnquist	Stevens	O'Connor	Scalia	Kennedy
1989 TERM									
Jimmy Swaggart Ministries v. Board of Equalization of California, 493 U.S. 378 (1990)	C	C	C	C	C	C	C (m)	C	C
Employment Division, Oregon Department of Human Res. v. Smith, 494 U.S. 872 (1990)	U	U	C	U (d)	C	C	C (c)	C (m)	C
Davis v. United States, 495 U.S. 472 (1990)	No deduction	ditto	ditto	ditto	ditto	ditto	ditto (m)	ditto	ditto
Board of Education of Westside Community Schools v. Mergens, 496 U.S. 226 (1990)	C	C (c)	C	C	C	U (d)	C (m)	C	C (c)

Case Name	Marshall	White	Blackmun	Rehnquist	Stevens	O'Connor	Scalia	Kennedy	Souter
1990 TERM									
EEOC v. Arabian American Oil Company, 499 U.S. 244 (1991)	Applies extrater-ritorially (d)	No extraterri-torial application	Applies extrater-ritorially	No extra-territorial application (m)	Applies extrater-ritorially	No extra-territorial application	No extra-territor-ial applica-tion (c)	No extra-territorial applica-tion	No extra-territorial applica-tion

Case Name	White	Blackmun	Rehnquist	Stevens	O'Connor	Scalia	Kennedy	Souter	Thomas
1991 TERM									
Lee v. Weisman, 505 U.S. 577 (1992)	C	U (c)	C	U	U	C (d)	U (m)	U (c)	C
International Society for Krishna Consciousness, Inc. v. Lee, 506 U.S. 805 (1992) solicitation of funds/distribution of literature (*per curiam*)	C C	U U	C (m) C (d)	U U	C (c) U (c)	C C	C (c) U (c)	U (d) U (c)	C C
1992 TERM									
Lamb's Chapel v. Center Moriches Union Free School District, 508 U.S. 384 (1993)	U(m)	U	U	U	U	U(c)	U(c)	U	U
Church of the Lukumi Babalu Aye, Inc. v. City of Hialeah, 508 U.S. 520 (1993)	U	U (c)	U	U	U	U (c)	U (m)	U (c)	U
Zobrest v. Catalina Foothills School District, 509 U.S. 1 (1993)	C	U (d)	C (m)	U	U (d)	C	C	U	C

Case Name	Blackmun	Rehnquist	Stevens	O'Connor	Scalia	Kennedy	Souter	Thomas	Ginsburg
1993 TERM									
Board of Education of the Kiryas Joel Village School District v. Grumet, 512 U.S. 687 (1994)	U (c)	C	U (c)	U (c)	C (d)	U (c)	U (m)	C	U

Case Name	Rehnquist	Stevens	O'Connor	Scalia	Kennedy	Souter	Thomas	Ginsburg	Breyer
1994 TERM									
Capitol Square Review and Advisory Board v. Pinette, 515 U.S. 753 (1995)	C	U (d)	C (c)	C (m)	C	C (c)	C	U (d)	C
Rosenberger v. The Rector and Visitors of the University of Virginia, 515 U.S. 819 (1995)	C	U	C (c)	C	C (m)	U (d)	C	U	U
1996 TERM									
Agostini v. Felton, 117 S.Ct. 1997 (1997)	C	U	C (m)	C	C	U (d)	C	U (d)	U
City of Boerne, Texas v. Flores, 117 S.Ct. 2157 (1997)	U	U (c)	C (d)	U (c)	U (m)	C (d)	U	U	C (d)

Supreme Court
Volume 1 pp. 261-276

TAKING DECISIONS OF THE U.S. SUPREME COURT: A CHRONOLOGY

Robert Meltz
Legislative Attorney
American Law Division

Once in the constitutional wings, the Takings Clause of the Fifth Amendment today stands center stage. No debate on the proper balance between private property rights and conflicting societal needs is complete without it.

The reasons for the Takings Clause's ascendancy are clear. Starting with the advent of comprehensive zoning in the early twentieth century, federal, state, and local regulation of land use has become pervasive. Beyond comprehensive zoning, recent decades have seen explosive growth in the use of historic preservation restrictions, open-space zoning, dedication and exaction conditions on building permits, nature preserves, wildlife habitat preservation, wetlands and coastal zone controls, and so on. In the Supreme Court, the appointment of several conservative justices since the Seventies has prompted a new scrutiny of government conduct vis-a-vis the individual.

As a result, the Court since the late Seventies has turned its attention toward the takings issue with renewed vigor, clarifying some issues and raising new ones. As a rough generalization, not without exception, the Court's decisions during this period evince a heightened concern for the property owner burdened by government-imposed property controls. Given this encouragement to property owners, and the inevitability of continued land use regulation, it is next to certain that takings issues will keep a high profile for the indefinite future.

By way of background, the Fifth Amendment of the U.S. Constitution states: "nor shall private property be taken for public use, without just compensation." Until the late nineteenth century, this clause was invoked only for **condemnation**: the formal exercise by government of its eminent-domain power to take property coercively, upon payment of just compensation. In such condemnation suits, there is no issue as to whether the property is "taken" in the Fifth Amendment sense; the government concedes so by filing the action. The only question, typically, is how much compensation must be paid.

Beginning in the late nineteenth century, the Supreme Court gave its imprimatur to a very different use of the Takings Clause. When the sovereign appropriated or caused a physical invasion of property, as when a government dam flooded private land, the Court found that the property had been taken just as surely as if the sovereign had formally condemned. So, it said, the property owner should be allowed to vindicate his constitutional right to compensation in a suit against the government. In sharp contrast with condemnation actions, then, such **takings actions** have the property owner suing government rather than vice-versa, hence the synonym "inverse condemnation actions." The key issue in takings actions is usually whether, given all the circumstances, the impact of the government action on a particular property amounts to a taking in the constitutional sense.

In 1922, in the most historically important taking decision,[1] the Supreme Court extended the availability of takings actions from government appropriations and physical invasions of property to the mere regulation of property use. This critical extension opened up vast new legal possibilities for property owners, and underlies most of the Supreme Court's takings decisions since 1922.

* * * * *

This report compiles only Supreme Court decisions addressing issues unique to takings actions, not those on condemnation or property valuation. A scattering of due process cases is also included where they address property-use restrictions or have been cited by the Court as authority in its takings analyses.

In the interest of brevity, we have mentioned no dissenting opinions, and almost no concurrences. Thus, the table does not reveal the highly polarized nature of many recent Supreme Court takings opinions, often decided on 5-4 votes.

Decisions are listed in reverse chronological order.

---

[1]Pennsylvania Coal Co. v. Mahon, 260 U.S. 393 (1922).

I. Takings Law Today: *Penn Central* (1978) to the Present

In 1978, the Supreme Court ushered in the modern era of regulatory takings law by attempting to inject some order into the ad hoc, case-by-case analyses that had characterized its decisions before then. In *Penn Central Transportation Co. v. New York City*, the Court declared that whether a regulatory taking has occurred in a given case is influenced by three factors: the economic impact of the regulation, the extent to which it interferes with reasonable investment-backed expectations, and the "character" of the government action. A related test for land-use regulation was announced by the Court in 1980, in *Agins v. City of Tiburon*. After these decisions, ad hocery in judicial taking determinations emphatically still remains, but arguably is confined within tighter bounds.

Penn Central also initiated a period of increased Supreme Court activity on the regulatory takings front. As the cases in this section reveal, quantum advances in the jurisprudence emerged in three areas: ripeness (chiefly, *Agins, Williamson County, MacDonald*, and *Riverside Bayview*); per se rules of takings liability (*Loretto, Hodel v. Irving, Babbitt, Lucas, Nollan*, and *Dolan*); and remedy (*First English*). Several decisions of this period evince a desire on the part of some justices, most notably Chief Justice Rehnquist and Justice Scalia, to extend greater protection to property rights (*Nollan, Dolan, Lucas*, and the dissents in *Penn Central, Keystone*, and *Pennell*).

Case	Action attacked	Holding/rationale
City of Monterey v. Del Monte Dunes at Monterey, Ltd., *cert. granted*, 118 S. Ct. 1359 (Mar. 30, 1998) (No. 97-1235)	City's failure to approve property owner's development plans after five, progressively smaller, applications (four by previous owner)	*Still pending:* Decision below, 95 F.3d 1422 (9th Cir. 1996), held that owner had right to jury trial under 42 U.S.C. § 1983 on whether taking occurred, and that City's development prohibition violated "rough proportionality" criterion of *Dolan, infra* page 4. City's petition for certiorari asks whether (1) section 1983 requires jury trial on liability issue; (2) jury or court can reweigh evidence on reasonableness of land use decision, and (3) "rough proportionality" test applies to taking claim based on regulatory denial.
Eastern Enterprises v. Apfel, 118 S. Ct. 2131 (1998)	Federal statute requiring company to fund health benefits of miner who worked for it decades earlier, where company left mining business before promise of lifetime benefits in collective bargaining agreements became explicit in 1974	Coal Industry Retiree Health Benefit of 1992 is unconstitutional as applied to Eastern. In opinion accompanying judgment, four justices find taking because statute imposes severe retroactive liability on a limited class of parties that could not have anticipated the liability, and the extent of liability is substantially disproportionate to the company's experience in mining field. This points to taking under *Penn Central* test, *infra* page 8. Also, remedy for taking based on generalized monetary liability is invalidation rather than compensation, supporting jurisdiction in district court. Remaining justice supporting judgment sees instead a substantive due process violation.

Case	Action attacked	Holding/rationale
Phillips v. Washington Legal Foundation, 118 S. Ct. 1925 (1998)	Texas' use of interest earned on lawyers' client trust funds to support organizations providing legal services to low-income persons	Interest is property of clients, not state. Despite fact that interest would not exist but for state's Interest on Lawyers Trust Accounts Program, state's rule that "interest follows principal" must be followed. Nor can interest be regarded as mere government-created value. Remanded to Fifth Circuit for decision on whether taking occurred.
Suitum v. Tahoe Regional Planning Agency, 520 U.S. 725 (1997)	Agency's ban on new land coverage in "Stream Environment Zones," under which plaintiff was barred from building home on residential lot	Taking claim is ripe despite plaintiff's not having applied for TRPA approval of her sale of transferrable development rights (TDRs). "Final decision" requirement of *Williamson County, infra* page 6, does not embrace such TRPA approval, since parties agree on TDRs to which plaintiff is entitled and no discretion remains for TRPA. TDRs' value here is simply an issue of fact, which courts routinely resolve without benefit of a market transaction.
Babbitt v. Youpee, 519 U.S. 234 (1997)	Federal statute's ban on descent or devise of small interests in allotted Indian land — as ban was narrowed by amendment	Taking occurred. The amendment, made in 1984, did not cure taking that *Hodel v. Irving, infra* page 6, found in pre-amendment version of statute. Amendment narrowed ban only as regards income-producing ability of the land, not its value. More important, amendment's allowance of devise to current owners in same parcel still offends *Hodel* by continuing to "severely restrict[]" Indian's right to direct descent of his property.
Bennis v. Michigan, 517 U.S. 1163 (1996)	Forfeiture of car, owned jointly by plaintiff and her husband, because of husband's illegal sexual activity in car	No taking (of wife's joint interest in car). To be sure, wife had no prior knowledge of husband's planned use of car. But government may not be required to compensate an owner for property which it has already lawfully acquired under authority other than eminent domain. Then, too, the cases authorizing forfeiture are "too firmly fixed" to be now displaced.
Dolan v. City of Tigard, 512 U.S. 374 (1994)	Conditions imposed by city for granting building permit, requiring applicant to dedicate public greenway along stream and adjacent bike/pedestrian pathway	Taking occurred. While greenway dedication condition rationally advanced a purpose of permit scheme (flood prevention), requiring landowner to allow public access to greenway did not. Hence, latter violated "nature of the permit condition" taking criterion in *Nollan, infra* page 5. Other condition, that pathway be dedicated, was not shown by city to impose burden on applicant that was "roughly proportional" to impact of applicant's proposed project on community. Hence, it violates the "degree of burden" taking criterion that Court announces here. Also, burden of proof is on government to demonstrate "rough proportionality."
Concrete Pipe & Products, Inc. v. Construction Laborers Pension Trust, 508 U.S. 602 (1993)	Federal statute requiring that employer who withdraws from multi-employer pension plan pay a fixed debt to plan	No taking. Taking claim not aided by fact that collective bargaining agreement predating statute protected employer from liability to plan beyond specified contributions. Three-factor *Penn Central* test, *infra* page 8, does not point to taking: (1) government action merely adjusted benefits and burdens of economic life; (2) withdrawal liability was not disproportionate; and (3) given longstanding federal regulation in pension field, employer lacked reasonable expectation it would not be faced with liability for promised benefits.
Lucas v. South Carolina Coastal Council, 505 U.S. 1003 (1992)	Development ban imposed on vacant lots under state's beachfront management statute	Government regulation of land that completely eliminates economic use is *per se* taking, even when legislature asserts prevention-of-harm purpose. There is a prior inquiry, however, as to whether proposed use is inherent in landowner's title under "background principles of the state's law of property and nuisance" existing when land was acquired. If not, there is no taking, since regulation does not take anything owner ever had.

Case	Action attacked	Holding/rationale
Yee v. City of Escondido, 503 U.S. 519 (1992)	Mobile home rent-control ordinance, combined with state law forcing mobile home park owner to accept purchasers of mobile homes in park as new tenants	No physical taking occurred. Neither state nor local law on its face requires landowner to dedicate his land to mobile home rentals, nor overly limits his ability to terminate such use. *Per se* rule in *Loretto*, *infra* page 7, applies only when permanent physical occupation is coerced. Claim that procedure for changing use of park is overly burdensome is not ripe, since plaintiff has not gone through procedure. Regulatory taking claim is not properly before Court, since not subsumed by questions in petition for certiorari.
Preseault v. ICC, 494 U.S. 1 (1990)	Federal "rails-to-trails" statute, under which unused railroad rights of way are converted to recreational trails notwithstanding reversionary property interests under state law	Premature for Court to evaluate taking challenge to rails-to-trails statute, because even if it causes takings of reversionary interests, compensation is available under Tucker Act (authorizing suits against U.S. for compensation). Nothing in rails-to-trails statute suggests the "unambiguous intention" to withdraw Tucker Act remedy which this Court requires. For example, Congress' expressed desire that program operate at "low cost" might merely reflect its rejection of a more ambitious federal program, rather than withdrawal of Tucker Act remedy.
United States v. Sperry Corp., 493 U.S. 52 (1989)	Statutory 1-1/2% deduction from awards of Iran-United States Claims Tribunal as reimbursement to United States for expenses incurred in the arbitration	No taking. 1-1/2% deduction is a reasonable "user fee" intended to reimburse United States for its costs in connection with tribunal. Amount of fee need not be precisely tailored to use that party makes of government services. Fee here is not so great as to belie its claimed status as a user fee.
Duquesne Light Co. v. Barasch, 488 U.S. 299 (1989)	State agency's refusal to allow inclusion of cost of canceled nuclear plants in utility's rate base	No taking. Under the circumstances, overall impact of preventing amortization of such costs was small, and not shown to be unjust or confiscatory.
Pennell v. City of San Jose, 485 U.S. 1 (1988)	Rent control ordinance allowing rent increases of greater than set percentage only after considering economic hardship caused to tenants	Not ripe. There was no evidence that hardship provision had in fact ever been relied upon to limit a rent increase. Also, ordinance did not require rent limit in event of tenant hardship, only that hardship be considered.
Nollan v. California Coastal Comm'n, 483 U.S. 825 (1987)	State's grant of building permit on condition property owners record easement allowing public to traverse beach on property	Taking occurred. Permit condition (recording easement) did not substantially advance a government purpose that would justify denial of permit (ensuring visual access to beach). Where such linkage exists, however, no taking occurs even if outright appropriation of the property infringement (here, the easement) would be a taking.
Bowen v. Gilliard, 483 U.S. 587 (1987)	Amendments to federal welfare program resulting in lower benefits and assignment of child support payments to entire family	No taking. Family has no property right to continued welfare benefits at same level. Child receiving support payments suffers no substantial economic impact, since payments were likely used for entire family before amendments.
First English Evangelical Lutheran Church v. County of Los Angeles, 482 U.S. 304 (1987)	Interim ordinance prohibiting construction of any structures in flood zone	If a regulation is held to have taken property, Takings Clause requires compensation for the time during which regulation was in effect — i.e., until the date of repeal or judicial invalidation. Mere invalidation of the regulation is not a constitutionality sufficient remedy. (Existence of taking assumed by Court owing to posture of case.)

Case	Action attacked	Holding/rationale
Hodel v. Irving, 481 U.S. 704 (1987)	Federal statute declaring that small interests in allotted Indian land may not descend by intestacy or devise, but must escheat to tribe	Taking occurred. Statute amounts to complete abrogation, rather than regulation, of right to pass on property — a right which, like the right to exclude others, is basic to the concept of property.
Keystone Bituminous Coal Ass'n v. DeBenedictis, 480 U.S. 470 (1987)	State regulation requiring that at least 50% of underground coal be left in place, where mining coal might cause subsidence damage to surface structures	No taking. Unlike the similar anti-subsidence law held a taking in *Pennsylvania Coal Co.*, *infra* page 12, the statute here has a broad public purpose and does not rule out profitable mine operation.
FCC v. Florida Power Corp., 480 U.S. 245 (1987)	Federal regulation requiring that utility greatly reduce rent charged cable TV company for attaching its cables to utility's poles	No taking. *Per se* rule in *Loretto*, *infra* page 7, applies only when permanent physical occupation is coerced, unlike here where utility voluntarily entered into contract with cable company. And new rent ordered by FCC was not confiscatory, hence not a taking.
MacDonald, Sommer & Frates v. Yolo County, 477 U.S. 340 (1986)	County's rejection of developer's first-submitted subdivision plat	Not ripe. Developer must first obtain "final and authoritative determination" of the type and intensity of development that will be permitted. County's rejection of first-submitted plat does not preclude possibility that submissions of scaled-down version of project might not be approved. Also, a court cannot determine whether compensation is "just" until it knows what compensation state or local government will provide.
Bowen v. Public Agencies Opposed to Social Security Entrapment, 477 U.S. 41 (1986)	Statutory repeal of provision in federal-state agreements allowing states to end social security coverage of state and local employees	No taking. Repealed provision is not "property," since Congress reserved right to amend agreements in enacting governing statute, and clause was not a debt or obligation of U.S.
Connolly v. Pension Benefit Guaranty Corp., 475 U.S. 211 (1986)	Federal act requiring that employers who withdraw from a multi-employer pension plan pay a fixed debt to the plan	No taking. Taking does not occur every time law requires one person to use his assets for benefit of another. Nor can statute be defeated by pre-existing contract provision protecting employers from further liability.
United States v. Riverside Bayview Homes, Inc., 474 U.S. 121 (1985)	Corps of Engineers' assertion of dredge and fill jurisdiction over certain freshwater wetlands	Not ripe. Mere assertion of regulatory jurisdiction by Corps is not taking; only when permit is denied so as to bar all beneficial use of property is there a taking. Also, fact that broad construction of statute might yield more takings is not reason to construe statute narrowly, since taking is unconstitutional only if no means to obtain compensation exists. Such means does exist here, since Tucker Act authorizes compensation for federal takings.
Williamson County Planning Comm'n v. Hamilton Bank, 473 U.S. 172 (1985)	County's rejection of developer's subdivision plat	Not ripe. Taking claim against state/local government in federal court is not ripe unless (1) there is final and authoritative decision by government as to type and intensity of development allowed, and (2) avenues for obtaining compensation from state forums have been exhausted. Here, developer failed to seek variances following initial denial, thus has not received a final decision. Nor did developer use an available state procedure for obtaining compensation. Absence of exhaustion requirement in 42 U.S.C. § 1983 distinguished.

Case	Action attacked	Holding/rationale
United States v. Locke, 471 U.S. 84 (1985)	Federal statute voiding unpatented mining claims when claim holder fails to make timely annual filings	No taking. Loss of claim could have been avoided with minimal burden. No taking when property can continue to be held through owner's compliance with reasonable regulations. *Texaco, Inc., v. Short, infra* this page, found controlling.
Ruckelshaus v. Monsanto Co., 467 U.S. 986 (1984)	Public disclosure and other use by EPA of industry-generated trade-secret data submitted with application for pesticide registration	Taking occurred. Trade secrets are property, but only those submitted 1972-78, when federal pesticide statute contained a confidentiality guarantee, were taken. Before and after this period, there was no investment-backed expectation of confidentiality, hence no taking. Tucker Act remedy (right to seek money from U.S. in Court of Federal Claims) was not withdrawn by pesticide act. Pesticide act reveals no such intention, and withdrawal would amount to disfavored repeal by implication of Tucker Act. Also, federal pesticide act sets up exhaustion of agency remedies as precondition to any Tucker Act claim.
Kirby Forest Industries, Inc. v. United States, 467 U.S. 1 (1984)	Filing of condemnation action by U.S. to acquire land for national park	No taking. Mere act of filing leaves landowner free, during pendency of condemnation action, to make any use of property or to sell it (but loss in market value from such action is not compensable).
Loretto v. Teleprompter Manhattan CATV Corp., 458 U.S. 419 (1982)	State statute requiring landlords to allow installing of cable TV equipment on premises, for one-time payment of one dollar	Taking occurred. Where as here government causes a "permanent physical occupation" of property, it is a *per se* taking — no matter how important the public interest served or how minimal the economic impact. In contrast, temporary physical invasions must submit to balancing of factors.
Texaco, Inc. v. Short, 454 U.S. 516 (1982)	State statute extinguishing severed mineral estates unused for long time unless owner filed statement within prescribed period	No taking. It is the owner's failure to use the mineral estate or timely file a statement, not the state's imposition of reasonable conditions on estate retention, that causes the property right to lapse.
Dames & Moore v. Regan, 453 U.S. 654 (1981)	President's nullification of attachments on Iranian assets in U.S., during hostage crisis	No taking. Attachments were revocable and subordinate to President's power under International Emergency Economic Powers Act. Hence, there was no property in the attachments such as would support claim for compensation. Also, possibility that suspension of claims against Iranian assets may effect taking makes ripe the question whether there is Tucker Act remedy here. We hold there is.
Hodel v. Indiana, 452 U.S. 314 (1981)	Restrictions in federal statute on surface mining of prime farmlands	No taking. Plaintiffs failed to allege that any specific property was taken. Mere enactment of statute was no taking, since prime farmland provisions do not on their face deny landowners all economic use of such land — *e.g.*, do not restrict non-mining uses thereof.
Hodel v. Virginia Surface Mining & Reclamation Ass'n, 452 U.S. 264 (1981)	Demand in federal act that surface miners restore steep slopes to original contour, and surface mining prohibitions therein	No taking. Plaintiffs failed to allege that any specific property was taken. Mere enactment of statute was no taking, since challenged provisions do not on their face deny landowners all economic use of affected land. In any event, taking claim is not ripe, since plaintiffs never used avenues for administrative relief in act — *e.g.*, variance from original-contour requirement.
San Diego Gas & Electric Co. v. San Diego, 450 U.S. 621 (1980)	City's adoption of open-space plan	No final judgment by state court below as to whether a taking had occurred, hence no Supreme Court jurisdiction under 28 U.S.C. § 1257.

Case	Action attacked	Holding/rationale
Webb's Fabulous Pharmacies, Inc., v. Beckwith, 449 U.S. 155 (1980)	County court declaring as public money the interest on interpleader fund deposited by litigants with the court	Taking occurred. On facts presented, interest could not be viewed simply as fee to cover court costs. State may not take interest simply by calling a deposited fund "public money."
Agins v. City of Tiburon, 447 U.S. 255 (1980)	Municipal rezoning under which property owner could build between one and five houses on his land	No taking. Enactment of ordinance is rationally related to legitimate public goal of open-space preservation, ordinance benefits property owner as well as public, and owner may still be able to build up to five houses on lot. As-applied challenge is not ripe, since owner never submitted development plan for approval under the new zoning.
Prune Yard Shopping Center v. Robins, 447 U.S. 74 (1980)	State constitutional mandate that persons be allowed to engage in political expression in private shopping center	No taking. Will not unreasonably impair value or use of property as a shopping center, since facility is open to public at large. And owner may restrict time, place, and manner of expression.
US v. Clarke,445 U.S. 253 (1980)	Municipalities' entering into physical possession of land without bringing condemnation action	Federal statute providing that allotted Indian lands may be "condemned" under state law does not allow cities to take land by physical possession in absence of formal condemnation proceeding. Term "condemned" refers only to filing of condemnation by government, not filing of "inverse condemnation" action by landowner.
Kaiser Aetna v. United States, 444 U.S. 164 (1979)	Federal order that owners of exclusive private marina, made navigable by private funds, grant access to boating public	Taking occurred. Infringement of marina owner's right to exclude others, particularly where there's investment-backed expectation of privacy, goes beyond permissible regulation. Navigation servitude does not grant government absolute taking immunity.
Andrus v. Allard, 444 U.S. 51 (1979)	Federal ban on sale of eagle parts or artifacts made therefrom, as applied to stock lawfully obtained before ban	No taking. Denial of one traditional property right (selling) does not necessarily amount to taking, even if it is most profitable use of property. Plaintiff retained right to possess, pass on, or exhibit for an admission price, the affected inventory.
Penn Central Transp. Co. v. New York City, 438 U.S. 104 (1978)	City's use of historic preservation ordinance to block construction of office tower atop designated historic landmark	No taking. Generally, three factors of "particular significance" in a takings determination are: (1) economic impact of regulation on property owner; (2) extent to which regulation interferes with distinct investment-backed expectations; and (3) "character" of government action (meaning principally that regulation of use is less likely to be taking than physical invasion). Here, landmark owner may earn adequate return from building as is, and more modest additions to building still might be approved. City's offering of transferrable development rights to building owner also weighs against a taking. Finally, city cannot segment air rights over building from remainder of property and claim that all use of air rights was taken.

II. The Dawn of Regulatory Takings Law: *Pennsylvania Coal Co.* (1922) to 1978

The principle that government may be held to have taken property in the Fifth Amendment sense merely through regulatory restriction of property use — that is, in the absence of any physical invasion or formal appropriation of the property — was first announced in 1922. In *Pennsylvania Coal Co. v. Mahon*, the redoubtable Justice Oliver Wendell Holmes ruled for the Supreme Court that a state law prohibiting coal mining that might cause surface subsidence in certain areas was a taking of the plaintiff's mineral estate.

The first steps taken by this new doctrine, however, were unsteady ones. Aside from making clear that takings occur only with the most severe of property impacts, the Court's opinions during this period display little in the way of principled decisionmaking. Moreover, the Court refused at times to part with its longstanding due-process approach to testing property-use restrictions, vacillating between the two theories.

Case	Action attacked	Holding/rationale
Regional Rail Reorganization Act Cases, 419 U.S. 102 (1974)	Federal statute directing transfer of bankrupt rail-roads' assets to federally created corporation and forcing continued operation of unprofitable lines	Availability of Tucker Act remedy (right to seek compensation from U.S. in Court of Federal Claims) if rail act effects "erosion taking" is ripe issue in view of distinct possibility that compelled rail operations at a loss would erode railroad's value beyond constitutional limits. Similarly, issue of remedy's availability if rail act effects "conveyance taking" is ripe, since act will lead inexorably to conveyance of assets. On merits, Tucker Act remedy is available for both alleged takings because rail act indicates no contrary intent; availability need not be stated.
Calero-Toledo v. Pearson Yacht Leasing Co., 416 U.S. 663 (1974)	Puerto Rico's seizure of yacht used for unlawful activity by lessee, but having innocent lessor	No taking. Forfeiture is not rendered unconstitutional because it applies to property of innocents. The property itself is treated as the offender, making owner's conduct irrelevant. Also, owner voluntarily entrusted the yacht to the lessee, and there was no allegation that the owner did all it could to avoid having property put to unlawful use.
Hurtado v. United States, 410 U.S. 578 (1973)	Pre-trial detention of federal criminal witnesses who are likely to flee and cannot post bond; payment of only one dollar per day	No taking. There is public duty to provide evidence; fact that pre-trial detention is involved here, and that financial burden may be great, is immaterial. Takings Clause does not make U.S. pay for performance of duty it is already owed. Hence, issue of whether one dollar is adequate compensation need not be reached.
YMCA v. United States, 394 U.S. 85 (1969)	Occupation of plaintiff's buildings by U.S. troops seeking to protect buildings from Panamanian rioters	No taking. Where private party is intended beneficiary of government activity, resultant losses need not be compensated even though activity was also intended incidentally to benefit public. Also, damage by rioters was not caused directly and substantially by government occupation.
Heart of Atlanta Motel, Inc. v. United States, 379 U.S. 241 (1964)	Federal statute banning racial discrimination in public accommodations	No taking. "The cases are to the contrary [of the taking claim]."

Case	Action attacked	Holding/rationale
Goldblatt v. Hempstead, 369 U.S. 590 (1962)	Ordinance barring excavation below water table	No taking. Fact that ordinance deprives property of its most beneficial use, even an existing one, does not render it a taking. No evidence that ordinance will reduce value of lot, and ordinance is valid police-power regulation.
Griggs v. Allegheny County, 369 U.S. 84 (1962)	Low and frequent flights over home near county-owned airport	Taking occurred of an air easement, per rule of *United States v. Causby*, *infra* page 12. County, rather than United States, must assume taking liability, since notwithstanding federal airport standards that must be met for receipt of federal funds, county promoted, built, owns, and operates airport.
Armstrong v. United States, 364 U.S. 40 (1960)	Required transfer to U.S. of title to unfinished boat, making a materialmen's lien unenforceable	Taking occurred. Destruction by government of all value of lien (which is property) is not mere consequential injury, hence non-compensable, but is rather a direct result of U.S.' exercising option under contract to take title to vessel.
United States v. Central Eureka Mining Co., 357 U.S. 155 (1958)	Federal wartime order requiring non-essential gold mines to close	No taking. Government did not occupy, use, or possess mines; rather it sought only to free up essential equipment and manpower for critical wartime uses. Such a temporary restriction during wartime is not a taking.
Tee-Hit-Ton Indians v. United States, 348 U.S. 272 (1955)	Removal by U.S. of timber from certain Indian-occupied lands in Alaska	No taking. Permissive Indian occupancy — *i.e.*, occupancy not specifically recognized by Congress as ownership — may be extinguished without compensation.
United States v. Caltex (Philippines), Inc., 344 U.S. 149 (1952)	Destruction by U.S. army of private oil terminal, to prevent its capture by advancing enemy	No taking. Wartime destruction of private property by U.S. to prevent imminent capture by an advancing enemy is exception to taking clause.
United States v. Pewee Coal Co., 341 U.S. 114 (1951)	Temporary seizure and operation of coal mine by U.S. during wartime to avert strike	Taking occurred. Government asserted total dominion and control over the mines.
United States v. Gerlach Live Stock Co., 339 U.S. 725 (1950)	Building of federal dam that ended seasonal inundation of plaintiffs' grasslands, turning them parched	Need not reach taking question, since Congress has not attempted to take, or authorized the taking without compensation, of any rights valid under state law.
United States v. Dickinson, 331 U.S. 745 (1947)	Flooding of land by federal dam in gradual, successive stages	When government takes by a continuing process of physical events, owner is not required to resort to piecemeal or premature taking actions. Date of taking occurs when situation becomes "stabilized."
United States v. Causby, 328 U.S. 256 (1946)	Frequent flights of military aircraft over chicken farm at low altitude	Taking occurred of air easement. Flights over private land that are so low and frequent as to be direct and immediate interference with use and enjoyment of land effect a taking.
United States v. Willow River Power Co., 324 U.S. 499 (1945)	Raising of water level by U.S., impairing efficiency of upstream hydro- electric dam	No taking. Dam operator's interest in river's water level is subordinate to paramount authority of U.S. to improve navigation.

Case	Action attacked	Holding/rationale
Bowles v. Willingham, 321 U.S. 503 (1944)	Federal statute authorizing restriction of rents in "defense areas" to levels that are "generally" fair, rather than fair to each landlord	No taking. Impossibility of fixing rents landlord by landlord and existence of war are germane to constitutional issue. Nothing in act requires offering accommodations for rent. Price control may reduce value of property, but that does not mean there is taking.
United States v. Chicago, M., St. P. & P. Railroad Co., 312 U.S. 592 (1941)	Raising of water level by U.S., forcing railroad to incur costs to protect embankment	No taking. Embankment was built on low-water mark in bed of navigable stream; government's navigation servitude covers entire bed of such streams to high-water mark.
Danforth v. United States, 308 U.S. 271 (1939)	Enactment of flood control statute authorizing condemnation	Mere enactment of statute authorizing future action cannot be taking, since "[s]uch legislation may be repealed or modified, or appropriations may fail."
United States v. Sponenbarger, 308 U.S. 256 (1939)	Enactment of flood control act and operations pursuant to act	No taking of land within floodway. Improvements under act had not increased flood hazard. Also, government effort to lessen flood hazard did not constitute taking of those lands not afforded as much protection as others.
Chippewa Indians v. United States, 305 U.S. 479 (1939)	Federal statute creating national forest on land held by U.S. in trust for tribe	Taking occurred. Mere enactment deprived tribe of all its beneficial interest in the land.
Shoshone Tribe v. United States, 299 U.S. 476 (1937)	Federal sanction of Arapahoe occupancy of land promised by treaty to exclusive occupancy of Shoshone	Federal guardianship of tribal land does not include requiring tribe to which exclusive occupancy has been pledged to share land with another tribe absent compensation.
Louisville Joint Stock Land Bank v. Radford, 295 U.S. 555 (1935)	Federal statute eliminating certain rights of mortgagees in property held as security	Taking occurred. Act as applied deprives mortgagee bank of its property rights under state law to retain lien until indebtedness is paid, to realize on the security through judicial public sale, to control property during default period, etc. Loss of these rights effects substantial impairment of the security. Act has taken from bank, and given to mortgagor, rights in specific property which are of substantial value.
Railroad Retirement Bd. v. Alton Railroad Co., 295 U.S. 330 (1935)	Required federal retirement scheme for interstate carriers	Due process violation occurred. Under scheme, a railroad must, in addition to making its own contributions to pension fund, act as insurer of contributions required of other railroads and railroad employees. Though property of railroads is dedicated to public use, it remains the private property of its owners, and may not be taken without compensation.
United States v. Creek Nation, 295 U.S. 103 (1935)	Portion of treaty lands taken by survey error of U.S., given to another tribe	Federal guardianship of tribal land does not allow appropriation by U.S. without compensation.
Norman v. B. & O. Rd. Co., 294 U.S. 240 (1935)	Federal mandate that obligations be dischargeable by payment of legal tender, voiding gold clause in pre-existing private contract	No taking. Relies entirely on *Legal Tender Cases*, *infra* page 15.

Case	Action attacked	Holding/rationale
Mullen Benevolent Corp. v. United States, 290 U.S. 89 (1933)	Acquisition by U.S. of lands, frustrating the replenishment of town's fund for repayment of bonds	No taking of bonds. No lien remained on land at time of purchase by U.S., and frustration of ability to replenish fund is merely consequential damage, hence noncompensable.
International Paper Co. v. United States, 282 U.S. 399 (1931)	Wartime requisition by U.S. of all power producible by power company from water in canal, cutting off paper company's lease right to use portion of such water	Taking occurred. Fact that requisition occurred by contract is of no moment, since power company was bound under governing requisition statute to obey. Paper company had water right, a property right, to use of canal water, and federal action terminated that right in its entirety. *Omnia Commercial Corp., infra* this page, can be distinguished, since here government took the property that petitioner owned, rather than merely frustrating future deliveries under contract.
Nectow v. City of Cambridge, 277 U.S. 183 (1928)	*Euclid*-style comprehensive zoning ordinance, as applied to designate portion of plaintiff's tract residential	Due process violation occurred. Because of industrial uses to which adjoining lands on two sides are devoted, subject land has little value for limited purposes permitted in a residential zone. Land-use restriction cannot be imposed where, as here, it does not bear substantial relation to public health, safety, morals, or general welfare.
Miller v. Schoene, 276 U.S. 272 (1928)	State order that cedar trees infected with infectious rust disease be cut down, so as not to endanger nearby cash crop	State did not exceed due process or proper bounds of police power. State may order destruction of one class of private property to save another of greater value to public.
Village of Euclid v. Ambler Realty Co., 272 U.S. 365 (1926)	Comprehensive zoning ordinance	No violation of due process. Zoning, as a general matter, is reasonable use of police-power to deal with increasingly crowded urban conditions. Fact that non-offensive as well as noxious uses are barred from a zone is not fatal.
Everard's Breweries v. Day, 265 U.S. 545 (1924)	Federal statute prohibiting doctors from prescribing intoxicating malt liquors for medicinal purposes	No taking of brewery's property. (No further discussion.)
Omnia Commercial Co. v. United States, 261 U.S. 502 (1923)	Wartime requisition by U.S. of steel plant's entire output, precluding plaintiff from buying steel at favorable price under preexisting contract with plant	No taking. Though contract rights are property, U.S. did not "take" those rights, but merely frustrated their exercise. The Constitution does not demand compensation for such consequential harm.
Pennsylvania Coal Co. v. Mahon, 260 U.S. 393 (1922)	State law barring coal mining that might cause subsidence of overlying land, applicable only where surface estate owner is different from mineral estate owner	Taking occurred. "While property may be regulated to a certain extent, if regulation goes too far it will be recognized as a taking." By eliminating right to mine coal, state law leaves the mineral estate owner with nothing. Moreover, because state law applies only where surface is in different ownership, it benefits a narrow private interest rather than a broad public one. And surface owners had expressly contracted away their right to subjacent support.

III. Appropriations and Physical Takings Only: 1870 to 1922

The 1870s marked the Supreme Court's first clear acknowledgment that the Takings Clause is not only a constraint on the government's formal exercise of eminent domain, but the basis as well for suits by property owners challenging government conduct not attended by such formal exercise. However, until 1922 the Court believed such "inverse condemnation" suits to be confined to government appropriations or physical invasions of property. Cases involving the impacts of government water projects (flooding, reduced access, etc.) were typical. When cases involving mere restrictions on the use of property reached the Court, they were tested under due process, scope of the police power, or ultra vires theories.

Case	Action attacked	Holding/rationale
Portsmouth Harbor Land & Hotel Co. v. United States, 260 U.S. 327 (1922)	Positioning of military guns for firing over private resort island, and actual firing on several occasions	Occasional firings and other evidence showed that U.S. might have installed guns not simply as wartime defenses, but to subordinate resort to right of government to fire across it at will, in peacetime. If so, effects an appropriation of a servitude and requires compensation.
Block v. Hirsh, 256 U.S. 135 (1921)	Statute allowing tenants to remain in possession at same rent upon expiration of lease	No taking. Validity of rate regulation in the public interest is well settled. Statute is justified only as temporary measure related to war effort. Landlord is assured of rents that are "reasonable."
Bothwell v. United States, 254 U.S. 321 (1920)	Government flooding of private land, forcing sale of cattle at low prices and destroying business	No taking as to cattle or business. The U.S. need only pay for property it actually takes.
Walls v. Midland Carbon Co., 254 U.S. 300 (1920)	State ban on non-heating uses of natural gas, forcing closing of plant that used gas to make carbon black	Within state's police power and does not take property without due process. State may curtail extravagant uses of a natural resource in which many have rights, limiting one person's rights in order that others may enjoy theirs.
Jacob Ruppert, Inc., v. Caffey, 251 U.S. 264 (1920)	Federal statute extending wartime ban on domestic liquor sales to beer, including supplies on hand at enactment	No taking. As in *Hamilton*, *infra* this page, there was no appropriation of private property, but merely a lessening of value due to a permissible restriction on its use. Nor is it significant that ban took effect immediately.
Hamilton v. Kentucky Distilleries & Warehouse Co., 251 U.S. 146 (1919)	Federal statute imposing wartime ban on domestic liquor sales, including supplies on hand at enactment	No taking. There was no appropriation for public purposes. Moreover, statute gave plaintiff nine months after enactment to sell liquor, and imposed no restriction at any time on export. Finally, restrictions here are less severe than ones upheld in state takings cases under Fourteenth Amendment.
United States v. Cress, 243 U.S. 316 (1917)	Federal lock and dam project that raised water above natural levels, periodically flooding private land	Taking of flowage easement occurred. Government's right to make navigational improvements is subject to taking clause when natural bounds of stream are exceeded.
Hadacheck v. Sebastian, 239 U.S. 394 (1915)	Ordinance barring brick manufacture in section of city, allegedly reducing value of land by 90%	Police power not exceeded. Only limit on police power is that it not be exercised arbitrarily.

Case	Action attacked	Holding/rationale
Reinman v. Little Rock, 237 U.S. 171 (1915)	Ordinance barring livery stables in section of city	Police power not exceeded; due process not violated. It is within police power to declare that in certain situations, a type of business shall be deemed a nuisance and prohibited, even if it is not a nuisance per se, as long as this power is not exercise arbitrarily or with unjust discrimination.
Richards v. Washington Terminal Co., 233 U.S. 546 (1914)	Harm to property from operation of nearby railroad located, constructed, and maintained under acts of Congress	Property owner's nuisance action against railroad may proceed. While Congress may legalize what would otherwise be a public nuisance, it may not immunize congressionally chartered railroad from private nuisance actions so as to amount to taking of private property. Private nuisances amounting to takings in this context are those where railroad operation subjects property owner to more than typical injury, as is the case here.
Peabody v. United States, 231 U.S. 530 (1913)	Positioning of military guns with capability of firing over private resort island, last fired in 1902	No taking. If U.S. had installed guns to establish right to fire over land at will in peacetime, would be a taking. But here, practice shots can be aimed elsewhere, and indeed, guns have not been fired for many years. Cf. *Portsmouth Harbor Land & Hotel Co.*, *supra* page 13.
Noble State Bank v. Haskell, 219 U.S. 104 (1911)	State statute requiring banks to pay assessment to fund designed to secure full repayment of deposits	No taking. A public advantage may justify a small taking of private property for what, in its immediate purpose, is a private use. In addition, benefit conferred on plaintiff bank through this scheme of mutual protection is sufficient compensation for correlative burden that it must assume.
United States v. Welch, 217 U.S. 333 (1910)	Flooding from government dam, cutting off right of way	Taking occurred. Destruction of an easement is as much a taking of it as is an appropriation.
Welch v. Swasey, 214 U.S. 91 (1909)	State statute limiting height of buildings in area containing plaintiff's land to lower height than elsewhere	No taking. Height limitation here, even though a discrimination, is not so unreasonable as to deprive owner of property of its profitable use without justification. The discrimination was justified by the police power.
Sauer v. City of New York, 206 U.S. 536 (1907)	Construction of elevated public viaduct in city street, impairing access, light, and air reaching plaintiff's property	No taking. Under New York law, public-highway abutter has easements of access, light, and air against erection of elevated roadway by private corporation, but not against erection of same for public use.
Manigault v. Springs, 199 U.S. 473 (1905)	Construction of state-authorized dam, compelling plaintiff to raise his dikes and impairing access to his lands	No taking. Flooding effects taking only where there is material impairment of flooded land's value — not, as here, where plaintiff is merely put to some extra expense in raising dikes (and even though dam's sole purpose is to enhance value of downstream lowlands for agriculture). No compensation for impaired access either, since within state's police power.
California Reduction Co. v. Sanitary Reduction Works, 199 U.S. 306 (1905)	Ordinance requiring that waste generated within city be disposed of at designated site, at transporter's expense	No taking. Imposing expense on waste generator (assuming transporter passes on disposal fees) was not taking, since it has always been generator's duty to have garbage removed from his premises. Nor did destruction of waste amount to taking, even if some of its constituents had value.

Case	Action attacked	Holding/rationale
Bedford v. United States, 192 U.S. 217 (1904)	Government revetments along river to halt widening, causing river to flow faster and erode/flood downstream property	No taking. Damage to land, if caused by revetment at all, was but an incidental consequence; distinguished from instance where government dam in river causes flooding of private land directly.
United States v. Lynah, 188 U.S. 445 (1903)	Flooding from government dam, completely destroying land's value	Taking occurred. Where government dam floods land so as to substantially destroy its value, there is a taking.
Meyer v. Richmond, 172 U.S. 82 (1898)	City-authorized railroad obstruction to street, reducing traffic at plaintiff's properties nearby	No taking. Obstruction was not on plaintiff's land. Hence, impact on plaintiff amounted only to consequential damages, which are noncompensable.
Gibson v. United States, 166 U.S. 269 (1897)	Construction of government dike near plaintiff's land, preventing ingress and egress of vessels to commercial wharf on plaintiff's land	No taking. No appropriation or direct invasion occurred, only incidental injuries from a lawful exercise of federal navigation servitude. No water was thrown onto plaintiff's land; dike did not physically touch the land or cause deposits thereon.
Mugler v. Kansas, 123 U.S. 623 (1887)	Ban in state constitution on manufacture or sale of liquor, greatly reducing brewery's value	No taking. A prohibition simply upon the use of property for purposes declared by valid legislation to be noxious cannot be deemed a taking.
United States v. Great Falls Mfg. Co., 112 U.S. 645 (1884)	Building of dam, which occupied plaintiff's land and took his water rights	Taking occurred. Where United States by its agents proceeds under act of Congress to occupy property for public use, it must compensate.
Transportation Co. v. Chicago, 99 U.S. 635 (1878)	Construction of tunnel under river, temporarily limiting access to wharf	No taking. Acts done in proper exercise of government powers, and not directly encroaching on private property, are not a taking.
Pumpelly v. Green Bay Co., 80 U.S. (13 Wall.) 166 (1871)	Dam that flooded plaintiff's land continuously	Taking occurred. It is not required that property be formally taken in order to implicate Takings Clause. Serious interference with the common and necessary use of property, as by continuous flooding, effects a constitutional taking.
Legal Tender Cases (Knox v. Lee), 79 U.S. (12 Wall.) 457 (1870)	Federal statutes making U.S. currency legal tender for payment of all debts, even those entered into before enactment	No taking. Takings Clause "has always been understood as referring only to a direct appropriation"; it has no bearing on laws such as this one that only indirectly cause loss. Overrules *Hepburn v. Griswold*, 75 U.S. (8 Wall.) 603 (1870) (finding legal tender acts violative of due process, but briefly raising taking issue).

INDEX

A

B

C

F

G

H

K

L

Q

R

U

V

W

Y

Z